AN INTRODUCTION TO
THE OLD TESTAMENT

AN INTRODUCTION TO
THE OLD TESTAMENT

Sacred Texts and Imperial Contexts of the Hebrew Bible

DAVID M. CARR

A John Wiley & Sons, Ltd., Publication

This edition first published 2010
© 2010 David M. Carr

Blackwell Publishing was acquired by John Wiley & Sons in February 2007. Blackwell's publishing program has been merged with Wiley's global Scientific, Technical, and Medical business to form Wiley-Blackwell.

Registered Office
John Wiley & Sons Ltd, The Atrium, Southern Gate, Chichester, West Sussex, PO19 8SQ, United Kingdom

Editorial Offices
350 Main Street, Malden, MA 02148-5020, USA
9600 Garsington Road, Oxford, OX4 2DQ, UK
The Atrium, Southern Gate, Chichester, West Sussex, PO19 8SQ, UK

For details of our global editorial offices, for customer services, and for information about how to apply for permission to reuse the copyright material in this book please see our website at www.wiley.com/wiley-blackwell.

The right of David M. Carr to be identified as the author of this work has been asserted in accordance with the UK Copyright, Designs and Patents Act 1988.

Library of Congress Cataloging-in-Publication Data

Carr, David McLain, 1961–
    An introduction to the Old Testament : sacred texts and imperial contexts of the Hebrew Bible / David M. Carr.
        p. cm.
    Includes bibliographical references and index.
    ISBN 978-1-4051-8468-7 (hardcover : alk. paper) – ISBN 978-1-4051-8467-0 (pbk. : alk. paper)   1. Bible. O.T. – History.   2. Bible. O.T. – History of contemporary events. 3. Bible. O.T. – Introductions.   I. Title.
    BS1130.C37 2010
    221.09–dc22
                                                                                                2009041256

A catalogue record for this book is available from the British Library.

Set in 10/13 pt Minion by Graphicraft Limited, Hong Kong
Printed in the USA

001   2010

CONTENTS

FIGURES

MAPS

BOXES

basics	**What is a Basics Box?**
	These boxes give a brief overview of basic information about a biblical book or other major text under discussion. This includes an outline of the book or text, information about the time(s) in which it was written, and (usually) a discussion of a major issue in interpretation of the book or text.

WHAT IS A MORE ON METHOD BOX?

These boxes give a brief introduction to methods used to interpret the Hebrew Bible. They detail the sorts of questions that each method attempts to answer, give an example of how the method has been applied, and include a reference to an article or book with more information about the method under discussion.

> ## What is in Miscellaneous Boxes?
>
> These boxes offer extra information relevant to the broader discussion. Some pull together relevant dates for a period, while others show parallels between texts, or summarize information on a theme or question that relates to the topic at hand. This information is not optional or superfluous. Instead, these boxes highlight topics that are worth focused attention.

PREFACE

This book introduces students to the books of the Hebrew Bible as shaped in the crucible of the history of Israel and Judah, as well as in the varied interpretations of later Jewish and Christian communities. A prominent theme throughout is the way the books of the Bible reflect quite different sorts of interaction with past and present empires that dominated the ancient Near East. At first both students and professors may find this approach jarring, since I do not begin with Genesis and do not proceed through biblical books in order. The group of texts introduced early on in this textbook is quite different from the Bible they now know. Moreover, this textbook incorporates advances in Pentateuchal criticism over the last decades that are unfamiliar to both students and many professors. Yet I can say on the basis of my and others' experience teaching this approach that the picture of the Bible's development comes into focus as the narrative of its formation unfolds. By the end students should find meaning in aspects of the Bible that they once overlooked, even as they also understand that much of the power of the Bible has been its capability to transcend the original contexts in which it was written. Moreover, through discussion of the history of Jewish and Christian interpretation of focus texts at the end of each chapter, students will gain a taste of how faith communities have used the Bible in creative, inspired, and sometimes death-dealing ways to guide and make sense of their lives.

I have been helped by many people in writing this textbook, first and foremost my wife, Colleen Conway. Versions of these chapters were originally written for a combined introduction to the Old and New Testaments that is co-authored with her, *Introduction to the Bible: Sacred Texts and Imperial Contexts* (also published by Wiley-Blackwell), and so she has read multiple versions of them, taught them in her courses, and offered many suggestions for improvement. Several colleagues – Benjamin Sommer, Kent Reynolds, Mark Smith, and Marvin Sweeney – went way beyond the call of duty to read and suggest revisions to excerpts from the manuscript relating to areas of their expertise. I cannot say that I incorporated every revision that they suggested, and they only looked at parts of earlier draft manuscripts, but I can affirm that this book is much stronger thanks to their gracious help. In addition, my students over the last two years have read earlier drafts of this textbook and suggested corrections. Some students and teaching assistants who have offered a particularly large volume of helpful corrections are Mary Ellen Kris, Candice Olson, Lizzie Berne-DeGear, Laurel Koepf, Meagan Manas, and Todd Kennedy. My thanks to all for their generous help in this project.

The date framework given in this textbook follows that of Anson Rainey and Steven Notley's *The Sacred Bridge: Carta's Atlas of the Biblical World* (Jerusalem: Carta, 2005). In many cases specific dates are uncertain, but Rainey and Notley provide a recent, solid framework to start from on an introductory level. Unless otherwise indicated, the Hebrew translations here are my own.

As with any such textbook, particularly a first edition, there is plenty of room for improvement. In particular, I am acutely conscious of the multiple ways in which virtually everything that is written here could be footnoted, qualified, and balanced with other perspectives. At particular points, such as my treatment of Pentateuchal source criticism, I explicitly summarize alternative perspectives that students may encounter when reading other resources. But inclusion of all alternative perspectives would have turned this into quite a different book, and one – I suggest – that would be much less suited for introducing students to academic study of the Bible. This introduction provides one general outline of the Hebrew Bible, which students can then supplement, correct, and balance in their future studies. All that said, I certainly invite all possible suggestions for correction and improvement so that any future edition of this textbook will be better.

David Carr
New York

ACKNOWLEDGMENTS

The author and publisher gratefully acknowledge the permission granted to reproduce the copyrighted material in this book:

Figure 0.1   © John C. Trever, Ph.D., digital image by James E. Trever.

Figure 0.2   Biblia Hebraica Stuttgartensia, edited by Karl Elliger and Wilhelm Rudolph, Fifth Revised Edition, edited by Adrian Schenker, © 1977 and 1997 Deutsche Bibelgesellschaft, Stuttgart. Used by permission.

Figure 2.1   Z. Radovan/www.BibleLandPictures.com.

Figure 2.3   bpk / Vorderasiatisches Museum, SMB / Gudrun Stenzel.

Figure 2.4   Jürgen Liepe.

Figure 3.1   © Lloyd K. Townsend.

Figure 3.2   William Schniedewind.

Figure 3.3   akg-images / Erich Lessing.

Figure 3.4   Courtesy of R. E. Tappy and The Zeitah Excavations Photograph by B. Zuckerman and M. Lundberg Overlay by P. K. McCarter, Jr.

Figure 3.5   Z. Radovan/www.BibleLandPictures.com.

Figure 4.1   © The Trustees of the British Museum.

Figure 4.2   The Granger Collection / Topfoto.

Figure 4.3   akg-images.

Figure 4.4   Image by © Francis G. Mayer/CORBIS.

Figure 5.1   Z. Radovan/www.BibleLandPictures.com.

Figure 5.2   akg-images / Erich Lessing.

Figure 5.3   Z. Radovan/www.BibleLandPictures.com.

Figure 5.4   Stiftung BIBEL+ORIENT.

Figure 5.5   Stiftung BIBEL+ORIENT.

Figure 5.6   Photo © The Israel Museum, Jerusalem.

Figure 6.1   Image by © The Gallery Collection/Corbis.

Figure 6.2   Stiftung BIBEL+ORIENT.

Figure 7.1   Stiftung BIBEL+ORIENT.

Figure 9.1   Z. Radovan/www.BibleLandPictures.com.

Figure 9.2   akg-images / Erich Lessing.

Figure 10.1   © The Natural History Museum, London.

Figure 10.2   Stiftung BIBEL+ORIENT.

Figure 11.1   Image by © Gianni Dagli Orti/CORBIS.

Figure 11.2   akg-images / Erich Lessing.

Figure 13.1   Photo © The Israel Museum, Jerusalem.
Figure 13.2   Courtesy of Carta, Jerusalem.

The Pharaoh Merneptah hymn in Chapter 3, page 65, and the Cyrus cylinder text in Chapter 11, page 210: PRITCHARD, JAMES; *ANCIENT NEAR EASTERN TEXTS RELATING TO THE OLD TESTAMENT – THIRD EDITION WITH SUPPLEMENT.* © 1950, 1955, 1969, renewed 1978 by Princeton University Press. Reprinted by permission of Princeton University Press.

At points throughout the book extracts have been used from the Revised Standard Version of the Bible: Revised Standard Version of the Bible, copyright 1952 [2nd edition, 1971] by the Division of Christian Education of the National Council of the Churches of Christ in the United States of America. Used by permission. All rights reserved.

The publisher apologizes for any errors or omissions in the above list and would be grateful if notified of any corrections that should be incorporated in future reprints or editions of this book.

ABBREVIATIONS

ANET   James Pritchard (ed.), *Ancient Near Eastern Texts Relating to the Old Testament with Supplement*. Princeton: Princeton University Press, 1969.

George   Andrew George, *The Babylonian Gilgamesh Epic: Introduction, Critical Edition and Cuneiform Texts*. New York: Oxford University Press, 2003.

Livingstone   Alasdair Livingstone (ed.), *Court Poetry and Literary Miscellanea*. State Archives of Assyria, 3. Helsinki: Helsinki University Press, 1989.

NJPS   *The New Jewish Publication Society Tanach Translation*. Philadelphia: Jewish Publication Society, 1985.

NRSV   *The New Revised Standard Version of the Bible*. New York: National Council of Churches, 1989.

NT   New Testament

OT   Old Testament

OT Parallels   Victor Matthews and Don Benjamin, *Old Testament Parallels*: *Laws and Stories from the Ancient Near East* (3rd revised and expanded edition). Mahwah, NJ: Paulist Press, 2007.

For Bible abbreviations, see the Miscellaneous Box on "Bible Abbreviations, Verses, and Chapters," in Chapter 1, p. 18.

Asterisks after Bible citations, e.g. "Genesis 12–50*," indicate that only parts of the cited texts are included.

// indicate that the texts before and after the slashes are parallel to each other.

OVERVIEW OF THE HISTORICAL PERIOD

This shows major periods and corresponding texts covered in this book.

DATES	1250–1000 BCE (13th–11th centuries)	1000–930 (10th century)	930–800 (10th–9th centuries)	800–700 (8th century)	700–586 (7th and early 6th centuries)	586–538 (6th century)	538–332 (6th–4th centuries)	332–63 (4th–1st centuries)
Chapter	2	3 and 4	5	5 and 6	7 and 8	9 and 10	11 and 12	12 and 13
MAJOR EVENTS (IN CHRONOLOGICAL ORDER)	Spread of villages in hill country; Tribal "Israel" emerges; Saul's chieftainship	Formation of Davidic monarchy; Jerusalem taken as capital of Judah/Israel; David and Solomon	Formation of northern kingdom of "Israel"; Rise and fall of Omride dynasty	Domination and destruction of northern "Israel" by Assyria; Domination of Judah by Assyria	Eventual decline of Assyrian power; Enactment of Josiah's "reform"; Decline of Judah into domination by Babylon; First wave of exile	Destruction of Jerusalem and its Temple; Second and third waves of exile of elites to Babylon	Persian victory, waves of return, rebuilding of Temple; Nehemiah's rebuilding of the wall; Divorce of foreign wives under Ezra and elevation of Torah	Hellenistic rule; Hellenizing crisis; Hasmonean kingdom
MAJOR WRITINGS (AND ORAL TRADITIONS)	(No writings, but oral traditions about exodus, trickster ancestors)	Royal and Zion psalms; Proverbs; J primeval history; ?Covenant Code; ?Song of Songs; ?Ecclesiastes	Jacob narrative; Joseph narrative; Exodus–wilderness story; Song of Deborah	Prophecy to the north by Amos and Hosea; Prophecy to the south by Micah and Isaiah	Early edition of Deuteronomistic history (Deut–2 Kings) that led from Deuteronomy to Josiah's reform (and no further); Nahum; Zephaniah; Early prophecies from Jeremiah	Exilic Deuteronomistic history; Lamentations; Ezekiel and Second Isaiah; L story of creation to Israel; P counter-story of creation to Israel	Haggai; Zechariah; Nehemiah memoir; Temple rebuilding/Ezra narrative; Third Isaiah; Combined L/P Pentateuch; Psalter	Early parts of Enoch; Ben Sira; Ezra–Nehemiah; Esther; 1–2 Chronicles; Daniel
MAJOR NEW IDEAS AND THEMES	Election theology	Royal/Zion theology			Exclusive devotion to Yahweh enforced (briefly) by Josiah	Monotheism	Dual Temple–Torah focus	Judaism

TIMELINE

Important texts are noted in **boldface**.

BCE	SOUTH (Judah)	NORTH ("Israel" in narrower sense)
1300	(Waning Egyptian domination of Canaan)	
		Spread of villages in Israelite hill county
		Merneptah Stela mention of "Israel"
1200		Battles of hill-country Israelites with neighbors
		Oral exodus traditions
		Oral ancestral traditions
1100		**Oral victory traditions**
	Saul's "chieftainship"	
	David (Hebron; 1010–1002)	
1000	David (Jerusalem; 1002–970)	
	Royal psalms, Zion psalms	
	Solomon (Jerusalem; 970–930)	
	Proverb collections, J primeval history	
	?Covenant Code, ?Song of Songs, ?Ecclesiastes	
	Rehoboam (Jerusalem)	Jeroboam founds northern monarchy
900		**Jacob narrative**
		Joseph narrative
		Exodus narrative
		(written) Song of Deborah
		Omride dynasty (880–841)
		Jehu's coup (841)
800		
		Jeroboam II (782–753)
		Amos
	Isaiah (early prophecy) Assyrian domination of Israel begins (745–)	
	Syro-Ephraimite war (735–4)	**Hosea**
	Assyrian domination of Judah (734–)	
	Micah, Isaiah (later prophecy)	
		Assyrian destruction of Israel (722)
	Hezekiah (715–686)	
	Hezekiah's rebellion and reform (705)	
700	Sennacherib's attack and mysterious withdrawal (701)	
	Manasseh (686–642)	
	Amon (642–640)	(Waning of Assyrian power)
	Josiah (640–609)	
	Zephaniah	
	Josiah's reform (623)	
	Josianic edition of Deuteronomistic history	
		(Fall of Nineveh, Assyria's capital)
	Nahum	
	Jeremiah	
	Domination of Judah by Babylonia	

600 First wave of exiles (586)
   Ezekiel's early prophecy
   Lay/Non-Priestly Pentateuchal Source
 Destruction of Jerusalem and second wave of exiles (586)
   Lamentations and Psalm 137
   Ezekiel's later prophecy
 Third wave of exiles (582)
   Exilic edition of Deuteronomistic history

   Lay Pentateuchal Source (incorporating modified
     forms of older J primeval history, Jacob–Joseph story,
     Moses story, and Deuteronomy)

   Priestly Pentateuchal Source

   Second Isaiah
Persian conquering of Babylonian empire (539)
 First wave of returnees (538)
 Another wave, beginning of Temple restoration (532)
 Another wave with Zerubbabel, completion of Temple rebuilding (520–515)
   Haggai and Zechariah (1–9)
500
 Nehemiah's return and governorships (445–425)
   (rebuilding wall, purification of priesthood)
   Nehemiah memoir
400 Return with Ezra, divorce of foreign wives, elevation of Torah (397–)
   Combined (L/P) Pentateuch
   Temple-rebuilding/Ezra narrative
   Third Isaiah
   Psalter
Greek conquering of Persian empire (332)

300 (Shifting domination of Palestine by Greek Ptolemies
(Egypt) and Seleucids (Mesopotamia); 332–142)

   Early parts of Enoch

   1–2 Chronicles

   Wisdom of Ben Sira
200
 Jason purchase of high priesthood, attempt to Hellenize Jerusalem (174)

 Menelaus purchase of high priesthood (171) and Judean rebellion against him

   Daniel

 Antiochus Epiphanes IV campaign to eradicate observant Judaism and beginning of Hasmonean-led
   rebellion against Hellenistic rule (167–)
 Purification and rededication of Temple (164)

 Hasmonean independence and rule (142–63)

   Ezra–Nehemiah

   Esther
100
 Roman takeover of Palestine (63)
CE
 Destruction of the Second Temple (70)

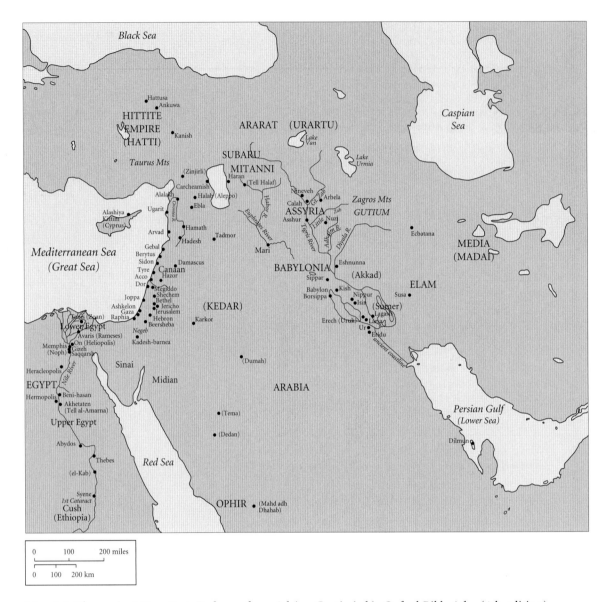

Map 0.1 The ancient Near East. Redrawn from Adrian Curtis (ed.), *Oxford Bible Atlas* (4th edition). Oxford, New York: Oxford University Press, 2007, page 67.

PROLOGUE

ORIENTATION TO MULTIPLE BIBLES AND MULTIPLE TRANSLATIONS

Chapter Outline

CHAPTER OVERVIEW

This chapter answers the questions: "What are the biggest differences between the scriptures revered in Judaism, Christianity, and Islam?" and "What should I know about in choosing an English translation of the Bible?" By the end of this chapter you should know the differences between the Bibles of Judaism and Christianity, as well as the relationship of the Muslim Koran to both sets of scriptures. You will also learn about how study of different readings of ancient manuscripts of the Bible, "textual criticism," and advances in knowledge of ancient languages have led to major progress in translation of the Bible since the King James Version was completed in 1611. Finally, you will learn some basic things to look for in choosing an up-to-date English translation of the Bible.

EXERCISE

Using the parallels provided at the end of the chapter in Appendix 1, compare the translations (and paraphrase) of Isa 52:13–15. What differences do you notice?

Take a look at two pages of a biblical book in your Bible. Make a list of *all* types of elements on those pages aside from the actual text of the Bible. Using the discussions in this chapter, identify where those elements came from.

The Different Scriptures of Judaism and Christianity

To begin, it is important to get acquainted with the different forms of the Old Testament/Hebrew Bible recognized by different faith communities. These are referred to as different "**canons**" of the Bible, with "**canon**" meaning a collection of books that are recognized as divinely inspired scripture by a given religious community. Such books are recognized as "**canonical**."

The Jewish people calls its Scriptures the "**TaNaK**" (or "**Tanach**," with the ch pronounced like the ch in Bach). This is a word formed out of the first letters of the three main parts of the Jewish Bible: **Torah** (Genesis, Exodus, Leviticus, Numbers, and Deuteronomy), *Neviim* ("prophets"), and *Ketuvim* ("writings"). See box on p. 4 for an overview of the contents of each of these three parts. The Torah, otherwise known as the **Pentateuch**, is the centerpiece of the Jewish Tanach, while the prophets and writings are understood as commentary on it. In accordance with the emphasis in Judaism on temple and purity, the Tanach concludes with the edict of Cyrus at the end of 2 Chronicles that authorizes the rebuilding of the Temple. The Jewish people looks with hope toward a new rebuilding of the Temple to accompany the coming of the messiah.

The Christian version of these scriptures, the "**Old Testament**" (OT) is organized quite differently from the Jewish Tanach. This is especially clear in the case of Protestant Bibles, which contain the very same books as the Jewish Tanach, but in a different order. Like the Jewish Bible, the Protestant "Old Testament" starts with the books of Genesis, Exodus, Leviticus, Numbers, and Deuteronomy, and then moves to Joshua through 2 Kings and then the parallel history found in 1–2 Chronicles and Ezra–Nehemiah. The rest of the books in the Old Testament are put in the order of their traditional authors, starting with the book of Job (an early Edomite sage), and moving through Psalms (David as traditional author), Proverbs, Ecclesiastes, and Song of Songs (Solomon as traditional author), and on to the major (Isaiah, Jeremiah, Ezekiel) and minor (Hosea, etc.) prophets. As in the case of the Jewish Tanach, the ending of the Christian Old

Contents of the Hebrew Bible/Tanach/Old Testament

Jewish Tanach	Protestant OT	Roman Catholic OT (*italics* = not in Tanach)	Eastern Orthodox OT (*italics* = not in Tanach)
Torah	**(Pentateuch)**	**(Pentateuch)**	**(Pentateuch)**
Genesis, Exodus, Leviticus, Numbers, Deuteronomy	Genesis, Exodus, Leviticus, Numbers, Deuteronomy	Genesis, Exodus, Leviticus, Numbers, Deuteronomy	Genesis, Exodus, Leviticus, Numbers, Deuteronomy
Prophets (Neviim)	**(Historical Books)**	**(Historical Books)**	**(Historical Books)**
Former prophets Joshua, Judges	Joshua, Judges, Ruth	Joshua, Judges, Ruth	Joshua, Judges, Ruth
1–2 Samuel 1–2 Kings	1–2 Samuel 1–2 Kings 1–2 Chronicles Ezra–Nehemiah	1–2 Samuel 1–2 Kings 1–2 Chronicles Ezra–Nehemiah	1–2 Samuel 1–2 Kings 1–2 Chronicles Ezra–Nehemiah *1 Esdras (2 Esdras in Russian Orthodox)*
Latter prophets *Major prophets*		*Tobit* *Judith*	*Tobit* *Judith*
Isaiah Jeremiah Ezekiel	Esther	Esther *(with additions)* *1–2 Maccabees*	Esther *(with additions)* *1–3 Maccabees*
Minor prophets/ book of the twelve	**(Poetical Books)**	**(Poetical Books)**	**(Poetical Books)**
Hosea, Joel, Amos, Obadiah, Jonah, Micah, Nahum, Habakkuk, Zephaniah, Haggai, Zechariah, Malachi	Job Psalms Proverbs Ecclesiastes Song of Solomon	Job Psalms Proverbs Ecclesiastes Song of Solomon *Wisdom of Solomon* *Sirach*	Job Psalms (with Psalm 151) Proverbs Ecclesiastes Song of Solomon *Wisdom of Solomon* *Sirach*
Writings (Ketuvim) Psalms Proverbs Job	**(Prophets)** Isaiah Jeremiah Lamentations	**(Prophets)** Isaiah Jeremiah Lamentations *Baruch* *Letter of Jeremiah*	**(Prophets)** Isaiah Jeremiah Lamentations *Baruch* *Letter of Jeremiah*
Five festal scrolls Song of Songs Ruth Lamentations Ecclesiastes Esther	Ezekiel Daniel Hosea, Joel, Amos, Obadiah, Jonah, Micah, Nahum, Habakkuk, Zephaniah, Haggai, Zechariah, Malachi	Ezekiel Daniel *(with additions)* Hosea, Joel, Amos, Obadiah, Jonah, Micah, Nahum, Habakkuk, Zephaniah, Haggai, Zechariah, Malachi	Ezekiel Daniel *(with additions)* Hosea, Joel, Amos, Obadiah, Jonah, Micah, Nahum, Habakkuk, Zephaniah, Haggai, Zechariah, Malachi
Daniel Ezra–Nehemiah 1–2 Chronicles			*4 Maccabees* (appendix)

Testament is revealing. It concludes with the last chapter of Malachi, a prediction of the second coming of Elijah (Mal 4:5). This ending leads nicely into the first book of the New Testament (NT), the Gospel of Matthew, which describes the coming of John the Baptist, who is clothed like Elijah and prophesies the coming of Jesus (Matt 3:1–6).

Other Christian churches organize their "Old Testament" similarly, but recognize additional books as part of it, books not included in the Jewish or the Protestant scriptures. For example, the Roman Catholic church also includes books such as 1 and 2 Maccabees, Sirach, and the Wisdom of Solomon. The Ethiopic church recognizes the book of Enoch as part of its Old Testament, and various forms of Orthodox Christianity likewise recognize slightly different groups of additional books. For the Roman Catholics, such additional books are "**deutero-canonical,**" which means that they belong to a "second canon." For Protestants, such books not in the Jewish Tanach are not considered true scripture, but "**apocrypha,**" which means "books hidden away." I will not hide such books away in this textbook, but neither will I be able to discuss them at length. Instead, I will discuss briefly a sampling of them: Sirach, Enoch, and the books of Maccabees.

"**Hebrew Bible**" is yet another term that is often used to designate the scriptures shared by Jews and Christians. Many people prefer the expression "Hebrew Bible" because it avoids the pejorative connotations that the term "Old Testament" has assumed in some Christian circles. Christianity has long struggled with a tendency toward what is called "**supersessionism**" – the idea that Christianity and the Christian church have superseded and thus replaced Judaism and the people of Israel. For Christians who subscribe to this idea, the Old Testament is often treated as the *Old* and superseded Testament. It is seen as the outdated book of the "law," as opposed to the New Testament, which is understood to be the truly scriptural word about Jesus, love, and grace. Such views reflect a lack of close reading of either the Old or the New Testament, but they are widespread and influential. Therefore, some avoid the term "Old Testament," with its possible implications of supersessionism, and prefer terms such as "Hebrew Bible" or "First Testament" instead. Other Christians find these terms odd and/or inaccurate (for example, several chapters in the Tanach/Old Testament are not in Hebrew, but Aramaic). They prefer sticking with the Christian term "Old Testament," but emphasize the more ancient understanding of "Old" as implying something good, rather than the more contemporary idea of "Old" being something that is outdated.

The important thing for academic study of the Bible is to understand the meanings of these different terms for the Tanach/Old Testament/Hebrew scriptures and the slight differences in contents and order of these otherwise similar collections. These differences reflect the fact that these scriptures have come to belong to multiple faith communities. In addition, the religion of Islam sees the scriptures of Judaism and Christianity as possessing a secondary authority to that of its central text, the **Koran**. From the Muslim perspective, the Koran represents in pure form revelations about the one true god, Allah (Arabic for "the God"), revelations present in diluted form in the Jewish Tanach and Christian Old and New Testaments. This Koran is quite different in contents from the Tanach/Old Testament, containing a set of Arabic poems attributed to the prophet Muhammad. It is not a parallel "Old Testament" or "Tanach." Nevertheless, parts of the Koran reflect post-biblical Jewish traditions about history up to Moses, and other Muslim traditions have elaborated on stories about Adam, Abraham, Ishmael, Joseph, and other biblical figures up to and including Moses. Thus Islam represents another strand of history of interpretation of scripture, alongside Judaism and Christianity.

Thus we see that there is no one "Bible" or "Old Testament" shared by Judaism and Christianity, let alone Islam. Despite major overlaps in the contents of the Jewish Tanach and Christian Old Testament, there are significant differences in order and (occasionally) content as well. This is an initial indicator of the quite different readings that Christians and Jews give to the texts they hold in common. We will see others along the way. Moreover, this diversity of Jewish and Christian Bibles is preceded by a diversity of perspectives and voices found within the Hebrew scriptures themselves. In the following chapters, we will see this diversity in texts written at different times and even in texts offering different perspectives on the same time.

Basics on Bible Translations

Since most students do not know Hebrew or Greek, they can only read a Bible in translation. There are several things that every user of such Bible translations should know about them in order to be an informed user.

First, every translation involves many decisions by the translator about the Hebrew, Greek, or (in a few cases) Aramaic text. Scholars are still not sure about the meanings of some words, and the biblical languages do not translate precisely into English (or other modern languages). In addition, we have no original manuscript of any biblical book, and the existing biblical manuscripts disagree with each other at many points. This means that scholars must use **textual criticism** to decide the best Hebrew or Greek text in each case where the manuscripts disagree with each other. Luckily, over the last several centuries much progress has been made in uncovering ancient manuscripts and learning to identify copying errors and other changes in such manuscripts. In addition, there has been a huge growth in knowledge about the biblical languages.

These advances in knowledge about the text and language of the Bible mean that academic study of the Bible requires use of up-to-date translations of the biblical text. The **King James Version** (also known as the "Authorized Version"), though beautiful and cherished by many, is not an up-to-date translation. It was done four hundred years ago. Scholars knew far less about Hebrew and Greek then than they do now. And the translation is based on manuscripts with more errors and expansions than the manuscripts used for translations today. Therefore, the King James Version should not be used for readings in a twenty-first-century academic course on the Bible.

Translations also vary in religious perspective. The New Jewish Publication Society translation (NJPS) obviously comes out of a tradition of Jewish interpretation of the Tanach. The New Jerusalem Bible (NJB) and New American Bible (NAB) were produced

Figure 0.1 One of our earliest manuscripts of the book of Isaiah, dated to the early first century BCE. Note how the letters are hung from lines on the parchment and a scribe has added a verse into the middle.

Figure 0.2 Scholarly edition of the same text as in Figure 0.1. In contrast to the early manuscript it has chapter and verse numbers along with scholarly notes at the bottom about alternative Hebrew readings to the ones given in the body of the text.

MORE ON METHOD: TEXTUAL CRITICISM

"Textual criticism" is not general study of a text. Instead, textual criticism focuses exclusively on getting the best textual reading for a given biblical text in its original language. Over the centuries scribes have introduced tens of thousands of minor changes into biblical texts as they copied them. Some were introduced by accident, as when a scribe might accidentally copy a given line twice. Other changes seem more intentional, where a scribe seems to have added a clarification of a place name or a theological correction or expansion.

In search of the best reading

Textual critics use two main methods to uncover the best reading for a Hebrew, Greek, or Aramaic biblical text. The first method is to compare ancient manuscripts of a given passage with each other, seeing if one or more **manuscript witnesses** to the passage seem to preserve a better reading. For example, one major witness for the Hebrew Bible is the **Masoretic text** (**MT**), the authoritative version of the Hebrew text that was produced by Jewish scribes in the medieval period. Other important witnesses for the Hebrew Bible are the biblical manuscripts found at the Dead Sea (Qumran), the Pentateuch preserved by the Samaritan community (around Samaria in the north), and even ancient translations of early Hebrew manuscripts, especially the **Septuagint** (**LXX**), an ancient set of translations of various biblical books into Greek.

On occasion, a biblical scholar may judge that all of the textual witnesses preserve an error. In such cases, that scholar may propose a reading that is not preserved in any manuscript. This second method of correction is called **conjectural emendation**.

by Catholic scholars. The New Revised Standard Version (NRSV; preceded by the Revised Standard Version – RSV) aims to be an ecumenical translation, but it is part of a line of Protestant revisions of the King James Version. The New International Version (NIV; now available in updated form as Today's New International Version) is also Protestant and was conceived as an evangelical alternative to the RSV/NRSV.

Translations also vary in style: whether they aim to stay as close to the biblical languages as possible or whether they aim for maximum readability. **Formal correspondence** translations aim to stay as close as possible to word-for-word translation of the Hebrew, Aramaic, or Greek text. This can make them good tools for study, but it also makes them more difficult to understand. Translations that tend toward formal correspondence include the NRSV, NIV, and the New American Standard Bible (NASB). Other translations tend toward **dynamic equivalence**, which aims for equivalent meaning, but not a word-for-word translation. This results in translations that are more readable, but also contain more interpretation on the part of translators. Examples of translations that tend toward dynamic equivalence include the NJB, NAB, and several other translations produced by Protestant groups, such as the Good News Translation (GNT); also known as the "Good News Bible" and as TEV – Today's English Version) and the Contemporary English Version (CEV). These translations should be distinguished from resources such as the Living Bible or Amplified Bible. The latter are not direct translations of the Hebrew and Greek texts, but paraphrases or expansions of other translations. For example, the Living Bible is a paraphrase of the nineteenth-century American Standard Version. Such paraphrase subtly adds yet another level of interpretation between the reader and the original text and is not helpful for academic work on the Bible.

One more way that contemporary Bible translations vary is in the extent to which they aim to use gender-neutral language, such as "humanity" instead of "mankind." Though older writing conventions endorsed the use of "man" for "human" or "he" for "he or she," many now argue that general use of such male-focused language reinforces male domination of women. This has led to two levels of revision of older translations that used such male-specific language. In some cases, past English translators had used male-specific words to translate Hebrew or Greek expressions that were gender neutral. The recent revision of the NIV translation, Today's New International Version, aims to correct such mistranslations to what is termed "gender-accurate" English expressions. Some other translations revise yet other references to people toward gender-neutral English terms, even in cases where the original biblical languages use masculine nouns. Examples of such translations include the NRSV, NJB, and the Contemporary Torah, a "gender-sensitive" revision of the NJPS. I generally follow that policy in this *Introduction*, using "God" rather than "he" or "him" and preferring gender-neutral references to human beings. Nevertheless, the Bible was formed in a culture that privileged masculinity and conceived its God in largely masculine terms, and this is reflected at points in the translations included in this textbook.

Finally, readers should recognize that all these translations are published in different editions, each with its own perspective and added resources. For example, the *New Oxford Annotated Bible* and the *HarperCollins Study Bible* are not different translations, but different editions of the NRSV. Each one has a different introductory essay, introductions to the biblical books, and brief commentary on the biblical text written by biblical scholars commissioned by the publisher. Indeed, whenever you use a given translation, it usually includes many other elements that were added by the publisher of the particular edition that you are using: headings for different sections of the biblical text, marginal references to other biblical passages, maps, and other additions. These can be helpful resources. Nevertheless, users of such editions should be aware of how these additional elements – none of which is actually part of the Bible per se – can subtly influence how one reads a given biblical passage. They should be used critically.

As time allows, it is often a good idea to compare multiple good translations with each other to see where there are significant differences. Some like to use online resources for this, such as Crosswire's "Bible Tool" (www.crosswire.org/study) or the Bible Gateway (www.biblegateway.com), though these resources are generally limited to older, out-of-date translations. Better alternatives are *The Complete Parallel Bible*, which contains four recent translations of the whole Bible (NRSV, NJB, New English Bible [NEB], and NAB), or a Bible software tool (such as Accordance, Bible Works, or Logos) that is equipped with multiple, recent translations. Such comparison can reveal major differences between translations, and the more one finds such differences, the more one wonders how to decide between the alternatives. This is ideally solved by learning biblical languages! Many students, however, lack time and/or interest in going that far with biblical studies. For those lacking knowledge of biblical languages it is important to know where a given translation is but one possible rendering in English of a phrase in Hebrew, Aramaic, or Greek that could also be rendered, perhaps better, in another way. Comparison of Bible translations shows this.

CHAPTER REVIEW

1. Know the meaning and significance of the following terms discussed
in this chapter:

- apocrypha
- canon and canonical
- conjectural emendation
- deutero-canonical boosks
- dynamic equivalence translation
- formal correspondence
  translation
- Hebrew Bible
- King James Version
- Koran
- LXX
- manuscript witness
- Masoretic text
- MT
- Old Testament
- Pentateuch
- Septuagint
- supersessionism
- Tanach or TaNaK
- textual criticism
- Torah

RESOURCES FOR FURTHER STUDY

Editions of translations

The first edition listed provides an overview of several
translations; some good editions follow.

The Complete Parallel Bible. New York: Oxford University
Press, 1993.

The New Jerusalem Bible. New York: Doubleday, 1985.
This is the NJB.

The New Oxford Annotated Bible (3rd edition), eds.
Michael Coogan et al. New York: Oxford University
Press, 2001. This contains the NRSV.

The Jewish Study Bible, eds. A. Berlin et al. New York:
Oxford University Press, 2004. This contains the NJPS.

The HarperCollins Study Bible (fully revised and updated),
eds. Harold W. Attridge et al. San Francisco: Harper-
SanFrancisco, 2006. This contains the NRSV.

One-volume commentaries

Mays, James L., ed. *HarperCollin's Bible Commentary*
(revised edition). San Francisco: Harper & Row, 2000.

Newsom, Carol A., and Ringe, Sharon H., *The Women's
Bible Commentary* (2nd edition). Louisville, KY: Westminster John Knox Press, 1998.

The formation of the Jewish and Christian scriptures

Barton, John. *How the Bible Came to Be*. Louisville, KY:
Westminster John Knox Press, 1997.

*Bible software packages for searches and initial
work with biblical languages*

For Mac (and Windows with a free Mac Emulator):
The "Introductory Level" of the "Scholars Collection"
of Accordance software from Oaktree Software (www.
accordancebible.com). Be sure to specify that you
want the NRSV, NJB, or other up-to-date translation.
Otherwise you are given the King James Version by
default.

Only for Windows:
Bible Works (www.bibleworks.com)
Bibloi (www.silvermnt.com; this was formerly "Bible
Windows")
Logos (www.logos.com)
You can also obtain free software for searching and
reading the Bible at www.crosswire.org.

Useful websites for translation comparison

Note that these mainly feature old translations.
Crosswire – www.crosswire.org/study
The Bible Gateway – www.biblegateway.com
Studylight (more up-to-date translations) – www.
studylight.org

APPENDIX 1: TRANSLATION AND PARAPHRASE COMPARISON OF ISA 52:13–15

ISA Chapter and Verse	Revised Standard Version	New American Standard Version	New International Version	Today's English Version (Good News Bible)
52:13	Behold my servant shall prosper, he shall be exalted and lifted up, and shall be very high.	Behold my servant will prosper, He will be high and lifted up, and greatly exalted.	See, my servant will act wisely; he will be raised and lifted up and highly exalted.	The Lord says, My servant will succeed in his task; he will be highly honored.
52:14	As many were astonished at him – his appearance was so marred, beyond human semblance, and his form beyond that of the sons of men –	Just as many were astonished at you, *My People*, so His appearance was marred more than any man, And his form more than the sons of men.	Just as there were many who were appalled at him – his appearance was so disfigured beyond that of any man and his form marred beyond human likeness –	Many people were shocked when they saw him; he was so disfigured that he hardly looked human.
52:15	so shall he startle many nations; kings shall shut their mouths because of him; for that which has not been told them they shall see, and that which they have not heard they shall understand.	Thus he will sprinkle many nations, Kings will shut their mouths on account of Him; For what had not been told them they will see, And what they had not heard they will understand.	so will he sprinkle many nations, and kings will shut their mouths because of him. For what they were not told, they will see, and what they have not heard, they will understand.	But now many nations will marvel at him, and kings will be speechless with amazement. They will see and understand something they had never known.

ISA Chapter and Verse	New English Bible	Living Bible	Tanakh	New Jerusalem Bible
52:13	Behold, my servant shall prosper, he shall be lifted up, exalted to the heights.	See, my Servant shall prosper; he shall be highly exalted.	Indeed, My servant shall prosper, be exalted and raised to great heights.	Look, my servant will prosper, will grow great, will rise to great heights.
52:14	Time was when many were aghast at you, my people;	Yet many shall be amazed when they see him – yes, even far-off foreign nations and their kings; [See the end of 52:15 for the rest]	Just as the many were appalled at him – So marred was his appearance, unlike that of man, His form, beyond human semblance –	As many people were aghast at him – he was so inhumanly disfigured that he no longer looked like a man –
52:15	. . . so now many nations recoil at the sight of him, and kings curl their lips in disgust. For they see what they had never been told and things unheard before fill their thoughts.	. . . they shall stand dumbfounded, speechless in his presence. For they shall see and understand what they had not been told before. They shall see my Servant beaten and bloodied, so disfigured one would scarcely know it was a person standing there. So shall he cleanse many nations.	Just so he shall startle many nations. Kings shall be silenced because of him, For they shall see what has not been told them, Shall behold what they never have heard.	so many nations will be astonished and kings will stay tight-lipped before him, seeing what had never been told them, learning what they had not heard before.

APPENDIX 2: CHARACTERISTICS OF SELECT ENGLISH TRANSLATIONS OF THE BIBLE

Translation	Background	Style	Use of MT (with translation of Isa 7:14 as indicator of theological leanings)	Gender language
NJPS (1985)	Jewish Publication Society	Formal correspondence, colloquial	No deviation from MT and uses Jewish chapter/verse numbering	Aims at "gender accuracy" (Note: 2006 JPS *Contemporary Torah* with more changes)
NRSV (1989)	Protestant, National Council of Churches	Formal correspondence, literary	Some deviation from MT in light of Dead Sea scrolls and LXX	Modest move toward inclusive language
NIV (1978)	Protestant Evangelical, International Bible Society	Formal correspondence literary	Very modest deviation from MT, mostly in notes. Modifies Hebrew of Isa 7:14 to match Matthew	
Today's NIV (TNIV) (2005)	Protestant Evangelical, International Bible Society	Formal correspondence, literary	Very modest deviation from MT, mostly in notes. Modifies Hebrew of Isa 7:14 to match Matthew	Modest move toward "gender-accurate" language
NASB (1971)	Protestant Evangelical, Lockman Foundation	Formal correspondence, quite literal and often awkward	Little revision of MT. Modifies Hebrew of Isa 7:14 to match Matthew	
GNT (formerly TEV) (1992)	Protestant, American Bible Society (particularly for missionaries)	Dynamic equivalence, colloquial and simple vocabulary	Little deviation from MT	Includes revisions toward gender-inclusive language
CEV (1999)	Protestant, American Bible Society	Dynamic equivalence, colloquial, yet more simple vocabulary and syntax	Little deviation from MT. Modifies Hebrew of Isa 7:14 to match Matthew	Moves toward gender-inclusive language for humans
REB (1989), revision of NEB (1970)	British Protestant and Roman Catholic churches	Dynamic equivalence, literary	Substantial deviations from MT	Moves in 1989 revision toward gender-inclusive language
NJB (1985)	European Roman Catholic	Dynamic equivalence, but literary	Some substantial deviations from the MT	Very modest moves toward gender-inclusive language
NAB (1991)	United States Roman Catholic	Mix of dynamic equivalence and formal correspondence (the latter especially in NT)	Some substantial deviations from the MT. Modifies Hebrew of Isa 7:14 to match Matthew	Modest moves toward gender-inclusive language in NT and Psalms

CHAPTER 1

STUDYING THE BIBLE

IN ITS ANCIENT

CONTEXT(S)

Chapter Outline

CHAPTER OVERVIEW

This chapter introduces the basic orientation of the textbook and sets the stage for what follows with three overviews: geographical, historical, and methodological. The beginning of the chapter answers the questions "What makes academic study of the Bible different from typical 'Bible study'?" and "Why is such academic study important?" Next you gain a bird's-eye view of the major regions of the land of Israel, the major periods of Israel's history, and the major methods used by scholars to analyze the Bible. Your future study will be helped in particular by learning the location of the two major regions of ancient Israel – the heartland of tribal Israel to the north and the area of David's clan, Judah, to the south (with the famous city of Jerusalem between these two areas) – and by memorizing the dates of the major periods in the history of Israel (see also the appendix to this chapter).

READING
Exodus 14–15.
Scholars see two
accounts of
deliverance in
Exodus 14: can you?

EXERCISE
Write a half-page to one-page statement or mini-autobiography of your past encounters with the Bible. Which parts of it have been most central in such encounters? Have you studied the Bible in an academic context before? Have you had unusually positive or negative experiences with the Bible or people citing it?

At first glance, the Bible is one of the most familiar of books. Most families own a copy. Every weekend, Jews and Christians read from it at worship. There are echoes of the Bible in all kinds of music, from Handel's *Messiah* to reggae and hip hop. Popular expressions, such as "Thou shalt not" or "Love thy neighbor as thyself," come from the Bible. Movies are often filled with biblical allusions. And you still can find a copy of the Bible, or at least the New Testament and Psalms, in many hotels.

AD, BC, BCE, and CE

The older expressions for dates, BC and AD, are explicitly Christian in orientation. BC comes from "Before Christ," and AD comes from the Latin *anno Domini*, which means "in the year of the Lord."

Over the last decades scholarly works have tended to use the more neutral terms BCE and CE, which refer to "Before the Common Era" and "Common Era" respectively. The year references are the same, but the labels are not specifically Christian.

This *Introduction* uses the standard scholarly BCE and CE abbreviations.

At second glance, the Bible is one of the most foreign of books. Its language, even in English translation, is often difficult to understand, especially if you are using the King James Translation (1611), with its beautiful, but often obscure, seventeenth-century cadences and words. The biblical texts that are translated in the King James and other versions are still older. The New Testament was written in Greek, and its texts date from about two thousand years ago (50–200 CE). The Old Testament was written in Hebrew, and some of its parts date as far back as three thousand years (1000–164 BCE). Both testaments reflect their ancient origins in many ways. They use ancient literary forms and images that are not common now. They come out of religious contexts much different from contemporary Judaism or Christianity. And they are addressed to historical struggles and circumstances that most readers of the Bible do not know.

Bible Abbreviations, Verses, and Chapters

When books and articles cite biblical passages by chapter and verse, they usually follow this order: abbreviation for the biblical book, followed by the chapter number, followed by the verse. An example is Isa 44:28 (chapter 44, verse 28). If more than one verse is cited, dashes and commas can be used: Isa 44:20, 28 or Isa 44:10–13, 28. When scholars want to refer to the bulk of a passage without detailing specific verses left out, they will add an asterisk to indicate that some verses are not meant to be included in the reference, e.g. Genesis 28*.

Here are standard abbreviations for biblical books shared by Jewish and Christian Bibles (given in the Old Testament order):

Gen = Genesis	(also known as Canticles, and Song
Exod = Exodus	of Solomon)
Lev = Leviticus	Isa = Isaiah
Num = Numbers	Jer = Jeremiah
Deut = Deuteronomy	Lam = Lamentations
Josh = Joshua	Ezek = Ezekiel
Judg = Judges	Dan = Daniel
Ruth = Ruth	Hos = Hosea
Sam = Samuel	Joel = Joel
Kgs = Kings	Amos = Amos
Chr = Chronicles	Ob = Obadiah
Ezra = Ezra	Jon = Jonah
Neh = Nehemiah	Micah = Micah
Esther = Esther	Nah = Nahum
Job = Job	Hab = Habakkuk
Ps or Pss = Psalms	Zeph = Zephaniah
Prov = Proverbs	Hag = Haggai
Eccl = Ecclesiastes	Zech = Zechariah
Song = Song of Songs	

The ancient aspects of the Bible are part of what give it its holy aura, but they also make biblical texts difficult to understand. If someone sees a reference to "Cyrus" in Isa 44:28 and 45:1, that person likely will have few associations with who "Cyrus" was and what he meant to the writer of this text. Most readers have even fewer associations with places and empires mentioned in the Bible, such as "Ephraim" or "Assyria." Usually, their only acquaintance with "Egypt" or "Babylonia" is a brief discussion in some kind of world history class. Furthermore, other aspects of biblical texts are often hard for readers to get much out of now – such as the genealogies of Genesis or the harsh words about enemies in the psalms. This means that large portions of the Bible mean little or nothing to many readers. Few people who try to read the Bible from beginning to end actually get very far, and those who do often fail to make much sense out of what they have read.

This book will give you keys to understand the often obscure parts of the Bible. Names (e.g. Cyrus), events (e.g. the liberation from Babylonian captivity), and general perspectives in the Bible that previously you might have skipped past or not noticed should come into focus and make sense. For many, the experience of reading the Bible in historical context is much like finally getting to see a movie in color that beforehand had only been available in black and white. It is not at all that the meaning of the Bible can or should be limited to the settings in which it was originally composed. On the contrary: along the way we will see how the Bible is an important document now thanks to the fact that it has been radically *re*interpreted over centuries, first by successive communities of ancient Israelites and later by Jewish and Christian communities who cherished the Bible. Still, learning to see scriptures in relation to ancient history and culture can make previously bland or puzzling biblical texts come alive.

The Origins of Verses and Chapters

The earliest Hebrew and Greek manuscripts of the Bible lack any chapter or verse markings or numberings. The Hebrew Bible/Old Testament was divided into sections for reading in the synagogue, and the Greek New Testament was divided into sections as well, but there were no numbers in these early manuscripts.

Verses were first added into the Hebrew Bible (without numbers) by the Masoretes, a group of Jewish scholars who worked in the seventh to tenth centuries CE and produced the standard edition of the Hebrew Bible now used in Judaism. The chapter divisions we now have were developed in 1205 by Stephen Langton, a professor in Paris and eventually an archbishop of the Church of England.

The first Old Testament and New Testament Bible with verses was produced in 1555 by a Parisian book seller, Robert Estienne (also known as Stephanus). He is reported to have divided a copy of his New Testament into the present 7,959 verses while riding horseback from Paris to Lyon. He also numbered the chapters and verses of both the Old and New Testament.

To pursue this historical approach, we will *not* read the Bible from beginning to end. Instead, we will look at biblical texts in relationship to the different historical contexts that they addressed. This means that rather than starting with the creation stories of

Genesis 1–3, this book starts with remnants of Israel's earliest oral traditions. These are songs and sagas from the time when Israel had no cities and was still a purely tribal people. Our next stop will be texts from the rise of Israel's first monarchies, particularly certain "royal" psalms that celebrate God's choice of Jerusalem and anointing of kings there. As we move on through Israelite history, we will see how biblical texts reflect the very different influences of major world empires: the Mesopotamian empires of Assyria and Babylonia, and then the Persian, Hellenistic (Greek), and Roman empires. The common thread will be historical, and this will mean starting most chapters with some discussion of the historical and cultural context of the biblical texts to be discussed there.

Overview: Order of Main Discussions of Biblical Books

Period of the Judges: Chapter 2. Oral traditions in Genesis 12–35, Exodus, and Judges 5.

Early monarchy/David and Solomon: Chapters 3 and 4. 1–2 Samuel, texts attributed to David and Solomon (Psalms [especially royal and Zion psalms], Proverbs, Ecclesiastes, Song of Songs), and Genesis 2–4 and parts of 6–11 (an early primeval history).

Later northern and southern monarchies: Chapters 5 and 6. Amos, Hosea, Micah and early parts of Isaiah (along with possible northern traditions in Exodus, Genesis 25–35, etc.).

Twilight of the Monarchy in Jerusalem: Chapters 7 and 8. Deuteronomy through 2 Kings, Jeremiah, Nahum, and Zephaniah.

Exile of Judeans to Babylon: Chapters 9 and 10. Lamentations, Ezekiel, Isaiah 40–55, and major parts of Genesis through Numbers (especially the Abraham story in Genesis 12–25 and the book of Leviticus).

Return of exiles and rebuilding: Chapters 11 and 12. Haggai, Zechariah, Isaiah 56–66, Jonah, Ruth, Job and the book of Psalms (along with parts of Ezra–Nehemiah and Genesis through Numbers).

The Hellenistic empires and crisis: Chapter 13. Sirach, Enoch, Daniel, Ezra–Nehemiah, 1–2 Chronicles, Esther and the final formation of the Hebrew Bible (along with some on Ecclesiastes and Song of Songs).

At first this approach may be disorienting, since it involves placing familiar biblical texts in a different order and in new contexts. Take the example of the story of creation in Gen 1:1–2:3. It seems straightforward enough as it is. Why wait to talk much about this opening story of the Bible until Chapter 9 of this *Introduction*? As we will see, one reason is that reading Gen 1:1–2:3 in relation to the Judeans' experience of forced exile in Babylonia (the focus of Chapter 9) explains the major emphasis in this text on the Sabbath. This is an aspect of the text that many people, especially non-Jews, completely miss, since it has little meaning for them. But the whole seven-day structure of the story is meant to lead up to one thing: God's rest on the seventh day and blessing of it (Gen 2:1–3). Reading this text in relation to the Babylonian exile highlights this important feature and makes sense of other aspects of the creation story as well.

This is just one way in which academic study of the Bible is quite a different thing from study of the Bible in Sunday school or even high school religion classes in parochial schools. Many people come to a university or seminary class on Bible expecting a summary of the contents of the Bible or indoctrination into biblical theologies or values. Others expect a devotional approach that they have learned in church Bible studies where the Bible often is read as a lesson book for life. All these approaches have their value and place, but they differ from the academic approach of a college or seminary course. Moreover, they are misleading indicators of what to expect out of such a course. Where a student might expect to work hard in a history or organic chemistry class, study of the "Bible" – especially if it's imagined on the basis of earlier experience with religious education – promises to be easy. Yet an *academic* course on the Bible offers its own set of challenges, somewhat similar to those of a good course in history or English literature. Indeed, some students find academic study of the Bible especially difficult because it offers alternatives to their past interpretations of biblical texts that they cherish. These students not only must learn the course material about the Bible, but must integrate this knowledge with their beliefs and values.

The benefits of such study are substantial. Familiar texts offer new meanings. Difficult biblical texts start to make better sense when placed in their original historical contexts. Where once the Bible might have seemed a monolithic, ancient set of rules, it becomes a rich variety of different perspectives that have stood the test of time. I encourage you to be open to this approach and learn for yourself what it has to offer.

The Geography and Major Characters of the Biblical Drama

Let us start by setting the scene for the drama of biblical history, looking at the geography of the biblical world, major nations, and major historical periods. This information is important, because it will orient you to the quite different world in which the Bible was created.

Asked to picture the land of Israel, many would conjure up images from TV specials or popular movies where biblical events occur amidst sand dunes, palm trees, and small villages. The reality is that the area of Israel encompasses sharp contrasts in topography, rainfall, and vegetation. Imagine Map 1.1 as divided into four narrow strips running up and down. The strip to the left is the *coastal plain* along the Mediterranean sea. It is low, flat, and fertile and receives relatively regular rainfall. Non-Israelites lived here through most of Israelite history, and it was ruled from Jerusalem only for short periods. The next strip is the *central hill country* and runs down the middle of the map, encompassing the hill country of Judah, hill country of Ephraim (Israel), and Galilee. This is an area of rocky hills, rising up to 3,000 feet, where most of Israelite history took place. It is drier and less accessible than the coastal plain to the west. The third strip is the *Jordan Valley*, encompassing the Dead Sea, Jordan River, and Sea of Galilee (from south to north). This is one of the lowest places on earth, about 1,000 feet below sea level, and – aside from some oases – it is very dry and barren. The fourth strip is

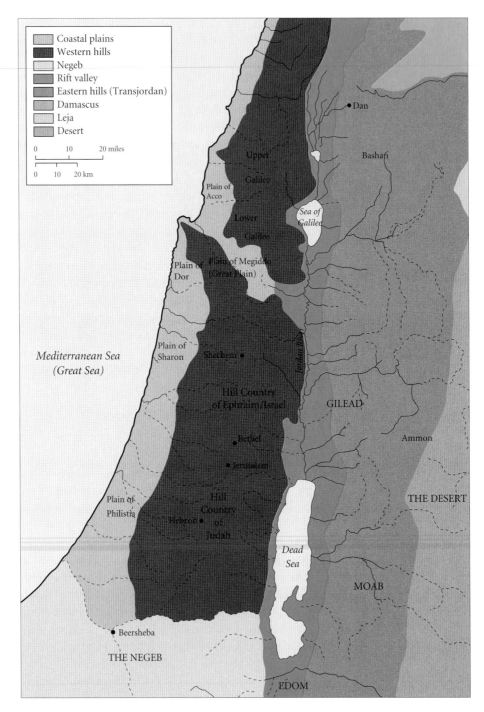

Map 1.1 The land of Israel and its surroundings. Redrawn from Adrian Curtis (ed.), *Oxford Bible Atlas*, 4th edition. Oxford, New York: Oxford University Press, 2007.

the *Transjordanian Plateau*, including Edom, Moab, Ammon, and the Gilead region (where Israelites settled). This plateau, now in the contemporary nation of Jordan, has similar characteristics to the central highlands of Israel. To the east of it (and off the map) lies the desert.

Before looking more broadly at the world of the ancient Near East, it is important to get a preliminary understanding of the different parts of the land of Israel and the peoples who lived there. Though people often apply the term "Israel" to this entire area, this term often refers more narrowly to the peoples who settled in the *northern* highlands described above ("Hill country of Ephraim/Israel" on Map 1.1, with Shechem at its center) along with parts of the Gilead of the Transjordan. For much of biblical history, this area and this people are to be distinguished from "Judah," which is located in the *southern* highlands of the map ("Hill country of Judah;" Hebron is a Judean city). Note that Jerusalem lay between Israel and Judah and was not "Israelite"/"Judean" until David conquered it by stealth at the outset of his monarchy. This distinction between "Judah" in the south and "Israel" in the north is important for much of Israel's early history. Later on, the term "Israel" came to encompass Judah as well, and the narratives of the Hebrew Bible – many of them written later – project that picture onto the earliest history of the people. Therefore, the word "**Israel**" has at least two major meanings in the Bible: a narrow sense referring to the ancient tribal groups settled in the northern highlands and a broader sense referring to Judah along with those other tribal groups. When people refer to the "land of Israel" or the "people of Israel," they usually are using the word "Israel" in the broader sense, but there will be numerous times in this *Introduction* when it will be important to remember the narrower sense of "Israel" (in the north) as opposed to "Judah" (in the south).

The "land of Israel" where most biblical events take place is actually relatively small. As you can see on Map 1.1, the Sea of Galilee is only 30 miles from the Mediterranean Sea, and the Dead Sea is only 60 miles away. The distance from the area around Shechem in the north to Beersheba in the south is about 90 miles. This means that the main setting of biblical history, the area of the central highlands (thus excluding the non-Israelite coastal plains), is about 40 miles by 90 miles – not much bigger than many large metropolitan areas. This tiny area is the site where texts and religious ideas were formed that would change world history. Notably, this highland area also encompasses many areas most in dispute in the contemporary Middle East, areas that are variously designated as "the West Bank," "occupied territories," and "Judea and Samaria." Before 1967 these regions were not part of the modern nation of Israel, but they were seized by Israel from Jordan during the 1967 war, and their status is a major issue in the ongoing Middle East conflict.

This recent dispute is only the latest chapter in thousands of years of struggles for control of this narrow strip of land. In ancient times, the land of Israel occupied a strategic location along the "Fertile Crescent" extending from Egypt in the southwest to the Mesopotamian empires of Assyria and Babylonia in the northeast. Because much of the area east of Israel was impassable desert, the major roads between Egypt and Mesopotamia had to cross the narrow strip of land between the Mediterranean Sea and the desert (see Map 1.2). Israel lay right along those roads and often got run over by

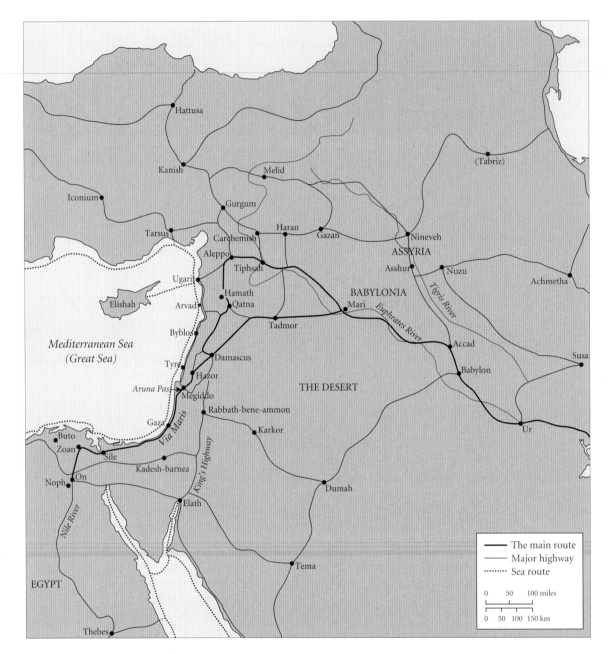

Map 1.2 The major routes of the ancient Near East. Note how the major routes move from Egypt on the left through Judah/Israel near the Mediterranean to Syria and Mesopotamia to the northeast and east. Redrawn from Yohanan Aharoni and Michael Avi-Yonah, *The Macmillan Bible Atlas* (revised edition). New York, Macmillan, 1977, map 9.

the armies of its more powerful neighbors. The various empires of the ancient Near East were almost always laying claim to Israel and the surrounding areas, and the peoples of Israel got caught in the middle.

Major Periods in the Biblical Drama

The major turns in biblical history can be seen in this context. The Egyptian empire dominated the area of ancient Israel from around 1450 to 1200 BCE, the years when most scholars think the biblical exodus may have happened. Then a series of catastrophes ended Egyptian rule over the area and inaugurated a power vacuum in the land of Israel. This is when we first see identifiable archaeological evidence of a "people of Israel." This people settled in small villages in the hill country of Judah and Israel during the **pre-state tribal period** (1250–1000 BCE, including the time of the chieftain, Saul), then kings David and Solomon ruled this whole area for about a century from their capital in Jerusalem (**united monarchy**, 1000–930 BCE), and finally the northern tribes split from this monarchy (930 BCE). Thus began the period of the **divided monarchy**, when there were two kingdoms in broader Israel: a kingdom of Israel in the north, and a kingdom of Judah in the south (930–722 BCE).

This window of freedom from imperial domination, however, was not to last. Especially in the late eighth century (745 BCE and onward), the Assyrian empire, based in what is now northern Iraq, gained control of both Israel and (later) Judah (see Map 1.3). This empire completely destroyed the kingdom of Israel in 722 BCE and dominated the kingdom of Judah for decades. Indeed, from 745 to 586 BCE, Israel and Judah were dominated by a series of brutal empires – Assyria, Egypt (for a couple of years), and Babylonia (based in middle Iraq). Though Judah enjoyed brief independence between domination by the Assyrians and Egyptians, the nation was dominated and eventually destroyed by the Babylonian empire, which reduced Jerusalem, along with its Temple, to rubble in 586 BCE (**destruction of Jerusalem**, ending a period of **Judah alone**, 722–586 BCE). Thus began one of the most important periods of biblical history, the **Babylonian exile** (586–538). At the outset of this period, most of the elite who had lived in Judah were forcibly deported to Babylon, and in many cases neither they nor their children ever returned.

The story of Israel and empires, however, was not over. Just decades later, the Persian ruler, Cyrus, conquered the Babylonian empire, ushering in a period of Persian rule of Judah that lasted from 538 to 332 BCE (the **Persian period**, the beginning of the **post-exilic period**, starting 538 BCE). The Bible records a number of ways in which Cyrus and his successors helped former exiles in Babylon rebuild the temple and rebuild their community. Later, Alexander the Great conquered the area in 333 BCE, beginning a period of Hellenistic rule, and it appears that he and his successors generally continued the Persian policies of support of Jerusalem and its leadership during their rule of Judah and Jerusalem (**Hellenistic period**, 332–167 BCE). Nevertheless, in the late second century (starting in 167 BCE), there was a major crisis in Judah, precipitated by the efforts of some elite Judeans to turn the city of Jerusalem into a Greek city. This

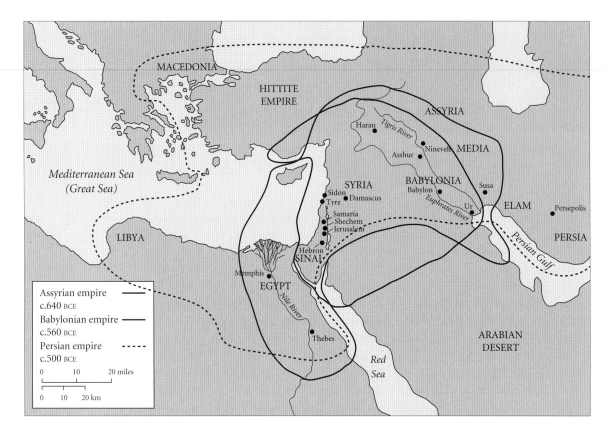

Map 1.3 The reach of three of the major empires that dominated Israel and/or Judah: the Assyrian, Babylonian, and Persian empires. Redrawn from www.bible.ca, Abingdon Press, 1994.

crisis eventually led to the formation, for a brief period, of another monarchy in Judah, this one led by a priestly family called the **Hasmoneans** (also known as the **Maccabees**). This **Hasmonean monarchy** continued from 142 to 63 BCE, when the Romans took control of the area, which they named "Palestine" and put under control of a series of governors. The year 63 BCE represents the **beginning of the Roman period** in Palestine.

With this, "Palestine" joined much of the surrounding world as part of the Roman empire. This is the time when Jesus lived, the early church formed in the wake of his crucifixion by the Romans, and the Christian movement spread across the Mediterranean Sea to cities around the Roman empire. This was also the time of multiple Judean revolts against Roman control that eventually led to the destruction in 70 CE of the Jerusalem Temple rebuilt under the Persians (**destruction of the Second Temple**) and the complete destruction of Jewish Jerusalem in 135 CE. Thus the Jewish temple state was completely destroyed. The main form of Jewish life to survive this catastrophe was rabbinic Judaism, which grew out of the scholarship and leadership of the earlier, popular movement of the Pharisees.

Later chapters of this *Introduction* will give details about all of these historical periods, correlating each of them with biblical texts. The aim here is to give a sense of how much Israelite history was shaped by relationships with various empires. Though "Israel" (and "Judah") emerged as recognizable peoples and states during an imperial power vacuum (1200–745 BCE), the books of the Bible were largely written during the periods of imperial domination by Assyrian, Babylonian, Persian, Hellenistic, and Roman empires. We gain a deeper understanding of the Old Testament the more we see how diverse biblical pictures of the "empire of God" were formed in response to domination by these powerful empires in the ancient world.

Multiple Contexts, Multiple Methods

Reading biblical texts in relation to their original contexts can make many aspects of them come alive, but the reason such texts are read now is that they have remained meaningful to diverse communities in much later contexts. These texts are in the Bible because they have consistently transcended their origins. This *Introduction* will discuss both aspects of the Bible: its origins in the ancient Near East and its later interpretation by Jewish, Christian, and even Muslim communities today. Knowing more about the Bible's early contexts gives some perspective on contemporary differences in interpretation. The more you know about the antiquity of the Bible, the more you may appreciate both the care and the creativity with which it has been read and reread over time by different communities.

This can be illustrated through a brief look at how different methods of biblical criticism might look at Israel's "exodus," the story of **Yahweh**'s (see box on p. 28) liberation of the people from Egypt that is now found in the first chapters of the book of Exodus (Exodus 1–15). To start, some scholars try to reconstruct whether and when this exodus actually happened. Such academic study of the history of Israel uses biblical texts as one among multiple sources for the reconstruction of "what probably happened." So far, the results of such study have been inconclusive. On the one hand, many scholars believe some sort of exodus out of Egypt happened, probably during the centuries just before the emergence of the people of "Israel" as a distinct group in the highlands of Canaan. On the other hand, most academic scholars of the Bible also believe that the written texts of the Bible are so far removed from the events that they describe that they are not useful for precise retelling of what actually happened back then: who said what, how many and who were involved, etc. The biblical texts are not reliable for such details because they have been filtered by centuries of oral retelling and written expansions by later Israelites. Imagine a game of "telephone" where hundreds of people over a period of five hundred years retell a story important to them, each one to the next generation, and then imagine trying to use the end result of the process for historical analysis. Because biblical texts are so shaped by time, scholars studying the history of Israel attempt to reconstruct what happened through analyzing them and comparing them – where possible – with archaeological records and non-biblical historical sources.

The Name of Israel's God: Yahweh/the LORD

The name of Israel's God in Hebrew is Yahweh, but you will not see this name written out in most English translations of the Bible. Instead, most translations have "the LORD" where the Hebrew manuscripts have a strange combination of the consonants for Yahweh (YHWH) and the vowels for the Hebrew word "lord." Why this combination?

The consonants are earlier, since the earliest Hebrew Bible manuscripts were written in all consonants. When Jewish scholars started producing manuscripts with vowels, the divine name Yahweh had become so holy that they did not pronounce it out loud (This is still true for many Jews.) Therefore, they added the vowels for "lord" in every

place where the consonants for Yahweh occurred so that readers would say "lord" rather than the holy name. English translations reflect this combination when they put "lord" in all capital letters (LORD), indicating that this particular "lord" is Yahweh. (Note "Jehovah" is the word that is produced when you simply pronounce the consonants of YHWH with the vowels for the Hebrew word for "lord.")

We will be focusing here on the state of the Bible before such prohibitions on pronouncing the divine name existed. So there will be occasions where it will be helpful to refer to Israel's God by the name Yahweh.

Historical criticism is a family of historical methods that analyzes how and where the biblical texts (and oral traditions in them) were composed. "Criticism" in this case does not mean that historical critics find fault with the biblical texts that they study, but that they use academically critical analysis to arrive at their conclusions rather than starting on the basis of faith assumptions. Through **tradition criticism** and **form criticism** biblical scholars attempt to identify early oral traditions standing behind the biblical text. For example, past tradition and form critics have supposed that the following song of Miriam may be one of the earliest traditions in the Bible to speak of the defeat of the Egyptian army at the Red sea:

> Sing to Yahweh, for he has been victorious
> Horse and rider, he has thrown into the sea. (Exod 15:21)

Form critics study different types of texts in the Bible and their likely social contexts. They would argue that the text above was the kind of "victory song" that was sung by women upon return of men from battle. Tradition critics investigate the telling and retelling process of early biblical traditions, often analyzing written texts to uncover the centuries-long evolution of oral traditions (and sometimes written traditions) about an event such as the exodus. **Source criticism** and **redaction criticism** attempt to reconstruct the literary development of such biblical texts. For example, more than two hundred years ago source critics discovered that the story of Israel's deliverance from Egypt in Exodus 14 is actually an interweaving of two, originally separate written accounts of the same event, one source which tells of the sea waters being driven back by a strong wind, and another source which tells of the Israelites being led through the sea between two walls of water. Redaction critics study the final formation of the biblical text through the combination of such sources and literary expansions of them. Where source critics study the written building blocks of the biblical text, redaction critics examine how those building blocks were put together and added onto. The broad term for this kind of study of the formation of the Bible out of both oral and written traditions is "**transmission history**."

Many scholars, however, focus not on how the Bible was formed, but on what it means and has meant to generations of readers of the Bible. For example, **literary criticism** has drawn on methods in the study of modern literature to study the plot, characterization, pacing, and shape of biblical texts. Such critics have examined Exodus 1–15 as if it were a novel, looking at *how* the story is artfully told: how is Moses introduced and characterized? How does this contrast with the characterization of the Egyptians and their leaders? What does the reader expect and learn as the narrative unfolds? Such study of the poetic and narrative dynamics of biblical texts is distinct from study of how such texts have been interpreted by later readers, which is the **history of interpretation**. Historians of interpretation study how the story of the Exodus is featured in Islam, as well as its becoming central to both Judaism and Christianity. The exodus story is the centerpiece of the Jewish celebration of Passover and is a founding story for the Christian practices of baptism and eucharist. Meanwhile, **cultural criticism** has studied ways the exodus story is not just read in faith communities, but has entered popular culture, through media such as reggae music or movies like *The Ten Commandments* and *The Prince of Egypt*. Both history of interpretation and cultural criticism are embraced in the overall study in **reception history** of how biblical texts have been used and consciously interpreted.

Finally, various forms of **ideological criticism** analyze ways that the exodus story can be, has been, and should be read in the midst of systematic structures of power. For example, early **feminist criticism** lifted up the importance of the story of the midwives in the lead-up to the Exodus (Exod 1:15–21), and later feminist critics have raised questions about the male focus of the exodus story and most other parts of the Bible. **Gender criticism** analyzes biblical depictions of both male and female gender in the Bible, including the implicit characterization of God in the exodus as a masculine, militaristic God, "a man of war" (Exod 15:3). Finally, **postcolonial criticism** has examined how texts like the exodus story were formed in response to imperial dynamics and later played a role in colonial imperialism. Thus, a postcolonial critic could look at how the biblical exodus story was written hundreds of years after the events it describes as a response to Assyrian, Babylonian, or other domination. But postcolonial critics have also looked at ways Christian missionaries and European colonial powers justified their domination of other peoples through depicting themselves as the true heirs of the "Israel" depicted as favored by God in the Exodus story. Thus "postcolonial" criticism adds a particular perspective to both study of the formation of the biblical text and study of its history of interpretation.

Conclusion

This chapter has given an overview which will be filled in by the following chapters. It may be disorienting to encounter so many terms and dates at once. Nevertheless, it is important to get this larger picture in order to understand the details of what follows. The remaining chapters of this *Introduction* will unfold the story of the Bible's creation. This story moves from discussion of oral traditions in pre-literate Israel all the way through to the final formation of the Hebrew Bible in the kingdom of the Hasmoneans. Though the first chapters will uncover a strange and different ancient Israel unfamiliar to many readers, this historical approach will illuminate many aspects of the Bible that otherwise make little sense. In addition, it will provide a starting point for engaging other scholarly methods of looking at biblical texts in new ways.

Of course, the analysis of the formation of the Bible and its texts is always in flux. Within the space of this brief *Introduction* I will only be able to touch on a few of the major debates. Nevertheless, scholars have been doing this kind of historical analysis of the Bible for about three hundred years, and these efforts have produced some interesting and important results. This textbook draws on the breadth of that scholarship in giving a historical orientation to the Bible that can be a starting point for further study, questioning, and correction.

CHAPTER ONE REVIEW

1. Know the meaning and significance of the following terms discussed in this chapter:

- cultural criticism
- feminist criticism
- gender criticism
- historical criticism
- history of interpretation
- ideological criticism
- Israel [two meanings]
- literary criticism
- postcolonial criticism
- reception history
- redaction criticism
- source criticism
- tradition criticism
- transmission history
- Yahweh

2. Be able to identify the following areas on a map and describe their general characteristics:

- coastal plain
- central hill country
- Jordan valley
- Judah
- Transjordan

3. Know the dates and basic significance of the following overall periods of history:

- pre-state tribal period
- united monarchy
- divided monarchy
- Judah alone
- destruction of Jerusalem
- Babylonian exile
- Persian period
- post-exilic period
- Hellenistic period

- Hasmonean (Maccabean) monarchy
- beginning of the Roman period
- destruction of the Second Temple

4. Know the order in which the following empires dominated Israel and Judah:

- Assyrian
- Babylonian
- Persian
- Hellenistic (or Greek)
- Roman

RESOURCES FOR FURTHER STUDY

Overviews of the history of Israel

Miller, J. Maxwell. *The History of Israel: An Essential Guide.* Nashville: Abingdon, 1997.

Shanks, Hershel. *Ancient Israel: From Abraham to the Roman Destruction of the Temple* (2nd edition). Washington, DC: Biblical Archaeology Society, 1999.

Geography of lands and places featured in the Bible

Atlas of the Bible Lands. (revised edition). Maplewood, NJ: Hammond, 1990.

Rainey, Anson F., and Notley, R. Steven. *The Sacred Bridge: Carta's Atlas of the Biblical World.* Jerusalem: Carta, 2006. Detailed. Much focus on reconstructing history.

Rogerson, John. *The New Atlas of the Bible.* London: McDonald, 1985. Organized not by historical periods, but by regions. Excellent photographs and art.

Discussions of methods in biblical interpretation

Barry, Peter. *Beginning Theory: An Introduction to Literary and Cultural Theory* (2nd edition). Manchester: Manchester University Press, 2002. Excellent, accessible overview of more recent literary theory and methods of interpretation.

McKenzie, Steven L., and Haynes, Stephen R. *To Each Its Own Meaning: An Introduction to Biblical Criticisms and Their Application* (2nd edition). Louisville, KY: Westminster John Knox Press, 1999.

Book of Exodus, problems of history, and history of interpretation

Johnstone, William. *Exodus.* Old Testament Guides. Sheffield: Sheffield Academic Press, 1990. Especially pp. 31–8.

Langston, Scott M. *Exodus.* Blackwell Commentary Series. Oxford: Blackwell, 2006. History of interpretation.

APPENDIX: ISRAEL'S HISTORY AND EMPIRES

(Prehistory of Israel: domination of Canaan by Egypt, 1450–1200 BCE)

Emergence of "Israel" in imperial power vacuum
    Appearance of Israelite villages in unsettled hill country (1250–1000 BCE)
    David and Solomon's united monarchy in Jerusalem (1000–930 BCE)
    Divided monarchy: southern Judah and northern Israel (930–722 BCE)

Oppression by successive empires: Assyria, Egypt, and Babylonia (745–586 BCE)
    Fall of northern kingdom (722 BCE)
    Destruction of Jerusalem and exile of its leadership (586 BCE; also other waves of exile)

Imperial sponsorship of (formerly exiled) Judeans: post-exilic period (starting 538 BCE)
    Persian-sponsored rebuilding and rule of Judah (538–332 BCE)
    Hellenistic continuation of Persian policies until Hellenistic crisis (332–167 BCE)
    Hellenistic crisis and emergence of Hasmonean/Maccabean monarchy (167–63 BCE)

Roman rule (starting 63 BCE with different dates of end)
    Destruction of the Second Temple (70 CE)
    Total destruction of Jerusalem (135 CE)

CHAPTER 2

THE EMERGENCE OF

ANCIENT ISRAEL AND ITS

FIRST ORAL TRADITIONS

Chapter Outline

CHAPTER OVERVIEW

This chapter addresses the questions "How did the earliest Israelites live?" and "What were some of Israel's most ancient traditions?" You will learn about ancient Israelite tribal life and how that form of social organization is distinguished from two other forms of social life important in later chapters of Israel's history: the monarchal city-state and the empire. The chapter discusses some unique characteristics of the kind of oral tradition typical of such tribal groups, and it finds evidence of such oral traditions embedded in biblical texts about Jacob, exodus from Egypt, and Deborah's victory over the armies of Hazor. In their early oral form (no longer available to us), these stories and poems, often celebrating devious "tricksters" who triumph over all odds, formed part of a "collective memory" that helped distinguish the tribal-culture Israelites from the Canaanites surrounding them. At the same time, despite these differences in social organization and tribal tradition, you will also discover in this chapter ways that early Israel was more "Canaanite" in its religion and culture than you previously thought. Read both for ways ancient Israel was different from its neighbors and for ways it was similar.

Imagining Early Israel

Let us begin with a look at the stories and songs treasured by Israel at the outset of its history. More than anywhere else in this book this requires a lot of imagination, since we have no Israelite writings from this period. Therefore, we must piece together a picture of Israel based on a combination of archaeology, some material from neighboring cultures, and distant echoes of early Israel in the much later writings now found in our Bible.

So we start with imagination – a creative reconstruction of the kind of village where Israel's first oral traditions might have developed. It is a journey back to the time described in the Bible in the books of Joshua and Judges. Nevertheless, there are major contrasts between what these books say about this "period of the Judges" and what historians reconstruct of it. Chapter 7 will discuss the later writing of Joshua and Judges, along with the Pentateuch that comes before them (Genesis–Deuteronomy). For now, however, the focus is not on the written books of the Bible, but on the oral culture that produced Israel's first traditions. Here is a picture based on archaeology and careful analysis of the Bible and non-biblical texts.

If we were to take a time machine back to Israel's beginnings, the journey probably would take us to one of the hilltop villages in the hill country that existed in the late second millennium (1250–1000 BCE) between the coastal plains and Jordan valley (see Figure 2.1). The early Israelites in the **village** lived on a subsistence level, surviving

Figure 2.1 Part of the hill country of central Israel. Notice the ancient terraces cut into the limestone hills to help in farming them.

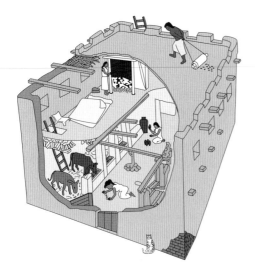

Figure 2.2 Typical pillared house of the Israelites. The bottom floor had stables for animals, cistern for water, and areas for cooking and food preparation. The top floor was where the family slept, dined, and entertained. Redrawn from Philip J. King and Lawrence E. Stager, *Life in Biblical Israel*. Louisville, KY: Westminster John Knox Press, 2001, page 29.

largely on the crops that they grew. Generally there were two main seasons: a dry summer–fall season and a rainy winter–spring season culminating in the harvest of barley, then wheat and other crops. The rain on which they depended was fickle. They would store water from the rainy season in sealed underground holes, "cisterns." They used large pottery jars to store food produced from the harvest. Nevertheless, about every three or four years there would be too little rain for crops. Life would be especially hard then, with families struggling to keep from starving until another year, a better rainy season, and the first harvests from that next year's crop. In such times they might sacrifice and eat one of their precious animals in order to survive. Otherwise, animals were primarily sources of milk and clothing (wool or skins).

Our village would have only a few homes, housing a handful of clans, settled in separate households where extended families lived together: grandparents, their sons and sons' wives, unmarried daughters, and dependents. Only about 50–300 people would have lived in each such village, and their lives were short and hard (as everywhere else in the ancient world). Though a few lucky individuals lived much longer, most males who survived early childhood typically lived into their mid-thirties, while most women died as early as their late twenties, half of them in childbirth. They were vulnerable to starvation, diseases, warfare, and (for women) the hazards of childbirth.

Because a village lacked a wall or many men of fighting age, it was vulnerable to raids from other areas or attacks by the organized armies of the city-states in the coastal areas and lowlands. Their only hope of defense was divine help, along with assistance from banding together with other villages in their tribe (e.g. Ephraim, Manasseh, Asher). In times of particular crisis, the villages of multiple tribes might join together in a temporary military alliance led by a charismatic individual. As we will see in the Song of Deborah, it was not always easy to pull together these scattered tribes and villages into a coordinated defense. Such texts show that – contrary to some other biblical portrayals – earliest "Israel" was a very loosely organized whole. Villages and tribes bonded together to counter the unpredictabilities of military or agricultural catastrophe. Still, the primary social reality for most people in early Israel would have been their village and its clans. They would have spent the vast bulk of their lives living and working within the confines of the village itself and the surrounding hills.

This way of life contrasted with that of non-Israelite **monarchal city-states** near Israel. Ancient Near Eastern city-states were territories controlled by a city, generally cities ruled by kings. Such cities could amass resources and achieve levels of organization that were impossible in more decentralized systems such as tribal Israel. The walls around cities gave them immense defensive advantages over forces attacking with superior numbers. City-states usually had a professional army, whose training and equipment

What Was Earliest "Israel" and Who Were "Judges"?

Though the Bible portrays "Israel" as a coherent group of 12 tribes descended from Jacob, most scholars now agree that this is not an accurate historical portrayal. Instead, as we will see later (in our look at Judges 5), earliest "Israel" was a loosely organized group of tribes who shared a way of life (in villages) and helped in each other's military defense. Anthropologists use the term "**segmentary society**" to describe the kind of decentralized social grouping that was early Israel.

One distinctive element of such segmentary societies is the lack of a permanent power structure, such as a kingship. Instead, the villages and larger groupings were guided in their day-to-day life by elders. In times of great need, charismatic leaders, such as Deborah, would arise to join the different groups of "Israel" into a common army. They are referred to in English biblical translations as "judges," but a better – though awkward – translation probably would be "temporary leaders."

gave them an advantage over more disorganized voluntary forces like those of Israel. Their greater military power and social organization allowed them to dominate surrounding areas, requiring peasants under their domination to help build fortifications in the city and provide regular deliveries of a certain amount of their produce. Even though the stories of the book of Judges come from a later time, we can read between the lines to see signs of struggle by Israelites against the attempts of surrounding city-states (e.g. Hazor) to dominate them. These threats, along with raids from groups such as the Midianites and Amalekites, created the need for charismatic leaders in crisis, "judges" such as Deborah or Samson, to rally disparate villages and tribes together, pooling their resources to repel a common enemy.

One enemy these Israelites did not have to face – in stark contrast to later periods in the history of Israel – was the might of a major ancient Near Eastern **empire** such as Egypt or Babylonia. The most this village culture would have known of such superpowers would have been distant echoes of Egyptian influence in some of the cities against which the villages had to fight for survival. Before the Israelite settlements emerged, Egypt had dominated the area for about two hundred years, subduing and demanding allegiance from the rulers of its major cities. We even have letters sent to and from the Pharaoh's scribes and rulers of city-states in Palestine such as Jerusalem, Shechem, and Megiddo. Jerusalem at this time was not inhabited by Israelites, but by Jebusites, and its king, Abdi-heba, writes the Pharaoh, "I am your slave, and I renew my covenant with you as my Pharaoh by bowing before you seven times seven times" (see Figure 2.3). Later he predicts that, if he is not sent enough troops, "The lands of Pharaoh, my lord, in Canaan, will be lost." It does turn out that Egypt lost control of the area. Nevertheless, Egyptian influence continued for centuries in major coastal cities such as Byblos, and elsewhere in Palestine.

Unlike the scribes who once wrote letters for king Abdi-heba of (pre-Israelite) Jerusalem, our hilltop villagers did not have time or need to learn to read and write.

Figure 2.3 Tablet containing a letter from Abdi-heba, the ruler of Jerusalem while it was still a Jebusite city, before David captured it. In it the ruler reports on the area to his overlords in Egypt.

We know from both comparative and archaeological evidence that writing – when it occurs – is primarily connected to centralized and hierarchical urban forms of social organization (e.g. Jerusalem). Nevertheless, like other small groups throughout time, our early Israelite villagers would have had a rich and varied cultural life. Rather than writing texts, they passed on traditions orally from one generation to another. These traditions would have included genealogical trees organizing clans and villages into tribal groups and sub-groups, stories of cultural heroes such as Jacob, and songs of deliverance about the exodus or the victory under Deborah.

These **oral traditions** were in flux, as they were sung and told from year to year amidst constantly cycling generations. At one time scholars used to think that non-literate cultures, such as the early Israelites, had unusual powers of memory that allowed them to memorize and precisely recite oral traditions over hundreds of years. Careful study of such cultures, however, has revealed that people who memorize traditions through purely oral means change them constantly and substantially. To be sure, some elements may be preserved because they are anchored in a name, topographical feature, or ongoing cultural practice. Nevertheless, the singers of oral cultures constantly adapt the traditions they receive, and they only partially can correct for this process of adaptation through consultation with networks of other oral singers and storytellers.

This means that the early traditions of ancient Israel, whatever they were, evolved in their journey across the centuries of the late second millennium, passing from one set of lips to another. A name such as "Moses" might stick, even the name of a long-abandoned Egyptian city – "Rameses" – but the story of the Israelites' exodus out of Egypt would evolve as they faced new enemies and challenges in later centuries. In the process of oral telling and retelling, the "Moses" of the story might start to resemble leaders or liberators at the time of retelling, and the "Egypt" of the retold story might resemble later enemies. Similarly, the story of Jacob wrestling God at the Jabbok (now in Gen 32:22–32) explains the place name "Penuel," and because the place name implies a divine encounter (Penuel is interpreted as Hebrew for "face of God"), that part of the story may have stayed stable over time while other details changed in the retelling process.

One characteristic appears to have been remarkably frequent, particularly in Israel's early traditions: the **trickster** – that is: a character whose ability to survive through trickery and even lawbreaking is celebrated in religion, literature, or another part of culture. Anthropologists have long noted that many cultures, particularly cultures of more vulnerable groups, celebrate such tricksters who survive against difficult odds through cunning and sometimes deceptive behavior. Figures such as the Plains Indian

History and the Books of Joshua and Judges

At this point we are discussing Israel's earliest history in the land. This is the time when Israel lived in villages and did not yet have a king, a period described in the biblical books of Joshua and Judges. These books, however, date from around 600 BCE at the earliest, at least five hundred years after the events they describe. They are different from each other, and each builds on diverse oral and written traditions to tell its stories. For example, the books tell up to three different stories of the conquest of several cities: e.g. Hebron in Josh 10:36–7, 15:13–14, and Judg 1:10 or Debir in Josh 10:38–9, 15:15–17, and Judg 1:11. Therefore, historians of ancient Israel are ever more careful about how they use information from Joshua and Judges. Also, the discipline of archaeology has provided an important control for helping such historians evaluate the historical usefulness of biblical traditions. Later in this *Introduction* we will return to look at the books of Joshua and Judges as theological texts addressed to the people of the seventh century.

MORE ON METHOD: TRADITION HISTORY AND TRANSMISSION HISTORY

Though traditions can be written as well as oral, many scholars use the term **"tradition history"** to refer to the history of oral traditions that existed before and alongside the written texts now in the Bible. Different versions of an oral tradition can be recognized by the combination of thematic or plot parallels on the one hand and variation in characters, setting, and especially wording on the other. Take the example of the parallel stories of Abraham and Sarah at Philistine Gerar with King Abimelech (Gen 20:1–18, 21:22–34) and Isaac and Rebekah at the same place and with the same king (Gen 26:6–33). Look at the similarities and differences! Though the two sets of stories are remarkably parallel, they diverge enough from each other that many believe them to be oral variants of the same tales.

Scholars can use the term "transmission history" to refer more broadly to the history of the transmission of oral *and written* biblical traditions. Later in this *Introduction* we will discuss numerous examples of the growth of written texts through combination or expansion of earlier sources.

Coyote demonstrate to their people how one can survive in a hostile environment where the rules are stacked against you. Throughout time people in vulnerable circumstances have celebrated such tricksters, who are often heroes within their own group. In home rituals, agricultural celebrations, weddings and other rites of passage, and other events, they would tell and sing stories of how their ancestors had triumphed against all odds, often tricking and defeating their more powerful opponents.

Problems in Reconstructing Early Israel

READING

The Merneptah
Stela, www.wiley.
com/go/carr (the
first non-biblical
mention of "Israel").

EXERCISE

Read Joshua 11. What impression do you get from this chapter of the
Israelites' military accomplishments? How does this compare with the
picture of these as summarized in Judges 1? As indicated in the discussion
below, both these narratives about Israel's origins were written centuries
after the events they describe and are historically problematic.

Figure 2.4 Stela listing Egyptian conquests,
dating to around 1200 BCE. It contains the
earliest mention of "Israel" outside the Bible.

The village described above is forever lost for us, if it ever
existed in anything like that form. At the most we have fragments of its existence. Archaeological surveys have uncovered
the remains of hundreds of settlements in the northern hill
country of Israel that suddenly spring up in unusual numbers
around 1250 BCE. Strikingly, this also happens to be around
the time when we see the first mention of the name "Israel" in
a datable ancient document. A stone monument or stela set
up by Pharaoh Merneptah (see Figure 2.4) celebrates his army's
victory over cities and other groups in Syria-Palestine, saying:

I have plundered Canaan from one end to the other, taken
slaves from the city of Ashkelon [a coastal Philistine settle-
ment] and conquered the city of Gezer. I have razed Yanoam
to the ground.
   I have decimated the people of Israel and put their children to death . . . All Canaan has been pacified. (Translation,
OT Parallels)

The stela commemorates an Egyptian campaign carried out
sometime around 1220 BCE. Interestingly, the Egyptian writing system clearly indicates that this "Israel" is a tribal people,
not a territory. The next securely datable mention of anything
specifically Israelite comes four hundred years later. So this
mention of a people, "Israel," in the Merneptah stela of 1207
is a precious clue. It helps us interpret the village settlements
across the hill country in 1250–1000 BCE as the earliest remains
of "Israel," the people who would later create the Hebrew
Bible/Old Testament.

The earlier history of this people cannot be recovered. This is as far back as we can go using academic methods of historical reconstruction. Through a combination of archaeological evidence for early hilltop villages and the Merneptah stela, we have good reason to think that some kind of village culture "Israel" already lived in the hill country of Palestine from around 1300 onward (see Map 2.1). Nevertheless, we do not have the kind of secure written or other sources that historians would typically rely on to tell us where these people came from or how they got there.

To be sure, the Bible tells a story of how this people was formed from ancestors of Jacob's sons, who went down into Egypt, emerged in the exodus, and wandered in the wilderness, before entering Canaan through a triumphant military conquest of all of the area and destruction of all its inhabitants. Scholars once thought that archaeological remains confirmed this picture of external origins and total conquest, since there are destruction layers in many Canaanite towns in the late second millennium. Some thought these destruction layers were evidence of an Israelite onslaught. Nevertheless, others have rightly argued that the cities where destruction layers were found are not generally cities mentioned in the Bible. Moreover, their destructions apparently occurred over a period of over one hundred years rather than in a single conquest as related in the book of Joshua. This calls into question the idea that they are the result of a coordinated Israelite conquest of the sort described in Joshua. Instead, many of these cities probably disappeared as part of a more widespread destruction of major urban centers that occurred toward the end of the second millennium, a destruction caused by a combination of environmental catastrophe and invasions of "sea peoples" from the western Mediterranean. Furthermore, of the nineteen cities mentioned in the Bible as destroyed by the Israelites, only three were clearly destroyed, while the rest either were not destroyed or were abandoned at the times when most scholars think the conquest could have occurred. In sum, the archaeological evidence, if anything, contradicts rather than confirms the picture of total destruction of the Canaanite people given in Joshua. Indeed, it better matches the picture of the coexistence of Israelites and Canaanites in the land given in Judges 1, a biblical text which contrasts with the account of total conquest in Joshua.

So, one might ask, where did the biblical stories in Joshua come from? There are different explanations for individual stories on the one hand and the broader account of total conquest on the other. For example, many scholars now understand individual stories such as the conquest of Jericho as tales of triumph that were built up to explain ancient ruins. Much later in Israel's history an Israelite storyteller, unaware that the ruins at Jericho long predated the presence of Israel in the land, told a story that explained those ruins as the remains of a great victory by God when Israel entered the land. This story developed over time until it was included in a broader story of Israel's conquest of the whole land under Joshua. This story of total conquest of the land (Joshua 1–12) in response to God's command (Deuteronomy 7) is even further from being a photographic reproduction of ancient events. The language and theology of Joshua 1–12 make clear that it was a story composed to empower a much later Israelite people who had been repeatedly humiliated and oppressed by the superpowers of their day. Chapter 7 of this textbook will feature more discussion of the biblical picture of conquest, since it focuses on the time in which the book of Joshua was written.

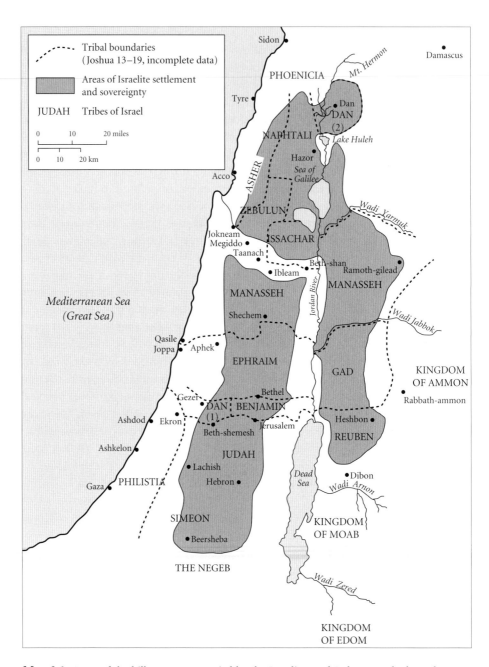

Map 2.1 Areas of the hill country occupied by the Israelites and Judeans, and where the tribes are said to have been located in the pre-state period. Redrawn from Norman Gottwald, *The Hebrew Bible: A Socio-Literary Introduction*. Minneapolis: Fortress, 1985, page 133.

All this leads us back to the origins of Israel – *in* Canaan. Our evidence shows every sign that the vast bulk of the earliest Israelites came from Canaan and shared its language, its material culture, and – to some extent – its religion. To be sure, there may have been a "Moses group," themselves of Canaanite extraction, who experienced slavery and liberation from Egypt, but most scholars believe that such a group – if it existed – was only a small minority in early Israel, even though their story came to be claimed by all. The rest of early Israelites did not come from outside the land through conquest or gradual settlement. The architecture and pottery of early Israelite settlements show close connections to pre-Israelite, "Canaanite" architecture and pottery. Prior attempts to identify a distinctively different "Israelite" pottery, house type, or other feature have failed. The Hebrew language, including its more ancient forms, is so closely related to neighboring languages that a student who learns Hebrew is well on his or her way to reading Phoenician, Moabite, Ammonite, etc.

Finally, both archaeological remains and the much later evidence from the Hebrew Bible indicate that the oldest forms of Israelite religion were not as distinct from non-Israelite, "Canaanite" religion as scholars once thought. The Canaanites worshipped various gods, such as the creator and father god **El**, his wife **Asherah**, the storm god **Baal**, and the goddess of love and war Anat. Anat is not particularly prominent in biblical traditions, but the other three all appear to have played significant roles in early Israel, alongside Israelite worship of a non-Canaanite God, "Yahweh." For example, ancient Israelites often expressed their theology by giving their children pious sentence-names. The Bible records that Saul, one of Israel's earliest leaders, had descendants named "Ishbaal" (Hebrew for "man of Baal") and "Mephibaal" ("from the mouth of Baal"). In this case, these names of Saul's descendants probably indicate reverence for Baal in his family. The name "El" is yet more prominent in biblical tradition, forming part of the name "Isra*el*," and of several important place names (e.g. Bethel – "house of El"). One biblical text even uses a frequent epithet of El, "the Most High," to describe how El assigned Yahweh to Israel:

> When the Most High assigned the nations,
>   when he divided humankind,
> He determined the boundaries of the peoples
>   according to the number of the gods.
> Yahweh's own portion was his people,
>   Jacob was his assigned share. (Deut 32:8–9)

The Name "Israel"

The name "Israel," like most ancient Hebrew names, is a sentence. It is formed from the divine name "El," and may mean "El rules" or "May El prove his rulership." It reflects the potential focus in earliest Israel on El's role in helping early tribal groups resist the "rulership" of surrounding cities and their armies.

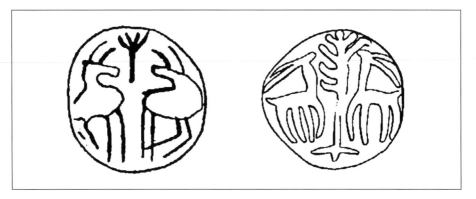

Figure 2.5 Animals feeding on trees, an early Israelite reflection of a yet earlier artistic pattern seen in pre-Israelite remains where the same animals were fed by a goddess figure, possibly Asherah. Redrawn from Othmar Keel and Cristoph Uehlinger, *Göttinnen, Götter und Gottessymbole: neue Erkenntnisse zur Religionsgeschichte Kanaans und Israels aufgrund bislang unerschlossener ikonographischer Quellen* (Quaestiones disputatae). Freiburg im Breisgau: Herder, 1992, page 134.

Israel's worship probably was not confined to male deities such as Baal, El, or Yahweh. Archaeologists have found remains in early Israelite settlements both of female figurines and of early Israelite depictions of trees, a frequent symbol in ancient Canaan of female reproductive power (see Figure 2.5). Many scholars think these early images of trees/ women were representations of the goddess Asherah, the wife of the creator god El. Worship of Asherah appears to have been widespread in earliest Israel. Each ancient village probably had its own hilltop sanctuary, a raised platform for sacrifice, featuring both a pillar to symbolize male deity and a tree to symbolize divine female power. Asherah, whose symbol is the tree, was the probable focus of the tree symbolism.

Traces of the Most Ancient Israelite Oral Traditions in the Bible

Such archaeological evidence helps us reconstruct aspects of Israel's origins not reflected in the Bible, which – after all – is a corpus of texts written down after the conclusion of the tribal period. It gives us a glimpse of tribal Israel that resembles the pre-Israelite culture from which it emerged. One might say that ancient Israelites were a sub-group of "Canaanites" living in hill-country villages. These ancient villagers, however, had their own traditions, passed down by word of mouth from generation to generation. These traditions, constantly evolving to fit the hopes and fears of the performers and their audiences, expressed the deepest values of their community. The following sections of this chapter discuss three sets of biblical texts that are good candidates for providing a view, however blurry and indistinct, of distinctive elements of early Israel's theology and traditions.

Exodus

As already suggested in Chapter 1, the narratives in Exodus 1–15 all come from centuries after this pre-state period in ancient Israel. Yet many indicators suggest that these traditions were present in ancient Israel from a very early period, probably when an "exodus group" of prisoners who had escaped from Egypt joined others living in hill-country villages and told their story of liberation from Pharaoh under the leadership of Moses. The indicators of historicity in the exodus story suggest that it was not made up by later authors, and those indicators point back to the late Bronze Age.

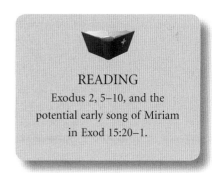

READING
Exodus 2, 5–10, and the potential early song of Miriam in Exod 15:20–1.

Yet, even assuming that some sort of exodus from Egypt occurred historically, the story about it would not have survived if it had not also spoken an important new word to the people living in the hill-country villages. And there are good reasons to think it did. For these village-culture Israelites had "pharaohs" of their own day, the rulers of the city-states surrounding them, whom they needed to resist. The Song of Deborah in Judges 5 (and the later accompanying story in Judges 4) vividly describes the kind of threat posed by such cities, with their professional armies and chariots. Furthermore, it is likely that some such formerly Egyptian-dominated cities, such as Jerusalem or Shechem, preserved remnants of the Egyptian culture. At the least, these former outposts of Egyptian domination of Canaan would have been perceived by villagers as the closest oppressive counterpart to the Egypt that had once dominated the area.

The story of Yahweh's deliverance of slaves from Egypt would have served as a powerful rallying cry for villagers now fighting for survival against such city-states. The story became the property of all "Israel," not just former slaves and their descendants. We see this sort of community claiming of an older story today, for example, in the way later African-Americans have claimed the stories of the Old Testament for themselves. In his August 2008 speech on race, "A More Perfect Union," Barack Obama drew on his autobiography to describe how he found hope in the merging of biblical stories and contemporary lives in the black church:

> People began to shout, to rise from their seats and clap and cry out, a forceful wind carrying the reverend's voice up into the rafters . . . And in that single note – hope! – I heard something else; at the foot of that cross, inside the thousands of churches across the city, I imagined the stories of ordinary black people merging with the stories of David and Goliath, Moses and Pharaoh, the Christians in the lion's den, Ezekiel's field of dry bones. Those stories – of survival, and freedom, and hope – became our story, my story; the blood that had spilled was our blood, the tears our tears; until this black church, on this bright day, seemed once more a vessel carrying the story of a people into future generations and into a larger world. Our trials and triumphs became at once unique and universal, black and more than black; in chronicling our journey, the stories and songs gave us a means to reclaim memories that we didn't need to feel shame about . . . memories that all people might study and cherish – and with which we could start to rebuild.

This claiming of older stories by new groups is hardly limited to the black church. Much as many Americans now claim for themselves the story of the *Mayflower* and the Puritan holiday of thanksgiving, despite the fact that many descend from immigrants of the last century, so also Israelite villagers of varied origins claimed the exodus story as their own. That story celebrated the god, Yahweh, who had liberated "them" from Egypt, and it expressed their confidence that this exodus God would also fight on their behalf against their contemporary "pharaohs," the local city-states.

Yet we should be clear, as was stressed in the first chapter of this textbook, that the exodus story (or stories) that ancient Israelites claimed almost certainly was not identical with the story found in the Bible in Exodus 1–15. No one would have been writing such texts in the villages of early Israel. Moreover, there are numerous signs – to be discussed elsewhere in this book – that these stories in the book of Exodus were shaped into their present form by much later Israelites rereading the story of exodus in relation to ever new "pharaohs": the "pharaoh" of Solomon and his kingdom, the "pharaoh" of Assyrian and Babylonian superpowers, etc. This process of merging of stories described by Barack Obama has been going on a very long time.

That said, there are some trickster elements in the biblical exodus story that may point to early oral elements lying in some form behind the text in Exodus 1–15. Take, for example, the tale of the tricky midwives, Shiphrah and Puah (Exod 1:15–22), who disobey Pharaoh's command to kill all male Israelite babies, claiming "Hebrew women are not like Egyptian women; they are so strong that they give birth before the midwife has a chance to get to them." Later on, fully intending to depart for good, Moses nevertheless tries to get the Israelites free by asking Pharaoh for a three-day vacation in the wilderness so they can fulfill God's command to worship there (Exod 5:1–5). Later, when Pharaoh agrees to let the Israelites have a three-day festival in Egypt rather than going away, Moses claims that they cannot do so because the Israelite sacrifices would be too distasteful to the Egyptians (8:21–3). When the plagues finally persuade Pharaoh to let the male Israelites go on their supposed worship pilgrimage, Moses slyly insists that the men cannot adequately observe this particular festival without all of their families and livestock along (10:7–10). All these elements are now found in much later, written biblical texts. Nevertheless, they reflect a tone of trickery particularly characteristic of early oral traditions. They indicate the persistence of trickster components later in Israel's history, but they may also be trickster tastes of early elements embedded in Israel's later exodus traditions.

Traditions surrounding Jacob

READING
Genesis 25, 27–35.

Such trickster elements are even more prominent in the traditions surrounding Jacob and his family in Genesis 25–35. Jacob cleverly gets a hungry Esau to sell his birthright for a pot of lentil stew in Genesis 25. Then, in Genesis 27, Rebekah, Jacob's mother, develops a tricky ruse to get Jacob's father, Isaac, to give Jacob the superior blessing that he meant to give to Esau. At Rebekah's urging, Jacob flees to escape Esau's plan to murder him, and he gets a taste of his own medicine in Haran, where his father-in-law, Laban, gets him to work seven years to marry Rachel, but then slips Leah into Jacob's marriage bed instead (Genesis 29). Soon Jacob turns the tables on Laban, using magical means to outwit Laban's plan to deprive Jacob of his wages in livestock (Genesis 30) and later escaping with Laban's daughters without Laban's knowledge (Genesis 31). In the process, Rachel shows her own capacity for trickery, stealing her father's household gods and then preventing him from finding them by sitting on them and then telling her father that she cannot get up because she has her period ("the way of woman is on me"; Gen 31:35). In these ways and others, the story depicts Jacob and his closest family as crafty tricksters, able to survive and flourish in the face of difficult odds. Not only is he himself a trickster, but his mother helped get him started, and he worked 14 years to marry a woman, Rachel, who continues the tradition.

Such traditions of trickery are not the sort of thing typically focused on in sermons and Sunday school lessons. Many within dominant cultures are not used to celebrations of culture heroes like this who trick and even lie to get their way. Nevertheless, such stories can be empowering to people who feel that they will inevitably perish if they play by "the rules" of their social context. Whether Native American or ancient Israelite, vulnerable people often gain empowerment through celebrating ancestors who made their way in the world through using cleverness to overcome impossible odds. For people on top, such trickster stories can appear to be embarrassing elements in an otherwise tidy Bible. For people on the bottom, such stories can be a major way of gaining hope and resisting domination.

In either case, the stories found in Genesis 25–35 are substantially different from Jacob, Rebekah, and Rachel stories told in villages of early Israel. On the one hand, we know that early Israel almost certainly told stories about Jacob, who happens to be a namesake of early "Israel." Moreover, the stories in Genesis are related in some way to those early tales. On the other hand, those stories changed radically over the centuries of oral and then oral-written tradition, and there are numerous elements in them that point specifically to later periods in Israel's history. For example, several place names that are now prominent in the Genesis Jacob story, e.g. Bethel and Penuel, may reveal a shaping of the story in the context of the later northern monarchy in Israel, where Bethel was one of the main royal sanctuaries and Penuel was a capital for a few years. In addition, in Chapter 10 we will see how people in exile probably added to the Jacob story the promise theme now found throughout Gen 26:1–33 along with several other isolated places in the Jacob story (e.g. 28:13–16, 32:10–13, 35:9–15).

In these and probably many other ways, the story of Jacob and his family has been so shaped by its journey through the centuries that we no longer can identify the parts that come from Israel's earliest history. The most we can say is that the people of Israel probably told trickster stories about Rebekah, Jacob, Rachel, and others from the beginning of their history, a time when they did not yet have a king and were living in vulnerable, unwalled villages of the hill country of Canaan.

basics Jacob Story

The Jacob story chiasm	A Encounter Jacob/Esau (25:21–34; 27:1–45)
	    B Divine encounter, departure (28*)
	        C Wives acquisition (29:1–30)
	            D Fertility: children (29:31–30:24)
	            D′ Fertility: flocks (30:25–43)
	        C′ Wives extrication (31:1–32:1)
	    B′ Divine encounter, return (32:22–32)
	A′ Encounter Jacob/Esau (33:1–17)

Defining "chiasm"	A **chiasm** is a circular literary form that moves through a set of themes to the center (e.g. A, B, C, D) and then goes through similar themes in reverse order after the center (e.g. D′, C′, B′, A′). Major emphasis is often put on the texts that occur at the center of a chiasm.
Major themes of the Jacob story	The center of this early Jacob story is the fertility of Jacob's family and flocks (Gen 29:31–30:43). This is a major theme of the story, alongside emphasis on his (and his women's) resourcefulness amidst conflict and danger.

FOCUS TEXT

READING
Judges 5 (note that this potentially early poem is different from the later account in Judges 4).

The Song of Deborah

The Song of Deborah in Judges 5 is the one of the best candidates for being a biblical text that might more closely reflect an ancient village-culture tradition than the (prose) narratives discussed so far. Unlike the above texts, the Song of Deborah is a poem, and its poetic – and perhaps sung – form could aid more precise memorization and recitation over the years. In addition, the song contains archaic elements of Hebrew language, and the list of tribes and other groups in Judges 5 only partially overlaps with later lists of tribes that made up early Israel. Judges 5 does not even mention some of the southern tribes, and it mentions other names not typically found in 12-tribe lists (e.g. Machir = Manasseh; and Meroz). These are among some of our first clues that this text may reflect a very early poem. Open up your Bible to Judges 5 and let us use this text as an evocative window to a time long before texts of our Bible began to be written down.

5:2–5: The song opens with a hymn of praise describing Yahweh's triumphant appearance from the southern desert regions of Seir and Edom (5:4–5). It is one of several potentially early texts that locate Sinai and Yahweh's origins in the desert regions south of Palestine (Deut 33:2; Hab 3:3; Ps 68:7–9). Our ancient text envisions Yahweh as a powerful storm god, whose arrival is marked by earthquakes and torrential floods. Yet there is also a focus here and throughout the poem on the people. The first verse of the poem celebrates the way leaders took the lead and the people responded willingly (5:2), and the second verse (5:3) calls on the powerful "kings and princes" of the world to hear this "song" about the triumph of a kingless group of tribal villagers.

5:6–12: The next section of the poem celebrates the emergence of leadership in this otherwise disorganized group: the rise of Deborah. Beforehand, trails had become unsafe, settlements were defenseless, and the people had no weapons (5:6–7a). But then Deborah arose "as a mother in Israel." The poem then again calls on those who volunteered in the effort to offer praise (5:9), along with other groups (5:10–11), and Deborah and Barak themselves (5:12).

5:13–18 and 5:23: The poem then details which tribal groups answered the call to battle willingly, and which did not. Six tribes came when called: Ephraim, Benjamin, Machir (related to Manasseh; Num 26:29), Zebulun, Issachar, and Naphtali. Four did not: Reuben, Gilead (perhaps in place of Gad in the standard lists of tribes), Dan, and Asher. Two southern tribes are not even mentioned: Judah and Simeon. Apparently at the time the Song was written they were not even envisioned as potential partners in this kind of military effort. Even the northern groups that appear here are clearly not unified. Only six out of ten answered the call to battle. Indeed, from the initial call to praise those who volunteered (5:2) to the contrast of those who volunteered and those who did not (5:13–18), much of Deborah's song seems aimed at encouraging the separate tribes to affirm their common destiny. It calls on villagers to sing praises to God for a victory where six tribes joined together to defeat – with God's help – the mighty forces of Sisera. And it soon calls on them to curse "Meroz," an unknown group who failed to answer the call (5:23).

5:19–22: The actual description of the battle occurs only in these four verses. They move beyond the conflict between Israel and Sisera to juxtapose the "kings of Canaan" and their horses, on the one hand, with the cosmic powers of Yahweh, on the other. The kings may have the superior military technology, but they have no chance against the power of stars fighting from heaven and the force of the Kishon river (5:19–21). Soon the once powerful stallions were fleeing (5:22).

5:24–31: In two scenes, 5:24–7 and 28–30, the poet concludes with vignettes about the aftermath of the battle. The first blesses Jael, of the Kenites, for aiding in the effort by cleverly tricking Sisera into enjoying her hospitality and then killing him with a mallet (5:24–7). Again, there is an element of the trickster here, since hospitality is otherwise celebrated as a profound value, not just in surrounding cultures, but in Israelite traditions as well. Nevertheless, Jael welcomes Sisera into her tent and feeds him, before killing him with a mallet. Like a slow-motion movie, the poetry uses repetition to focus in on the moment.

> Between her feet he sank, he sank, he fell
> He lay between her feet, he sank, he fell
> Where he sank, there he fell, killed.

Meanwhile, in 5:28–30 the poet offers another vision featuring a woman, this time the mother of Sisera, waiting for him to return triumphant from battle, not knowing of his recent death. As she wonders at his delay, her "wise women" speculate that he is probably delayed by dividing spoil: a few Israelite maidens for each warrior and some nice cloth to bring back to the women at home.

In this way, "Deborah's song" uses two scenes involving women to illustrate the contrast between the destinies of Yahweh's friends and enemies. Yahweh's enemies will perish and their women (like Sisera's mother) will mourn, but those who join in the effort to fight, like Jael, will be "like the sun when it rises with all its might" (5:31).

This belief in the triumph of the people that God chooses is an early form of what is often termed: "**election theology**" – that is, the idea that God has chosen a particular people to care for and defend. This idea is present in the affirmation of the exodus tradition that Yahweh delivered Israel from Egypt. And it is implicit in the stories of God's protection and provision for Israel's trickster ancestor, Jacob, and his family. In all these traditions, God chooses not a place, nor a territorial nation, but a people, and protects them against seemingly impossible odds. This belief in God's choosing of a particular people, rooted in tribal traditions like the Song of Deborah and the exodus story, is a fundamental bedrock of later Israelite theology, especially in the northern part of Israel. Moreover, this idea of the distinctiveness and chosenness of a *people*, election theology, may have distinguished early Israel from some of the monarchal nation states that surrounded it. Those states were more focused on how their gods chose a particular city and/or royal-priestly dynasty.

The Creation of "Israel" Through Cultural Memory of Resistance to Domination

All this is a prelude to the gradual creation of the Hebrew Bible/Old Testament. At this point in the history of Israel no books, not even chapters, had been written. "Israel" was only a very loose association of village-tribal groups. These villages shared, however, a common way of life. They aided each other in times of famine, and charismatic leaders such as Deborah rose up in times of crisis to fight common enemies. Whatever their diverse origins, these village-dwellers came to claim a common story of liberation from Egypt. They claimed a common ancestor, Jacob, along with the rest of his trickster family. And through poems like the Song of Deborah, they celebrated those occasions where they joined together to experience Yahweh's deliverance against the more powerful city-states around them.

Some scholars, such as Maurice Halbwachs (*On Collective Memory* [Chicago: University of Chicago Press, 1992]) and Jan Assmann (*Religion and Cultural Memory* [Stanford: University of Stanford Press, 2005]), have argued persuasively that such common memories are what form groups of people. Such **cultural memory** is reinforced through parental teaching, schools, festivals, and other practices in which people in groups recite or act out their common heritage. For example, national holidays, such as July 4 in the US, are occasions when national identity is reinforced through various festivities, in this case marking the day when the nation was born. New citizens are required to learn the common story before they can become "Americans." Similarly, the worship year in Jewish synagogues and Christian churches continually reminds those communities of their stories, having them relive the events of the Torah (for synagogues) or the life of Jesus (for churches) and reinforce their sense of a particular religious identity. You become a "Jew" or "Christian" partly through learning the story of that group and claiming it as your own.

We do not know exactly how the oral versions of the texts about exodus, Jacob's family, and Deborah's victory were used, but they appear to have served a similar purpose in helping to create and reinforce a sense of common "Israelite" identity out of varied groups. Whether taught to children, recited at clan worship, sung at festivals, or used in some other way, the ancient oral traditions discussed in this chapter helped turn the people living in the hill country of Syro-Palestine into the "Israelites" who would create the later Bible.

The shared oral memories discussed in this chapter made for a particular kind of community: one that celebrated powerful work by God on the one hand and the clever action of tricksters on the other. In the midst of the pluralistic Canaanite religious environment, these traditions praise the liberative work of Yahweh, a god known from the southern deserts. Yet they also celebrate Israelite resourcefulness and wit. In particular, they empower people living on the margins by celebrating clever underdogs such as Jacob or Jael. Women are quite prominent in these traditions, as mothers, tricksters, and even military leaders (Deborah). Meanwhile, "kings" and their representatives are the opponents in these village-culture traditions, whether Pharaoh or Hazor's general Sisera.

Even when Israel developed writing, the stories of these oral traditions – in highly varied forms – continued to be told and sung among Israelites, many of whom never learned to write. We must keep in mind that our written Bible is but the tip of the iceberg of a largely lost oral tradition in ancient Israel. The process started not with writing, but with telling tales of Israelite liberation, survival, and victory.

CHAPTER TWO REVIEW

1. Know the meaning and significance of the following terms discussed in this chapter:

- Asherah
- Baal
- cultural memory
- El
- election theology
- empire
- monarchal city-state
- oral traditions
- segmentary society
- trickster
- village

2. Know the main differences between the following three ancient forms of social organization:

- empire
- monarchal city-state
- village

3. What is "tradition history," and what is an example of the sort of phenomenon in the Bible that it would study? What is the difference between "tradition history" and "transmission history"? Do the terms overlap?

4. What do anthropologists now know about the character of oral traditions? How does this affect their usability for reconstructing early traditions? How specifically are such oral traditions reflected in Genesis 12–25 or Exodus 1–15?

5. What are the main issues surrounding the reconstruction of a historical "conquest" of all of Canaan by all of Israel?

RESOURCES FOR FURTHER STUDY

Commentaries and other books on Joshua

Hawk, Daniel L. *Every Promise Fulfilled: Contesting Plots in the Book of Joshua*. Literary Currents in Biblical Interpretation. Louisville, KY: Westminster John Knox Press, 1991.

Nelson, Richard D. *Joshua: A Commentary*. Old Testament Library. Louisville, KY: Westminster John Knox Press, 1997.

Niditch, Susan. "Joshua" in the *Oxford Bible Commentary* (revised edition), eds. John Barton and John Muddiman. New York: Oxford University Press, 2007.

Commentaries and other books on Judges

Hamlin, John E. *At Risk in the Promised Land: A Commentary on the Book of Judges*. Grand Rapids: Eerdmans, 1990.

McCann, J. Clinton. *Judges*. Interpretation. Louisville, KY: Westminster John Knox Press, 2002.

Soggin, J. Alberto. *Judges*. Old Testament Library. Philadelphia: Westminster Press, 1981.

Trible, Phyllis. *Texts of Terror: Literary-Feminist Readings of Biblical Narratives*. Philadelphia: Fortress, 1984. Chapters on the Levite's wife and Jephthah's daughter.

Everyday life in ancient Israel

King, Philip J., and Stager, Lawrence E. *Life in Biblical Israel*. Library of Ancient Israel. Louisville, KY: Westminster John Knox Press, 2001.

The history of Israelite religion

Keel, Othmar, and Uehlinger, Christoph. *Gods, Goddesses, and Images of God in Ancient Israel*, trans. Allan W. Mahnke. Minneapolis: Fortress, 1997. Difficult, but good.

CHAPTER 3

THE EMERGENCE OF THE

MONARCHY AND ROYAL

AND ZION TEXTS

Chapter Outline

CHAPTER OVERVIEW

This chapter examines the rise of a monarchy in ancient Israel and surveys biblical texts connected to this period. The first part gives a historical reconstruction of the early monarchy and its rise, a reconstruction that only partially agrees with the much later and highly theological narratives (in Samuel and Kings) about these events. Apparently David and Solomon, the first figures with much claim to being real "monarchs" in ancient Israel (not Saul), borrowed elements of foreign monarchies when they set up their monarchy in Jerusalem, particularly elements from Egypt, which had dominated the region up until a few centuries prior to their rule. One major element that they borrowed from earlier monarchies was the use of written texts to reinforce more stable forms of "cultural memory" across their realm, indeed texts that often promoted the value of the monarchy and its capital, Zion. This chapter concludes with a survey of some pro-royal and pro-Zion texts in the Bible that may come from this period, some of which show similarities to older monarchal traditions in Egypt and Mesopotamia. These royal and Zion psalms, whose pro-royal perspective contrasts with the harsh judgments of later authors of Samuel and Kings, are the first of several biblical echoes of ancient empires to be discussed in this and the next chapter. Read this chapter with an aim to penetrate beyond the depiction of the monarchy in the stories of Samuel and 1 Kings to hints of a distinctly different sort of early Israelite monarchy that can be found through reading between the lines of those narratives and analyzing biblical texts (especially royal psalms) potentially from that period.

Imagining Early Monarchal Israel

Once again, let us start with an imaginary reconstruction of the context in which these biblical traditions were written down. Our sources are few, varied, and disputed. Although the Bible describes Israel as a world power at the time of David and Solomon, archaeologists have not succeeded in finding extensive remains of their kingdoms. Some even suspect that the Bible's entire picture of their glory is a fictional creation of an Israelite golden age. This book, however, takes another perspective. Certainly, the stories surrounding David and Solomon grew over time, and their reputation was enhanced. Nevertheless, a combination of archaeology and a critical reading of biblical texts suggests that Israel under David and Solomon did develop the beginnings of a city-state monarchy, a monarchy that apparently included short-lived domination of some neighboring nations as well. The following imaginary reconstruction is based on this combination of archaeological and biblical evidence.

Our journey takes us back to another hilltop in ancient Canaan, this time Mount **Zion**, a hilltop to the south of the heartland of tribal Israel. Generally speaking, "Zion" and the city associated with it, "Jerusalem," are synonymous in the Bible. What is less well known is that Jerusalem had a long history as a city before David conquered it and made it the capital of his kingdom. In Chapter 2, we discussed a letter from Abdi-heba, a king of pre-Davidic Jerusalem. This letter is but one sign that Jerusalem before David had its own cultural and political traditions. Moreover, David and his successors may have adapted some of the traditions of this ancient city in the process of setting up their fledgling kingdom. For example, the Bible contains a tantalizing suggestion that the pre-Israelite (Jebusite) inhabitants of the city already had a belief in Jerusalem's invulnerability. When David laid siege to Jerusalem, the Jebusites are said to have told David that "you will not come in, even the blind and lame will ward you off" (2 Sam 5:6). Such a claim that Jerusalem was unconquerable anticipates later Biblical **Zion theology** – that is, theology about Jerusalem's specialness and invulnerability – that we will see in some of Israel's psalms and other literature.

Let us return now to imagining the Jerusalem of later, Solomonic, times. As it turned out, the Jebusites were wrong. David conquered Jerusalem by stealth and made it the capital of his kingdom, uniting Judah in the south and Israel in the north. In our imagining exercise, we visit Jerusalem at the time of Solomon, David's son and successor. By this time, Jerusalem has become the center of a fledgling mini-empire. Not only does the city have its ancient wall and traditions, but Solomon has built a new palace for the king and a temple to Yahweh (see Figure 3.1). The temple contains the "ark of the covenant," a symbol of older Israel's tribal-Exodus god.

Solomon, the king, serves as both high priest and commander of the army. Below him is a small but expanding class of priestly, royal, and military officials. This is a new form of leadership, showing an evolution under David from tribal structures to foreign models of monarchy, particularly as seen in Egypt. Solomon's court bears a strong resemblance to the Egyptian royal court, and many of its positions are filled by the sons of officials who served in David's court. Indeed, one of Solomon's scribes may even

Figure 3.1 Artist's reconstruction of Solomon's Jerusalem. The Temple is on the upper right, next down is the palace, and then the citadel of David with a stepped-stone structure supporting it.

have had an Egyptian father, David's scribe "Shisha," whose name is quite similar to the Egyptian word for "scribe." These officials and those under them administrated the complex kingdom. They were the glue that held this broad kingdom of varied tribes and territories together.

This nation, indeed this mini-empire, had many provisions for continuity across space and time. Where tribal culture had charismatic leaders such as Deborah who galvanized the people in a time of crisis, this kind of monarchy achieved political stability through an ongoing royal dynasty. Where tribal culture depended on tribes volunteering to join others in resisting enemies, this monarchy had a standing army. And where groups in tribal culture shared ever-fluid *oral* traditions, this monarchy resembled other such monarchies in using *written* texts to reinforce and standardize oral memory. These written texts were not accessible to everyone in a largely non-literate society, but they provided an essential way to educate the new ruling class for this more expansive realm. By memorizing a specific collection of written texts, youths preparing to be leaders learned a common worldview that persisted across space and time. David's and Solomon's scribes are the probable authors of the first such collection of Hebrew, written, literary-theological texts.

The Rise of the Israelite Monarchy and Resistance to It

READING

1 Samuel 8–12, 16–20, 31; 2 Samuel 2–10 and 1 Kings 1–10.

EXERCISE

The readings above are narratives about the rise of kingship told centuries after the events they describe. The authors of these narratives reveal much about their values in the different reasons they give for why a monarchy rose in Israel. As you read 1 Samuel 8–12 make a list of the different reasons given for the rise of the monarchy (including chapter and verse) and note any other clues you can find to whether the authors of these texts approved or disapproved of the monarchy. Extrapolating from these narratives, do you think the authors of these texts thought the monarchy was a good idea?

Before looking at the earliest Hebrew texts, we need to appreciate the city-state context in which they were created. In Chapter 2 we saw how Israel emerged as a loose association of villages organized into tribes, settled largely in the northern hill country of Palestine. They were a "people," not a city-state or nation. Their limited resources and social organization made it difficult for them to resist raids by neighboring tribes or attempts to dominate them by nearby city-states. Aside from the rise of temporary leaders in times of crisis, "judges" in the Bible, there were no elite classes. The people shared common access to the orally transmitted "cultural memory" that helped identify them as Israelites.

The book of 1 Samuel, written hundreds of years after the period it narrates, gives many explanations for why this tribal existence under judges came to an end: the people requested a king because Samuel's sons were corrupt, or because they wanted to imitate other nations, or because they wanted a human king instead of Yahweh as king (see the exercise at the outset of this section). Nevertheless, the explanation for kingship that most scholars find compelling is the following: the Israelites accepted kingship because it was the only form of social organization that was centralized enough to repel the Philistine invasions into the hill country of central Palestine. The Bible records clashes between Israelites and Philistines in stories about Samson (Judges 14–16), the time of Samuel (1 Sam 4:1–7:1), Saul (1 Samuel 13–31), and David (2 Samuel 5 and 8). Saul, a member of the tribe of Benjamin, was anointed as "king" to repel the Philistines; he really was little more than a warlord. He did not develop a city capital or a professional army, and he achieved only limited success before being killed in battle with the Philistines, along with his heir Jonathan (1 Samuel 31//2 Chronicles 10). Saul's leadership was not the sort of "kingship" needed to repel the Philistines. It was really more of a "chieftainship."

Kingship would come under David and especially his heir, Solomon. Within the much later biblical texts, David is remembered as a paradoxical mix. On the one hand, several texts depict him as a king "faithful" to Yahweh (e.g. 1 Kgs 3:6). On the other hand, he is flawed enough to seduce an officer's wife, Bathsheba, and send her husband to certain death in order to be able to marry her (2 Samuel 11–12). In the broader scheme of things, however, David appears to have been an extraordinarily gifted military commander who took the first steps in establishing a monarchy that would last over four hundred years.

Timeline: Rise of the Monarchy	
Saul's chieftainship	1025–1010 BCE (Note this date range is particularly uncertain because of incomplete preservation of 1 Sam 13:1.)
David's reign	1010–970 BCE
In Hebron	1010–1002 BCE
In Jerusalem	1002–970 BCE

David started as an officer in Saul's Israelite army, and he was so militarily successful against the Philistines that he had to flee Saul's jealous wrath (see 1 Samuel 16–29). Later, when Saul died, David ruled his tribe, Judah, for a few years from the Judean town of Hebron, while Saul's son Eshbaal ruled Israel (2 Samuel 2–3). Then, when Eshbaal was assassinated, the Israelite leaders anointed David as king over them, so that David became king of both Judah and Israel (2 Sam 4:1–5:5). One of the first things he did as ruler of both peoples was to start a series of campaigns against the Philistines that permanently ended their threat to Judah and Israel (2 Sam 5:17–25; 8:1; see also 2 Sam 21:15–22).

Yet David did much more than defeat the Philistines. In contrast to (warlord) Saul, David introduced societal changes associated with true kingship: establishment of a state based in a walled city, organization of a professional army, and enforcement of taxes on the people to support the fortified city (or cities) and army. First, David captured the Jebusite city of Jerusalem, by stealth, and made it the capital of his new kingdom (2 Sam 5:6–16). This was a politically smart move for a Judean king claiming authority over Israel. Jerusalem was not identified with the southern tribe of Judah the way that Hebron was. Second, David solidified Jerusalem's claim as the new capital of "Israel" by bringing into it the ark of the covenant, an object sacred to all the Israelite tribes (2 Samuel 6). Third, he achieved additional military success, subduing neighboring kingdoms such as Moab, Edom, Ammon, and even Damascus (which was allied with Ammon; 2 Samuel 8, 10–12). This allowed him to pay members of his army with land grants and support his fledgling state with tribute from neighboring groups. Fourth and finally, he started to build longer-term city-state structures: he started plans for a temple (2 Sam 24:18), solidified ties with neighboring groups through marriage alliances (2 Sam 3:2–5), developed a professional army, and prepared for formal taxation through instituting a census of the people (2 Sam 24:1–9). He even appears to have followed Egyptian models in developing a royal court, eventually one that included a position for "forced labor" of his citizens to help with fortifying the country (2 Sam 20:23–6; compare with 2 Sam 8:16–18). Map 3.1 surveys his kingdom.

David's successor, Solomon, went yet further in developing a city-state based in Jerusalem. After being put in power by a virtual coup d'etat implemented by his mother, Bathsheba (working in concert with several of David's close associates; see 1 Kings 1–2), Solomon began building a full-fledged ancient Near Eastern city-state. He continued and expanded the royal cabinet, appointing sons of David's officials to several crucial positions, and adding some new positions, again along the Egyptian model. He expanded the army and added chariots. He made marriage alliances with foreign kings. He started lucrative trade exchanges with Tyre, Arabia, and others. He engaged in major construction projects in Jerusalem and several fortress cities, Hazor, Gezer, and possibly Megiddo (see Map 2.1, p. 42). Most importantly, drawing heavily on the material and technical resources of the Tyrian king Hiram, Solomon built the Jerusalem Temple for Yahweh and a palace for himself.

To do this, Solomon required significant resources. He divided the kingdom into 12 districts, each with a governor and each responsible for providing for the royal apparatus for one month. Many scholars see this 12-district system, organized in correspondence with the lunar monthly cycle, as the beginning of the idea that Israel originated as *12* tribes. Only later was this 12-tribe idea projected back into Israel's earlier history – the time of the judges and before. The most important shift for village-culture Israelites was that they now had a new burden to add to the struggle for everyday existence. Not only did they need to find a way to provide for their kin each year, but they also had to provide substantial resources to the king and his city-state.

Not all Israelites were happy with the changes that came with David's and Solomon's kingship. Though surely they were glad to see the Philistine threat contained, many perceived David and especially Solomon as Judean versions of the oppressive kings they had just defeated. This led to several rebellions, mainly centered in the north, where people in the heartland of ancient tribal "Israel" were the least happy with being ruled by Judah. One was led by Absalom, David's own son; another was led by Sheba, a leader from the Israelite north; and the final and successful one was led by Jeroboam, who will be discussed more in Chapter 4. What is important for our purposes now is an appreciation that the leaders in this early monarchy had to contend with opponents, particularly those associated with the Israelite north, who doubted the benefits of this new monarchy. The monarchy was a major new form of communal life, with many foreign elements, that involved many costs as well as benefits.

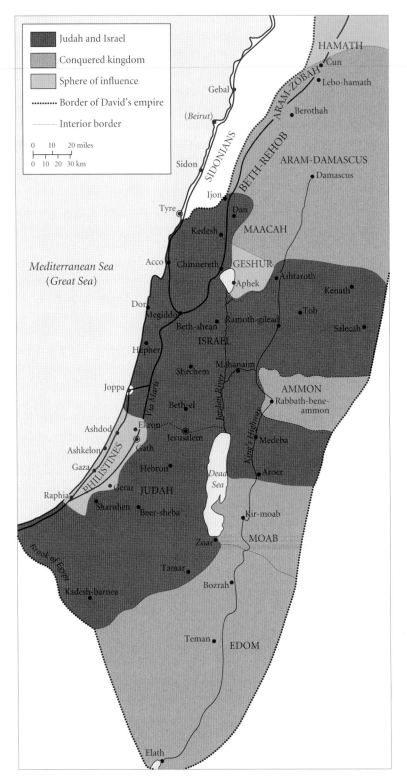

Map 3.1 Areas ruled and dominated by David and Solomon. Redrawn from Yohanan Aharoni and Michael Avi-Yonah, *The Macmillan Bible Atlas* (revised edition). New York: Macmillan, 1997, map 104.

Influence of Ancient Empires on Early Israel's Monarchy and Writings

David and Solomon did not start from scratch when they started to develop the Israelite monarchy and associated Jerusalemite city-state. They were adopting a more ancient social form that was known elsewhere. After all, city-states had been around in Mesopotamia, Syria, Egypt, and even Palestine from the third millennium onward. Indeed, as we have seen, Jerusalem itself was the site of a small, pre-Israelite, Jebusite city-state which had once been dominated by Egypt. There are numerous signs that David and Solomon drew deeply on older Egyptian and other models in building the monarchy in Jerusalem: the make-up of their royal court, the models used for construction of temple and palace, etc. These are non-textual "echoes of empire" seen in the emergent Davidic monarchy in Jerusalem.

Yet there is another sort of "echo of empire" to be discussed here, and that is the way some biblical texts appear to echo pre-Israelite texts that were used in the much older empires of Mesopotamia and Egypt. One thing that distinguished many ancient monarchies from the tribal groups surrounding them was their use of written texts, including the sorts of texts found in the Bible: wisdom sayings, psalms, myths, and stories (see Figure 3.2). These written texts were a form of cultural memory like the oral traditions that continued to exist. Nevertheless, there were important differences. Most importantly, the relative firmness of written traditions made them good tools for shaping elites across time and across space. Written texts do not change as readily as oral traditions do. This was important in city-states and empires, which spanned large distances and joined disparate groups together. An empire or even a centralized city-state could bind together its different parts by making sure that its leaders all learned writing and memorized the same educational texts.

Our best examples of such literary education come from Egypt and Mesopotamia, much larger civilizations whose texts are better preserved (in Egypt because of climate, in Mesopotamia because they used clay tablets). The evidence from Egypt and Mesopotamia shows how students learned in family-based schools, often learning to read texts from either their own fathers or teachers whom they called "father." Ancient education in Egypt and Mesopotamia followed a similar pattern, a pattern probably common across the ancient world. Students started by learning to write and read basic symbols. The next step was memorizing and reciting basic "wisdom" instructions on how to live, and the final and most advanced stage was internalizing and performing other types of texts, such as royal hymns or stories of creation and flood. Careful analysis of student exercises such as that seen in Figure 3.3, has allowed scholars to see how students in these cultures were taught to memorize their culture's texts line by line. Only a few in any ancient society had time to acquire such knowledge, but it was an important means by which Egypt, Mesopotamia, and other cultures trained future leaders.

This background from the cultures of Egypt and Mesopotamia is important because their educational-literary systems were used as models for the monarchies of Syro-Palestine in the centuries just before Israel emerged. During the thousand years before

Figure 3.2 Scribe standing before the king of a small neighboring kingdom with a scroll in his hand, dating from about a century after David and Solomon. The image shows the prestige attached to scribal writing even in the small kingdoms of the area.

Israel's emergence many local city-states had scribes who had learned to read and write Mesopotamian texts, even using Akkadian (a Mesopotamian language) to correspond with rulers in Egypt. In addition, Egypt itself exercised cultural influence in the area, especially in the coastland cities of Phoenicia. The Bible itself records how Solomon was dependent on the Phoenician city of Tyre for supplies and know-how in construct-ing the temple (1 Kgs 5:15–25; 7:13–47). We now have ancient inscriptions from the time of David and Solomon – such as the alphabet found at Tel Zayit (see Figure 3.4) – that likewise document the adoption of the 22-letter Phoenician alphabet in Judah, Israel, and surrounding nations. They are precious clues to the adoption, during the early Israelite monarchy, of a major ancient means for uniting broader kingdoms: systems of writing and education (see Figure 3.5).

The kingdom of David and Solomon was far too small to develop its own brand-new counterpart to the massive literatures of those ancient empires. Thus when scribes began writing the first Hebrew texts in the time of David and Solomon, it seems that they did *not* focus on creating textual versions of earlier Israelite oral traditions about ancestors, exodus, or the like. Instead, the earliest authors of Hebrew literature were dependent on *foreign* models for literary education and imitated *foreign* texts from Egypt and Mesopotamia. Why? Perhaps because in creating Israel's first written literature these early Judean scribes were most interested in adapting earlier examples of such writings (all of which were foreign), rather than transforming properly oral traditions from the Israelite north. So they wrote Hebrew versions of the sorts of texts used elsewhere to educate leaders for their emergent monarchy: creation and flood myths, hymns about the king, instructions on proper living, etc.

In this chapter we will look at two types of texts that show particularly close links to the monarchy and some reliance on

Figure 3.3 Student exercise tablet where the teacher wrote a couple of lines of an educational text on the top half and the student copied below.

Figure 3.4 Letters inscribed into the surface of a stone, with overlay indicating their shape. The stone was found embedded in a wall from the tenth century BCE.

Figure 3.5 The "Gezer Calendar." This may be a school exercise from the time of Solomon. It lists what was done in the months of the agricultural year of ancient Canaan.

foreign models as well: royal and Zion psalms. Though some of these texts are attributed to David or Solomon (see box on p. 66), we cannot be sure that all come from that time. This chapter starts from the above-mentioned principle that the earliest authors of Judean and Israelite texts probably were the most dependent on pre-Israelite models in authoring early monarchal texts. Therefore, biblical texts with the most chance of being early are those which feature the clearest echoes of educational texts used in pre-Israelite Mesopotamian and Egyptian education. Whatever the date of the texts to be discussed here, a study of them in relationship to their non-biblical counterparts can teach us much about how these biblical texts were used and what made them special.

Echoes of Near Eastern Royal Theology in the Royal and Zion Psalms

One of the main emphases in the literature of ancient empires was the monarchy. For example, Egyptian enthronement texts describe the new king (Pharaoh) receiving a document on which was written his throne names, climaxing with the throne name that marked his status as the only begotten son of the sun god, Re. Temple reliefs show the process by which Re conceived the king, not through intercourse, but through spreading his aroma over the king's mother. By the end of the process Re equipped the king with all he needed to rule the world in Re's place, proclaiming:

EXERCISE
Read the following (royal) psalms and make a list of ideas that come up two or more times in them: 2 Sam 23:1–7; Psalms 2, 21, 72, and 110. Include citations in your notes of where each idea occurred. Then read the following (Zion) psalms and list ideas that occur two or more times in them: Pss 9, 15, 46, and 48. Finally, how do all these texts contrast with the values implicit in the narratives about the rise of kingship in 1 Samuel 8–12? Make a list of similarities and (especially) differences.

Son of my body, beloved, lord of the righteousness [Maat] of Re, whose body I have made with me in the palace, I give you all life and wellbeing, to appear as the king of upper and lower Egypt on the throne of Horus.

Meanwhile, we also have hymns used in Egyptian education that taught students to celebrate the Egyptian king's power to vanquish wrongdoing and establish prosperity. The following one focuses on the Pharaoh Merneptah:

Be glad of heart, the entire land! The good times have come. A lord – life, prosperity, health – is given in all lands, and normality has returned to its place. The king of Upper and Lower Egypt, the lord of millions of years, great of kingship like Horus ... he who bestows happiness on Egypt, the son of Re, most competent of any king, Merneptah – life, prosperity, health.

All you who are righteous, come that you may see! Right has banished wrong. Evildoers have fallen on their faces. The oppressors are ignored. (ANET 378, adapted)

Similar themes appear in the royal literature of ancient Mesopotamia. For example, we find the following proclamation to the king in an ancient Babylonian coronation ritual:

May Assur and Ninlil, the lords of your crown, set your crown on your head for a hundred years! May your foot in Ekur and your hands stretched toward the breast of Assur, your God, be pleasing! May your priesthood and the priesthood of your sons be pleasing to Assur, your god! With your straight scepter widen your land! May Assur give you authority, obedience, concord, justice and peace! (Translation: Livingstone, 472)

Royal texts from both ancient Mesopotamia and Egypt emphasized the choosing of the king by the high god of the pantheon, the king's appointment as the highest authority and priest of the land, his overcoming of all enemies in the name of the god, and his bestowing of justice and peace on the land through his rule. Together, these and other themes comprise what is meant here by "**royal theology**."

Many elements of Egyptian and Mesopotamian royal theology are common in the **royal psalms** of the Hebrew Bible (Psalms 2, 18, 20, 21, 45, 72, 89, 110, and 144; along with 2 Sam 23:1–7). These poetic texts feature a distinctive focus on the king and his relationship with God. For example, Psalm 110 opens with a call for the king to sit at the right hand of God (Ps 110:1), a common motif in ancient Egyptian royal art. Its picture of the king subduing his enemies (Ps 110:1–3a) is typical of ancient royal literature, whether Egyptian or Mesopotamian. The latter part of verse 3, however, contains an obscure text whose meaning may be clarified when we look back to Egyptian royal ideology. God proclaims to the king: "from the womb of dawn, I fathered you like dew." Recall that the sun god, Re, in Egypt conceived the king through spreading his aroma over the king's mother. The Egyptian word for "aroma" rhymes with the word for "dew."

Labels (e.g. "Psalm of David"): What They (Don't) Tell Us

Though many psalms are attributed to David (e.g. 21, 110) and a few even to Solomon (e.g. 72), we must be careful about how much weight we put on such ancient attributions of authorship. Ancient texts could be attributed to authors for a variety of reasons – to continue a stream of tradition associated with a given ancient figure, to gain authority through being associated with an ancient figure, etc.

Therefore, when we see a text such as Psalm 110 assigned to David, this may mean that it was written at the time of David by one of David's scribes, or it may just mean that this psalm was seen as part of a longer tradition of Davidic psalms. Similarly, labels that assign the Song of Songs, Ecclesiastes, and most parts of Proverbs to Solomon probably do not mean that Solomon wrote all these texts. Instead, some may have been written at the time of Solomon, while others may just be part of a broader stream of "Solomonic" tradition extending even to apocryphal texts, such as the Wisdom of Solomon.

That said, the Bible's attribution of texts to figures such as David or Solomon can still be significant. For one thing, they are the first Judean or Israelite figures in the Bible to have whole biblical texts attributed to them (Moses only becomes the author of the Pentateuch in *post*-biblical tradition). The attributions of texts to David and Solomon may be recollections, preserved in the Bible, that David and Solomon's time was the first phase of the development of Israelite literature.

The same is not true for the smaller collection of superscriptions that place certain psalms at particular points in David's life, such as the superscription to Psalm 51 (a confessional psalm) that locates that psalm in David's life just after Nathan had confronted him about having an affair with Bathsheba and arranging to have her husband, Uriah, die in battle (story in 1 Sam 11:1–12:23). These historicizing superscriptions are marked by their language and theology as later additions to the Psalter and represent examples of early biblical interpretation.

In speaking of Yahweh "fathering" the king "like dew" (see "aroma" in the Egyptian materials) "before the womb of the dawn," Psalm 110 seems to apply these ideas to the Judean king. The psalm then hearkens back to the pre-Israelite royal traditions of Jerusalem in reporting God's oath to give the king eternal priesthood "according to the order of Melkizedeq" (110:4), a figure remembered elsewhere in the Bible as one of Jerusalem's kings in the time before David (Gen 14:18). Next come pictures of the king destroying his enemies (Ps 110:5–6) that are quite typical of ancient royal literature, before the psalm concludes with a reference to the king's drinking from Jerusalem's spring (Ps 110:7). Apparently the Judean king was anointed by the Gihon spring in Jerusalem (1 Kgs 1:33–4, 38–9). Thus Psalm 110 is a good example of a psalm whose obscure references can be understood when we see how it adapts ancient ideas about kingship recalled from pre-Davidic Jerusalem and the yet older royal theologies of Egypt and Mesopotamia. It does not depend on any specific pre-Israelite text, but in a broader way it contains "echoes of ancient empires."

The same can be said of many other biblical royal psalms. Just as the Egyptian king received a written decree from the gods proclaiming his status as the "son of Re," so Psalm 2 has the king report receiving a similar decree from Yahweh:

> I will proclaim the decree of Yahweh.
> He said to me, "You are my son,
>   I have fathered you today.
> Ask me, and I will give nations as your birthright,
>   The entire world as your possession." (Ps 2:7–8)

This theme of God offering the king whatever he wants, especially military victory (Ps 2:8), is found in other royal psalms as well (Ps 21:2; see also 1 Kgs 3:5), and is a major feature of ancient Egyptian and Mesopotamian royal theology. Over and over again the texts of these ancient empires emphasize that it is the king who is authorized to call on God for military help. The king, and the king alone, is authorized by God to ask for and achieve military success for his people, and one of the main jobs of the king in ancient Egyptian and Mesopotamian royal texts is to destroy the people's enemies.

This emphasis in royal psalms on the king's violent power can seem harsh to contemporary readers, particularly those in Europe or North America who have not experienced the direct threat of military attack. To ancient Israelites, however, such words sounded differently. Though many may have been inclined to follow calls such as Absalom's or Sheba's to reject the monarchy, these royal psalms insist that the king was appointed by God and would protect and defend them against any threat like that of the Philistines. In the process, the psalms draw on older Near Eastern royal imagery – e.g. divine "fathering" of the king, setting the king at God's right hand, the grant of the king's wishes – to justify the Jerusalem monarchy to skeptical Israelites.

One other important theme in these royal psalms is the emphasis on the importance to the kingship of "social responsibility" – Hebrew **tsedeqah**. This Hebrew word is usually translated into English as "righteousness," but it refers more specifically to the virtue of fulfilling one's social obligations to others, particularly defending those most vulnerable in ancient society: the orphan, widow, and foreign immigrant (the "stranger" or "alien"). For example, 2 Sam 23:3 notes that the king must rule with such "social solidarity" to dawn on his people like the morning light, and virtually all of Psalm 72, a "psalm of Solomon," is a prayer that God may give the king the power to rule his people with such tsedeqah:

> Give the king your justice, O God,
>   and your social solidarity to the royal son!
> May he judge your people with social solidarity [tsedeqah],
>   and your poor with justice! (Ps 72:1–2)

These texts show that Israelite kingship aimed to be an institution that protected the formerly vulnerable peoples of Israel's hill country and provided true justice. As we will

basics | **Book of Psalms: Part 1**

(For basics on "Book of Psalms: Part 2," see box on p. 224.)

Multiple levels in the book of Psalms

The book of Psalms was created over a very long period of time. It contains some of Israel's earliest texts. Yet it was still being expanded late into Israel's history. This mix of ancient and later texts in Psalms reflects the fact that these texts were integrally linked to and reflected shifts in the lives of Israelites as they faced ever different individual and national challenges.

Tracking down the earliest psalms

It is impossible to be sure whether a given psalm comes from the pre-exilic period, let alone from the time of David and Solomon. Nevertheless, most scholars agree that some psalms are good candidates for being among Israel's earliest literature. Some hymns, such as the praise of the storm god in Psalm 29, may have originated as pre-Israelite hymns to other gods before being adapted for Israelite use. Some other potentially early psalms mention the king, ark, or Zion, such as the celebration in Psalm 132 of Yahweh's choice of Zion and David's moving of the ark there. It is relatively unlikely that an author wrote such references after the destruction of the monarchy and the Zion Temple with its ark.

Other potentially early psalms?

The examples discussed above point to the probable existence of early psalms across the book of Psalms. They stand as potential indicators that *some* of the other psalms that lack such historical references, such as some psalms of lament or trust, may also date from Israel's early periods. Such texts about individual suffering or rescue are inherently difficult to date. Luckily, such dating is relatively unimportant for their interpretation.

see, the monarchy – like all human institutions – did not always live up to its highest aims, and Israelites rebelled against the monarchy several times. Nevertheless, these psalms show how Israel's kingship was meant to be an institution through which God provided both protection and care for the most vulnerable of God's people.

These same values of justice and social solidarity are also prominent in another group of psalms, often termed "**Zion psalms**" because of their common emphasis on the special significance of Zion/Jerusalem, the capital of the new monarchy. For example, Psalm 9 describes how God who dwells in Zion "judges the peoples with social solidarity" (9:8) and is "a stronghold for the oppressed" (9:9). Psalms 15 and 24 are ancient liturgies for those making a pilgrimage to Zion. These psalms bar from Zion those who cannot affirm that they have "clean hands and a pure heart" (24:4) and do not exploit others through lending practices (15:5). Zion, at the heart of ancient Jerusalem, was the mountain where God dwelt. Those who would come there had to hold themselves to a higher standard of behavior. They were expected to be just as the God of Zion is

MORE ON METHOD: POETIC ANALYSIS

Poetry in the Bible does not have the kind of sound rhymes found in much English-language poetry. Instead, it is characterized by a phenomenon called "**seconding**," where the second line of a poetic **couplet** – or pair of lines – builds on the idea or imagery of the first line, but somehow takes it further. Some poems may have a **triplet** (or more). In triplets the stress is on the final, third line, which builds on and advances the idea(s) or imagery of the first two. Take the example of the following triplet from Psalm 110, a royal psalm:

> 2) The LORD sends out from Zion
> your mighty scepter
> *Rule in the midst of your foes.* (NRSV)

Note how a translation like the NRSV marks a triplet like this through slightly indenting the second and third lines. These indentations of about 2 spaces indicate where the translators locate the Hebrew line breaks.

The example above uses italics for the third and climactic, seconding, line of the triplet. If you are analyzing a couplet or triplet, it is a good idea to write it out this way and underline or highlight the final line. Look at the parallels and differences between this final line and the two lines that precede it. How do the first two lines prepare for the final line and what is the impact of concluding the triplet this way? Can you identify an emotional impact of this poetic couplet in addition to summarizing it?

Take a Bible with the NRSV and try to find and analyze the poetic units in verse 3 of Psalm 110. (Hint: according to the NRSV, there is a triplet and a couplet here.)

For more see Robert Alter, *The Art of Biblical Poetry* (New York: Basic Books, 1985).

just. Furthermore, these and other psalms repeatedly assert what will be one of the most important claims of Zion theology: that Jerusalem, the dwelling place of God, is invulnerable to foreign attack. See, for example, the description of Jerusalem/Zion in Psalm 46:

> There is a river whose streams bring joy to the city of God,
> The holy dwelling of the most high.
> God is in the midst of her [the city], she shall not fall.
> God will rescue her at the break of day. (46:4–5)

Though parts of these royal and Zion psalms may have been written at later points in the history of the Jerusalem monarchy, they stand as excellent examples of how early Israelites – who had lived for hundreds of years in hilltop villages – made theological sense of this new social form: a new monarchy set in a new capital city, Jerusalem. Later Jewish and Christian interpreters, of course, have reinterpreted many of these psalms, so that – for example – the king praised in texts such as Psalm 2 or 110 is understood to be the Messiah. Such reinterpretations can be legitimate, since these texts would not have survived and become part of the Hebrew Bible if later readers had understood them only to be relevant to a monarchy that would eventually perish. Yet these texts should also be understood in their historical context. As such, they are a witness to some of Israel's earliest ideas about power and community, ideas which would prove very important to the later writers of prophecies and histories.

CHAPTER THREE REVIEW

1.   Know the meaning and significance of the following terms discussed in this chapter:

- couplet
- royal psalms
- royal theology
- seconding
- triplet
- *tsedeqah*
- Zion
- Zion psalms
- Zion theology

2.   Can you take a translation that marks poetic couplets and triplets (such as the NRSV, NIV, or NAB) and identify couplets and triplets in biblical poems?

3.   What was the major reason that scholars think a monarchy arose in Israel? How is this different from other reasons given in the stories of 1 Samuel?

4.   What role did writing play in the emergent monarchy? How was this related to orality and memorization?

5.   What do the mentions of David in psalm superscriptions tell and not tell us?

6.   Some scholars working from a liberation perspective believe that the rise of the monarchy was a "counter-revolution" – a step back from struggle for justice. For them, royal and Zion theology are an oppressive strand of biblical tradition that must be distinguished from liberative strands of biblical theology such as those seen in the exodus story (or biblical prophets such as Amos). Others argue that justice and righteousness stand at the heart of royal and Zion theology and that the survival of Israel and its traditions (including traditions about exodus and justice) depended on the emergence of a monarchy. Which perspective do you find more compelling and why?

RESOURCES FOR FURTHER STUDY

McCarter, P. Kyle. *I Samuel: A New Translation; II Samuel: A New Translation*. Anchor Bible. Garden City: Doubleday, 1980.

CHAPTER 4

ECHOES OF PAST EMPIRES IN BIBLICAL WISDOM, LOVE POETRY, LAW, AND NARRATIVE

Chapter Outline

CHAPTER OVERVIEW

In this chapter we look at some texts in the Bible that contain strong "echoes" of past ancient empires in biblical texts. These echoes may indicate that these texts were written during the early monarchy when scribes were most dependent on foreign models in creating the first Israelite written corpus. Some texts discussed here are attributed to Solomon (e.g. Proverbs, Song of Songs, and Ecclesiastes – see Chapter 3, box on p. 66) while others are originally anonymous. For example, the latter part of the chapter will discuss scholars' discovery (over three hundred years ago) of an early strand of stories about creation and flood, the "J primeval history," embedded in parts of Genesis 1–11. It should be emphasized that some of these texts may come from a time later than the early monarchy (many scholars think so). Nevertheless, they all lack the hostility toward foreign influence typical of much later biblical tradition. Early or late, a study of them in relation to their non-biblical counterparts can teach us much about how these biblical texts were used and what made them special.

Echoes of Past Empires in Writings Attributed to Solomon

Some of the most striking echoes of ancient empires in the entire Old Testament are found in books associated with Solomon, David's successor: Proverbs, Song of Songs, and Ecclesiastes (for more on what this association means, see Chapter 3, box on p. 66). This is a bit of a surprise, since virtually all historical critics do not think Solomon actually wrote all three books, and most would date these books to widely different periods. Nevertheless, despite their differences, these "Solomonic" books all echo traditions that were prominent in the Ancient Near East.

READING
Prov 6:20–8:36; 10:1–32;
22:17–29.

Instruction of
Amenemope (www.
wiley.com/go/carr).

Ecclesiastes 1:1–3:22 and
Song of Songs 1:1–2:7.

---

basics   Song of Songs

It has proven difficult to find a systematic pattern in the loosely connected love poems that make up the Song of Songs. The following is a rough overview based particularly on the striking set of parallel refrains across the Song (2:7; 3:5; 8:4).

Outline

I	Introduction of themes	1:1–2:7
	Seeking day/night scenes	2:8–3:5
	Riches and praise	3:6–5:1
	Seeking night scene	5:2–6:3
	Riches and praise	6:4–8:3
II	Concluding statements on themes	8:4–14

Date

Most scholars would date the Song of Songs to the third or fourth centuries BCE, centuries after Solomon, particularly because of late features in its language. A minority see indicators of earlier origins of these materials, such as the way they resemble Egyptian and other early love songs.

Theme: sex, God, and the poetics of the Song

Many readers insist that one must decide that the Song is *either* about human desire *or* about divine–human love. The poetry of the Song, however, is more elusive. The dense metaphors and disconnected dialogues invite readers to build their own images of what is happening. The lack of explicit divine references and other features of the Song suggest that the book was meant to evoke the drama of human love. Still, the poetry allows multiple readings, especially now that the Song stands in a Bible that elsewhere depicts God's love for God's people (e.g. the book of Hosea, to be discussed later in this textbook).

Take, for example, the Song of Songs (otherwise known as Song of Solomon or Canticles), an often overlooked book of passionate love poetry at the heart of the Old Testament. Though early Jewish and Christian communities often read this book as a love dialogue between God and God's beloved community (whether church or synagogue), the book's closest parallels are secular love songs found in Egypt just before the emergence of Israel. Those ancient Egyptian love poems and their parallels in the biblical Song of Songs do not describe the love affairs of gods. The Song of Songs does not ever clearly refer to Yahweh! Instead, like the Egyptian love poetry it most resembles, the Song of Songs is focused on the drama of human physical love: desiring, seeking, losing, and seeking again human passion with one's true love. Moreover, like the love literature that it echoes, the Song of Songs presents a positive, not fearful, picture of female desire. The woman of the Song of Songs is a powerful figure, not afraid to ask her lover for what she wants and speaking more than half of the words of the book. Nowhere in the book is she judged for her desire, nor is her lover, even though their love remains frustratingly secret and forbidden (Song 8:1–2).

Scholars are not sure when to date the Song of Songs, though its links to early Egyptian love poetry might point to an early core. Ecclesiastes (also known by its Hebrew name "Qohelet") is similarly difficult to date, and it likewise echoes literature from the ancient Near East. The book, attributed to "the teacher, the son of David in Jerusalem," is a combination of skepticism about wisdom and affirmation of life's small joys. Its main idea is the way all values are called into question by the fact that everyone dies and "you can't take it with you." During ancient Israel's history, there was no belief in a heaven or hell where people would be rewarded or punished for their behavior during life. In light of this, the "teacher" of Ecclesiastes ends up deciding that "emptiness, emptiness, all is emptiness" (Eccl 1:2, 14; 2:1; etc.). Since everyone dies sooner or later, both frantic pleasure seeking (Eccl 2:1–11) and excessive wisdom and righteousness (2:12–23) are pointless, "chasing after wind." Rather than getting too attached to any great project, the teacher of this text urges all to enjoy each day's moderate pleasures:

> Go, eat your food with pleasure, and drink your wine with a happy heart; for God has long approved what you do. Let your clothing always be white, do not let oil be lacking on your head. Enjoy life with the woman you love, all the days of your empty life that you are given under the sun. For that is your portion in life and your work which you work under the sun. (Eccl. 9:7–9; see also 2:24–5; 5:18–20; 8:15)

This kind of day-to-day living, eating, drinking, and enjoying romantic love, this "imperative of joy" (as one scholar has called it), is the "teacher's" prescription for life lived in a world where "emptiness, emptiness, all is emptiness."

I have not called this "teacher" of Ecclesiastes "Solomon" because historical-critical scholars agree that Solomon was not the author of this enigmatic book. Many would even date it centuries after the time of Solomon, partly because of resemblances they see between the ideas of Ecclesiastes and the Greco-Roman idea of *carpe diem* (Latin for "seize the day"), an idea that might be paraphrased "drink up, for tomorrow you

basics	Ecclesiastes/Qohelet	
Outline: **counter-wisdom** **instruction**	I Introductory royal testament II Instruction in skeptical wisdom III Epilogue with later affirmations	1:1–2:26 3:1–12:8 12:9–14
Date	Most scholars consider Ecclesiastes/Qohelet to be among the latest books in the Hebrew Bible. The Hebrew in which it is written is unusual for an early text, and many would see its perspective to be Greek. As in the case of the Song of Songs, however, there are some reasons to think a form of Ecclesiastes may have been earlier, such as its resemblance to the older form of the Gilgamesh epic (see below).	
Major themes: **Qohelet's** **contradictions**	The lead themes through most of Ecclesiastes are the absurdity of all human striving (Eccl 1:2, 14; 2:1; etc.) and the benefits of daily pleasures in life (2:24–5; 5:18–20; etc.). Yet the last verses of the book (12:13–14) as well as isolated sections in its midst (e.g. 2:26; 3:17) affirm the more traditional idea that good eventually is rewarded and evil punished. Many would take these more traditional affirmations to be late additions to the book.	

may die." Others, however, see an echo of a much more ancient text here in Ecclesiastes, an echo of the Mesopotamian epic of Gilgamesh. An ancient version of this epic has a scene where its hero, Gilgamesh, is beside himself with grief and despair after seeing his closest friend, Enkidu, die. Having just seen the "fate of all humankind" in the death of his friend, Gilgamesh tells a barmaid, Siduri, of his desperate fear of death and wish that he could be immortal. In response, she speaks words that sound much like the "imperative of joy" of Ecclesiastes:

Gilgamesh, where are you wandering? You cannot find the life that you seek.
　　When gods created humankind, for humankind they established death. Immortality they reserved for themselves.
　　You, Gilgamesh, let your belly be full. Keep enjoying yourself day and night! Every day make merry, dance and play every night! Let your clothes be clean. Let your head be washed, may you be bathed in water. Gaze on the little one who holds your hand. Let a wife enjoy your repeated embrace! Such is the destiny of mortals. (Translation: George, vol. 1, 279)

This text was written about a thousand years before the time of Solomon, yet it was passed down to later times as one of the most commonly used educational texts both inside and outside Mesopotamia. The ancient speech of Siduri in Gilgamesh anticipates Ecclesiastes not only in the response to death through an "imperative of joy," but in the detailed sequence of pleasures it endorses: food, wine and partying, good clothing, good hygiene ("oil" washing), and sexual partnership. It is possible that the author of Ecclesiastes drew on this part of the ancient epic of Gilgamesh, rather than later Greco-Roman ideas, in formulating his solution to an empty universe.

MORE ON METHOD: COMPARISON WITH NON-BIBLICAL TEXTS

Biblical scholars learn much through comparing biblical texts with similar texts found elsewhere in the ancient world. Sometimes, as in the case of parallels between Prov 22:17–24:34 and the Egyptian Instruction of Amenemope, scholars are comparing a biblical text with a possible source of that text. As suggested at the outset of the chapter, this can have implications for the dating of that text. At other times, however, such comparison with other ancient texts simply allows a biblical scholar to put a biblical text in a broader cultural context. Through it, we can see distinctive features of the biblical version of a broader Near Eastern tradition and gain possible data on the sorts of social contexts where texts of a given type (e.g. royal psalms, proverbs, or love songs) were produced and used (e.g. education).

Useful resources for comparison

For translations of texts: Victor H. Matthews and Don C. Benjamin, *Old Testament Parallels: Laws and Stories from the Ancient Near East* (3rd edition). New York: Paulist, 2006.
For background on texts: Kenton L. Sparks, *Ancient Texts for the Study of the Hebrew Bible: A Guide to the Background Literature*. Peabody, MA: Hendrickson, 2005.

One thing is clear: Ecclesiastes is responding with skepticism to older wisdom of the kind seen in Proverbs, the "Solomonic" book with the best claim to being datable (at least in part) to the time of David and Solomon. This one biblical book actually contains multiple collections, many of which are identified by separate headings: "the Proverbs of Solomon, son of David, king of Israel" (Prov 1:1–9:18), "the Proverbs of Solomon" (Prov 10:1–22:16), "the Proverbs of Solomon that were collected by Hezekiah's men" (Prov 25:1ff.), and so on. What we have in Proverbs, then, is a collection of collections of ancient Israel's educational materials.

This collection of collections in Proverbs contains some of the clearest echoes of foreign educational texts found in the Bible. For example, we find a collection of "words of the wise" in Proverbs 22:17–24:22 whose "thirty sayings" (Prov 22:20) loosely adapt and echo some of the 30 chapters of the Egyptian Instruction of Amenemope (see Figure 4.1). Both collections begin with a call to memorize the following instruction

Figure 4.1 Copy of the Egyptian Instruction of Amenemope, dated approximately 1200 BCE. The topics of its 30 sayings (cf. Prov 22:20) loosely parallel those found in Prov 22:17–24:22.

(Amenemope chapter 1; Prov 22:17–21), and continue with similar instructions not to oppress the poor (Amenemope 2; Prov 22:22–3), not to move boundary stones (Amen 6; Prov 22:28), not to get tied up in pursuing wealth (Amenemope 7; Prov 23:4–5), to avoid fools (Amenemope 9; Prov 22:24–5), and to take care in eating in front of nobles (Amenemope 23; Prov 23:1–3). To be sure, the author of Proverbs did not translate the ancient Egyptian instruction. The existing parallels between the texts are parallels in general content, and there are many parts of Prov 22:17–24:22 that have no counterpart in the Instruction of Amenemope. Nevertheless, the shared concept of 30 sayings and multiple parallels between these texts are good reason to conclude that the author of Prov 22:17–24:22 knew of and loosely appropriated parts of the Egyptian Instruction of Amenemope, along with other wisdom traditions, in composing his own version of "30" sayings. In this sense Prov 22:17–24:22 is an important "echo of ancient [Egyptian] empire" in the Bible.

The book of Proverbs also shows the importance of female wisdom in ancient Israel, an importance reflected in different ways by the Song of Songs and Ecclesiastes. Proverbs starts and continues with calls for students to attend to both the father's *and* the mother's wisdom (Prov 1:8; 6:20; 23:22). The early chapters of Proverbs feature a powerful depiction of wisdom as a female, semi-divine figure (e.g. Prov 1:20–33; 8:1–36). And Proverbs concludes with an instruction attributed to King Lemuel's *mother* (Prov 31:1–9) and an A–Z praise of the "woman of power" which Jewish men often sing to their wives over the table of the Friday evening Sabbath meal (Prov 31:10–31). Some have seen echoes of the Egyptian goddess of order, Maat, in the depiction of female wisdom in Proverbs, but this broader association of women with wisdom in Proverbs may reflect the prominent role that mothers played in teaching children, both in Israel and in the rest of the ancient Near East. This prominent role of mothers as teachers may also be reflected in the Gilgamesh scene (possibly echoed in Ecclesiastes) where the barmaid teaches Gilgamesh. Note also the teaching voice given to the female lover in Song of Songs, where she makes the daughters of Jerusalem swear not to "awaken or arouse love until she is ready" (Song of Songs 2:7; 3:5; 8:4). In these and other ways, women were viewed as unusually wise in the Bible and its surrounding world, and this is reflected in the Bible.

basics   Book of Proverbs

Outline: treasury of ancient Israelite wisdom

I	Introductory instruction: seek wisdom!	1:1–9:18
II	Additional wisdom collections	10:1–31:9
III	A good woman as embodiment of wisdom	31:10–31

Date

Most scholars see a great diversity of date in the material of Proverbs. Sections such as Proverbs 1–9 are dated many centuries after Solomon, while parts of other sections, such as Prov 22:17–24:22, are thought to be among the earliest parts of the Bible. A minority of scholars, however, find indicators of early date in sections such as Proverbs 1–9 as well.

Major themes

Since Proverbs is a collection of collections, it is particularly difficult to summarize with a single theme or set of themes. Nevertheless, major features of the book include its prominent focus on female figures toward the beginning (Proverbs 1–9) and end (Prov 31:10–31), and its repeated emphasis on the importance of "fear of Yahweh" (Prov 1:7, 29; 2:5; etc.) throughout.

Alongside all this, there also is a religious element. Both the instructions and proverbs in the book of Proverbs have a distinctive emphasis on the "fear of Yahweh" as crucial to the successful life (Prov 1:7, 29; 14:26–7; 23:17; etc.). Nevertheless, the collections of educational texts in Proverbs are broader instruction in how to succeed with both god and human beings. Combined with assertions of the importance of fearing Yahweh (e.g. Prov 14:26) are pragmatic sayings such as the affirmation in Prov 17:8 that bribes often work well. All these materials in Proverbs (in contrast to Qohelet) affirm the basic idea of **moral act-consequence**: the idea that fear of God and/or good actions produce good results, while bad behavior leads to disaster. The task of the student is to walk the path toward success, not toward death.

Uncovering Echoes of Past Empires Elsewhere in the Bible

READING

Genesis 1–11, Gilgamesh (tablet 11), and Atrahasis (www.wiley.com/go/carr).

EXERCISE

Before reading this section, read Gen 6:5–9:17 and note every place where the same or quite similar event is narrated twice. An example would be God's announcement of the flood both in Gen 6:13 and in 7:4. Another is Noah's multiple entries into the ark in 7:7 and 7:13. Once you have developed a list of such doubly narrated events, see whether "God" or "LORD" is used to refer to God in any of these doublets. Come up with your own theory about how the biblical flood story ended up this way.

So far we have found echoes of ancient empires in entire texts (e.g. royal psalms; see Chapter 3) or books (e.g. the Song of Songs) that are associated in different ways with the time of David and Solomon. Nevertheless, other texts from the Bible also contain strong echoes of ancient Near Eastern literature, many of which si milarly may be datable to the beginnings of the monarchy. For example, recent scholarship by David Wright (*Inventing God's Law* [New York: Oxford University Press, 2009]) has identified multiple and specific parallels between the ancient Mesopotamian Code of Hammurabi and a collection of biblical laws in Exodus 20:22–23:33 called the "**Covenant Code**" (see Exod 24:7). For over a century scholars have judged that this "Covenant Code" was one of the earliest collections of laws in the Bible, because its laws about topics such as building altars (Exod 20:24–6) and celebrating festivals (Exod 23:14–17) reflect early practices of offering sacrifices all over the land and not just in Jerusalem. Only recently, however, have scholars seen ways that the Covenant Code may be loosely modeled on parts of the Code of Hammurabi (see Figure 4.2), much as Prov 22:17–24:22 was modeled partially on the Instruction of Amenemope. Indeed, it is likely that many of the purity and ritual regulations of Leviticus and Numbers also had ancient precursors, since we have extensive examples of similar sorts of documents about priestly matters found among the remains of the peoples preceding and surrounding ancient Israel. Law, whether royal decree or priestly instruction, was one of the most important forms of ancient writing.

Perhaps the most famous echoes of texts from ancient empires are found at the very beginning of the Bible, in the **primeval history** (Genesis 1–11), which tells stories about the whole earth and its peoples. Before looking at these echoes, however, it is important to realize that these chapters of Genesis contain *two* parallel sets of stories about the early history of the world. Lots of things are described twice in these chapters. "God" creates plants, animals, and humans (male and female) in Genesis 1, and then "Yahweh God" creates the first man, animals, and then woman in Genesis 2. Genesis 3–4 tell

Figure 4.2 The Hammurabi stela. The king shows respect before the enthroned Mesopotamian god of justice, Shamash. The text describes his appointment by the gods to give justice and quotes his proclamation of laws that roughly parallel (in topic) parts of the Covenant Code in Exod 20:22–23:33.

stories about these first humans and their descendants up to the time of Noah, and then Genesis 5 gives a genealogy from Adam to Noah. Then, the flood story of Genesis 6–9 is full of doubly narrated events: two descriptions of the problem leading to the flood (6:1–4 and 6:11), two descriptions of God's perception of the problem (6:5 and 6:12), two assertions that Noah was exceptional in his righteousness (6:8 and 9), and so on. Looking at these duplicate narratives in the flood and across Genesis 1–11 more generally, it appears as if an Israelite author had two complete, written stories of creation and flood, and that author wove those older written stories, these ancient "sources" of Genesis, together to create the present biblical text.

Over the last two hundred years, biblical scholars have reached a high level of agreement on how to untangle these interwoven creation and flood writings (sources) embedded in Genesis 1–11. They call one of these sources "**P**" or the **Priestly Source**, because its sequence of stories (Gen 1:1–2:3; 5:1–32; 6:9–22; 7:6, 11, and other parts of the flood up through 9:1–17) links with other parts of the **Tetrateuch** (Genesis, Exodus, Leviticus, and Numbers) that focus on priests. The other source starts with the garden of Eden story in Genesis 2:4–3:24, continues with the Cain and Abel story and genealogies of Genesis 4, includes its own flood narrative (Gen 6:1–8; 7:1–5, 10, 12, and other parts up through 8:20–2), and contains an epilogue about Noah and his sons (Gen 9:18–27). This source is often called "**J**" or the "**Yahwistic Source**," since this source uses the holy Hebrew name Yahweh to refer to God. (The German scholars who first discovered the J source two hundred years ago used the letter "j" for their "y" sound and spelled the name Yahwist "Jahwist.") As will be discussed later, in Chapter 10, many scholars see this J source, like P, continuing across the Tetrateuch, but there are good reasons to be skeptical of their claims. Instead, this textbook considers any early "J" source to be limited to a "J primeval history" found exclusively in Genesis 1–11.

Both of these sources, J and P, echo texts from ancient empires that preceded Israel. For example, the P creation story in Genesis 1:1–2:3 echoes aspects of the ancient Mesopotamian Enuma Elish epic (www.wiley.com/go/carr). Both texts describe the beginning of creation as a watery chaos before the god(s) spoke the world into being:

Enuma Elish	Genesis 1:1–3
When on high no heaven had been named, when no earth had been called, When there were no divine elders . . . When there was nothing, nothing but . . . Godfather Apsu and Mummu-Tiamat, Godmother of All Living, two bodies of water becoming one . . . When there were no divine warriors, When no names had been called, When no tasks had been assigned . . . (Translation: *OT Parallels* 12)	When God first created the heaven and the earth, and the earth was completely without form and darkness was on the face of the deep, and a divine wind howled over the face of the water . . .

God said, ["let there be light . . ."] |

MORE ON METHOD: SOURCE CRITICISM

The term "source criticism" refers to the scholarly attempt to identify separate sources standing behind the existing biblical text. As discussed in the main text, we have no manuscripts of these earlier sources. Instead, scholars must examine the biblical text we now have and look for clues to earlier sources, such as doublets, contradictions, and major shifts in language. Sometimes scholars can achieve substantial consensus in reconstructing hypothetical earlier documents, such as the Priestly/P and Yahwistic/J primeval history sources discussed in this chapter. As we will see in later chapters, the picture is less clear as we move beyond Genesis 1–11.

The Enuma Elish goes on to describe the creation of the inhabited world out of a conflict between the gods, including the triumph of the god Marduk over the goddess of the primeval salt water, Tiamat. Such a focus on divine conflict is absent from the biblical story, but Tiamat is distantly echoed in the Hebrew word for "deep" that appears in the initial description of chaotic waters in Gen 1:2. Moreover, the biblical chapter shares with its Mesopotamian counterpart a picture of creation that moves from watery chaos to the creation of light, then a heavenly domed ceiling to separate the two primeval oceans (the "firmament" of Gen 1:6 and following), dry ground, and humans. In these and other ways the story of creation of the cosmos in Genesis 1 echoes multiple elements of the Enuma Elish epic, even as the biblical story also has its own distinctive emphases, some of which will be discussed when we return to the P document in Chapter 10.

Meanwhile, the echoes of ancient empires are just as widespread in the J primeval history. Many scholars have noted that this strand of Genesis 1–11 links at multiple points with the ancient Mesopotamian Atrahasis epic, written almost one thousand years before the time of David and Solomon. That epic starts with a creation story that resembles parts of the garden of Eden story (Gen 2:4–25), continues with various accounts of human multiplication that anticipate the biblical report of human multiplication (Gen 6:1), and concludes with an ancient Mesopotamian story of the flood with several links to the story of Noah and the flood. In Atrahasis the gods ordain a flood, the flood is announced to a flood hero, the hero builds an ark and survives the flood, the flood eventually abates and the ark lands on a mountain, the flood hero offers a sacrifice, and the god(s) resolve never to send another flood once they smell the sacrifice. Sometimes, the links can be very specific. For example, a version of the Atrahasis flood narrative that was included in the Gilgamesh epic (see Figure 4.3) tells of how the flood hero, Utnapishtim in that story, sent forth a dove, a swallow, and a raven to find out if the flood was over, closely paralleling the story (in J) of Noah sending birds to find out the same thing (Gen 8:6–12). These and other parallels have convinced

Figure 4.3 Tablet of the Gilgamesh epic containing the flood narrative.

many scholars that the author of the J primeval history knew some form of these ancient Mesopotamian traditions. He may even have been crafting his own distinctively Israelite version of the Atrahasis primeval history.

We do not know for sure when the authors of the J and P narratives did their work. Most would date the overall P source to a relatively late period in Israelite history, but there are signs that some parts of the P source, including some form of the Genesis 1 creation story, may have existed much earlier. Meanwhile, many would date the J primeval history early in Israelite history, possibly as early as the time of Solomon. Its widespread and specific dependence on older non-biblical Mesopotamian texts makes good sense in the early period of the monarchy, and it does not clearly anticipate or refer to themes of Torah and law that are important in later periods of Israelite history. In sum, if there is material from around the time of David or Solomon in the book of Genesis, the J primeval history is one of the most likely places to find it.

FOCUS
TEXT

The Garden of Eden Story (Gen 2:4–3:24)

We turn next to look more closely at the text that opens the J/Yahwistic source discussed above: the garden of Eden story in Gen 2:4–3:24. Most people approach this text with presuppositions shaped by its history of interpretation. For example, if asked to name the fruit that Adam and Eve ate in the garden, most would instantly reply "an apple." The Genesis text, however, does not say this. Similarly, though many assume that the snake in the garden was "Satan," that is never specified in the Bible. These and other elements were added to the biblical story by later interpreters (see Figure 4.4).

This history of interpretation of the garden of Eden text has also influenced what people think the whole story is about. For example, many have understood Paul in Rom 5:18–21 to imply that Genesis 2–3 is a tale of how sin entered the world, putting all humans under the curse of death. In the post-Pauline letter of 1 Timothy, this tragedy is blamed on women, who must now pay the price by bearing children:

> For Adam was formed first, then Eve; and Adam was not deceived, but the woman was deceived and became a transgressor. Yet she will be saved through childbearing, provided they continue in faith and love and holiness, with modesty. (1 Tim 2:13–15; translation: NRSV)

Later Christian interpreters expanded on this type of interpretation, with the early theologian Gregory Nazianzen talking of how Eve "beguiled the man by means of pleasure" and Tertullian saying to a group of nuns, "Are not each of you an Eve? . . . You are the Devil's gateway." With these and many other interpretations setting the stage for contemporary readings, it is little wonder that many people today assume that this text is an anti-female text blaming Eve for seducing Adam and introducing sin and death into the world.

Yet particularly thanks to groundbreaking work by Phyllis Trible (*God and the Rhetoric of Sexuality* [Philadelphia: Fortress, 1978]) and others in the mid-1970s, scholars have

Figure 4.4 Titian's painting of Adam and Eve taking the apple from a snake-tailed cherubic Satan. It well illustrates how later interpretation of Genesis 2–3 influenced people's visions of the scene.

gradually recognized that there is no more basis for that reading in the text itself than there is for the idea that the fruit which the first humans ate was an "apple" (that word never occurs in Genesis 3). Both of these ideas are later interpretations that have been laid on a text that has very different concerns. Trible and others have pointed out that the text actually celebrates the woman as the culmination of creation. "Sin" is never mentioned in it, and the woman and man share responsibility for the garden crime. Moreover, the consequences for this act that come on them are depicted in the text as tragic, not divinely willed elements of creation. Let us now take a new look at this often-interpreted text.

The story is organized into three main parts: a description of God's creation of a deeply connected partnership of men and women working the earth (Gen 2:4–25), a crime scene describing their disobedience of God's one prohibition (3:1–6), and an account of the tragic loss of original connectedness to each other and the earth as a result of the crime (3:7–25). The story opens with God creating the first "human" (Hebrew *Adam*) out of the earth (Hebrew *adamah*), and giving him life through breathing the divine breath into him. God sets him in the garden to work and protect it, and the word play on *Adam/Adamah* (much like "human" and "humus") emphasizes the original connectedness of the human to the earth he was destined to work.

Yet God immediately recognizes that there is a problem with this picture: "It is not good for the human to be alone" (Gen 2:18). God then decides to create a partner "corresponding to him." God creates the animals, and brings each to the human for him to name them, but none truly "corresponds" to him (Gen 2:19–20). So God tries a new approach, anesthetizing the first human by putting him to sleep, removing a rib, and "building" the woman out of it. When the human awakens and sees the woman, he sings the first song of creation, one that emphasizes the connectedness they share:

> This is it! Bone of my bones, flesh of my flesh;
> This one will be called woman [Hebrew *ishah*]
> for out of man [Hebrew *ish*] she was taken. (Gen 2:23)

The text concludes by saying that this is the origin of love and marriage, it is the reason a man leaves his parents and "clings to his wife and they become one flesh." In stark contrast to many other world-creation stories, sex is not connected at all here to having children. Instead, sex is a sign of the original connectedness of the man and the woman created out of a part of him so that they would truly correspond to each other. This is a story of God's will that humans be in close relationship with each other and the earth. In the wake of this creation, both man and woman "were naked and not ashamed" (Gen 2:25). They may work the garden together and eat of its fruit, with one exception: they may not eat of the "tree of knowledge of good and evil" on penalty of death (Gen 2:17).

The scene shifts in Gen 3:1–6 to a new cast of characters, the man, woman, and now a "clever" snake in place of God (Gen 3:1). Again, the history of interpretation has often pictured Satan as the snake, but there is no basis for that in the Hebrew text. Instead, the snake stands as an ancient symbol of wisdom and immortality, and the adjective used to describe him – *arum* ("clever") – is a virtue frequently praised in the wisdom writings of Proverbs. Furthermore, though interpreters have often supposed that the sin of the first humans somehow consisted of sex or desire, there is no hint of that here. As we saw, Genesis 2 already explains the first sexual partnership of humans as the result of God's creation of a woman out of part of a man. Instead, the issue is human acquisition of godlike "wisdom." Not only is the "clever" snake associated with wisdom, but the "tree of knowledge of good and evil" is a symbol of wisdom's fruits. This then is underlined when the snake convinces the woman to consider eating of the tree, and she sees that the "tree was good for food, a delight to the eyes, and good for becoming wise" (Gen 3:6). She eats of the fruit of wisdom, gives fruit to her husband and he does the same, and the text says that "the eyes of both were opened" (Gen 3:7). This is a frequent expression for gaining education. Thus Gen 3:1–7 describes the first act of human disobedience as the defiance of God and the gaining of a form of "wisdom" that shows many signs of being associated with the ancient Israelite textual wisdom we have seen in books such as Proverbs.

This then sets in motion a tragic unraveling of much of the connectedness that God had created at the outset. The text already illustrates this when God arrives in the garden, the humans hide, and when questioned about why they are hiding, begin to blame each other. The man blames both the woman and God who made the woman (3:12), and the woman blames the snake (3:13). In response, God proclaims consequences for all three. The snake will now crawl on the ground and be an eternal enemy of humans. The woman will no longer enjoy idyllic life in the garden, but God will "multiply her toil and pregnancies" (not "increase pangs in childbearing" as often translated). And the idyllic life of the man likewise will come to an end. His toil is to work the ground from which he was made until he dies and returns to it. Where once there was mutual desire, now the woman's desire will be for her husband, and where once there was mutuality between corresponding partners, now the husband will "rule" over his wife (3:16). The story goes on to describe Adam's naming of his wife "Eve" (a name made from the Hebrew word for "life") to reflect her new job of producing children (3:20). God gives the human pair clothes (3:21) – a sign of human civilization that is also seen in ancient non-biblical texts such as the Gilgamesh epic. Finally, God expels them from the garden for fear that they might gain godlike immortality much as they already gained godlike wisdom (Gen 3:22–4).

In this way the text accurately depicts the non-ideal world that actual Israelites lived in, but with a twist. Most Israelites still lived lives closely tied to the land, working it by the sweat of their brow until they returned to it. The work was hard, famine was frequent, and death came much sooner than it does for people in the developed world today. Women lived in patriarchal marriages, sustaining the household with their work, while undergoing an endless series of pregnancies, many of which were very dangerous. Analysis of female remains has suggested that as many as half of women eventually died in childbirth. In this sense, the realities described in the latter part of Genesis 3 all held true for the ancient Israelite men and women. Yet what is remarkable about this text is its suggestion that this often harsh and patriarchal reality is not what God originally intended for humans. God originally made humans for fruitful farming, long life, and mutual, truly corresponding life and desire between men and women. It was only with the human step toward godlike wisdom that they emerged into the harsh reality that they experience today. "Wisdom" – not women – is the source of the tragic endless labor, patriarchy, and death that characterize the present.

This kind of narrative about human origins is as timeless as many texts discussed above, but it may also stand as a reflection on what "wisdom" was coming to mean in monarchal Israel. Though most still lived in villages, Judah and Israel were increasingly dominated by urban elites who were educated in new literary traditions modeled on non-biblical sources. The leaders of Israel during this period underwent a momentous shift in their collective memory. Before this monarchy, tribal villages all had their oral traditions, such as tales of trickster ancestors, the exodus, or military triumph. But now

– with the monarchy – we have seen the emergence of an early Israelite literary tradition recited and memorized from *written* texts: royal psalms, stories of royalty, royal wisdom and (possibly) early love literature, stories of creation and flood. Moreover, many of these written texts were based on educational literature from outside Israel, such as Egyptian wisdom and love songs or Mesopotamian traditions about creation and flood. This growing Israelite literary corpus, so difficult to identify precisely now, was the means by which a small and growing number of literate Israelites gained "knowledge of good and evil" and had their "eyes" "opened."

Read in this context, the garden of Eden story – itself a text – suggests that wisdom is both an essential part of human growing up and a source of many human ills. On the one hand, it suggests that there is no return to an idyllic life in the garden, munching on fruit and obeying God's one clear command – not to eat of the tree of knowledge of good and evil. On the other hand, this enlightenment, this human journey to mature civilization, has brought many of the ills of adult life with it: endless pregnancies and agricultural work. The marks of original creation persist, such as the way humans still are drawn to "cleave to each other" and "become one flesh." Yet the story recognizes that adult life also has its toil and tragic imperfections. The journey out of the garden has brought a life where humans have work in place of leisure, "wisdom" in place of the single garden command, and – all too often – male rule over women in place of the connectedness that God originally wished.

Conclusion

Ultimately, we cannot know for sure whether any of the texts discussed in this chapter date from the time of David or Solomon's monarchy. Some texts are associated with David or Solomon, but this is not a sufficient basis for dating them to that time. The form of the Hebrew language can be another clue, but it is not reliable for dating texts transmitted – often by memory – over centuries. Even the tracing of "echoes" of ancient non-biblical texts in the Bible is not a sure sign of early dating. In sum, there are no sure guideposts for dating biblical texts, particularly to a period so long before our earliest manuscripts. The most we could do in this chapter is focus on a few biblical texts, some associated with David and Solomon and some not, that show a distinctive "echoing" of foreign, pre-Israelite traditions. Such non-polemical echoing, I am suggesting, would be most typical of writings formed at the outset of Israelite writing and less typical of later times when hostility toward foreign culture was greater.

These echoes of ancient texts can teach us about how ancient Israelites used the sorts of written texts now in the Bible. For example, the Instruction of Amenemope, the epic of Atrahasis, and the laws in the Code of Hammurabi were all used in ancient Egyptian or Mesopotamian education. Mesopotamian and Egyptian leaders were qualified for their jobs by learning to read and memorize these texts. When we turn to similar biblical texts, such as the "words of the wise" in Prov 22:17–24:34 that echo Amenemope, it is logical to hypothesize that such biblical texts likewise were used to educate leaders in the early monarchy. Whatever the original function of earlier oral traditions now embedded in such biblical texts, as *writings* they probably helped educate the leadership elite in an emergent monarchy.

Meanwhile, the differences between biblical texts and their non-biblical counterparts are as important as the similarities. We can learn much about the particular values and perspectives of biblical authors through comparing the Covenant Code with Hammurabi, the "words of the wise" in Prov 22:17–24:34 with the Instruction of Amenemope, the J source in Genesis 1–11 with Atrahasis, and so on. Biblical authors did not just copy major texts of Mesopotamia and Egypt. They reframed non-biblical traditions in light of their particular values. There is a major difference, for example, between the biblical story of the flood in Genesis 6–9, where just one god brings the flood and rescues a human from it, and the polytheistic tale in Atrahasis, where most of the gods bring the flood while one god rescues a human from it. In this and other biblical texts discussed here, we see ancient Israelite authors building freely on and yet radically adapting more ancient literary traditions from elsewhere. These unknown authors, the earliest of whom worked in the time of David and Solomon, are responsible for writing the first building blocks of what would much later become the Hebrew Bible.

CHAPTER FOUR REVIEW

1. Know the meaning and significance of the following terms discussed in this chapter:
- Covenant Code
- J
- moral act-consequence
- P
- Priestly Source
- primeval history
- Tetrateuch
- Yahwistic Source

2. Know the basic character of the following ancient Near Eastern texts and how they are related by scholars to biblical texts that were discussed in this chapter:
- Atrahasis Epic
- Code of Hammurabi
- Egyptian love songs
- Gilgamesh epic
- Instruction of Amenemope

3. What are two different ways in which comparison of a biblical text with an ancient non-biblical text can be useful? Give two examples of such comparison from this chapter.

4. What are the multiple clues to the presence of two sources in Genesis 1–11?

RESOURCES FOR FURTHER STUDY

General introductions to wisdom literature

Crenshaw, James. *Old Testament Wisdom: An Introduction.* Louisville, KY: Westminster John Knox Press, 1998.

Murphy, Roland. *The Tree of Life: An Exploration of Biblical Wisdom Literature.* New York: Doubleday, 1990.

Proverbs

Fox, Michael V. *Proverbs.* 2 volumes. Anchor Bible. New York: Doubleday, 2000, 2009.

Leeuwen, Raymond C. Van. "Proverbs." Pp. 17–264 in vol. 5 of the *New Interpreters Bible.* Nashville: Abingdon, 1997.

Newsom, Carol A. "Woman and the Discourse of Patriarchal Wisdom: A Study of Proverbs 1–9." Pp. 142–60 in Peggy L. Day (ed.), *Gender and Difference in Ancient Israel.* Philadelphia: Fortress, 1989.

Ecclesiastes

Brown, William. *Ecclesiastes.* Interpretation. Louisville, KY: Westminster John Knox Press, 2000.

Crenshaw, James L. *Ecclesiastes.* Old Testament Library. Philadelphia: Westminster Press, 1987.

Gordis, R. *Kohelet: The Man and His World: A Study of Ecclesiastes* (revised edition). New York: Schocken Books, 1988.

Lohfink, Norbert. *Qohelet: A Continental Commentary,* trans. Sean McEvenue. Minneapolis, MN: Fortress, 2003. Translation of a 1980 original.

Song of Songs

Exum, Cheryl. *Song of Songs.* Old Testament Library. Louisville, KY: Westminster John Knox Press, 2005.

Keel, Othmar. *Song of Songs: A Continental Commentary,* trans. Frederick J. Gaiser. Minneapolis: MN: Fortress, 1997. Translation of a 1986 original.

Weems, Renita. "Song of Songs." Pp. 361–434 in vol. 5 of the *New Interpreters Bible.* Nashville: Abingdon, 1997.

Genesis 1–11

Carr, David. *Reading the Fractures of Genesis.* Louisville, KY: Westminster John Knox Press, 1996. For more detail on indicators of sources in Genesis 1–11.

Gowan, Donald E. *From Eden to Babel: A Commentary on the Book of Genesis 1–11.* International Theological Commentary. Grand Rapids: Eerdmans, 1988.

Discussion of Song of Songs, Genesis, and other texts relating to sexuality

Carr, David M. *The Erotic Word: Sexuality and Spirituality in the Hebrew Bible.* New York: Oxford University Press, 2003.

CHAPTER 5

NARRATIVE AND PROPHECY

AMIDST THE RISE AND FALL

OF THE NORTHERN KINGDOM

Chapter Outline

CHAPTER OVERVIEW

Chapter 4 traced echoes of past empires in the Hebrew Bible, while this one focuses on the reverberations of an imperial onslaught. The time to be reviewed here is the ninth and eighth centuries BCE (800s and 700s). The attacking empire was **Assyria**, a Mesopotamian state based in what is now northern Iraq. By this point there was no longer a "kingdom of Israel and Judah" based in Jerusalem. Instead, there were two kingdoms. A new kingdom of Israel had risen up in the north, while a southern kingdom of Judah was still ruled by descendants of David in Jerusalem. Initially, this northern kingdom (Israel) became stronger than its southern counterpart, while developing its own corpus of texts that were largely distinct from those used in the south. Yet ultimately the northern kingdom was destroyed by Assyria, and the southern kingdom barely survived the decades it spent under Assyrian domination.

The Hebrew Bible reflects this initial imperial encounter in at least two main ways. First, although the Hebrew Bible is a collection of Judean texts, it preserves some remnants of texts from the destroyed northern kingdom, texts that have been appropriated and adapted by Judean scribes. Second, the Bible's first prophetic books came from this time of imperial encounter. The books of Amos, Hosea, Micah, and Isaiah all contain early prophecies that reflect the crises faced by Judah and Israel leading up to and during the Assyrian onslaught. Knowing more about the origins of these texts – whether northern texts now embedded in the Hebrew Bible (e.g. an early Jacob story) or prophetic writings formed in the crucible of imperial crisis – can help us understand them in new ways.

Setting the Stage: The Rise of the Northern Kingdom of Israel and Its Texts

READING
1 Kings 12; 2 Kgs 14:23–9;
15:17–31; 17:1–6 (from
Jeroboam of Israel to the fall
of the north). Review Genesis
25–35 and Exodus 2–14.

EXERCISE
Compare 1 Kgs 11:26–8, 40, and 12 with Exodus 2 and 4–5.
What parallels do you see between how 1 Kings 11–12
describe Jeroboam's story and how Exodus 2 and 4–5
describe the story of Moses?

Our journey toward greater understanding of these texts starts with the story of the emergence of a monarchy in the Israelite north. This monarchy was the ultimate outgrowth of a long process of tribal rebellion. Groups in Israel had tried in the past to gain liberty from the Davidic monarchy, but they did not succeed in breaking free until Solomon's death, around 927 BCE.

According to the description of this event in 1 Kings 12 (//2 Chronicles 10), Solomon's son, Rehoboam, went to the ancient tribal center of Shechem to be anointed by the elders of northern Israel. Instead, they ended up having a confrontation. The elders asked if Rehoboam's "yoke," that is his domination of them, would be as heavy as that of his father. Against the advice of his older advisors, Rehoboam is reported to have said: "I will add to your yoke; my father disciplined you with whips, but I will discipline you with scorpions" (1 Kgs 12:11//2 Chr 10:14). As one might expect, this did not get a good response. The elders called for withdrawal of support of the Davidic monarchy in Jerusalem, saying "To your tents, oh Israel. Look to your own house, David" (1 Kgs 12:16; cf. 2 Sam 20:1). When Rehoboam sent his chief of forced labor to bring the northerners back in line, they stoned him to death (1 Kgs 12:18).

The elders of Israel, however, appear to have started a new monarchy rather than trying to return to the tribal life they had before kingship. In place of Rehoboam, they anointed as king one of their own countrymen, Jeroboam, who was a man from the tribe of Ephraim. Earlier he had worked for Solomon as chief of forced labor, but rebelled and fled to Egypt when Solomon tried to kill him (1 Kgs 11:26–7). As a new king of Israel, Jeroboam first established Shechem as his capital, then moved to Penuel, and he established royal sanctuaries at the towns of Bethel (toward the south of Israel) and Dan (in the north; see Map 5.1). He installed statues of calves at each sanctuary and proclaimed "Here are your gods, Oh Israel, who led you out of Egypt." (1 Kgs 12:28).

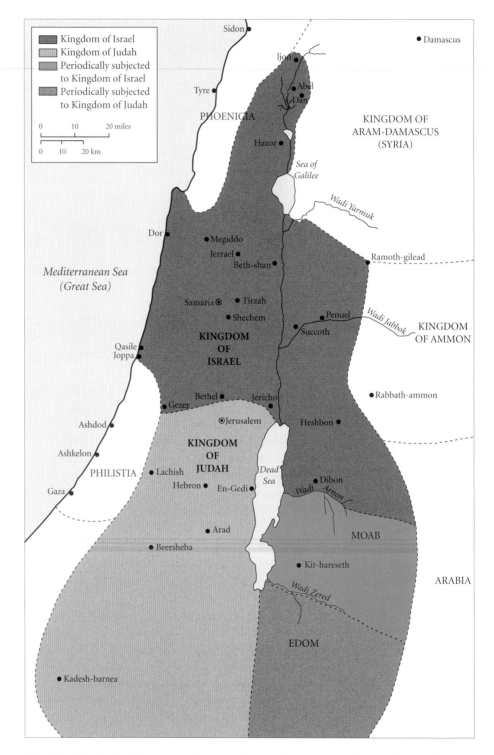

Map 5.1 The divided kingdoms of Israel and Judah. Redrawn from Norman Gottwald, *The Hebrew Bible: A Socio-Literary Introduction*. Minneapolis: Fortress, 1985, page 291.

This narrative in 1 Kings 12 represents a perspective by later southern scribes on how awful it was that Israel in the north broke away from Judah. Nevertheless, even this unsympathetic narrative preserves a memory that this Israelite northern monarchy was different from the Davidic monarchy in the south. Having gained liberty, Jeroboam invoked exodus traditions in setting up royal sanctuaries in Bethel and Dan ("Here are your gods . . . who led you out of Egypt"). He picked ancient northern cities as capitals for his new kingdom, cities such as Shechem and then Penuel. And though Jeroboam's "calves" are viewed negatively in these chapters of the Bible, archaeological finds of ancient statues of bulls in Israelite sites suggest that they were one of the most ancient symbols of divinity known in early Israel.

There is one other way in which Jeroboam and other northerners forged a new path in founding the northern monarchy: *they appear to have developed their own corpus of written texts*. This corpus could have been a "counter-curriculum" to replace many of the Davidic and Zion texts that had been taught in the north during David and Solomon's rule. Those texts remained important in Judah, and many are preserved in the Bible. The split-off kingdom of "Israel," however, created its own distinctive texts, featuring northern themes, places, and heroes.

Indeed, some chapters in the Bible probably were written in the north as part of this distinctive counter-curriculum. A good example is the story of Jacob found in Genesis (Genesis 25–35). It features Jeroboam's royal sanctuary city of Bethel and early northern capitals such as Penuel (where Jacob wrestles God – Gen 32:22–32). Indeed, the story of Jacob in Genesis counters the claims of the older monarchy in Jerusalem. Where Jerusalem Zion traditions claimed that Yahweh dwelled at Mount Zion (Pss 9:12; 135:21), the Jacob story embedded in Genesis has God (quoted by Jacob) say, "I am the God who dwells in Bethel" (Gen 31:13). These clues suggest that the bulk of the Jacob story now in Genesis was written in the north as a counterpoint to the writings of the Davidic monarchy in the south. To be sure, as we saw in Chapter 2, the Genesis Jacob story builds on more ancient trickster and other oral traditions about Jacob and his family. Nevertheless, most of the *written* story of Jacob probably originates from the time of the early northern monarchy as part of Jeroboam's counter-curriculum. It even seems as if the northern prophet, Hosea, studied this story and could refer specifically to it (Hos 12:3–4, 12).

It is difficult to know exactly what other biblical texts were composed in the north, but there are many other chapters of the Old Testament that show strong northern connections. Chapter 2 of this textbook discussed one of those chapters, Deborah's victory song in Judges 5, which focuses exclusively on northern tribes. This early song probably was written down in the northern kingdom started by Jeroboam. Some form of the book of Deuteronomy may have started in the north as well. It includes a scene of covenant making on northern mountains (Deut 27:1–13) that almost certainly would not have been composed by later Judean scribes.

We may even have hints of fragments of an early northern exodus story in the book of Exodus. As you may have seen in the exercise comparing 1 Kings 11–12 and Exodus 2, 4–5, the story in Exodus is written in a way that makes Moses's liberation of Israel from Egypt sound a lot like Jeroboam's liberation of Israel from Rehoboam.

More on Method: The Joseph Story and Literary Approaches

The Joseph story as a potential early northern text

The Joseph story (minus probable later additions such as chapters 38, 46, and 48–9) is another good candidate for being an early northern text. These chapters tell a tale that starts with a pair of dreams that Joseph has. In one, the sheaves of grain belonging to Joseph's brothers bow down in obedience to Joseph's sheaf. In the other dream, 11 stars and the sun and moon bow down to Joseph. His (11) brothers interpret these dreams as claims by Joseph that he will dominate them, and their murderous resentment about these claims results in Joseph being taken into slavery in Egypt (Genesis 37). There he rises to prominence, is able to provide food for his family when they flee a famine in Israel, and is reconciled to his brothers (Genesis 45 and 50).

Especially since Joseph was an ancestor of Jeroboam, tribal groups of the north could have seen this narrative as an allegory of power. It may have been designed to help them recognize Jeroboam's ultimate destiny to rule and provide for them the way Joseph, Jeroboam's ancestor, was destined to rule and provide for his brothers. As such, an early form of the Joseph narrative now in Genesis may have been part of the early northern literary corpus.

Literary approaches and Joseph

Meanwhile, the Joseph story has been a major focus of literary study of the Bible. No matter when one dates the Joseph story (and there is debate), there is much room for analysis of its characterization of Joseph and his brothers, the contrast between what the storyteller says happened at points and what different brothers report about what happened, and the move of the plot from brotherly resentment to reconciliation. Literary study of biblical narrative draws on the study of modern literature to reach insights about texts like the Joseph story that are not related to particular theories about dating or social context.

Such literary approaches to biblical narrative have grown ever more varied as study of literature in the humanities itself has evolved. For more on diverse literary approaches to narrative, see David Gunn, "Narrative Criticism," pp. 201–29 in S. McKenzie and S. Haynes (eds.), *To Each Its Own Meaning* (Louisville, KY: Westminster John Knox Press, 1999).

Both grow up in privileged households, identify with the people being oppressed, flee from the oppressive ruler, return when that ruler dies, appeal to the new ruler to lighten the oppression, and eventually lead their people out from under oppression when the new ruler refuses. It is possible that Jeroboam's liberation of the north just happened to parallel Moses's liberation of Israel. It is more likely, however, that these parallels in stories came about because scribes working for Jeroboam in the early northern kingdom shaped the ancient exodus traditions of the north in light of the recent "exodus" they had experienced under Jeroboam from oppression by Solomon and his son, Rehoboam.

Does this mean that the ancient northern scribes just "made up" stories about Jacob or Exodus in the process of writing their counter-curriculum? Not really. There is a contemporary analogy to this process of shaping ancient stories in light of recent experience. In the 1950s and 1960s, many fighting for civil rights would cite the biblical story of the exodus as a warrant for their struggle for freedom. In doing so, they selectively drew on the parts of the story that most matched their current experience. An example was Martin Luther King Jr.'s famous final speech in Memphis, just before he died, about standing, like Moses, on the mountain, looking over into a promised land that he would not get to see himself. The parallels between the biblical stories of Moses and Jeroboam probably were caused by a similar process of linking past to present. northern scribes who were writing down ancient oral traditions about the exodus retold the story so that it celebrated a "Moses" who now looked much like Jeroboam, their new king. The written results of their work, an early northern "exodus story," are preserved – very fragmentarily – in parts of Exodus 2, 4–5.

It should be no surprise that there are many traces of northern texts in the Bible, in Genesis, Exodus, and many other books of the Old Testament. There is much archaeological evidence that the kingdom of Israel, during its two centuries of existence, was more powerful and prominent than the kingdom of Judah to the south. In particular, the northern kingdom reached a zenith of power during the time of king Omri and his son, Ahab (see Figure 5.1). Omri established a massive new capital in Samaria, made a major marriage alliance with Phoenicia (Ahab's wife Jezebel was from Sidon), and

Figure 5.1 One of the ivory carvings found in Samaria, the site of Ahab's famous "ivory palace" (1 Kgs 22:39). Originally covered in gold, these objects illustrate the kind of wealth and power possessed by the northern kingdom, particularly under Omri and Ahab.

Figure 5.2 Detail from a wall-sized panorama, in the palace of the Assyrian king Sennacherib, of the defeat of the town of Lachish in Judah. The Assyrians are pushing a siege engine up a ramp to break a hole in the wall of Lachish while the Judean defenders attempt to set the engine on fire by throwing torches down from the wall.

dominated the smaller, southern kingdom of Judah, which was still ruled by descendants of David. Though the Omride dynasty was eventually brought down through a coup d'etat led by a general Jehu (841 BCE), years afterward, Mesopotamian kings would still refer to the whole area as "the house of Omri." The northern kingdom of Israel could achieve such prominence during this time partly because it had more land and population than the kingdom of Judah and controlled more central trade routes. Judging from this, many scholars believe that the northern kingdom of Israel had a more active literary tradition during this time than Judah did. The kingdom of Israel became the central place for writing and developing written traditions common to north and south, while Judah played a more peripheral role until the late eighth century.

Imperial clouds, however, were on the horizon. In the second half of the eighth century, the Assyrian empire under King Tiglath-Pileser III began extending its reach westward to secure access to resources and trade routes in the area of Israel. The Assyrians had long been a major trading power in the Near East, but by this time they also had assembled an extremely efficient army that was the terror of their neighbors. Figure 5.2 shows an Assyrian depiction of an attack on a Judean city in 701. Other parts of the same set of reliefs show Judean resisters being impaled and inhabitants of the town being led away in chains. Through such attacks, and reports and depictions of them, the Assyrians terrorized the area and enforced their domination. One Assyrian king brags, "Many of the captives . . . I took alive; from some of these I cut off their hands to the wrist, from others I cut off their noses, ears, and fingers; I put out the eyes of many of the soldiers." Another reports, "I fixed up a pile of corpses in front of the gate. I flayed the nobles, as many as had rebelled and spread their skins out on the piles of corpses." It was in the face of threats like these that central parts of the biblical tradition were formed.

Facing the prospect of possible Assyrian invasion, many countries voluntarily submitted to Assyria and promised to send regular tribute to the Assyrian king. This happened first in the north, perhaps as early as the ninth century with Jehu (as in Figure 5.3), but first in an ongoing way when King Menahem of Israel started paying substantial

Significant Dates: The Northern Kingdom ("Israel")

Jeroboam, founding kingdom	930–910 BCE
The Omride dynasty (Omri, Ahab, Ahaziah, Joram)	880–841 BCE
Coup d'etat by Jehu (Jehu pays tribute to Assyria sometime around 841–814 BCE)	841 BCE
Jeroboam II (relative prosperity)	782–753 BCE
Assyrian domination/destruction of Israel (Menahem, Pekah, Pekahiah, and [king] Hoshea)	745–722 BCE

Figure 5.3 Panel from the Black Obelisk of the Assyrian king Shalmaneser III, depicting the Israelite king Jehu offering tribute to and kissing the ground before the Assyrian king. It documents the brief subservience of the northern kingdom to Assyria about a hundred years before Assyria dominated and eventually destroyed the kingdom of Israel in the late eighth century.

tribute to Assyria around 738 BCE. But Menahem died, and the kingship was soon taken over around 735 BCE by Pekah, who aimed to join Syria and other nations in rebelling against Assyria and stopping payment of the onerous tribute. In what is called the **Syro-Ephraimite war** (735–734 BCE) this new anti-Assyrian coalition even laid siege to Jerusalem in the south in an attempt to force similar anti-Assyrian policies on Ahaz, who was king of Judah at the time. Ahaz escaped the Israelite and Syrian forces by appealing for Assyrian help, thus defeating those besieging him, but also falling under Assyrian domination himself. Thus began a process by which the northern kingdom was gradually reduced in size and eventually totally destroyed in 722, while Judah barely survived its period of Assyrian rule.

This whole process decisively affected the formation of the Hebrew Bible. Whatever texts we now have from the northern kingdom probably were preserved in the later southern kingdom. Moreover, this drama of Assyrian invasions, anti-Assyrian coalitions, and switching between pro-Assyrian and anti-Assyrian kings forms the backdrop for much of Israel's earliest written prophecy. Prophets such as Hosea are difficult to understand without a sense of the political turmoil their countries were facing. Even the harsh prophecy of Amos, which was delivered prior to the worst of Israel's encounters with Assyria, became as important as it did as an explanation of the disaster that eventually overtook that kingdom.

In sum, much of the Hebrew Bible was formed in the shadow of Assyria's imperial domination of Israel and Judah. The rich literature of the north was destroyed as such, only to be preserved in fragments strewn across Judah's later Bible. In addition, this Assyrian crisis was the starting point for the development of written prophecy in ancient Israel and Judah. Prophets such as Hosea and Amos, Micah and Isaiah, may not have gotten much of a hearing in their own day. Nevertheless, the writings attributed to them became very important to later generations of Judeans who had to endure yet more catastrophes like the eighth-century Assyrian onslaught. Let us turn now to look at the phenomenon of such written prophecy.

Ancient Near Eastern Prophecy

Prophecy was a widespread phenomenon in the Near East. Egypt, Phoenicia, Syria, and the kingdoms of Mesopotamia all knew people, some amateurs and some professionals, who pronounced oracles from the gods. This was part of a broader system by which kings and others tried to divine the future. Much as some people learn to read scrolls, these scholars aimed to learn to "read" clues in the cosmos to the gods' intentions, clues encoded in dreams, omens, parts of special animals sacrificed to divine the future, and other means. Life was unpredictable, and the people of the Near East marshaled every resource they could to understand more about what the gods were doing and what they wished. Verbal prophecies from human mediums were a major way of gaining such information.

Most such prophecies were oral, but sometimes they were written down. The archives at Mari, a Syrian city that became very powerful in the second millennium BCE, contain hundreds of records of prophecies given there, just in case such prophecies might be useful later. Later Mesopotamian archives likewise contain careful records of prophetic oracles and even a few small collections of oracles. Perhaps one of the most interesting written prophecies, however, is an early eighth-century wall inscription dating from just a few decades before the time of the biblical prophets and found in the Trans-Jordan, just across from Israel, in a crossroads village now known as Deir Alla. Part of the inscription reads as follows:

> This is the story of Balaam, son of Beor and a seer. The divine assembly appeared to Balaam, son of Beor at night. He dreamed he heard El pronounce a death sentence on his city. He watched as the divine assembly announced the beginning of a drought that would burn the land of his city like a raging fire. When Balaam got up the next morning, he began to fast and to lament bitterly. The people of the city asked, "Balaam, son of Beor, why do you fast? Why do you mourn?" So Balaam agreed to tell them about his dream. "Sit down and let me tell you what the mighty ones have done. Let me show you what the divine assembly has decided. (Translation: *OT Parallels*, 132–3)

This text is interesting from a variety of angles. The "Balaam, son of Beor" mentioned here is also seen in a biblical text, Numbers 22–4. In Numbers, Balaam is hired to curse Israel, but ends up prophesying Israel's glory instead. In the Deir Alla inscription, however, Balaam's prophecy sounds more like the judgment prophecies of Amos and other biblical prophets. It describes how Balaam saw a vision where the gods announced a devastating drought. A few decades later Amos, Isaiah, and others would receive divine visions and other messages about devastating judgments about to hit their peoples.

Perhaps yet more interesting, the Deir Alla text may give clues as to how such written prophecies were used. To begin with, the wall inscription shows signs that it once was written on a scroll, much like the books of the biblical eighth-century prophets. In addition, there is a good chance that students were educated at Deir Alla where the inscription was found. An alphabet exercise was found there, and the room where the inscription was found had benches, possibly for students learning texts such as the prophecy of Balaam written there. Perhaps the written prophecies of Amos and other late eighth-century prophets likewise were taught to students, first the prophets' own children and a few other students, later to many others. Let us turn now for a closer look at their "teachings."

Amos, Prophet of Justice

READING
Amos 1–2 and 7–9.

The prophet Amos may be best known right now – insofar as he is known at all – as a prophet of social justice. No other prophet packs so much social critique into so little space. The book starts and finishes with similar divine critiques of elites of northern Israel taking advantage of their power to exploit the poor:

> For the three crimes of Israel and for four,
>   I will not turn back the punishment.
> Because they sell those who act rightly for silver
>   And the poor for a pair of sandals.
> They trample the head of the poor into the dust of the earth
>   And push the oppressed out of their way. (Amos 2:6–7; also 8:4–6)

Later, Amos proclaims disaster for the women of the capital city of Samaria, who "oppress the poor and crush the needy" (4:1). He announces disaster for those "who turn justice into wormwood and bring down social solidarity" (5:7). In a passage later echoed by Martin Luther King and others, he calls for "justice [to] roll down like waters and righteousness like an everflowing stream" (5:24).

This prophecy by Amos does not seem to have been received positively in his own time. To start with, he was an outsider in northern Israel. The Bible records that he came from Judah, having been a shepherd near the small town of Tekoa (Amos 1:1; 7:14). Moreover, most of his prophecies to the north were uncompromisingly harsh, often undermining the ancient traditions most dear to his audience. The Israelites might have thought they were safe because the God of the Exodus was on their side, but Amos suggested that this exodus was nothing special:

> Are you not like the Ethiopians to me, Oh Israel?
> Did I not bring Israel out of Egypt
> And the Philistines from Caphtor
> And the Arameans from Kir? (Amos 9:7)

The Israelites might have thought that God's choosing of them would protect them ("election theology"), but the book of Amos quotes God giving an interesting twist on such northern election theology:

> You only have I known among all the nations of the earth,
> Therefore, I will hold you accountable for all your crimes. (Amos 3:2)

A later story about Amos in Amos 7:10–17 gives a vivid picture of one response to his message. It starts by telling how Amos went to the royal sanctuary at Bethel, and announced that the king of Israel at the time, Jeroboam II, would die by the sword, while his people would go into exile. The high priest at Bethel, Amaziah, sent a message about this to the king and then said to Amos:

> Go away, seer, flee to Judah
>   Eat bread there and prophesy,
> But don't ever again prophesy at Bethel because it is the king's
> sanctuary and the temple of the kingdom. (7:12–13)

Amos in this story responds that he is – or was – not a professional prophet just trying to prophesy anywhere. Instead, God called him from his farmwork in Tekoa to go prophesy to "God's people, Israel" (Amos 7:14–15). But now that Amaziah has told him to stop prophesying in Israel, Amos adds to his former prophecy that the priest's wife will become a city prostitute, his sons will die in battle, and he, a priest, will die "in an unclean land" (7:17).

There is no hint in this and many other prophecies that Amos aimed to change the ways of his Israelite audience. To be sure, there are some isolated calls for the people to change in chapter 5 (Amos 5:4, 6, and 14) and some predictions of hope for Judah added to the end of the book (Amos 9:8b, 11–15). These fragments, however, hardly outweigh the book's general tone of doom. It starts with a set of prophecies where God proclaims that "for three crimes and for four" God will not turn back the punishment (Amos 1–2). It ends with a series of four visions: in the first two Amos turns back God's punishment through his pleas on Israel's behalf (Amos 7:1–6), but in the "third" and "fourth" visions God will not turn back the punishment (7:7–9; 8:1–8). Instead, God has a "plumbline of justice" by which he has measured Israel (7:7–9), and it will be struck by a horrible earthquake (8:8; see also 2:13).

basics   **Book of Amos**

Outline:
Judean prophetic
judgment on
Israel

I	Sayings against the nations: setting the judgment of Israel in context	1:1–2:16
II	Elaboration of judgment: the inversion of Israel's election	3:1–9:8a
III	Final qualification: future for "Israel" in a revived Davidic kingdom	9:8b–15

How Amos was
adapted for
the south

Most specialists in Amos agree that the book of Amos contains numerous additions that adapted his prophecy to the north so that it could speak to the south as well. For example, the oracle of judgment against Judah in Amos 2:4–5 stands out from the other oracles in 1:3–16 and is probably an addition designed to include Judah among the nations judged by Amos. Likewise, the concluding promise that the "booth of David" will be rebuilt (Amos 9:11–15, also introduced by 8b) was probably added to provide a word of hope for Judah (and "Israel" in the wider sense) in contrast to the word of judgment throughout the rest of the book on the northern kingdom of Israel.

More
information:
Amos and praise

The middle of the book is punctuated by three similar praises of Yahweh: 4:13; 5:8–9; 9:5–6. Read them and see the similarities. These late elements of Amos challenge the reader to praise the awesome God who brings such judgment on Israel and set that judgment in the context of God's creation.

As it turns out, Israel actually was hit by an earthquake around the time of Amos, and this fulfillment of Amos's prophecy was never forgotten (Amos 1:1). Yet his prophecies of disaster proved to be correct in a broader way as well. As Amos had predicted (Amos 2:13–16; 3:11–15; 6:1–7), the northern kingdom was completely destroyed, though not in a way he envisioned. Amos prophesied in a time before the Assyrians' dominance and does not mention them, but in 722 they invaded, destroyed Israel's sanctuaries and palaces, and carried into exile its surviving leaders.

By this time Amos had returned to Judah, and his written prophecy was a form of prophetic "teaching" that Judeans could reinterpret – now in relation to the threat (and later reality) of Assyrian domination. Like teachings seen in Proverbs, these sayings by Amos followed a format of "three and four" (Prov 30:15–31; cf. Amos 1–2; 7:1–9; 8:1–8), rhetorical questions (Amos 3:4–6), and riddles (Amos 3:12; 6:12). Yet this written prophetic teaching of Amos consists of quotations of God, not a sage like Solomon. And the focus of the teaching is on social acts and their national consequences, not the smaller-scale "moral act-consequence" of an individual student emphasized in Proverbs (see Chapter 4 on moral act-consequence). In the end, this written form of Amos's prophecy had a more lasting effect than any oral words that he delivered. Though he was told to go home by the northern high priest Amaziah, Amos's words are still being read more than two and a half thousand years after they were written.

Hosea, the Northern Prophet, Calling for Israel's Devotion to Yahweh Alone

The book of Hosea was also addressed to the kingdom of Israel around this time, but it is quite different from the prophecy of Amos. Where Amos emphasized judgment for Israel's injustice, Hosea pleaded for his own people to change, to "sow social solidarity" (10:12) and "protect justice" (12:6). Where Amos announced irreversible disaster, Hosea predicted restoration on the other side of God's punishment. And where Amos inverted and critiqued his audience's deep belief in their chosenness (ancient "election theology"), Hosea found new ways of describing that chosenness, ways that emphasized God's love for Israel and God's wish for Israel's devotion to God. For Hosea, Israel's main failing was a lack of devotion to God and a love of false gods instead.

READING
Hosea 1–2 and 11–12.

This is most vividly illustrated at the outset of the book with Hosea's image of God's broken marriage to Israel. The book starts with the story of a rather remarkable and personal act of symbolic prophecy – yet one that we will see also has disturbing overtones. Hosea is called by God to marry and have children by a promiscuous woman, giving these children Hebrew sentence-names that symbolize what God plans to do with Israel, such as "not pitied" and "not my people" (Hos 1:2–9). Then, after the brief insertion of a yet later text reversing this prophecy of judgment (Hos 1:10–2:1), we encounter one of the most powerful passages of the whole book: God's agonized speech to Israel in the wake of Israel's spiritual promiscuity (Hos 2:2–15). In this speech God, not Hosea, is the husband, and the nation of Israel is the wife. God starts with an address to the children of this "Israel," telling them – in effect – that God has divorced their mother:

> Protest to your mother, protest,
>   For she is not my wife
>   And I am not her husband. (Hos 2:2a)

Yet God in Hosea 2 is not as done with this relationship as first appears. God's speech immediately turns toward a plea for the children to get their "mother," their nation, to end her adulterous ways, lest she be subject to the sort of stripping and shaming that wives suspected of adultery had to endure at the hands of their husbands:

> [Tell her to] put away her promiscuity,
>   and remove her adultery from between her breasts.

Lest I strip her naked,
    And display her like the day she was born,
Make her bare as the desert,
        and make her dry like parched earth,
    And let her die of thirst. (Hos 2:2b–3)

This Israel, this wife of God, is facing the prospect of drought and famine (the "stripping") because she has gone after "other lovers" in search of love gifts. Yet Yahweh in Hosea's speech insists that she was mistaken about who was providing for her. In actuality, it was really Yahweh, her husband, who was giving her the things a man was to give to his wife: food, clothing, and oil (Hos 2:5, 8).

This list of gifts suggests that Hosea sees Yahweh as betrayed by Israel's worship of other gods, such as Baal (Hos 2:13). According to Hosea, the problem is that Israel sought grain and other benefits from these other gods rather than relying on Yahweh alone. Such worship of multiple gods, of course, was quite common in ancient cultures, and we even see signs that people worshipped other gods alongside Yahweh from the time of earliest Israel (see Chapter 2) through Hosea's time (see Figure 5.4). Nevertheless, Hosea proclaims to his people that Yahweh is as offended by such worship of other

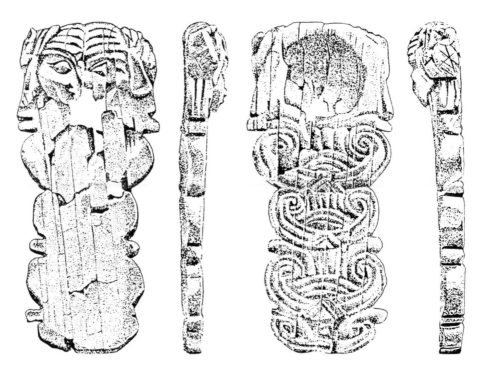

Figure 5.4 Ivory spoon found at Hazor, uniting images of a woman on one side with a tree of life on the other. It illustrates ongoing reverence for a goddess in the form of tree imagery.

gods as a husband would be by his wife's adultery. Like a good husband, he provided his wife with good things, and she undermined his manhood by giving her love to others who she thought could provide better.

In response, Yahweh says that he will block Israel's way to her lovers so that – like the woman of the Song of Songs – she will "seek" her lovers and not "find" them (Hos 2:6–7). Much of the rest of the speech elaborates on how Yahweh will devastate the land of Israel for its unfaithfulness. Nevertheless, it concludes not with judgment, but with hope – in this case Yahweh's plan to seduce Israel and bring back the early times when Israel was in the wilderness and fully in love with God:

> Therefore, look, I will seduce her,
>   and I will lead her in the desert,
>   And speak tenderly to her.
> I will give her vineyards from there,
>   and the valley of Achor as a gate of hope.
> She will respond there as in her youthful days,
>   As when she came out of the land of Egypt. (Hos 2:14–15)

In this way, Hosea's image of marriage between Yahweh and Israel is meant to depict not just Yahweh's pain at what Hosea saw as Israel's betrayal, not just Yahweh's intent to bring consequences, but also Yahweh's enduring love, a love which means that God cannot bear to let Israel go for good and aims to bring her back into relationship with him. As if this were not enough, the book further underscores this point through having Hosea himself describe another act of symbolic prophecy. As a symbol of God's intent to take back Israel despite what "she" has done, God tells Hosea to pay a price to hire a woman known for promiscuity and then specify that she not seek any lovers – not even be with Hosea – for a long time (Hos 3:1–5).

The narratives of symbolic prophecy in Hosea 1 and 3 have led many readers to psychologize Hosea's message, believing that his bold new vision of God was prompted by problems in his personal life, perhaps a propensity to end up with the wrong kinds of women. There are clues elsewhere in the book, however, that suggest a more important background: the power politics surrounding Assyrian domination of Israel going all the way back to the time of King Jehu. In Hos 5:8–6:6 we see Hosea's critique of Israel and Judah's lack of steadfast "love" for Yahweh (6:4). Hosea sees this lovelessness proven when Israel (called "Ephraim" here) pursued "futile" plans (5:11) and even sent away to Assyria to save itself (5:13). In Hos 7:3–7 Hosea condemns as "adultery" (7:4) the constant shifting of kings, largely in response to the Assyrian threat. In Hos 8:7–10 Hosea likens the kingdom's tribute payments to a case where a prostitute is actually paying her clients ("Ephraim hires its lovers," 8:9). Finally, Hos 9:1–6 mixes images of agricultural plenty and international politics. The prophet tells the people at a harvest festival not to rejoice, because they are like a promiscuous woman who has loved her wages for sex at threshing floor and winepress (9:1–2), and who will soon go into exile in Assyria and Egypt (9:3–6). In these passages, Hosea critiques the multitude of ways that Israel (and Judah) tried to manipulate or buy their way out of

basics Book of Hosea

Outline: prophecy of judgment and hope

I	Introduction of judgment and hope by way of family imagery	1–3
II	Elaboration of prophecy of judgment and hope by way of other images	4–14

How Hosea was adapted for the south

Hosea himself may have spoken about Judah in the south (one example is 5:8–15), but there are signs that later Judean authors adapted Hosea's sayings so that they included Judah in Hosea's judgment (examples are 5:5; 6:4, 11). Still other additions resemble the conclusion to Amos (Amos 9:11–15). Like that conclusion, they see future hope for destroyed "Israel" being located in a broader "Israel" that is centered in Judah and its Davidic monarchy (1:11; 3:5; 11:12).

Hosea's prophecy for the ages

This adaptation of Hosea was but the first step in having the book's images speak to new communities which Hosea had not addressed. Whatever personal or cultic background there once was to Hosea's marriage and other imagery, it gained a symbolic life of its own. Within the present form of the book, the marriage imagery of Hosea 1–3 introduces Hosea's prophecy more generally and then fades into the background. Later, Hosea quotes Yahweh as saying that "by the hand of the prophets I gave analogies" (Hos 12:10; probably mistranslated in the NRSV). These analogies in Hosea – marriage, parent, covenant – have been applied and reapplied by centuries of later readers.

oppression by Assyria. According to Hosea, they should have been devoted to and trusted in Yahweh instead of pursuing such power politics.

There may be some critique of Israel's cult practices as well, especially given the frequent references to "Baal" throughout Hosea. The people of Israel had worshipped various gods alongside Yahweh, long before Hosea's time, and apparently continued to do so. Indeed, scholars have not been able to reconstruct an early period when the tribes of Israel did not worship other gods. Ancient tribal and later sites have yielded female statues that many interpret to be goddess figurines. Early Israelites appear to have borne names formed from the names of various deities, including "Baal" and "El." And a couple of early inscriptions from around the time of Hosea feature blessings "by Yahweh and his asherah [or Asherah]" (see Figure 5.5). Though there is debate about how to interpret these blessings, many understand them to imply that Yahweh had taken over Asherah, formerly El's wife, as his own. In all these ways, Hosea faced a much more diverse religious landscape than we often picture for early Israel (see Figure 5.6). What was new was that he argued that this religious diversity, this lack of pure worship of

Figure 5.5 Drawing and inscription found at a desert trading post called Kuntillet Adjrud used by eighth-century Israelites. Interpretation of the drawings is disputed, but note the figure playing a lyre on the upper right. The inscription toward the top is understood by many to refer to "Yahweh and his Asherah."

Yahweh, was one reason for Israel's ills. He believed that the religious diversity of his time was a falling away from Israel's past pure devotion to Yahweh in the wilderness. That is how most contemporary readers of the present Bible perceive the matter. Yet his audience probably perceived his calls for pure worship of Yahweh alone as something *new*.

Overall, Hosea's main point seems to be that his people is displaying a massive unfaithfulness – whether in international policy or in religious practice. Such unfaithfulness, for Hosea, is like a wife's unfaithfulness to her husband. Yahweh's response is a mix of emotions typical of wronged husbands: agony and jealous wrath at his wife's betrayal combined with a wish to have her back again. In this way Hosea suggests to his fellow Israelites oppressed by Assyria that Yahweh did not fail or abandon Israel; rather Israel abandoned Yahweh first.

Readers over the years have responded differently to Hosea's picture of God and Israel. For many, the book stands as a powerful picture of God's longing for steadfast love and his willingness to go to any length to bring the people back. Yet others are disturbed by ominous parallels between God's behavior in Hosea's prophecy and the cycle of spousal abuse: a husband's anger at his wife and/or jealous accusations of adultery, physical beating and/or sexual humiliation of the wife, and wooing of the wife back. Hosea used the image metaphorically, believing that Israel had actually been spiritually promiscuous and that God was fully in the right to punish her before

Figure 5.6 Pillar figurines of a sort common in archaeological remains of the eighth century. They indicate to many scholars that some kind of goddess worship continued to prevail in the time of Hosea and Amos.

bringing her back. Many now would reject this image of God as a husband stripping and beating his sinful, human wife (before taking her back again). Furthermore, such metaphors can be and have been extended to justify human spouse abuse. Some husbands and religious professionals have taken Hosea's picture to be a biblical endorsement of the right of human husbands to beat or sexually humiliate wives whom they suspect of adultery or other wrongs. Finally, Hosea's use of the image of a sexually promiscuous woman as an image of sin also had consequences. Even though he was critiquing male leaders as much as or more than females, his particular association of feminine sexuality with sin is echoed in several later prophets, the New Testament, and later traditions as well. In light of these concerns, these images in Hosea and later prophets are too painful to serve for some readers as images of a God of love.

There are, however, other images in Hosea that offer alternative ways of envisioning God's agony and passion for reconciliation. Consider, for example, the picture in Hosea 11, where God now is Israel's parent, agonizing over his son's disobedience after God's tender care for him. As before in Hosea, God addresses Israel here as "Ephraim," the main tribal territory that was left after the Assyrians stripped the nation of Israel of its more distant holdings:

> When Israel was a child, I loved him
>> From Egypt I called my son.
> They were called that, but they went their own way,
>> Sacrificing to baals and making offerings to images.

> But I taught Ephraim how to walk,
>> I took them up in my arms.
>> They are unaware of my healing care.
> I led them with human ties,
>> With cords of love.
> I was like one who takes an infant to their cheeks,
>> I bent down to them and fed them. (Hos 11:1–4)

Yahweh's first response to his son's betrayal after such tender care is threats of exile and destruction. Once again we see distant echoes of Israel's struggles in international politics:

> He will return to Egypt,
>> and Assyria will be his king;
> A sword devours his cities,
>> and it will consume his limbs.
>> It will eat because of his schemes. (11:5–6)

Yet for Hosea, unlike Amos, this is not the final word. Like a parent who could never give up a child, God relents:

> How can I give you up, oh Ephraim?
>> How can I surrender you, oh Israel? . . .
> I have changed my mind.
>> My compassion is warm and tender.
> I will not act on my wrath,
>> I will not again attack Ephraim.
> For I am God, not a man.
>> I am the holy one in your midst.
>> I will not come in anger. (Hos 11:8–9)

Here Hosea draws on the metaphorical power of the parental relationship, yet clearly distinguishes this picture of God from that of a human "man." God here is deeply hurt and angered by the faithlessness of his people. Yet God cannot bear to destroy the child whom he once embraced in Egypt and taught to walk in the wilderness. Even if a father could bear to destroy his son, God here is "not a man" (11:9). For Hosea, God's infinite compassion can be imaged, but only partially so, by the powerful compassion a parent feels for his or her child.

We see one more important image appear in Hosea, again one that is intricately tied to the power politics in which Israel was embroiled: **covenant**. Although this word is sometimes loosely used to designate any relationship of mutual obligation, the word "covenant" (*berit* in Hebrew) had more specific connotations in the world of Hosea's day. A covenant was a contract between political parties that was sealed by oaths and

Hosea and the "Book of the Twelve Prophets"

The book of the Twelve Prophets

Hosea is the first in the **book of the Twelve Prophets**, a collection of 12 shorter prophetic books that is usually placed in bibles after Ezekiel or (Ezekiel and) Daniel. The books are attributed to so-called "**minor prophets**" – Hosea through Malachi. The word "minor" is applied to these prophets not because they are thought to be unimportant, but because the books attributed to them are relatively short. Each of these short books has its own character, but they also show signs of being edited into a larger whole by later scribes.

Hosea 14:9 and prophetic teaching

One possible sign of such editing is the last verse of Hosea, Hos 14:9. It stresses that the "wise" will understand the words of Hosea, and it praises the ways of Yahweh as "right." Such mention of the "wise" is otherwise typical of books such as Proverbs. This verse marks the book of Hosea as a form of prophetic "teaching," much like Solomon's teaching in Proverbs and Ecclesiastes.

At the same time, since Hosea is the first book of the 12 minor prophets, this framing of Hosea's book as a teaching has implications for understanding the 11 books that follow. With this conclusion to Hosea in Hos 14:9, they too stand as prophetic teaching to be understood by the "wise."

curses. When someone entered into a covenant with another, they would pronounce curses on themselves if they broke the agreement. Indeed, the word for "make" a covenant in Hebrew is "cut" (Hebrew *karat*). This may be because the parties to the covenant would cut apart a living animal and walk between the bleeding pieces, proclaiming something like "so may this happen to me and more if I break the words of the covenant." The Assyrians imposed such covenants on the peoples they dominated in the form of **vassal treaties** (a type of international covenant), forcing peoples – their vassals – to act out curses of destruction if they failed to keep the terms of these covenants. Hosea seems to refer to these vassal treaties when he attacks Israel for making a "covenant" with Assyria and sending oil (probably to seal a vassal treaty) to Egypt (Hos 12:2). Yet Hosea also refers in Hos 6:7 and 8:1 to another sort of "covenant," this time a treaty with Yahweh that Israel has broken. These are our first datable references to a "covenant" between Yahweh and the people. Hosea may have developed this idea of God's treaty with Israel partly in response to what he saw as false treaties that Israel was making with superpowers such as Egypt and Assyria. If so, Hosea's theological adaptation of the idea of covenant" or treaty stands as an important early example of the phenomenon of hybridity that will be discussed further in Chapter 7: where an oppressed people takes a cultural form of their oppressor (the vassal treaty) and transforms it so that it can express resistance (a vassal treaty with Yahweh).

Conclusion

This discussion of Hosea is particularly important because his prophecy proved so influential in later biblical writings. We will see elements of his picture of divine–human marriage appear in several other prophets. His development of the picture of God's covenant with Israel also becomes important, especially as Judah and Israel endure decades of oppression under the severe vassal treaties of Assyria and then Babylonia. And his call for exclusive devotion to Yahweh was foundational for later Israelites. Although the present Bible contains much later narratives that project this call for devotion back into earlier periods of Israel's history (such as Exod 20:1–3), the book of Hosea is our earliest datable witness to this idea, and it probably was not well received at first. Nevertheless, this belief in God's exclusive claims on God's people grew in importance, particularly as Israel and Judah had to grapple with Assyrian and Babylonian oppression, destruction, and exile. The people suffering through these experiences asked themselves what they could learn from them. They looked back to traditions such as Hosea, spoken out of the crucible of imperial oppression, and concluded that they needed to learn to be more faithful to Yahweh and Yahweh alone. They believed they must reject any other lord (human or divine) and choose Yahweh's boundless love instead.

Meanwhile, it turned out that Amos's prophecy about the north proved more right than Hosea's, at least regarding the northern kingdom. Readers often find the doom aspect of Amos's prophecy difficult to take. "What," they ask, "is the point of announcing irreversible doom on a people if they cannot do anything about it?" In this respect, Hosea's images of hope on the other side of judgment are attractive. Yet there turned out to be no hope on the other side of judgment for the kingdom of Israel to which Hosea addressed his words. Instead, Amos's words proved "prophetic" in the predictive sense of the term. Though Amos was rejected in his own time, and he may well have judged himself a failure, his prophetic writings were adopted and adapted so that readers now, more than twenty-seven centuries later, are trying to learn the lesson he had to teach.

CHAPTER FIVE REVIEW

1. Know the meaning and significance of the following terms discussed in this chapter:
- Assyria
- book of the Twelve Prophets
- minor prophet.
- Syro-Ephraimite war

2. What are the different sorts of indicators of northern origins in the Jacob story of Genesis on the one hand and in the Moses story on the other?

3. What was an ancient "covenant," and what did it mean to "cut" it?

4. What was special about a "vassal treaty," and how is it related to a "covenant"?

5. How did Amos and Hosea relate in different ways to the ancient Israelite idea of election?

6. If they were to speak today to the same contemporary community, how would Amos and Hosea address that community differently? Would there be an equivalent in that community to the idea of election theology? How would Amos's and Hosea's different feelings about election theology be reflected in their different contemporary prophecies?

7. Try rewriting one of the following three prophecies so that it now addresses a contemporary community that you know and care about: Amos 2:6–16; 8:1–8; or Hos 11:1–12. Try to match it sentence for sentence, image for image, metaphor for metaphor.

RESOURCES FOR FURTHER STUDY

General works on prophecy and all of the prophets

Heschel, Abraham. *The Prophets*. 2 volumes. New York: Harper & Row, 1962.
Koch, Klaus. *The Prophets*. 2 volumes. Philadelphia: Fortress, 1983.
Lindblum, J. *Prophecy in Ancient Israel*. Philadelphia: Muhlenberg, 1962.

Commentaries on all of the 12 minor prophets

Limburg, James. *Hosea – Micah*. Interpretation. Atlanta: John Knox Press, 1988.

Sweeney, Marvin. *The Twelve Prophets*, vols. 1 and 2. Berit Olam. Collegeville, MN: Liturgical, 2000–1.

Hosea

Mays, James Luther. *Hosea: A Commentary*. Old Testament Library. Philadelphia: Westminster Press, 1969.

Amos

Mays, James Luther. *Amos: A Commentary*. Old Testament Library. Philadelphia: Westminster Press, 1969.

CHAPTER 6

MICAH, ISAIAH, AND THE

SOUTHERN PROPHETIC

ENCOUNTER WITH ASSYRIA

Chapter Outline

CHAPTER OVERVIEW

In this chapter we move from the world of the northern kingdom of Israel back to that of the southern kingdom of Judah, but the theme of imperial attack remains the same. The people of Judah faced Assyrian attack with faith in Jerusalem's invulnerability, a faith based in ancient Zion theology and soon deepened by an experience of Assyrian withdrawal from a siege of Jerusalem. Addressing this overall situation, Micah critiqued his audience's faith in Zion's invulnerability and proclaimed doom, while Isaiah offered a vision of God's purging of Zion that combined judgment with hope. Both messages were unpopular at the time they were spoken, but became important later. Indeed, the present books attributed to Micah and Isaiah are a mix of early prophecies actually from Micah and Isaiah and prophecies written centuries later. This chapter focuses primarily on texts from both books that can be traced to the eighth-century prophets, while other chapters will discuss later parts of the book of Isaiah. For now, gain a sense of context from this chapter's historical review and then focus on the assigned readings from Micah and Isaiah to see how the early prophecies in each book represent contrasting visions of Yahweh's plans for Zion.

The Historical Context for Micah and Isaiah

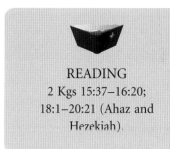

READING
2 Kgs 15:37–16:20;
18:1–20:21 (Ahaz and
Hezekiah).

Micah and Isaiah worked in a completely different world of ideas from that seen in Hosea. It is a world similar to that seen in the royal and Zion psalms discussed in Chapter 3 of this textbook. And that should be no surprise, since Micah and Isaiah both prophesied in Jerusalem and Judah, the home of royal and Zion theology. Their audiences were more familiar with ideas that Zion was special and invulnerable than they were with Israelite exodus or wilderness traditions. The tradition of Davidic kingship was deeply rooted there too, along with the hopes in royal theology that the Davidic king would bring justice and blessing to the people.

The Judeans drew on such beliefs in royal and Zion theology as they confronted their own version of threats from the Assyrian onslaught. At first, these threats were indirect. In the Syro-Ephraimite war (735–734), Israel and Syria laid siege to Jerusalem in hopes of forcing King Ahaz (735–715) to join their anti-Assyrian alliance. Ahaz appealed to Assyria for help, and the Assyrian armies eventually arrived, defeated Israel and other allied nations, and imposed tribute on Judah. From this point forward Judah, along with Israel, was under Assyrian domination. A few decades later another king was in power, Hezekiah (715–686), and he saw an opening amidst chaos in Assyria to get out from under Assyrian domination. He improved the fortifications of Jerusalem and other major outposts, including building a tunnel to Jerusalem's water supply. Moreover, he appears to have tried to rally the people around Yahweh and insure Yahweh's support through a religious reform involving purification of the Jerusalem Temple (destruction of a bronze snake there) and elimination of competing sanctuaries outside Jerusalem (2 Kgs 18:4; compare with 2 Chr 29:3–19).

Eventually, however, the Assyrian armies came again, laid siege to Jerusalem, and threatened to wipe out the kingdom of Judah much as they destroyed the northern kingdom decades earlier. But here the story takes a different turn. The Assyrian army turned back, apparently to deal with urgent military threats that had developed at home. Subsequent Assyrian and biblical sources talk quite differently about this withdrawal (see box on p. 118 for the Assyrian view), but at least two things are clear. First, after this apparently miraculous deliverance of Jerusalem, the people of the kingdom of Judah had an even deeper and more unshakable belief in Zion theology, particularly the idea that Zion was invulnerable. Second, despite this deliverance, Hezekiah and his successors, Manasseh (686–642) and Amon (642–640), remained Assyrian vassals, suffering under Assyrian domination for several more decades until Assyria's power began to wane.

The prophets to be discussed in this chapter both addressed this situation. Though they came from different parts of Judah, they both probably addressed the citizens of Jerusalem, which at that time was a walled city about the size of a few city blocks. They both prophesied in the last decades of the eighth century and touched on similar themes. This closeness of the two prophets, both geographically and chronologically, makes the contrasts between them all the more striking.

A View from the Assyrian Imperial Court: The Annals of Sennacherib

The following is a quotation from the text of the prism shown in Figure 6.1, where Sennacherib, king of Assyria, describes his invasion of Palestine and siege of Jerusalem during the reign of Hezekiah, king of Judah.

Figure 6.1 The Sennacherib prism.

Because Hezekiah of Judah did not submit to my yoke, I laid siege to forty-six of his fortified cities, and walled forts, and to the countless villages in their vicinity. I conquered them using earthen ramps and battering rams. These siege engines were supported by infantry who tunneled under the walls. I took 200,150 prisoners of war, young and old, male and female, from these places. I also plundered more horses, mules, donkeys, camels, large and small cattle than we could count. I imprisoned Hezekiah in Jerusalem like a bird in a cage. I erected siege works to prevent anyone escaping through the city gates.

The cities in Judah which I captured I gave to Mitinti, King of Ashdod, and to Padi, King of Ekron, and to Sillibel, King of Gaza. Thus I reduced the land of Hezekiah in this campaign, and I also increased Hezekiah's annual tribute payments.

Hezekiah, who was overwhelmed by my terror-inspiring splendor, was deserted by his elite troops, which he had brought into Jerusalem. He was forced to send me 420 pounds [Akkadian 30 talents] of gold . . . and all kinds of valuable treasures, his daughters, wives, and male and female musicians. He sent his personal messenger to deliver this tribute and bow down to me. (Translation: *OT Parallels* 191–2)

Exercise

How does this description compare with Isaiah 36–37 (parallel to 2 Kgs 18:13, 17–19:37)? How about to 2 Kgs 18:14–16 (material not found in Isaiah)?

Significant Dates: Judah under Assyrian Domination	
Ahaz	735–715 BCE
Syro-Ephraimite war	735–734 BCE
Hezekiah	715–686 BCE
Beginning of Hezekiah's rebellion	705 BCE
Attack of Sennacherib	701 BCE
Manasseh	686–642 BCE
Amon	642–640 BCE

Micah, a Southern Prophet, Predicting Judgment for Judah and Jerusalem

The first prophet to be discussed is Micah, a southern prophet like Amos. Just as Amos spoke to Israel as an outsider from Judah, so Micah spoke to Jerusalem as a Judean refugee coming from an area decimated by Assyria (the town Moresheth). Moreover, both prophets spoke words of judgment to their audiences, attempting to pierce their false sense of security. Yet the differences between these prophets are striking as well, and they point once again to the different traditions held dear by their different audiences. Where Amos undermined northern Israelite ideas of election, Micah attacks southern trust in Zion theology, particularly the idea that Zion/Jerusalem was invulnerable to all attacks, a belief manifest in biblical texts such as Psalm 46: "God is in the midst of the city, it shall not be moved" (Ps 46:5 NRSV).

READING
Micah 1–3 and 5–6.

The book of Micah starts with judgment, as Micah proclaims to the people of Judah that they are not immune from the Assyrian disaster that has hit the north. The first oracle describes an awesome **theophany** (divine appearance) of Yahweh coming from the Temple (Micah 1:2), yet it quickly becomes clear that this is no cuddly God:

> Yahweh is treading on the sanctuaries of the earth,
> Then the mountains will melt under him,
>   And the valleys will burst open
>   Like wax on a fire.
> Like waters cascading down a slope.

All this, Micah says, is happening because of the "crime of Jacob and the sins of the house of Israel" (1:5). The reader may ask, "What is this crime?," and the text soon answers that it is the capital cities of Samaria and Jerusalem. In a section that sounds much like Hosea, Micah announces that God is about to destroy Samaria, the capital of the northern kingdom, because of its "idols," which he sees as "wages of a prostitute" (1:6–7). But, lest his country-people think they are immune from this disaster, Micah concludes by saying that Judah will be hit by the same destructive power, with the "wound" even reaching the gate of Jerusalem (1:8–9). The next saying (1:10–12) makes a similar point – tracing the path of the invading Assyrian army as it moves from Gath, town by town, to the gate of Jerusalem.

Obviously Micah, like Hosea, is speaking in the context of Assyrian invasion, but he insists that the impending destruction at Assyrian hands is actually caused by God's judgment of the inner ills of the people of Judah. In a social critique reminiscent of Amos, he pronounces a lament over those who:

> plan evil and acts of evil on their beds,
> When morning comes, they do it,
>   Because they have the power to do so,
> They covet fields, and seize them
>   Houses, and they take them away.
> They defraud others of their homes
>   And people of their land. (2:1–2)

Such critiques continue, as in Micah's attack on those who make women and children homeless (2:9) or in his quotation of God's vivid judgment on the leaders who "devour my people's flesh, flay the skin off them, the flesh off their bones, and . . . breaking their bones to bits, chop them up like soup meat in a pot, like flesh in a caldron." (3:2–3).

Apparently, the powers that be in Micah's time did not like this message. He quotes others as telling him "stop preaching . . . that's no way to preach, shame will not overtake us! Is the house of Jacob really condemned? Is God's patience really so short?" (2:6–7). Apparently there were others proclaiming more hopeful messages, and Micah proclaims Yahweh's judgment on those who "cry 'peace' when they have food in their mouths, but launch war on the one who takes food from them" (3:5). In a climactic message, Micah announces an end to all of the leaders who "build Zion with blood and Jerusalem with malice" (3:10):

> [Jerusalem's] leaders administer justice for bribes,
>   Her priests give rulings for a fee,
>   And her prophets predict the future for pay.
> And then they rely on Yahweh, saying,
>   "Isn't Yahweh in our midst?
>   No disaster will come on us!" (3:11)

For Micah, these leaders and their trust in ancient Zion theology are bringing about the very disaster they consider unthinkable:

> Therefore, because of you,
>   Zion shall be plowed as a field
> Jerusalem will become heaps of ruins,
>   And the mountain of the house of Yahweh will be a wooded height. (3:12)

Up to this point, Micah sounds a lot like Amos. He maintains that Jerusalem's corruption is so deep that Yahweh will let the Assyrians destroy it. The book so far explains Judah's oppression by Assyria as a result of its deep-seated iniquity.

Nevertheless, much of the rest of the book, including some of its most famous passages, sounds a much more hopeful note. Micah 4 starts with a famous prophecy (4:1–3), also seen in Isaiah 2:2–4, that God will make Zion/Jerusalem the center of world justice, so that – in a reversal of the usual transformation of farmers into fighters (see Joel 3:10) – nations will "hammer swords into plowshares and spears into pruning hooks" (4:3). The rest of Micah 4–5 contains prophecies of how Yahweh will redeem "daughter Zion," who has endured pain like a woman in labor, bringing her exiles back to her (4:6–7, 8–10). The book goes on to say that when "[Zion] who is in labor has brought forth" (5:3), a powerful ruler will arise from tiny Bethlehem of Ephratah to reign in glory from Jerusalem (5:2–4). This prophecy, often understood by Christians to be a prophecy of Jesus's birth in Bethlehem, is part of a series of prophecies about how Zion will triumph over the Assyrians and other enemies who dominated her (4:11–5:15).

These words of hope for exiles and promise of victory in Micah 4–5 contrast sharply with the proclamation of absolute doom on Zion in Micah 1–3. Chapters 4 and 5 hardly sound like the words of the prophet who announced that "Zion shall be plowed as a field, and Jerusalem will be heaps of ruins" (3:12). Because of this, most scholars believe that much of Micah 4–5, and possibly 6–7 as well, was added by later – anonymous – prophets to the book of Micah. As discussed in Chapter 4 (in the review of sources in Genesis 1–11), to copy and expand an earlier work was an ancient way of recognizing its ongoing importance and apply its message to later times. In this case, these prophets had seen Micah's earlier prophecies of destruction come true, had come to treasure his prophecies, and yet addressed an audience in Babylonian exile who needed new words of comfort to balance Micah's words of judgment. These later prophets declared to their exilic (or post-exilic) audience that Yahweh had a grand future for Zion/Jerusalem and for them. These visionary words of hope – both of a glorious ruler (5:2–4) and of a world where people would not "study war any more" (4:1–3) – have been as important or more important to later communities as the earlier words of judgment on which they were built.

The rest of the book of Micah, however, is not all words of hope. Micah 6:9–16 accuses Jerusalem of succumbing to the same social ills as its northern neighbor: "You have kept the statutes of Omri and the works of the house of Ahab" (6:16). This

basics | Book of Micah

Outline: cycles of judgment and salvation – Judah

I   Destruction up to the gates of Jerusalem (1:1–2:11) and prediction of the in-gathering of exiles (2:12–13)

II   Destruction of Zion (3:1–12) and its restoration along with the Judean monarchy and people (4:1–5:15)

III Judgment of Israel (6:1–7:7) and prophetic prayer for restoration (7:8–20)

Theme

Whereas the original prophet, Micah, stressed God's impending judgment on Zion, the book now emphasizes salvation on the other side of such judgment. It was addressed to much later Judeans who had experienced many of the disasters that Micah described. The book encouraged them and later communities to have hope for the future. Though God might destroy everything they held dear, God also could restore them.

More information

Micah's words of judgment were not forgotten. A story in the book of Jeremiah, Jeremiah 26, describes how the later, seventh-century prophet Jeremiah was almost executed for proclaiming the destruction of the temple. At this point, the elders reminded the people of Micah's proclamation of Zion's destruction, a prophecy given a century before the time of Jeremiah (Micah 3:12). In addition, they tell a story – not found elsewhere in the Bible – of King Hezekiah listening to Micah's prophecy and repenting (Jer 26:19). Jeremiah's life was spared.

may be another saying from the same eighth-century prophet (Micah) who proclaimed that the wound of Israel was coming to the gate of Jerusalem (1:9, 12). Most famous of all is the speech in Micah 6:1–8, which responds to people's complaints that God has burdened them (6:3) by saying that God's requirements are simple: "to do justice, love kindness, and walk wisely with your God" (6:8). Soon afterward, the book insists that "it is true wisdom to fear your [God's] name" (6:9), reflecting the fact that the book of Micah, like Amos and Hosea, is prophetic *teaching* or *wisdom*. It is not clear that Micah 6:2–8 came from the same eighth-century prophet who spoke most of Micah 1–3, but it is quite clear that this saying has served for many as a powerful distillation of the long-term significance of the message of the prophets. The saying in 6:2–8 well exemplifies the way the book of Micah has been enriched over time by multiple voices that could be considered "inspired." As a result, the book of Micah now is a powerful mix of Micah's eighth-century words of judgment and much later prophetic teachings about hope and God's true wishes for God's people.

Isaiah's Vision of Hope for Jerusalem/Zion
Embedded in the Book of Isaiah

READING
Isaiah 1–11 and
28–32.

EXERCISE
Using the Appendix to this chapter, compare and contrast Psalm 46 (a Zion psalm) with two prophecies about Jerusalem/Zion – Isaiah 1:21–6 and Micah 3:9–12. Which is closer to Psalm 46?

The book of Isaiah was one of the first places where scholars recognized this kind of mix of earlier prophecy and later expansion. Isaiah starts with a superscription that identifies what follows as "the vision of Isaiah, son of Amoz, which he saw concerning Judah and Jerusalem during the time of Uzziah, Jotham, Ahaz, and Hezekiah, kings of Judah" (1:1; see also 2:1) – that is, as the revelation given to Isaiah about the southern monarchy during the last few decades of the eighth century. Nevertheless, scholars have found many signs that the book was written over centuries. As early as nine hundred years ago, the Jewish scholar Abraham Ibn Ezra noted that the reference to the Persian king Cyrus in Isa 41:25 seems to indicate that its author not only knew of this king ruling two hundred years after the time of Isaiah, but could describe him to a contemporary audience as one "foretold from the start." Over the last two hundred years, scholars have used these and other observations to distinguish between the words of the eighth-century prophet Isaiah in the book of Isaiah and layer upon layer of prophecies by later writers now in the book as well.

This research has helped scholars see both the complexity and the grandeur of the book of Isaiah. On the one hand, scholars now believe that most sayings actually from "Isaiah ben Amoz" can be found in *parts* of Isaiah 1–11 and 28–32, with *most* of the rest of the book (and all of Isaiah 36–66) coming from later authors. On the other hand, scholars also have an ever increasing appreciation of the insight and artistry of the entire 66-chapter book, later portions included. Certainly later communities of faith have found inspiration in Isaiah as a whole. Virtually all of the later prophecy in Isaiah 40–66 appears in the cycle of readings used in Jewish synagogues, and the same visions of comfort and restoration have been central to Christianity from the outset. There will be occasion to return to both the design and interpretation of these portions of the book of Isaiah in Chapters 9 and 12 of this *Introduction*.

For now it is important to recognize that this is another place where modern presuppositions about authorship and "inspiration" can mislead us in reading the Bible.

Often modern interpreters assume that the *real* inspiration can only lie with an original author, a prophet in this case, while all later materials must be corruptions of the original, pure message. What emerges, however, from a look at the book of Isaiah and its history of interpretation is that Isaiah – the eighth-century prophet – provided a dynamic and complex vision that was only the start of a much bigger process. Ultimately, the power of his vision *increased* as later authors, addressing quite different times, expanded on and adapted it so that it would speak to those times. The result was a grand book of 66 chapters, the first of the three books of the "**major prophets**" (Isaiah, Jeremiah, and Ezekiel).

Let us turn now to take a closer look at the early eighth-century vision of Isaiah ben Amoz. Much of this vision is focused on Yahweh's message amidst threats related to the Assyrian onslaught. The first such major threat was the attempt by Syria and Israel in 735 to force Ahaz of Judah into joining an anti-Assyrian alliance by laying siege to Jerusalem (the Syro-Ephraimite war). The book of Kings describes Ahaz as responding to the siege by asking for help from Assyria (2 Kgs 16:5–9). As we can see in Isaiah 7–8, Isaiah saw this request by King Ahaz as a fatal failure to trust in Yahweh's protection of Zion. In Isa 7:1–9 Isaiah assures Ahaz that the coalition against Judah will not stand and that Ahaz should "not be afraid." Ahaz in 7:10–17 rejects Isaiah's offer of a sign from Yahweh, and Isaiah announces that the result of this rejection will be an imminent attack by the king of Assyria. Finally, Isa 8:1–8 continues these themes, proclaiming disaster on the attackers from Israel and Syria (8:1–4), but also on the people of Judah for refusing to trust in God's protection of Zion (= "the flowing waters of [Jerusalem's spring] Shiloah," 8:6). Each of these stories features a child with a Hebrew name that signifies the core of Isaiah's message: "a remnant shall return" (7:3), "God with us" (7:14), and "speedy comes the booty" (8:1). In light of the rejection of his message, Isaiah tells in 8:10–18 of Yahweh's command to "seal" his prophetic "teaching" in his "students" (8:16), so that these students can serve as a sign for future generations of "Yahweh who dwells in Zion" (8:18). Perhaps some of these students were Isaiah's own, strangely named children, since literate fathers often taught their own children. In this case, Isaiah is passing on to his children a "teaching" and a "witness" that his own generation would not hear. We probably have this process to thank for the initial preservation of Isaiah's words and the beginnings of the book.

The story of Isaiah's commission in Isaiah 6 reflects his experience of rejection during the time of Ahaz. Many readers are well familiar with the beginning of this text, where Isaiah actually sees Yahweh's terrifying presence in the Jerusalem temple, surrounded by "seraphim" (see Figure 6.2 for more on these) – an Egyptian symbol. Awed by the spectacle, he proclaims a lament, "woe upon me, for I am a man of unclean lips in a people of unclean lips, looking onto the king of kings, Yahweh of armies!" (6:5). One of the winged cobras then burns his lips with a fiery coal, saying that this has removed the prophet's sin and bloodguilt (6:6–7). The rest of the passage then describes how Isaiah's people are about to be subjected to a similar burning process, starting with the prophet's commission to deliver a message that will not be heard:

Figure 6.2 Judean seals from the time of Isaiah and Micah, showing strong Egyptian influence. Note especially the winged cobras, which probably were the referent for the "seraphim" mentioned in Isaiah 6.

Isaiah 6 and the "Call Narrative"

Many scholars would call Isaiah 6 a **prophetic call narrative.** Such a narrative is a story, told in the first person by the prophet ("I," "me"), where he tells of how he was authorized by God to be a prophet and deliver God's message. Other examples are Jer 1:4–10 and Ezekiel 1–3.

Here are the typical parts of a prophetic call narrative, with illustrations from Isaiah 6:

1	A divine appearance	1–4
2	An introductory word by God	5–7
3	The call of the prophet (or leader)	8–10
4	An objection from the prophet	11a
5	A divine reassurance/answer	11b–13
6	A sign reinforcing the answer	[not present]

These prophetic call narratives stand toward the outset of a prophetic book (Jeremiah and Ezekiel) or collection in a prophetic book (the Isaiah memoir in Isaiah 6–8) and emphasize God's authorization of the message in that book. They are as different as the books that they authorize, and some

scholars dispute the application of the term "call narrative" to some of these texts (particularly since the word "call" has its home in later Christian theology). Sometimes these texts lack one or another part of the typical form. Nevertheless, they share with each other the idea that the idea for the prophet's message arose not with him, but with God. The prophet was but a messenger.

Isaiah 6 probably was written as an introduction to his memoir, insisting on God's role in authorizing his prophecy during the Syro-Ephraimite war even though it was rejected. As this text became part of the larger book of Isaiah, it came to authorize the book as a whole.

Other call narratives: an exercise

Judg 6:11–24 and Exod 3:1–4:17 are call narratives for other figures, Gideon and Moses. Compare these texts with Isa 6:1–13. What is similar and what is different about the form of these texts? What is similar or different about the role they play in the biblical books where they occur?

> Go and say to this people:
> "Keep listening, but do not comprehend.
>   Keep looking, but do not understand."
> Make the mind of this people senseless,
>   And stop up their ears,
>   And shut their eyes,
> Lest they see with their eyes,
>   And hear with their ears,
>   And understand with their mind
> And change their ways and be healed. (6:9–10)

Isaiah is understandably upset at receiving this commission and asks "how long?" The answer is that Judah is about to be laid waste – again a probable reference to Assyrian attacks. Only after successive invasions is there any sign of hope. It is a "stump," which Isaiah is told is a "holy seed" (6:13).

We see this image of the "stump" used elsewhere in Isaiah to communicate that there is hope on the other side of apparent absolute destruction: for an apparently dead stump can have a shoot spring forth from it (see Job 14:8–9). At the end of Isaiah 10, Isaiah describes Yahweh as coming through the whole area, cutting down the tallest trees and chopping off their branches (Isa 10:33–4). Since "trees" were an image for royal dynasties, many understand this to be Isaiah's prediction that Yahweh is about to send the Assyrian army through the area, "cutting off" all of the royal dynasties and thus terminating the monarchies of Judah, Israel, and their neighbors. Yet Isaiah sees a future on the other side of this awful event. Though the Davidic dynasty in Jerusalem might seem like a completely dead stump, Isaiah proclaims that a "shoot shall spring forth from the stump of Jesse [David's father]" (Isa 11:1). This "shoot" will be an ideal king:

> With social solidarity he will judge the poor,
>   And he will rule the oppressed fairly.
> He will strike the earth with the rod of his mouth,
>   And he will kill the wicked with the breath of his lips. (Isa 11:4)

Although many later interpreters, particularly Christians, now see this text as relating to Jesus, it originally stood as an ancient prophecy that a new king would arise over Judah who would fulfill all the promises of royal theology: a king who judges justly and successfully defends his people. The passage then turns to a grand vision of peace centered in Zion:

> The wolf will sojourn with the lamb,
>   The leopard will lie down with the calf . . .
> They will not hurt or destroy in all my holy mountain,
>   For the earth shall be as full of the knowledge of Yahweh
>   As waters cover the sea. (Isa 11:6a and 9)

This whole complex of texts (Isa 10:33–11:9) beautifully displays Isaiah's affirmation of the royal and Zion theology that was so important to Judah, even as he proclaims an awesome, forest-felling destruction of its current leadership. His words, both in Isaiah 6 and Isa 10:33–11:9, helped explain why Judah had undergone such suffering, even as they also offered images of hope that Yahweh eventually would restore Zion and its kingship.

The uniqueness of Isaiah's message is nicely illustrated through comparing Isaiah's words about Zion in Isa 1:21–6 with Micah's proclamation that Zion will be "plowed as a field" (Micah 3:9–12; see the Appendix to this chapter for a side-by-side comparison with Isa 1:21–6). Where Micah presents God as utterly rejecting Zion (/Jerusalem) as having been built "with blood" (3:10), Isaiah's God sounds more like Hosea's, in agony over how his city – envisioned as female – has been corrupted by violent, corrupt leaders:

> How she has become a promiscuous woman,
>   The city that once was faithful!
> She that was full of justice,
>   Social solidarity made its home in her,
>   And now murderers! (Isa 1:21)

To be sure, Isaiah does resemble Micah in his understanding of Jerusalem's ills. He, like Micah, criticizes a loss of "justice" (Isa 1:21; see Micah 3:9) caused by its leaders' robbery (1:23, "companions of thieves"; see Micah 2:2), taking of bribes, and perversion of due process due to the most vulnerable people (Isa 1:23; see Micah 3:11). Yet Isaiah does *not* proclaim a final end to Jerusalem as a result of these misdeeds by its leaders. Instead, in an echo of Isaiah's own burning purification process (Isa 6:6–7), Isaiah announces that God is about to purify Jerusalem as metal alloy is purified in a hot forge (Isa 1:25). Once again, this image of a refining fire is Isaiah's way of announcing grand hope for Zion on the other side of painful judgment:

> I will restore your judges as at the first,
>   And your counselors as at the beginning.
> Then you will be called "city of social solidarity"
>   "The faithful settlement." (Isa 1:26)

Again, Isaiah contrasts here with Micah. Where Isaiah affirms that Yahweh dwells in Zion and will defend and restore it (Isa 8:18), Micah directly attacks its leadership for saying "Isn't Yahweh in our midst? No disaster will come on us!" (Micah 3:11). It is even possible that Micah had prophets such as Isaiah in mind when he blamed Jerusalem's future destruction on those who would affirm Zion theology in this way (Micah 3:12).

Apparently Isaiah's message evolved decades later when he prophesied during the time of King Hezekiah, son of Ahaz. This was the time, described in 2 Kings 18–20//

Isaiah 36–9 (and 2 Chronicles 29–32), when Hezekiah joined an anti-Assyrian coalition and barely escaped destruction when the Assyrian army of Sennacherib laid siege to Jerusalem (only to withdraw). The narratives about this event found in Kings and Isaiah depict Hezekiah as a positive contrast to his father Ahaz and Isaiah as more affirming of this later king. Where Ahaz refused the sign offered by Isaiah and failed to trust in Yahweh's care for Zion (Isaiah 7–8), Hezekiah actually consulted with Isaiah, and – as a result – the city was rescued (2 Kgs 18–19//Isaiah 36–7; compare with 2 Chronicles 32). The oracles found in Isaiah 28–31, however, show that Isaiah was more critical in this time than these narratives indicate. He repeatedly announces judgment on leaders like Hezekiah who go to Egypt to form anti-Assyrian alliances (30:1–5; also 28:14–22) and rely on military strength for salvation (30:15). Yet again, Isaiah seems to have experienced rejection, with people telling him to shut up or preach more comfortable words (30:10–11). This is why, he says, God commanded him to write these prophecies down, preserving them in scroll form as a witness against the people of Hezekiah's time (30:8).

Conclusion

All this suggests that one major impetus for the initial *writing* of prophecies such as those of Isaiah was the experience of rejection. None of the prophets discussed in this or the previous chapter seems to have been a major success in his own time. Yet their words were preserved for a later time by their closest students and/or associates. Moreover, as the words of Isaiah and other prophets appeared to come true over time, the significance of their written prophecies grew. For example, what started as Isaiah's counter-wisdom to the false wisdom of Jerusalem's leaders (see Isa 29:14; 31:1–2) was treasured by later Judeans and expanded in subsequent centuries. Eventually, the smaller groups of sayings seen in Isaiah 1–11, 28–32, and elsewhere grew into the 66-chapter book we now have.

This highlights the multi-layered quality of interpretation of such biblical texts. If the significance of these writings had been exhausted in the time of Amos and Isaiah, we probably would not be reading them now. We have these books because later communities found their sayings so helpful that they copied and expanded them. Moreover, this process of rereading and creative reworking continued in Jewish and Christian communities even after the texts of these prophetic books were fixed. For example, later readers reinterpreted predictions of the imminent arrival of a just Judean monarch (e.g. Micah 5:2–4; Isa 11:15) as predictions of a royal messiah who would overcome Rome or some successive oppressive empire. These and other prophecies have retained a lasting significance because problems of injustice and imperial rule did not cease after the Assyrian onslaught in the eighth century.

CHAPTER SIX REVIEW

1. What is a theophany? Where does one occur in Micah? Is it good?

2. What is a "prophetic call narrative," what does it do, and what are its typical parts? Give an example.

3. Which prophets are among the "major prophets," and in what order do these books appear in the Bible?

4. Which chapters in the books of Isaiah and Micah have the largest amounts of material from the eighth-century prophets, and which parts of each book are made up virtually exclusively of texts added by later authors?

5. What differences do you see between the views of these two eighth-century Judean prophets on what is wrong with Jerusalem? What are the main differences in their views of Jerusalem's future? Is either of these identical with Zion theology as seen in Psalm 46?

6. Do you think the eighth-century prophet Isaiah might have been one of the "prophets" whom Micah criticized for "leaning on Yahweh and saying 'Surely Yahweh is with us, nothing will happen to us'" (Micah 3:11)? Why or why not?

7. What differences do you see between Micah (as seen in Micah 1–3) and Amos?

8. What differences do you see between the message of the eighth-century prophet Isaiah (as seen in eighth-century parts of the book) and Hosea?

RESOURCES FOR FURTHER STUDY

Micah

Mays, James Luther. *Micah: A Commentary*. Old Testament Library. Philadelphia: Westminster Press, 1976.

Isaiah 1–39

Blenkinsopp, Joseph. *Isaiah: A New Translation and Commentary*, parts 1–3. Anchor Bible. New York: Doubleday, 2000–3.
Childs, Brevard. *The Book of Isaiah: A Commentary*. Old Testament Library. Louisville, KY: Westminster Press, 2001.
Clements, R. E. *Isaiah 1–39*. New Century Bible Commentary. Grand Rapids: Eerdmans, 1980.

The history of interpretation of the (whole) book of Isaiah

Childs, Brevard. *The Struggle to Understand Isaiah as Christian Scripture*. Grand Rapids: Eerdmans, 2004. This forms somewhat of a response to Sawyer (next entry).
Sawyer, John. *The Fifth Gospel: Isaiah in the History of Christianity*. Cambridge: Cambridge University Press, 1996.
Stern, Elsie. "Beyond Nahamu: Strategies of Consolation in the Jewish Lectionary Cycle for the 9th of Av Season." Pp. 180–204 in *SBL Seminar Papers 1998*. Atlanta: Scholars Press, 1998. If you can find a copy of it, this article provides useful coverage of Jewish interpretation of the book of Isaiah, particularly Isaiah 40–55.

APPENDIX: COMPARISON OF A ZION PSALM (PSALM 46) WITH MICAH 3:9–12 AND ISA 1:21–6

Psalm 46:1–7 (a Zion Psalm)

God is our refuge and strength, a very present help in trouble. Therefore we will not fear though the earth should change, though the mountains shake in the heart of the sea; though its waters roar and foam, though the mountains tremble with its tumult.

There is a river whose streams make glad the city of God, the holy habitation of the Most High. **God is in the midst of her, she shall not be moved**; God will help her right early. The nations rage, the kingdoms totter; God utters God's voice, the earth melts. **Yahweh of armies is with us**; the god of Jacob is our refuge [refrain repeated in verse 11].

Micah 3:9–12	Isaiah 1:21–6

Hear this, you heads of the house of Jacob
and rulers of the house of Israel,
 	
who abhor justice
      and pervert all equity
who build Zion with blood
      and Jerusalem with wrong.
Its heads give judgment for a bribe,
its priests teach for hire,
its prophets divine for money;
 	
yet they lean upon the Lord and say,
"Is not the Lord in the midst of us?
No evil shall come upon us."
	The faithful city,
	      What a harlot she has become!
	Zion once full of fair judgment,
	Where saving justice used to
	      dwell,
	but now assassins!
	Your silver has turned to dross,
	      Your wine is watered.
	Your princes are rebels,
	      Accomplices of brigands.
	All of them greedy for presents
	      and eager for bribes,
	They show no justice to the
	orphan,
	and the widows' cause never reaches them.
	
	Hence the Lord Yahweh of armies,
	the Mighty One of Israel, says this,
	"I shall get satisfaction from my enemies,
	I shall avenge myself on my foes.

Therefore, because of you
Zion shall be plowed as a field
Jerusalem shall become a heap of ruins
and the mountain of the house,
a wooded height.
	I shall turn my hand against you,
	I shall purge your dross as though with potash,
	      I shall remove your alloy.
	And I shall restore your judges as at first,
	      Your counselors as in bygone days,
	
	After which you will be called 'City of Saving Justice'
	      'Faithful City'."

CHAPTER 7

TORAH AND HISTORY

IN THE WAKE OF

THE ASSYRIAN EMPIRE

Chapter Outline

CHAPTER OVERVIEW

Chapters 5 and 6 featured prophecies responding to Assyrian attack in the eighth century, while this chapter focuses on biblical texts formed in the wake of the collapse of Assyrian domination in the seventh century. Foremost among these is the first text to be known as a "Torah of Moses." This first "Torah," however, is not Genesis–Deuteronomy, but rather an earlier, seventh-century edition of the book of Deuteronomy. In this chapter of the textbook we will see how Deuteronomy shows the impact of Assyrian oppression even after the Assyrians had lost control of Judah. The same is true of the books that follow Deuteronomy – Joshua, Judges, Samuel, and Kings. Each of these books reframes earlier traditions about Israel's history in light of Judah's recent experiences of Assyrian oppression. This long experience of imperial domination forms the background for the hostility toward foreigners and foreign influence in Deuteronomy–2 Kings and the emphasis in these books on the importance of exclusive loyalty to Yahweh and Yahweh alone.

The Seventh Century: The Space Between Empires

The late seventh century was a brief window of time when Judah enjoyed the hope of independence. This was the time when Judah moved from domination by Assyria to eventual domination (and destruction) by Babylonia. At the outset of this period in the 620s BCE the people of Judah already had experienced over seven decades of oppression and humiliation at the hands of the Assyrian empire. During these decades they had been ruled by kings loyal to Assyria, first Manasseh and then (briefly) his son Amon. Then, in the mid-seventh century, cracks began to appear in the once invincible empire. Several regions successfully broke away from Assyria. Amon was assassinated in a palace conspiracy, perhaps by an inner elite hoping to take advantage of the emerging power vacuum. The Bible says that the assassins were themselves killed by the "people of the land," who anointed his 8-year-old son Josiah as king in his place (2 Kgs 21:19–26).

Though he started as a boy king, Josiah reigned for over thirty years (640–609). Important things appear to have happened during his reign, particularly the latter part of it. Thus 2 Kings tells a story of how, in the eighteenth year of his reign, Josiah funded a renovation of the Temple. At some point in the process the priests told him that "the book of the Torah" had been found there (2 Kgs 22:3–10). When it was read to him, Josiah realized his nation faced curses for disobeying the Torah, and he immediately sent to have its authenticity verified by a prophet named Huldah. She prophesied that the words of the book were true, but that King Josiah would die in peace (2 Kgs 22:14–20). Josiah then had the book read to the elders and the rest of the people, and he led the people in making a "covenant" to follow all the words of the book of the Torah that had just been found (2 Kgs 23:1–3). This then started a process that is often described as "**Josiah's reform**" (623 BCE). Josiah commanded the priests to remove the statue of the goddess Asherah from the temple in Jerusalem along with all elements related to Baal and all deities other than Yahweh (2 Kgs 23:4, 6–7). He also destroyed all the sanctuaries ("high places") outside Jerusalem and removed their priests (2 Kgs 23:5, 8–14). In an apparent move to restore David and Solomon's united kingdom (see Map 7.1), he even defiled the ancient royal altar at Bethel and destroyed sanctuaries throughout the area of the former northern kingdom (2 Kgs 23:15–20). Finally, he commanded a national Passover in which people from the entire kingdom, north and south, were to come on pilgrimage to the temple in Jerusalem (2 Kgs 23:21–3). Such a Passover had not been celebrated "from the days of the judges who judged Israel through to the days of the kings of Israel and Judah" (2 Kgs 23:22).

This final note indicates that many elements of Josiah's reform were new. Where the Jerusalem Temple had once been the home of worship of various deities alongside Yahweh, now Josiah dedicated it to worship of Yahweh and Yahweh alone. Where the people of Judah and Israel had worshipped in local sanctuaries since the time of the judges, Josiah destroyed those sanctuaries and had them worship in Jerusalem. And where Passover previously had been a local festival celebrated by clans in their villages, Josiah required all now to come to Jerusalem, the capital city, in a national pilgrimage

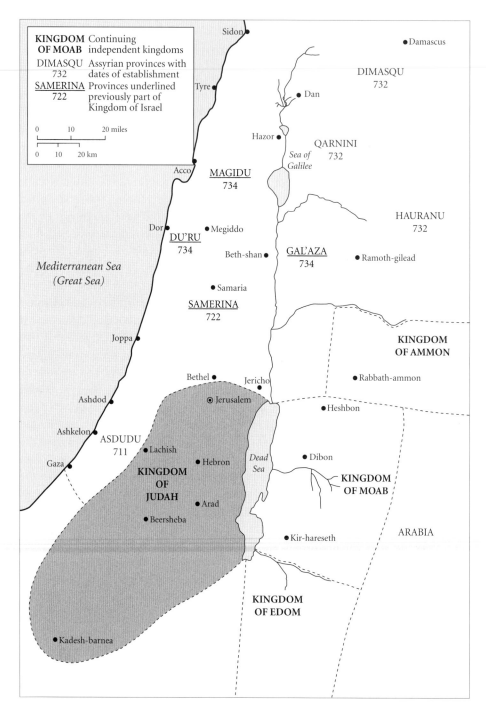

Map 7.1 The Judean kingdom after the fall of the north. Redrawn from Norman Gottwald, *The Hebrew Bible: A Socio-Literary Introduction*. Minneapolis: Fortress, 1985, page 291.

festival. Contemporary scholars see a strong element of political centralization in these moves of religious reform, with Josiah aiming to restore David's Jerusalem-centered kingdom spanning north and south and achieve independence from the Assyrian empire. Nevertheless, the biblical text itself focuses on another rationale for his actions: 2 Kgs 23:24 asserts that all of Josiah's actions were done to implement "the words of the Torah that Hilkiah, the priest, found in the house of Yahweh."

Indeed, there are strong links between Josiah's reform and a book of "Torah" found in the Hebrew Bible. In 1805 the German scholar Wilhelm De Wette noticed that these elements of Josiah's reform are rooted in central emphases of the book of Deuteronomy. The laws in Deuteronomy start with a regulation to destroy all non-Yahwistic worship items and local sanctuaries and worship Yahweh in only one place (Deuteronomy 12). This sounds like an authorization for the temple purification and sanctuary destruction that Josiah implemented. Deuteronomy also includes laws for festivals that require all to come to the central worship place (Deuteronomy 16). This sounds like the background for Josiah's Passover. Deuteronomy concludes with curses that will come upon a people that does not follow its stipulations (Deut 28:15–68). This sounds like the curses that Josiah feared would come upon his people for not obeying the Torah found in the temple (2 Kgs 22:13). Throughout, the book of Deuteronomy refers to itself as the "Torah" or the "scroll of the Torah" and so on (Deut 1:5; 31:9–12, 24–6; etc.), much as 2 Kings refers to the scroll reported by the priest Hilkiah and implemented by Josiah as "the scroll of the Torah" (2 Kgs 22:8, 10, 13, 16; 23:2–3; etc.). In sum, it looks as if the "scroll of the Torah" in Deuteronomy – with its instructions for centralized worship and Passover – is the "Torah" that 2 Kings 22–3 describes Josiah as reading and implementing in his reform.

This description of Josiah's reign in 2 Kings 22–3 is not just a fictional glorification of his reign, but reflects actual historical changes that took place during the late monarchy of Judah. Prior to this point, we have tax documents from ancient Samaria and some other early texts that include a significant proportion of deity names other than Yahweh. After this point, the names found in caches of late Judean letters show virtually exclusive devotion to Yahweh. Archaeologists have found a number of sanctuaries that were used for sacrifice outside Jerusalem from the time before Josiah. In the time of Josiah and afterwards, however, the evidence for such sanctuaries diminishes considerably. Finally, there is a massive shift in the diversity of art around the end of the seventh century. In previous chapters we saw examples of female figurines and images, animals, etc. from earlier periods in Israel and Judah's history. Now our archaeological finds – seen in Figure 7.1 – are heavy on text and light on images. The few images that appear are an isolated human or plant. Thus, not only does the Bible testify to a purification and reform, but the archaeological record seems to confirm that this was a time of a radical revolution. A similar revolution in our own setting would mean the elimination of all but one religion in the US and the destruction of all worship places outside Washington, DC, so that all had to travel there to celebrate any major holiday.

What might have caused such a revolution in the religious and political life of ancient Judah? The first thing to affirm is that this reform was built on older roots. For example, the emphasis on pure worship of Yahweh alone and elimination of Baal worship

Figure 7.1 Seals and other images from the late seventh century. They well illustrate the decline in use of images in Judah and the rise in importance of texts.

is a major focus in Hosea's prophecy in the northern kingdom of the eighth century, discussed in Chapter 5. In that chapter we also saw signs that Deuteronomy itself, like Hosea, probably originated as a northern text. Judging from this and similar emphases on cultic purity in narratives about the northern prophets Elijah and Elisha (1 Kings 17–2 Kings 10), it appears that some groups in the Israelite heartland in the north had already strongly advocated pure worship of Yahweh.

Late in the eighth century, the north was destroyed and Judah became the sole place for the preservation of the values and texts of these groups advocating pure worship of Yahweh. As we have seen, Hezekiah was the king in the south then and instituted some cultic centralization and purification while attempting independence from Assyria as well (see 2 Kgs 18:4 and the later descriptions in 2 Chronicles 29–31). This religious reform by Hezekiah is not explained in the biblical narratives, but may have been motivated by Hezekiah's wish to avoid the mistakes of the northern kingdom as identified by Hosea and other northern traditions. Decades later his religious changes were reversed by his successor, Manasseh (2 Kgs 21:3–7//2 Chr 33:3–7), but they were not forgotten. Indeed, Josiah's reform can be seen as a reinstatement of ancient northern emphases on cultic purity and centralization that had already been introduced to Judah, preliminarily, by Josiah's great-grandfather, Hezekiah.

Even as we recognize the precursors to Josiah's reforms, there are also important new elements. First, the biblical reports are more clear in Josiah's case than in Hezekiah's about how Josiah extended his reforms to encompass areas of the former northern kingdom (2 Kgs 23:15–20//2 Chr 34:6–7; compare with 2 Kgs 18:4//2 Chr 31:1 on Hezekiah). By the time of Josiah's reform the Assyrian empire had collapsed. This left a power vacuum in the area of the former northern kingdom where there once had been an Assyrian province. In response, Josiah tried to revive David and Solomon's ancient united monarchy, claiming the north once again as part of a kingdom based in the south. His stress on centralization of worship related to this. Now all, in both north and south, were required to come to Jerusalem for worship at festivals such as Passover.

Josiah's reform is distinguished in another way from Hezekiah's: it appears to be connected to a text, in this case a text sounding much like Deuteronomy. To be sure, there are signs that some kind of reform was already underway before the "scroll of the Torah of Yahweh" was brought to light. Chronicles suggests that Josiah's purification and centralization preceded the discovery of the scroll (2 Chronicles 34), and even 2 Kings implies that temple renovations were already underway when Josiah was informed about it (2 Kgs 22:3–10). Yet the biblical tradition is clear that this book played an important role in Josiah's reign. This does not necessarily mean that everyone agreed immediately on the authenticity of the book that Josiah put at the center of his reform. Rather, he seems to have felt a need to have the book authenticated (2 Kgs 22:14–20//2 Chr 34:22–8), indicating some doubts about its origins (note also a possible critique of this "Torah" in Jer 8:8–9, a potential seventh-century text discussed in Chapter 8). Indeed, these doubts about the authenticity of Josiah's book have been shared by some contemporary scholars. Nevertheless, whatever the origins of the "scroll" announced by the priest, Hilkiah, it appears to have come to play a pivotal role in Josiah's inauguration of a new era in Judah's monarchy. Let us now take a closer look at Deuteronomy, a probable revision of that ancient scroll.

The Deuteronomic Torah of Moses and the Phenomenon of Hybridity

The book of Deuteronomy reveals a remarkable blend of ancient Israelite law and radical adaptation of the Assyrian vassal treaty form. To start, the book appears to have ancient roots. Not only does it show signs of northern origins (discussed previously), but many of its laws are revisions of older laws seen in the "covenant code" of Exod 20:22–23:33. For example, the altar law in Deuteronomy 12 emphasizes the importance of one altar, while its parallel in Exod 20:24–5 provides instructions for building altars around the land. Similarly, the law about festivals in Deuteronomy 16 parallels the rules about them in Exod 23:14–17 (see box on p. 138), making sure that they are celebrated in only one place. In this way and many others the book of

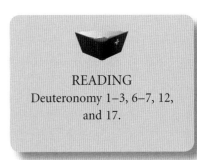

READING
Deuteronomy 1–3, 6–7, 12, and 17.

Deuteronomy builds on and revises older legal teachings in Israel. And the Deuteronomic "Torah"-teaching builds on other ancient traditions as well. For example, the law about moving boundary markers in Deut 19:14 builds on a virtually identical teaching in Prov 22:28 (see the box opposite on "Proverbs and Deuteronomy"), which in turn parallels a similar ruling in the Egyptian Instruction of Amenemope. At the same time, Deuteronomy adds a theological rationale not found in the Proverbs teaching.

Overview: The Three Pilgrimage Festivals in the Covenant Code and Deuteronomy

Note the crucial additional note in Deut 16:16 about making a pilgrimage to only one place. Otherwise, the introduction to the pilgrimage festivals in Exod 23:15 and the concluding overview in Deut 16:16 are fairly similar:

Exod 23:15	Deut 16:16
Three times a year you shall make a pilgrimage. You shall observe the festival of unleavened bread . . . You shall not appear empty-handed before me.	Three times a year every male shall appear before Yahweh your God **in the place that I choose:** at the feast of unleavened bread, the feast of weeks, and the feast of booths. And none should appear empty handed . . .

Comparison exercise

Compare and contrast other parts of Exod 23:14–17 and Deut 16:1–17.

That said, Deuteronomy is an example of another, quite remarkable form of revision: the theological adaptation of the Assyrian **vassal treaty** so that it now expressed God's – not the Assyrian king's – rule of Israel. During the century that Assyria dominated Israel and Judah, it subjugated many nations through a vassal treaty form. This was a text form that kings under domination and their subjects had to copy and recite, where they called down on themselves an array of curses if they failed to show exclusive loyalty – "love" in the treaties – toward the Assyrian king. These treaties followed a standard format where the vassal lord, the Assyrian king, reminded his vassal king and that king's people of their obligations toward him. A typical treaty started with a preamble and historical prologue, where the Assyrian king introduced himself and reminded the vassal people of the things he had done on their behalf. Next was the core of the treaty, the requirement by the Assyrian king for the vassal to give exclusive allegiance – "love" – to him. This was followed by a set of instructions on how the vassal king was to express this exclusive allegiance/love. The treaty concluded with elements designed

Proverbs and Deuteronomy

Compare and contrast:

Prov 22:28	Deut 19:14
Do not ever move a boundary marker which your fathers made.	Do not move a boundary marker which earlier generations set **In the inheritance which Yahweh your God is giving you to inherit.**

basics Deuteronomy (and the Ten Commandments)

Outline: farewell teaching of vassal treaty with Yahweh

I	Introduction of Yahweh's acts, Ten Commandments, and exhortations Deut	1:1–11:32
II	Central rules of the treaty with Yahweh (organized by the order of the Ten Commandments)	12:1–26:19
III	Means of remembrance and enforcement of the Treaty with Yahweh	27:1–31:29
IV	Moses's farewell	31:30–34:12

Date(s)

Late pre-exile and exile: Deuteronomy is a combination of an earlier, pre-exilic Deuteronomic lawbook and later, exilic additions to that lawbook. The Deuteronomic lawbook probably includes yet earlier northern materials, but these are impossible to identify precisely.

The Ten Commandments and Deuteronomy

The Ten Commandments in Deut 5:6–21 are classic teaching materials, short and easily memorized by using your fingers. Their form is similar to the "instruction" form found in Proverbs and other teachings. Like such instructions, the Ten Commandments are difficult to date. They almost certainly do not derive from Moses, but do represent many of Israel's deepest shared values.

The importance of these commandments in the book of Deuteronomy is reflected in the fact that the topics at the center of Deuteronomy (Deuteronomy 12–26) follow about the same order as the topics of the Ten Commandments found in Deuteronomy 5. In this sense, the Ten Commandments form the core of the Mosaic "teaching" given in Deuteronomy.

to enforce this set of stipulations: calling of witnesses to the agreement, curses for disobedience, provisions for copying and reading the treaty to the people, etc.

Several biblical texts follow parts of this vassal treaty form, but the book of Deuteronomy follows it almost exactly. Like the other treaties, Deuteronomy starts with a preamble and historical prologue, but now Yahweh is Israel's sovereign lord who has given Israel its land. Deuteronomy resembles the Assyrian treaties in emphasizing the requirement of allegiance – "love" – that Israel is to offer, but now Israel must offer allegiance to Yahweh "with all [its/your] heart, life strength, and might" (Deut 6:4–6). The laws of Deuteronomy include prohibitions of treason against Yahweh (Deuteronomy 13) that resemble Assyrian prohibitions of treason against the Assyrian king. Finally, Deuteronomy, like the Assyrian treaties, concludes with a call for witnesses (now "heaven and earth" 30:19; 31:28), blessings for obedience and curses for disobedience (28 and 29:9–28), and provision for the safekeeping, copying, and regular reading of the treaty (Deut 31:9–13, 24–6; also 17:18–19). Moreover, some of the curses in Deuteronomy 28 are

Overview: The Covenant Code and Deuteronomy

The laws below cover similar topics, but read a few and see how they treat these topics differently! Though Deuteronomy covers topics not found in the Covenant Code (Exod 20:22–23:33), most topics in the Covenant Code are covered in Deuteronomy. Deuteronomy is thought to be the later of the two.

Law about altars	Exod 20:22–6	Deut 12:13–28
Slave release laws	Exod 21:1–11	Deut 15:12–18
Cities of Asylum	Exod 21:12–14	Deut 19:1–13
Kidnapping	Exod 21:16	Deut 24:7
Consequences of sex with a virgin	Exod 22:16–17	Deut 22:28–9
Penalty for unlawful religious practices	Exod 22:18	Deut 18:9–14
Penalty for sacrifice to other gods	Exod 22:20	Deut 17:2–7
Prohibition of charging interest	Exod 22:25	Deut 23:19–20
Requirement to return a cloak taken as collateral	Exod 22:26–7	Deut 24:10–13
Requirement of first-born sons and livestock	Exod 22:29–30	Deut 15:19–23
Legal justice rules	Exod 23:2–8	Deut 16:18–20
Returning livestock	Exod 23:4–5	Deut 22:1–4
Prohibition of oppressing foreign workers	Exod 23:9	Deut 24:17–18
Sabbath year rules	Exod 23:10–11	Deut 15:1–11
Sabbath command	Exod 23:12	Deut 5:12–15
Pilgrimage festivals	Exod 23:14–17	Deut 16:1–17
Requirement to bring first fruits	Exod 23:19a	Deut 26:1–10
Not boiling a calf in its mother's milk	Exod 23:19b	Deut 14:21b

almost exact replicas of curses found in the treaties that the late eighth-century Assyrian king Sennacherib used to insure loyalty by his vassals to his successor.

Thus, in the wake of Assyrian oppression, it appears that the authors of the book of Deuteronomy envisioned Israel as in a vassal treaty relationship with Yahweh, their God. This was what "covenant" (Hebrew *berit*) with Yahweh meant to them. It was a formal relationship, sealed by blessings and curses. Its core was a requirement of exclusive allegiance to a lord. Yet the authors of Deuteronomy made a revolutionary shift vis-à-vis the vassal treaties that they knew: where before Judah had to be exclusively obedient to the Assyrian king, now they were to be exclusively faithful to Yahweh. Where before the Assyrian king was jealous and would tolerate no rivals, now Yahweh is depicted as jealous and intolerant of any rival gods. Before the people feared the invasion of the massive Assyrian army if they were disobedient. Now they faced direct divine punishment, the "curses of the treaty covenant" (Deut 29:20), if they failed to be faithful to the words of Deuteronomy. Thus when Josiah read some form of Deuteronomy to the people and led them in a covenant ceremony based on it (2 Kgs 23:1–3//2 Chr 34:29–31), he was moving them from one vassal relationship to another. Previously they had known subjugation to Assyria by means of written vassal treaties. Now Josiah was leading them – by means of an early written edition of Deuteronomy – into a vassal relationship with Yahweh.

MORE ON METHOD: POSTCOLONIAL CRITICISM

The term "**postcolonial criticism**" embraces a wide range of approaches that look at how texts and their interpretations are interrelated with structures of colonial domination. Within biblical studies it has taken two main forms.

First, many scholars have taken categories developed in earlier postcolonial studies of contemporary literature and used those categories to illuminate the production of ancient biblical literature in relation to imperial domination. This chapter's discussion of Deuteronomy as an example of "hybridity" would be an example of this approach.

Second, other scholars have looked at how the Bible itself has been used as a tool for colonial domination. For more on this approach, see R. S. Sugirtharajah, *Postcolonial Criticism and Biblical Interpretation* (New York: Oxford University Press, 2002).

We will never know the precise manner in which some yet older form of Deuteronomy was crafted into an Assyrian-like vassal treaty, but scholars do know analogies to this overall process. In particular, postcolonial theorists have uncovered many examples of writers, artists, and others who appropriate the cultural forms of their former oppressors in the process of trying to develop their own, *post*colonial expressions. For example, even after India achieved independence from Britain in 1947, Indian writers developed a rich tradition of distinctively Indian novels in English. In doing so, they adopted their colonial oppressor's language and an originally non-Indian cultural form, the novel. Yet they used these tools to build a distinctively Indian literature. This is but one example of the way that peoples who must redefine themselves in the wake of oppression often find it helpful to revise and even invert the cultural forms of their former oppressors. Postcolonial theorists refer to this process of adaptation and inversion of oppressors' cultural forms as "**hybridity**." This concept will come up again in this *Introduction* because it is useful in understanding how many biblical texts were formed in relation to non-biblical textual forms.

For now, it is important to recognize that Deuteronomy, this hybrid vassal treaty with God, presents itself as the most important "teaching" Israel could ever have. It bears the label of "Torah," which is the Hebrew equivalent of "teaching," and the book names numerous ways in which the people of Israel are to insure that this Torah/teaching is foremost in their hearts and minds. They are to memorize this Torah's words

---

basics Book of Joshua

Outline: the conquest and settlement of the promised land

I	Exodus-like, holy war conquest	1–12
II	Distribution of the land	13–22
III	Joshua's covenantal farewell	23–4

Date Late pre-exilic (especially Joshua 1–12) and exilic/post-exilic (13–24).

Theme Though the book of Joshua starts with an apparent total conquest of the land (Josh 11:23) in fulfillment of Yahweh's command (Deuteronomy 7), chapters 13–22 hint that the conquest was *incomplete* (Josh 13:1–7; 15:63; 16:10; 17:12–13) and show a diversity in the make-up of the people that threatens to split them by the end (Joshua 22). This, then, is the context for Joshua's exhortations to the people in Joshua 23 and 24, where he urges them to avoid the worship practices of the foreign peoples among them (Josh 23:5–13; 24:14–15). Instead, they should, like Joshua, be devoted to Yahweh and the book of the Torah (Josh 23:6; 24:26; compare Josh 1:7–8).

More information: Joshua and Moses Joshua is Moses's appointed successor in Deuteronomy (Deuteronomy 31), and he is presented in the book of Joshua as a second Moses. Like Moses, he presides over the people crossing water "on dry ground" (Joshua 3–4; compare Exodus 14), and he celebrates a Passover preceded by a circumcision of the new generation of males who were born in the wilderness (Joshua 5; compare Exodus 12). In these and other ways, Joshua is presented as the last semi-Mosaic leader before things fall apart during the time of the judges.

(Deut 6:6; 11:18), recite them constantly to their children (Deut 6:7; 11:19), bind copies of Torah commands on the entryways of their houses and on their bodies (Deut 6:8–9; 11:20), make sure that the king reads and obeys this Torah/teaching constantly (Deut 17:18–20), and carefully copy the Torah and read it aloud to the entire community (Deut 31:11–13). As the Assyrian vassal treaty used some of the same means to instill absolute loyalty to the king of Assyria, so also Deuteronomy uses a yet fuller array of these strategies to insure memorization of this Torah/teaching and loyalty to Yahweh alone.

The Deuteronomistic History (Deuteronomy–2 Kings)

READING
Joshua 1–2, 11; 23–4; Judges 1–2; 1 Samuel 12; 1 Kings 8; 2 Kings 17, 22–3. Review readings from Judges–2 Kings done for earlier chapters. (Note: Deuteronomy is also part of the Deuteronomistic history, but was read in relation to the preceding section.)

EXERCISE
Pick some of the texts above and make a list of the chapters and verses in those texts where you see the following themes (from Deuteronomy) appear: (1) the importance of faithfulness to the LORD (Yahweh) alone; (2) the belief that Yahweh will punish unfaithfulness; (3) the importance of pure worship and sacrifice in only one place; and/or (4) hostility toward foreigners and/or foreign influence.

Most scholars agree that Deuteronomy originally stood at the beginning of a larger history that is termed the "**Deuteronomistic history**" and included the books of Deuteronomy, Joshua, Judges, 1 and 2 Samuel, and 1 and 2 Kings. Though Deuteronomy includes Moses's reviews of stories now in Exodus and Numbers, these reviews are probably there because those books did not yet stand before Deuteronomy as part of a broader Pentateuch. Deuteronomy was the starting point of a larger whole. The rest of that whole is found in the **books of the former prophets:** Joshua, Judges, Samuel and Kings. These books often refer back to the Torah in Deuteronomy (examples are Josh 1:7–8 and 2 Kgs 23:24–5). Moreover, as you saw in doing the exercise at the outset of this section, these books continue many of the values seen at the heart of Deuteronomy: the importance of faithfulness to Yahweh alone, the belief that Yahweh will punish unfaithfulness, the importance of pure worship and sacrifice in only one place, and hostility toward foreigners and/or foreign influence. These are stipulations of the Deuteronomic vassal treaty with Yahweh. The books of the former prophets describe the extent to which the kings and people of Israel were faithful or unfaithful to these stipulations.

basics | **Book of Judges**

Outline: decline of order/ obedience in the time of judges	I Prologue: incomplete conquest and overview of 1:1–3:6 disobedience after Joshua
	
	 II Specifics on spiraling chaos: 3:7–21:25
	     A Worsening judges: Othniel to Samson 3:7–16:31
	     B People on their own with no king 17:1–21:25

Date	Pre-exilic and exilic/post-exilic.
Theme	Though Judges includes older traditions, they have been radically adapted to fit a theological framework that expresses the values of Deuteronomy. The shape of this framework is given in a narrative overview (Judg 2:11–22) that follows the death of Joshua (Josh 2:6–10). We hear in this text of a recurring cycle of punishment and rescue that is repeated in many of the following chapters.: 1 Israel disobeys Yahweh and his commands. 2 Yahweh lets them be conquered by a foreign people. 3 They cry out and Yahweh sends a judge to deliver them. 4 The judge dies, and the people start disobeying again. The stories in Judg 3:7–16:31 roughly follow this framework, but they also diverge in minor ways that show a spiraling decline of order and obedience in Israel. Moreover, the judges progress from unblemished figures, such as Othniel and Deborah, to less impressive leaders, such as Jephthah and Samson. The final chapters, Judges 17–21, show how bad things get when the people are without a king and "do what is right in their own eyes" (Judg 17:6; 21:25).

It is important to realize, however, that the authors of these historical books drew on older traditions in the process of writing a history of Israel's faithfulness and unfaithfulness. The book of Joshua frames older stories of local military victories with new descriptions of total destruction of all Canaanites in the land (Joshua 11–12), certifying that Israel had taken the land just as Yahweh commanded it in Deuteronomy (Deuteronomy 7). The book of Judges radically adapts older texts about the tribes of Israel – such as the song of Deborah – so that they now fit into a cyclical pattern of the people forgetting to be faithful to Yahweh, Yahweh letting them fall into oppression, the people crying out, and Yahweh rescuing them. The books of Samuel contain large blocks of probable older compositions, such as an "ark narrative" (1 Sam 4:1–7:1; 2 Sam 6) and a "**succession narrative**" (2 Samuel 9–20 along with 1 Kings 1–2) that may have been written around the time of David and Solomon. To these and other older traditions the authors of Samuel added their own perspective on the monarchy in 1 Samuel 12, and on parts of the oracle to David in 2 Samuel 7:1–16. Finally, one finds a similar combination of old and new in the books of Kings. Here the authors cite earlier books such as the "Acts of Solomon" (1 Kgs 11:41), the "Annals of the Kings of Israel" (1 Kgs 14:19; 15:31; etc.) and the "Annals of the Kings of Judah" (1 Kgs 14:29; 15:7, 23; etc.). Yet they put their own stamp on the whole, particularly through inserting major theological speeches at important junctures. These speeches concern themes such as the dedication of the temple (1 Kings 8), the theological rationale for the destruction of the northern kingdom (2 Kings 17), and Josiah's reform and attempt to reunite the north and south in a kingdom centered on Jerusalem (2 Kings 22–3). As you saw in the exercise that opened this section, these and other speeches express central values seen in the book of Deuteronomy. Such close links to and dependence on Deuteronomy are what lead scholars to call these materials "**Deuteronomistic**."

basics	**Books of Samuel**	
Outline: the beginnings of the Davidic kingship (1–2 Samuel)	I Transitions to kingship	1 Samuel 1–31
	A Samuel: a judge who anointed kings	1 Samuel 1–8
	B Samuel to Saul: a failed king	1 Samuel 9–15
	C Saul to David: the dynastic founder	1 Samuel 16–31
	II David's reign as Israel's first king	2 Samuel 1–24
Date	Late pre-exile and exile, with some early pre-exilic sources.	
Theme	This book spread over two scrolls (1 and 2 Samuel) presents an ambivalent picture of the origins of the monarchy. The reign of David is presented as an improvement on that of Saul. Nevertheless, in episodes such as the affair with Bathsheba and murder of her husband (2 Samuel 11–12), David proves to have flaws of his own. Deuteronomistic speeches at points such as 1 Samuel 12 and 2 Samuel 7 present the move to the Davidic monarchy as a negative development, but one that Yahweh accepted. Such Deuteronomistic speeches reflect the much lower monarchal expectations of scribes looking back at three centuries of Davidic rule.	

This chapter focuses on these historical books because there are signs that they originally concluded with Josiah's reform. If so, then the Deuteronomistic history originally started with the Deuteronomic Torah and ended with Josiah's implementation of Deuteronomy in his reform, Huldah's prediction that he would die in peace, and a praise of him that echoes Deut 6:4–5 (2 Kgs 23:25). As it turned out, Josiah did not

basics Books of Kings

Outline: obedience and sin in the history of the monarchies

I	Solomon's rule: devotion and sin	1 Kings 1–11
II	Divided monarchy: northern sin and southern obedience and sin	1 Kings 12–2 Kings 17
III	Decline of Judah: Hezekiah to exile	2 Kings 18–24

Date

Pre-exilic edition and exilic/post-exilic redaction.

Theme

The books of Kings were divided for space reasons across two scrolls, 1 and 2 Kings, but they tell one story of the rise and fall of the monarchy of Israel, from Solomon to the exile. The story starts with Solomon's building of the Temple in Jerusalem (1 Kings 6–8), which becomes the one place that Israel is allowed to sacrifice, according to the law in Deuteronomy (Deut 12:13–28). The narrative goes on, however, to describe Solomon's fall toward disobedience (1 Kings 11), which is quickly followed by the revolt of the northern tribes and their building of their own altars outside Jerusalem (1 Kings 12).

From then on, each king of Israel and Judah is measured by his faithfulness to the commands in Deuteronomy to worship Yahweh alone and to sacrifice at only one place. The destruction of the Israelite monarchy is explained by the failure of Israel and its kings to follow these rules (2 Kings 17). Despite some ideal leaders, such as Hezekiah and Josiah, most kings in Judah likewise fail. From the perspective of Kings, the final result of such disobedience of Deuteronomic laws is the destruction of Jerusalem and the exile (2 Kings 24).

More information: the pre-exilic and exilic editions of Kings

As we have them now, the books of Kings are late compositions that explain the destruction of the north and exile of the south as resulting from disobedience of the law of Deuteronomy. Yet there are numerous signs that these books are only the latest stage of a long process of revision and growth. Royal narratives elsewhere in the ancient Near East were typically written in the royal court to promote the king. An earlier, pre-exilic version of these books may have ended with Josiah, or even Hezekiah. Rather than explaining disaster, such earlier versions promoted the initiatives of those kings. Only later were these Hezekian and/or Josianic versions modified to explain the destruction of the kingship itself.

die in peace, as we see in a later expansion of this history starting in 2 Kgs 23:29. Nevertheless, the major narrative arc of the Deuteronomistic history leads from Deuteronomy on the one end to Josiah's implementation of Deuteronomy on the other. This formed the scope of the pre-exilic edition of the Deuteronomistic history. Only later did editors long after Josiah's time extend this history from Josiah's (violent) death to the destruction of Jerusalem and exile of its inhabitants. This expanded exilic edition of the Deuteronomistic history will be discussed in Chapter 9 of this *Introduction*.

In the present context we should view much of Deuteronomy through 2 Kings as a pre-exilic history of Israel and Judah that was written in the wake of decades of oppression by Assyria. Like Deuteronomy, this history is an example of hybridity. It seems to represent a nationalistic appropriation by Josiah's scribes of a form of history writing that was used in the Assyrian empire to instill pro-royal sympathies in leadership near and far. Starting in the tenth century, both Babylonian and Assyrian educational centers started to rely more and more on epics and narratives that celebrated certain past kings such as Sargon as ideals of kingship, while denigrating others. We also see the increasing use of longer histories of kings, histories that included notes about their major achievements. Some Judean officials probably were required to memorize such royal narratives and histories during the times of Hezekiah and Manasseh. Yet there are crucial differences between those Mesopotamian histories and the Deuteronomistic history in the Bible. Rather than insuring loyalty to a foreign king, the Deuteronomistic history was aimed at insuring loyalty to Yahweh alone. As part of this, it aimed to support Josiah's move from worship of multiple deities at multiple places to pure worship of Yahweh alone in Jerusalem.

This retelling of Judah's story is analogous to the kind of retelling of individual stories that many people do on the other side of a major crisis. A person may tell their own life story one way for a long time, and then something happens – divorce, a near-death experience, struggle with addiction, or another crisis – that makes them realize that some things that they thought were important were not, and other things that they had ignored were very, very important. In light of this experience, that person will tell their life story differently. For example, someone recovering from addiction might find healing through telling others in self-help groups about his or her struggle with addiction, what happened to make him or her seek recovery, and what things are like now. Indeed, many alcoholics and other addicts have found the power to stay free of their addiction by telling and retelling their new stories of addiction and recovery.

Building on this analogy, the Deuteronomistic history might be viewed as ancient Judah's equivalent to this sort of retelling of a personal story. Judah was on the other side of the crisis of Assyrian oppression, and the retelling of its story was aimed at gaining and maintaining freedom from Torah disobedience and oppression by foreign powers. Like someone retelling their own personal story, this retelling of Israel's story incorporates earlier elements, such as the succession narrative or older lists of kings and their years of rule. But the retelling as a whole is now reframed in light of the experience of liberation from Assyria. It is a retelling of the people's history that is completely reoriented toward their new chance to achieve permanent freedom through obedience to Yahweh's Torah.

Each book of the Deuteronomistic history now reflects central themes of that Torah, from hostility to foreign influence to valuing of pure and centralized worship of Yahweh alone. Much like the memorizing of the Torah in Deuteronomy, this retelling of the people's story was aimed at reshaping the communal soul of Israel. Previously, literate Israelites would have memorized other historical traditions (e.g. the succession narrative). As mentioned before, some officials during the time of Hezekiah and Manasseh may even have learned pro-royal Mesopotamian historical traditions. But this Deuteronomistic history represented a new form of cultural memory, aimed at replacing its predecessors. It grounded Josiah's reform with an overview of life in the land that extended from the Deuteronomic Torah on the one hand to Josiah's reform on the other.

The Conquest and Ancient Holy War

The books of Deuteronomy and Joshua describe Israel as conquering all of Canaan and destroying *all* of its inhabitants (Deuteronomy 7; Joshua 1–11). This is a description of an ancient "holy war" (Hebrew *herem*); that is, a sacred war engaged in not for purposes of gaining booty or wives, but at divine command. Biblical rules for the conduct of such sacred wars are found particularly in Deuteronomy 20. One gruesome mark of the "not-for-profit" character of such a war was the destruction of all living beings, human and animal, of the conquered people.

We see this idea outside Israel as well. One example is found in the ninth-century inscription of King Mesha of Moab. He describes a holy war commanded by his god, Chemosh, against a town in Israel called Nebo.

At that time, Chemosh said to me, "Go, take Nebo from Israel." So I deployed my soldiers at night and attacked Nebo from dawn until noon. I won a great victory and I sacrificed seven thousand men, women and children from Nebo to Chemosh as I had vowed I would do. (Translation: *OT Parallels, 168–9*)

One key difference between this inscription and the biblical book of Joshua is that the Mesha text is reporting on a recent killing of people that actually happened. In contrast, Joshua (along with Deuteronomy) draws on the concept of "holy war" to imaginatively depict a conquest centuries before that probably never happened in this way.

All this can give us a new perspective on some of the most troubling parts of the Deuteronomistic history, such as its report of a divine command to eliminate all foreigners in the land (Deuteronomy 7) and description of the Israelites' fulfillment of that command, killing all Canaanites (Josh 10:40–2; 11:16–23). For many people, these are some of the most disturbing texts in the Bible, and they have been used in destructive ways to justify the killing or displacement of Native Americans and others.

Yet as we read these texts in Joshua, we should realize that they are not historically factual reports of the Israelites' total conquest of the land. (The Bible itself contains traditions to the contrary, such as the overview in Judges 1 of non-Israelites still in the land.) Rather, these narratives were designed to help the people of Josiah's time believe in a God who could help them succeed in a battle against all odds. Like the rest of the Deuteronomistic history, the conquest stories were written with the idea that Judah's past oppression was caused by its failure to obey Yahweh's Torah and eliminate foreign influence. Writing from this perspective, the authors of Joshua crafted a narrative that could empower Judah of Josiah's time to eliminate every trace of foreign influence that might cause them to fall back into oppression. Like many disempowered peoples, these authors wanted a God who could fight and fight successfully on their behalf. Perhaps Josiah even trusted the help of such a warrior God in his fatal confrontation with the Egyptian Pharaoh (2 Kgs 23:29–30//2 Chr 35:20–6). In any case, contemporary readers who interpret these texts from a position of privilege should recognize their dangers, but should also note how differently such warlike texts can be perceived by people fighting for liberation against more powerful foes.

Deuteronomy 6:4–9

FOCUS TEXT

Having completed an overview, let us turn now to a specific text that exemplifies many of the central dynamics of seventh-century biblical literature, Deut 6:4–9. Many scholars have seen in this text a possible beginning of an early form of Deuteronomy, before later authors added the review of history in Deuteronomy 1–3, the teaching in Deuteronomy 4, and the Ten Commandments in Deuteronomy 5. Whether or not Deut 6:4–9 started an early form of the book, it certainly sums up many of its major themes, along with themes that play a major role in the rest of the Deuteronomistic history.

The first sentence is marked off in the Hebrew of the Masoretic text tradition by unusually large final letters at the end of its first and last words. Such letters are often used elsewhere in the Bible to mark the outset of a biblical book (examples are found in Genesis, Proverbs, Chronicles) or an important point in a biblical book. Here they mark the beginning of what is known in Judaism as the "Shema," named after the first Hebrew word in the verse: *shema* – "Hear!" The rest of the sentence can be translated in two ways. One could translate it, "Hear, oh Israel, Yahweh is our God, Yahweh alone." This translation emphasizes that Israel should have one and only one God. The other, equally correct translation (in terms of the Hebrew) is, "Hear, oh Israel, that Yahweh, our God, is one Yahweh." We know from earlier inscriptions that earlier Judeans and Israelites worshiped different forms of Yahweh, "Yahweh from Teman" or "Yahweh from Samaria." According to this translation of Deut 6:4, such local manifestations of Yahweh are false. The Yahweh who belongs to Israel is one and only one deity. This would reinforce Josiah's push to centralize and standardize worship of Yahweh. Both translations link with other traditions in Deuteronomy and the Deuteronomistic history. Perhaps part of the power of this verse was its capacity to express both meanings.

The next verse expresses a core commandment in Deuteronomy and beyond. The people are to "love" God with all that they are and have. The list is often translated as "all your heart, soul and might" (NRSV) or the like, but these English words are a pale reflection of the Hebrew. The first word in the series, *lebab*, is not just the "heart," but also the "mind." For ancient Israel and other ancient Near Eastern peoples, the "heart" and "mind" were connected, not distinct as they so often are in Western culture. The second word that is often translated as "soul," Hebrew *nephesh*, actually refers to the vital life strength that infuses an entire person. It is the power that distinguishes a living person from a corpse, that powers desire, thought, will, and movement. Deut 6:4 calls on all Israel to devote that entire life strength to love of Yahweh. Finally, the word often translated as "might," Hebrew *meod*, refers to power or strength. Most often it appears in the Bible as an adverb, meaning "very." It may serve a similar function in this series in Deut 6:5, emphasizing how very much Israel must "love Yahweh, your God," with all Israel's heart/mind and life strength.

This call to love connects to other texts, both inside and outside the Bible. One of the places in the Bible outside the Deuteronomistic history where we see a similar description of someone "loving" another with their "life strength" (*nephesh*) is the Song of Songs. Several times the woman in the Song of Songs describes her lover as the one whom her "life strength loves" (Song 1:7; 3:1–4). Whether or not one believes that the Song of Songs pre-dates Deuteronomy, the author of this text in Deuteronomy probably expanded on this more general expression for a lover found in ancient love poetry. Where such ancient love poetry spoke of one's love as the one whom one's "life strength" loved, the author of this text speaks of love with one's "whole heart/mind, life strength, and power." Furthermore, similar to Hosea (which also shows possible links to ancient love poetry), this expanded description of love is focused on the people's love of Yahweh, rather than on one human's love for another.

We see this expanded version of the description of love at one other, strategic location in the Deuteronomistic history, the description of Josiah at what would have been the conclusion of a Josianic edition of the Deuteronomistic history:

> Before Josiah there was no king like him who turned to Yahweh with all his heart/ mind, all his life strength, and all his power, in accordance with the Torah of Moses, and after him there was never another like him. (2 Kgs 23:25)

This is the highest praise given any king in any part of the Deuteronomistic history. It marks Josiah as the superlative example of a king who followed the law of the king seen in Deut 17:14–20, which specifies that the king must study and follow the "Torah" as he leads his people in faithfulness. Later authors added material after this text to explain why the exile still happened despite Josiah's virtues (2 Kgs 23:26–7), but that does not appear to be in view here. Nor does Josiah's strange and seemingly pointless death at the hands of the Egyptians fit with the preceding materials about him (2 Kgs 23:29–30). Rather, this final evaluation of Josiah's reign in 2 Kgs 23:25 concludes a narrative arc that began with the call to "love" in Deut 6:4–5.

This call to "love" in Deut 6:5 also connects, however, to yet another discourse, and that is the Assyrian requirement that vassal kings and their people "love" the Assyrian king. In this case, the "love" required was far from the sort of passionate love envisioned in love poetry like the Song of Songs. Rather, the "love" – Akkadian *ramu* – required in Assyrian treaties was faithful obedience to the Assyrian king: paying tribute, not joining alliances with other nations against Assyria, reporting traitors and extraditing them to Assyria, etc. As a hybrid response to this experience of Assyrian domination, Deuteronomy 6:5 and the rest of the Deuteronomistic history reflect this dimension of "love" as well. But now Israel is to show faithful obedience to Yahweh and Yahweh alone. The people must not follow other gods (//alliances), and they must report and try prophets who encourage betrayal of Yahweh (//traitors). Thus the "love" envisioned in Deuteronomy is not a passionate or romantic emotion that one feels at one time and might not feel at another. It is a basic attitude of loyalty and devotion to one far more powerful than one's self; in this case, Yahweh, the god of Israel. Deut 6:5 represents a basic reorientation of such loyalty and devotion from the Assyrian king to Yahweh in the wake of the collapse of Assyrian empire.

The rest of the passage, Deut 6:6–9, aims to reinforce that reorientation through making sure that the people internalize the commands of Yahweh that are expressed in the Torah. Wisdom texts, such as the adaptation of the Instruction of Amenemope in Prov 22:17–18 (also Prov 3:3 and 7:3), urged the student to memorize the sayings of the teacher and recite them – "establish them firmly on your lips." The Torah of Moses in Deuteronomy represents a new form of "wisdom," which likewise should be memorized – "put on your heart/mind" (Deut 6:6) – and recited constantly in the presence of one's children, sitting at home, going on one's way, lying down and getting up (Deut 6:7). This constant repetition of the words of the Torah is not just aimed at reinforcing the loyalty of adult Israelites, but it is also intended to teach children the Torah as well, almost like a language that they hear spoken by parents at home. As if this were not enough, the words of Yahweh's commandments are also supposed to be worn on the bodies of Israelites and inscribed on their doorways and gates. Every aspect of their lives is to reflect Yahweh's commands, particularly the call to honor one and only one God, Yahweh, and love Yahweh with all one's heart/mind, life strength, and power (Deut 6:4–5).

Over the long haul, these injunctions appear to have been effective, since this passage ended up being one of the most important texts in both Judaism and Christianity. A version of this command – "you shall love the Lord, your God, with all your heart, your soul, and your mind/energy" – is named as the greatest commandment of all by Jesus in the Christian gospel of Mark and later parallels to it in Matthew and Luke (Mark 12:28–9//Matt 22:34–7; Luke 10:25–7). This corresponds to the honoring of this command in Judaism as one of the holiest of all. Jews are required to recite this command and then others in Deut 11:13–21 (more on love and memorization) and Num 15:37–41 (on wearing fringes) twice a day, when rising and when going to bed. The great Jewish rabbi, Akiba, is reputed to have died at the hands of the Romans with the words of the Shema on his lips, and Jewish martyrs in later centuries have followed his example, reciting Deut 6:4 and following verses while dying during medieval riots associated with the crusades, in the Spanish inquisition, and in Nazi gas chambers. Ironically and tragically, many of these Jewish martyrs have died at Christian hands while reciting what Christians recognized as the "greatest commandment." Deut 6:4–5 has been important in both traditions, but that has not prevented centuries of deplorable Christian persecution of Jews.

CHAPTER SEVEN REVIEW

1. Know the meaning and significance of the following terms discussed in this chapter:
- books of the former prophets
- Deuteronomistic
- Deuteronomistic history
- hybridity
- Josiah's reform
- succession narrative

2. What is a vassal treaty and what are its major parts? How is the book of Deuteronomy similar to and yet different from a vassal treaty?

3. What is postcolonial criticism and what are two different ways in which biblical scholars draw on or engage it? What is an example of the use of postcolonial criticism to analyze Deuteronomy and the Deuteronomistic history?

4. Compare any of the following sets of laws that are parallel between Deuteronomy and the Covenant Code: altar, judges, slavery, pilgrimage festivals. What do the new elements in the laws of Deuteronomy tell us about the book's distinctive values?

5. How is the pre-exilic edition of the Deuteronomistic history different from the exilic edition?

6. What did DeWette hypothesize about Josiah's lawbook? When and why?

7. What is the ancient concept of "holy war"? How does this concept function in the Deuteronomistic history?

RESOURCES FOR FURTHER STUDY

Discussion of the Deuteronomistic history as a whole

Nelson, Richard D. *The Historical Books.* Interpreting Biblical Texts. Nashville: Abingdon, 1998.

Weinfeld, Moshe. *Deuteronomy and the Deuteronomic History.* Oxford: Clarendon Press, 1972.

Deuteronomy

Mayes, A. D. H. *Deuteronomy.* New Century Bible. Greenwood, SC: Attic Press, 1979.

Miller, Patrick. *Deuteronomy.* Interpretation. Louisville, KY: John Knox Press, 1990.

Tigay, Jeffrey. *Deuteronomy.* Philadelphia: Jewish Publication Society, 1996.

Joshua and Judges

See "Resources for Further Study" in Chapter 2.

1 and 2 Samuel

McCarter, P. Kyle. *I Samuel: A New Translation; II Samuel: A New Translation.* Anchor Bible. Garden City: Doubleday, 1980.

1 and 2 Kings

DeVries, Simon. *1 Kings.* Word Biblical Commentary, no. 12. Waco, TX: Word Books, 1985.

Gray, John. *I & II Kings* (2nd revised edition). Old Testament Library. Philadelphia: Westminster Press, 1970.

Nelson, Richard. *First and Second Kings.* Interpretation. Atlanta: John Knox Press, 1987.

CHAPTER 8

PROPHECY IN THE TRANSITION FROM ASSYRIAN TO BABYLONIAN DOMINATION

Chapter Outline

CHAPTER OVERVIEW

In this chapter we continue our look at the seventh century through discussing three prophets from that period. Though two of these prophets, Nahum and Zephaniah, are often overlooked by readers of the Hebrew Bible, they provide helpful insight into Judah just before and during the time of Josiah's reform. The third prophet to be discussed is Jeremiah, another "major prophet," to whom one of the largest books in the Hebrew Bible is devoted. As we will see, this is only partly due to the fact that Jeremiah had a long career, spanning from Josiah's reform until the beginning of Judah's exile in Babylon. The other reason that his book is long is that it was expanded over time by some of the same scribes who preserved and expanded the Deuteronomistic history. Apparently Jeremiah's unrelenting message of doom, though unpopular in his day, proved especially powerful to later generations who found it helpful in understanding their experiences of oppression and exile. In contrast, Nahum's and Zephaniah's more comforting messages did not receive the same attention and expansion.

Nahum

The first prophet to be discussed, Nahum, gives us a sense of the hostility toward Assyria that was felt by Judeans around the time of Josiah. Where some prophetic books are made up in part by oracles against various nations – examples are Isaiah 12–23, Jeremiah 46–51, and Ezekiel 25–32 – *all* of Nahum is devoted to oracles against *one* nation: Assyria. The book appears to have been written during Josiah's reign. Assyria was in decline and the Babylonians and Medes were about to destroy Assyria's capital, Nineveh, in 612 BCE. The reading from Nahum 3 powerfully expresses the rage against the brutal Assyrian empire after decades of Assyrian oppression. Building on older prophetic uses of the metaphor of the adulterous female (such as in Hosea), Nahum envisions Nineveh as a sexually promiscuous woman about to be punished for her sinfulness through exposure, isolation, and destruction (3:5–7). The impetus behind this vicious imagery is given at the end of the poem:

READING
Nahum 3.

> There is no easing of your [Nineveh's] pain,
>   your wound is fatal,
> All who hear the report of you,
>   Clap their hands in celebration.
> For who has escaped your continual cruelty? (Nah 3:19)

The Assyrian empire had cultivated a reputation for cruelty in an attempt to terrorize its vassals into submission. Here we see the flip side of it. Having endured such cruelty and terror for so long, dominated nations such as Judah had a deep store of anger toward Assyria that powered the celebration of Assyria's destruction in Nahum. People who have not experienced such long-term oppression by an empire are often baffled by such rage, seen even now in anti-American sentiments in the Arab world and elsewhere. Yet such rage helps explain the deep and persistent anti-foreign sentiment that runs through so much of the Deuteronomistic history.

basics Book of Nahum

Outline:
proclamation
of the end of
Assyrian Nineveh

I	Hymn: Yahweh, destroyer of oppressors	1
II	Taunt song: destruction of Nineveh	2–3

Themes

Though the poem in Nahum 2–3 celebrates the downfall of a specific imperial city, Nineveh, the poem at the outset makes this book into a more general celebration of Yahweh's ability to destroy imperial oppressors and restore the oppressed. For the later revisers of this book, the destruction of Nineveh was but one demonstration of Yahweh's power to destroy oppressive empires.

Zephaniah

READING
Zephaniah 1.

Our second seventh-century prophet, Zephaniah, is dated to the reign of Josiah and gives us a window into the time before his reform. Zephaniah proclaims Yahweh's irreversible judgment, a "day of Yahweh," against Judah and Jerusalem for impure cultic practices: worship of Baal and heavenly objects, swearing by the god of Ammon (Milkom), and failure to seek Yahweh (Zeph 1:4–6). These are the sorts of practices that Josiah stopped during his reform, but they were popular up to that point. (Indeed, Manasseh, Josiah's grandfather, is said to have restored many of these practices after Hezekiah's earlier reform, and they probably continued during the early years of Josiah's reign as a boy king – he was anointed at age 8.) But Zephaniah proclaims that Yahweh is about to destroy the officials and royalty who promote such impure worship. Echoing the anti-foreign sentiment we saw in Nahum, Zephaniah says that "the officials and king's sons who wear foreign clothes" are about to bear the brunt of Yahweh's judgment. Where others might think of the "**Day of Yahweh**" as a time when Yahweh comes to rescue the people, Zephaniah (Zeph 1:7–2:2) – echoing Amos (Amos 5:18–20) – proclaims that this "Day of Yahweh" will be a time of great punishment and sorrow.

basics   Book of Zephaniah

Outline:
judgment and
exhortation to
Jerusalem

I	Announcement: "Day of Yahweh" against Judah	1:2–18
II	Exhortation to repentance	2:1–3:20
	A Call for repentance amidst judgment of nations	2:1–3:8
	B Reason for repentance: impending restoration	3:9–20

Themes   This book provides another example of how an earlier prophet's words of judgment (e.g. Zeph 1:2–18) now introduce words of hope for later Judeans. It is difficult to know which words in the book actually addressed people of the time of Josiah and how they were received. What is clear is that Zephaniah's earlier words are now part of a prophetic book relevant to later Judeans. It teaches the need for people in God's holy city, Jerusalem, to repent in light of Yahweh's judgment of other empires.

To be sure, like the book of Isaiah, the book of Zephaniah now contains promises of hope, promises that were probably added during the exilic and later periods. The second chapter is a call to repentance (2:1–3) in light of Yahweh's punishment of other nations (2:4–15), and the third chapter features a series of promises of salvation that much resemble later prophecies (3:9–20). These probable later materials show how later readers of Zephaniah fit his words into a broader picture of hope for exiles and later returnees from exile, while the earlier materials in Zephaniah 1 give us insight into a Judah that stands on the eve of Josiah's reform.

Jeremiah

READING
Jeremiah 1:1–3:5; 7:1–15 (compare with Jeremiah 26); 20:7–18; 28 and 36.

EXERCISE
Rewrite Jeremiah's prophecy in Jer 7:1–15 so that it addresses a community important to you and its own form of belief in its invulnerability. Match sentence for sentence, image for image, metaphor for metaphor as much as you can. What would it be like to hear this message as a member of that community

Jeremiah's career probably overlapped those of Nahum and Zephaniah, but it continued well into the time of Josiah's reform and beyond. Like the book of Zephaniah, the book of Jeremiah contains critiques of the sorts of worship of other deities that Josiah eventually eliminated. Yet Jeremiah's early prophecy is distinguished from Zephaniah's in several ways.

First, Jeremiah's prophecy is directed at people in both north (Israel) and south (Judah), probably reflecting the push toward unification of north and south that we see in Josiah's reform. For example, in Jer 3:12–14, 19–23, Jeremiah receives a call to prophecy "to the north," and he calls people in the former kingdom of Israel to repent and come to Jerusalem. This northern focus is present in numerous parts of the book of Jeremiah.

Second, the speeches in Jer 2:2–3:11 that precede the Jer 3:12–23 prophecy to the north echo and intensify the husband-and-wife imagery that we saw in the northern prophet Hosea. As in Hosea, Jeremiah's Yahweh fondly remembers early times when Israel was his bride in the wilderness (Jer 2:2; see Hos 2:14–15). Jeremiah, like Hosea, sees the people's seeking of foreign alliances (2:18) and of other gods (2:10–11) as like a woman's sexual promiscuity (2:20–5, 33). Yet Jeremiah goes beyond Hosea, in his pictures of both his people's misdeeds and Yahweh's response to them. For Jeremiah, God's people has been like a woman with anyone anywhere, "on every high hill and under every green tree" (Jer 2:20; also 3:2), like a wild donkey in heat whose lust cannot be contained (Jer 2:24), like a woman so skilled in planning sexual rendezvous that she can teach the most wicked women new tricks (Jer 2:33). In response, Yahweh promises to permanently divorce her (Jer 3:1–5; contrast Hos 2:14–15). "Israel" has not admitted her guilt (3:13), and there is no independent future for her. Instead, Jeremiah urges her "children" (literally "sons") to reject their mother's ways and come south to Zion (3:14).

Looking more broadly, Jeremiah has harsh words for the south (Judah) as well as the north (Israel), and these words are directed against false worship, futile political alliances, injustice, and false prophecy of hope. These themes continue throughout the book. The critique of injustice starts in Jer 2:34, where the prophet – in a disturbing extension of the female metaphor for the people – claims that female Israel has "blood" on "her skirts," not menstrual blood but here the "blood of the innocent poor." Finally, a series of prophecies in Jer 23:9–22 attacks fellow prophets for reassuring those who do evil (23:14), announcing hope and security when there is no basis for it (23:16–17), and missing a crucial opportunity to help the people repent their evil and avoid destruction (23:21–2). Biographical narratives about Jeremiah, such as Jeremiah 28, continue this theme of conflict between him and other prophets.

Jeremiah seems to have grown ever more pessimistic about his people's prospects. Here we should recall that his career spanned the time from the high hopes of Josiah's reform to the total destruction of Jerusalem about thirty-five years later. Early in his career Jeremiah shared Josiah's focus on the importance of pure worship of Yahweh, and some have found affirmations by Jeremiah of Josiah's program of reunification of north and south in passages such as Jer 3:12–14, 19–23 (discussed above), and 30:18–21. Yet there is a tantalizing hint in a judgment speech in Jer 8:4–13 that Jeremiah rejected the authenticity of the Deuteronomic Torah that came to stand at the center of Josiah's reform:

> How can you say, "we are wise,
>   And we have the Torah of Yahweh,"
> When, in fact, the false pen of the scribes,
>   has made it into a lie?" (Jer 8:8)

For Jeremiah, the Torah of Moses – probably some form of Deuteronomy – is the product of contemporary authors, "scribes." It does not represent a truly ancient word. Though Jeremiah would later recognize Josiah as a king of justice in comparison with his son, Jehoiakim (Jer 22:15–16), in this central respect – the recognition of the authority of a form of Deuteronomy – he appears not to have been convinced by part of Josiah's reform.

While Jeremiah may have supported parts of Josiah's program, his relationship with Josiah's successors was resolutely bad. A particularly large number of his prophecies are associated with the time of Jehoiakim, who was appointed over Judah by the Egyptians on their way back from their fight with Babylon (2 Kgs 23:34–5). Early during Jehoiakim's reign, Jeremiah delivered a sermon against the Jerusalem Temple that is described twice in the book of Jeremiah, once in Jer 7:1–15 and again in Jeremiah 26. Both versions of this "Temple sermon" feature a frontal attack on Zion theology, especially the idea that Jerusalem and its Temple were invulnerable. To those who continually affirm "this is the temple of Yahweh, the temple of Yahweh, the temple of Yahweh," Jeremiah proclaims that Yahweh will make it a heap of ruins, much like the ruins of the ancient tribal sanctuary at Shiloh, where the ark of the covenant once was (Jer 7:14//26:6). Such a claim was virtual blasphemy to the people of the time, since the belief in Zion's invulnerability had been reinforced all the more in the wake of the Assyrian king Sennacherib's withdrawal from besieging Jerusalem during the time of Hezekiah. According to Jeremiah 26, the people were ready to kill Jeremiah for speaking such words. Nevertheless, some recalled that Micah had earlier proclaimed that "Zion shall be plowed as a field" (Jer 26:18; see Micah 3:12). Ultimately, Jeremiah was protected by Ahikam, the son of Josiah's former scribe, Shaphan (Jer 26:24).

Another biographical narrative, Jeremiah 36, preserves a fascinating picture of the delivery and writing of Jeremiah's prophecy. It describes how Jeremiah was commissioned by God in Jehoiakim's fourth year to write a scroll containing all of his oracles up to that point in hopes that Judah might hear it and repent (36:1–3). Nevertheless, when the scroll was read to Jehoiakim, he was not pleased with its contents. As each column of the scroll was read, the king cut it off and threw it into the fire. After this, Jeremiah received a commission to write "another scroll." So Baruch, Jeremiah's scribe, produced a new scroll with the words of the original one, along with "many words like them" (Jer 36:27–32). Many scholars believe that much of what is now chapters 1–25 of the book of Jeremiah are the remnants of that new scroll (see Jer 25:13). This scroll, like Isaiah's memoir of rejected prophecies a century earlier (Isaiah 6:1–8:16) and other prophetic writings, is another example of how the writing of biblical prophecies was prompted by the rejection of those prophecies in the prophet's own time.

Yet Jeremiah, partly because of his long career, appears to have experienced more than his share of rejection. Chapters 26–45 of Jeremiah contain biographical narratives that chronicle Jeremiah's difficult experiences, starting with his brush with execution after the Temple sermon (Jeremiah 26; cf. Jer 7:1–15), and continuing with episodes such as his battle with Hananiah over falsely hopeful prophecy (Jeremiah 28), the burning of his scroll (Jeremiah 36), his imprisonment during the Babylonian siege of Jerusalem as a possible traitor (Jeremiah 37), his being dumped in a cistern to die by opponents (Jeremiah 38), and finally his being carried off into Egypt by rebels against Babylonian rule (Jeremiah 43). Though these narratives about him postdate the prophet, they probably reflect his increasing isolation as he prophesied judgment throughout Judah's long slide from dreams of glory under Josiah to total destruction by the Babylonians.

The difficulty of Jeremiah's career is also reflected in a set of laments in the book where Jeremiah protests to God about the unfair job that God has given him. For example, in the lament assigned for this section, Jeremiah 20:7–18, the prophet describes being "taken advantage of" by God, who has required him to proclaim a harsh message that leads to his own rejection:

> O Yahweh you have seduced me, and I let myself be seduced.
>> You have overpowered me and won.
> I'm a laughingstock all day,
>> Everyone makes fun of me.

For every time I speak, I cry an alarm.
  I call out, "Violence and ruin."
For the word of Yahweh has become for me
  A cause of embarrassment and criticism all the time. (Jer 20:7–8)

Jeremiah goes on to say that he has no choice, because every time he tries to stop speaking God's message, the word becomes "like a burning fire raging in my bones; I cannot keep holding it in" (Jer 20:9). The lament continues and even reaches a fairly hopeful point, where Jeremiah envisions his eventual restoration and praises Yahweh for it (20:11–13), but then we hear another lament, perhaps originally a separate text, where he curses the day he was born and those who announced his birth (20:14–18). These and other laments chronicle the fact that Jeremiah's work was difficult and did not reach a happy ending (see also Jer 11:18–20; 12:1–6; 15:10–21; 17:14–18; 18:18–23).

The growth of the book of Jeremiah

Though Jeremiah's prophecy was rejected in his own time, his written words became important to later generations of Judeans. His prophecies of disaster appeared in a different light in the wake of the destruction of Jerusalem, removal of the monarchy, and exile of thousands of Judeans to Babylon. Baruch or a later author wrote biographical accounts about Jeremiah, and additional authors enriched the writings about Jeremiah with prose versions of Jeremiah's sayings.

basics	**Book of Jeremiah**		
Outline: (of the Masoretic Jeremiah)	I First scroll: oracles against Judah (and Israel)		1–25
	II Biography: Jeremiah's call for submission and hope		26–45
	III Oracles against foreign nations		46–51
	IV Historical appendix (adapted from 2 Kings)		52
Themes	The book of Jeremiah aims to make sense of the destruction of Jerusalem (described in the historical appendix, Jer 52) through looking back at Jeremiah's once unpopular prophecy of judgment and call for submission to the Babylon empire. In addition, it contains words of judgment on other nations and – particularly in the "book of consolation" in Jeremiah 31–2 – words of hope for Judah.		

In the case of Jeremiah, we are unusually lucky in having ancient manuscripts that reflect an earlier version of Jeremiah that is quite different from the one now translated in most Bibles. These ancient manuscripts – both old Hebrew manuscripts found near the Dead Sea (at Qumran) and an ancient Greek translation of manuscripts much like them, the Septuagint of Jeremiah – reflect a version of Jeremiah that was about one-eighth shorter than the standard Hebrew edition of Jeremiah (the Masoretic text translated in your Bible). Most scholars agree that this shorter version of Jeremiah was an earlier version of the book, before many words, phrases, and even longer passages (e.g. Jer 33:14–26; 39:4–13; etc.) were added to the book by later scribes. Moreover, this older version is quite differently organized from the standard – Masoretic text – version. It proceeds from the scroll of Jeremiah in 1–25 directly to the oracles against the nations (see Jeremiah 46–51 in your Bibles), and only then to the biographical narratives found in Jeremiah 26–45 and historical materials of Jeremiah 52. Apparently the Hebrew version of Jeremiah now found in the standard Jewish (Masoretic) Bible was produced by moving the oracles against the nations from their original position to a concluding position in the book (46–51). This meant that the biographical narratives about Jeremiah (26–45) now stood close to the sayings attributed to him (Jeremiah 1–25). This reorganization of the book of Jeremiah and the addition of one-eighth of its present material was done centuries after the time of Jeremiah, probably around the third and/or second century BCE.

Unfortunately, we have no manuscripts to help us trace the earlier history of the development of the book, but scholars do think that much of it was the creation, not of Jeremiah, but of exilic authors who were heavily influenced by the language and ideas of the book of Deuteronomy. That is why so many passages in Jeremiah, such as the version of the temple sermon found in Jeremiah 7, sound so much like the Deuteronomic Torah. Ironically, though Jeremiah himself appears to have rejected that Torah (Jer 8:8–9), these post-Jeremiah texts quote him as announcing Yahweh's judgment on those who reject God's "Torah" (e.g. Jer 26:4). Such associations with Deuteronomy have led scholars to speak of a "Deuteronomistic redaction" throughout the book. This exilic redaction starts with the description of Jeremiah's call in Jer 1:4–10 (compare with Isaiah 6 and Ezekiel 1–3) and includes many other texts across the rest of the book. We even see the incorporation into the book of Jeremiah (Jer 39:1–10; 40:7–41:18; 52:1–34) of texts also seen in the Deuteronomistic history (2 Kgs 24:18–25:30). In sum, when we look at the book of Jeremiah, much of it reflects the words of Baruch and these exilic Deuteronomistic authors rather than the words of Jeremiah himself.

FOCUS
TEXT

Jer 31:31–4

As in the case of Isaiah, we should not judge that such later parts of the book of Jeremiah are of little worth. On the contrary, some of the most important texts for Jewish and Christian communities have been ones that scholars have identified as coming from these later "Deuteronomistic" redactors.

One example is Jeremiah 31:31–4, a prose text that builds on multiple parts of Jeremiah's prophecy to give a word of hope to later communities. Like Jeremiah's earlier prophecy, this later text includes both Israel and Judah in its scope, starting with Yahweh's promise to make a "new covenant" with the "house of Israel" and the "house of Judah" (31:31). The text then contrasts this new covenant with the older covenant that Yahweh made with the exodus generation, a covenant which this text asserts was broken. Yahweh in this text is particularly pained by this breaking of the covenant because he had "married" Israel, a subtle reference to earlier images of divine–human marriage in Jeremiah's prophecies (31:32). But this text is moving toward hope, not judgment. The next part, Jer 31:33–4, describes Yahweh's solution. Rather than waiting for the people to memorize teachings as is urged in older wisdom texts (Prov 3:3; 7:3) and the Deuteronomic Torah (Deut 6:4–7; 11:18–19), Yahweh will write these words on the people's hearts himself, so that they no longer will need to encourage each other to be obedient. It will come naturally.

It is impossible to be sure about these things, but the contents and prose form of the text have led most scholars to conclude that it was not authored by Jeremiah, but by a later, anonymous prophet who was addressing later Judeans of the exilic period. As we will see in Chapter 9, the Judeans in exile were in despair over the destruction of their nation and wondered what kind of future Yahweh had in store for them. This addition to the book of Jeremiah in Jer 31:31–4 provides an answer. It insists that Yahweh is making a new covenant with Israel that Yahweh will help them obey. Unlike the older covenant, it will not depend on the weak will of Yahweh's very human people. Rather, Yahweh will write this new covenant on the heart of Yahweh's beloved, espoused people, so that they will naturally know and follow it.

Later communities were powerfully affected by this vision in Jer 31:31–4 of Yahweh's willingness to go to any lengths to make a covenant that would really work for his beloved people. For example, the Jewish community at Qumran who collected the Dead Sea scrolls saw themselves as a community of the "new covenant" mentioned in Jeremiah. Just a century or two later, the expression "new covenant" came to play a very important role in the early Christian movement as well. Texts in Paul and Luke quote Jesus as telling his disciples that the wine of the Christian eucharist was the "new covenant in my blood" (1 Cor 11:25; Luke 22:20). In 2 Corinthians 3, Paul goes beyond this, drawing on Jer 31:31–4 to describe how the "Spirit of the living God" has written a "new covenant" on the hearts of the people at his church in Corinth (see especially 2 Cor 3:6). Much as Jer 31:31–4 contrasted the older covenant and the newer one, Paul now contrasts this spiritual writing on "tablets of human hearts" with the writing "on tablets of stone" by Moses. Such language allows Paul to stress God's role in making the Corinthians righteous, rather than their righteousness being anything that they themselves could boast about (2 Cor 3:2–6). By this point in the Christian movement, the "new covenant" of Jer 31:31–4 was reinterpreted as a covenant allowing both Jews and gentiles to be in a relationship with God that revolved around faith in Christ.

Eventually, later Christians applied a derivative of the term "new covenant" – that is, "New Testament" – to the specifically Christian scriptures associated with their move-ment: e.g. Matthew, Mark, Luke–Acts, John, etc. In addition, they labeled earlier Jewish scriptures with the corresponding term "Old Testament." Read in the light of Jer 31:31–4, this would imply a replacement of the "old testament" with the new, since this passage describes Yahweh's replacement of an older covenant that was broken with a new one. Yet by the point at which these labels – "Old" and "New Testament" – were developed, both sets of scriptures were important in Christianity. Church leaders rejected attempts by some, such as the early theologian Marcion, to have the church authorize only New Testament texts, and theologians found multiple ways in which the texts of the Old Testament pointed toward values and beliefs central to Christianity.

In sum, the words about the "new covenant" in Jer 31:31–4 provided the terms for the later division of scriptures into "Old Testament" and "New Testament," while also defining a major challenge for Christians. Were Hebrew scriptures such as Jer 31:31–4 now themselves to be understood as part of an outdated "covenant?" Or might these scriptures be used to learn more deeply about aspects of the gospel now written on the hearts of Christian believers?

Conclusion to the Pre-Exilic Period

Other chapters in this book have included an imaginary overview of the sorts of texts (and some traditions) that were in circulation at a given time in ancient Israel and Judah. This chapter concludes with a picture of two different groups of texts that probably were prominent in different groups in late seventh-century Judah. On the one hand, many in ancient Judah continued to study older sorts of texts: proverbs and wisdom instructions, royal and other sorts of psalms, love poetry, creation and flood myths, along with assorted traditions with strong northern connections, such as the story of Jacob and Joseph found in Genesis 25–50. On the other hand, the book of Deuteronomy laid claim to be a new kind of "wisdom." Some, such as Jeremiah, seem to have been skeptical of Deuteronomy's claims to be true Torah wisdom (Jer 8:8–9), and our historical evidence suggests that kings after Josiah did not take the Deuteronomic Torah very seriously. Nevertheless, the book of Deuteronomy lays claim to be a potential replacement of older forms of teaching, and the rest of the Deuteronomistic history retells all of the people's history from that perspective. Though Deuteronomy echoes older wisdom texts, it calls on the people to devote all their time to memorizing Moses's Torah teaching (Deut 6:6–9). There is little room in Deuteronomy or the history that follows it for competing claims or texts.

With Josiah's death, many probably dismissed the claims of Deuteronomy and the rest of the Deuteronomistic history, but at least one family appears to have continued to treasure and expand those writings: the family of Shaphan. Shaphan was Josiah's scribe, and he is described as very involved in the process leading to the introduction of the Deuteronomic Torah to the king and the people (2 Kgs 22:3–10) and the verification of it through the prophet Huldah (2 Kgs 22:14–20). Shaphan may have been involved in the revision of the Deuteronomic Torah at the time of Josiah and the Deuteronomistic reframing of other historical traditions to bolster Josiah's reform. Furthermore, his family played a particular role in later Judean history. His son, Ahikam, sheltered Jeremiah when people wanted to kill him after his Temple sermon (Jer 26:24), and Shaphan's grandson was the first one to hear Jeremiah's scroll of oracles and make sure it was passed on to officials in the palace (Jer 36:10–13). By this point, the family of Shaphan no longer seems to have been part of the Judean inner circle. Yet one of their members, a grandson of Shaphan's named Gedaliah, is put in power by the Babylonians after the last king is removed (2 Kgs 25:22), and he gives a message of cooperation with Babylon that sounds somewhat like Jeremiah's prophecy (2 Kgs 25:23–4//Jer 40:7–12). Gedaliah was soon killed (2 Kgs 25:25//Jer 41:1–3), but his family is the most likely group to have cherished and protected the texts discussed in this and the previous chapter. In the twilight of the Judean monarchy, when others may have dismissed texts like Deuteronomy or Jeremiah, they expanded the Deuteronomistic history and revised/expanded Jeremiah's oracles so that the Jeremiah scroll agreed more with the values of that history.

Thus the late seventh century is a time when major traditions in the Bible were introduced, but all these texts still had a journey to make before becoming the biblical texts they now are. They do not seem to have been broadly recognized as important until total disaster struck Jerusalem, with the destruction of the Temple and the monarchy. Moreover, Jeremiah and the Deuteronomistic history were revised in light of this catastrophe, so that the Deuteronomistic history, for example, now extends up through the first part of exile in Babylonia. Chapter 9 examines the impact of this catastrophe across a broader stretch of biblical traditions.

CHAPTER EIGHT REVIEW

1. How does Zephaniah understand the "Day of Yahweh" differently from the conventional view? With what other prophet does he share this innovation?

2. What shifts in meaning do you think were produced when the biographical narratives (now in Jeremiah 26–45) were moved from the end of the book to between the words of Jeremiah in 1–25 and the oracles against foreign nations now in Jeremiah 46–51?

3. How was the response to Jeremiah's prophecy similar to or different from that of eighth-century prophets?

4. Comparing Jeremiah to earlier prophets, such as Hosea or Isaiah, which do you think has more to say to your contemporary community? Why? What would they say now?

RESOURCES FOR FURTHER STUDY

Carroll, Robert. *Jeremiah*. Old Testament Library. London: SCM, 1986.

Clements, R. E. *Jeremiah*. Interpretation. Atlanta: John Knox Press, 1988.

Thompson, John. *The Book of Jeremiah*. New International Commentary on the Old Testament. Grand Rapids: Eerdmans, 1979.

CHAPTER 9

LAMENTS, HISTORY, AND PROPHECIES AFTER THE DESTRUCTION OF JERUSALEM

Chapter Outline

CHAPTER OVERVIEW

T he exile is the central point of ancient Israelite history, the period around which all others are oriented. Josiah's reform is a crucial turning point in the pre-exilic period, but already that formulation – "pre-exilic" – shows that the period of the exile is more important still. Most discussions of the history of the Hebrew Bible revolve around three periods: the pre-exilic, exilic, and post-exilic. The post-exilic period, as we will see in Chapter 11, is defined particularly by those who returned from exile to Judah. Yet for most others whose families had left Judah, there was no return from "exile" to life in the land, and many "Jews" have lived away from the land of Judah ever since the exile. Thus, the exile of waves of Judeans, first in 597 and then in 586 (and yet another in 582), introduced a new era in the history of the Israelite people and development of the Bible. From this point onward, they had no nation state. In the wake of the exile and destruction of Jerusalem, those scriptures now were scriptures for exiles and returnees living in a land dominated by others. The link between texts and a city-state monarchy was broken. The Bible would never be the same.

This is the first of two chapters focusing on biblical texts that can be linked to the Babylonian exile. In this chapter we look at laments in the wake of Jerusalem's destruction, prophecies addressed to exiles found in Ezekiel and chapters 40–55 of Isaiah, and the rewriting of parts of the Deuteronomistic history in light of the destruction of Jerusalem. These texts provide clues to the increasing importance during the exile of Israel's traditions about its pre-land origins and the emphasis in many exilic traditions on Yahweh's promise and ability to work with the people no matter how sinful. We will see these elements again in the next chapter's discussion of Pentateuchal traditions.

The Sixth Century: The Neo-Babylonian Destruction of Jerusalem and Exile

READING
2 Kgs 23:29–25:30.
Exilic laments: Ps 137;
Lamentations 1; Isa 63:7–64:12.

EXERCISE
Before reading this section, read the "exilic laments" listed above and then write down five words that these texts from the exile evoke for you.

Despite high hopes during the time of Josiah, the kingdom of Judah never achieved an extended period of independence, nor was its control over the north firm for any length of time. Instead, Josiah was killed in 609 in a confrontation with the Egyptian Pharaoh Necho as Necho was traveling through Israel on his way to assist Assyria in trying to contain a rising military power in Mesopotamia.

That power was the emergent "Neo-Babylonian" state (distinguished from the "Old Babylonian" empire of the early second millennium), a state ruled by a group of Aramean people called "Chaldeans". Thus began a period of Judah and its kings struggling under the shadow of Neo-Babylonian domination. Though the Egyptian Necho appointed one of Josiah's sons, Jehoiakim, as Josiah's successor, Jehoiakim quickly became a Babylonian vassal. A few years later, he sought to get out from under Babylonian domination with Egypt's help, but the Babylonian army eventually came and laid siege to Jerusalem. In an attempt to avert the wrath of the Babylonians, the people of Jerusalem apparently killed Jehoiakim and replaced him with his son, Jehoiachin, but the Babylonians still took young Jehoiachin and several thousand elite Judeans into exile (in 597), the first of several waves of forced resettlement of Judeans in the Babylonian empire. In place of Jehoiachin, the Babylonians appointed as king his uncle, Zedekiah, a son of Josiah. As a Babylonian appointee, Zedekiah was a weak ruler who was not recognized by many of his country-people. After about ten years he, like his brother Jehoiakim, tried to get free of Babylon by joining an anti-Babylonian coalition of nations.

This rebellion by Zedekiah was the final straw for the Babylonians. Nebuchadnezzar marched on Jerusalem in 586 BCE and breached the walls (see Figure 9.1). He destroyed the Temple that Judah had thought was invulnerable, took yet more of Judah's elite into exile (though fewer than in 597), and installed Gedaliah, the grandson of Shaphan, Josiah's scribe, as governor in Mizpah, a town a few miles northwest of Jerusalem. Our last historical records point to the collapse of power structures in the land. In Judah things went from very bad to worse. Gedaliah was assassinated, his assassins fled to Ammon before Gedaliah's forces, and Gedaliah's forces fled to Egypt out of fear of Babylonian reprisals, forcing Jeremiah to come with them (2 Kgs 25:25–6//Jeremiah 41–2). The last we hear

Figure 9.1 Ashes and arrowheads left from the Babylonian attack on Jerusalem.

of life in Judah, the Babylonians had attacked again and taken a third wave of Judeans into exile in 582 BCE (Jer 52:30; see Map 9.1).

Meanwhile, life went on in Babylonian exile for the thousands of upper-class Judeans who had been forcibly resettled. The books of Kings (and Jeremiah) end with a brief account of how the king, Jehoiachin, was taken out of prison during his thirty-seventh year of exile in Babylon, given a place at the Babylonian king's table, and given rations (2 Kgs 25:27–30; appropriated in Jer 52:31–4; cf. Ezek 1:2). This narrative was written by the exiled authors who extended and expanded the Deuteronomistic history written back in Josiah's time, and is confirmed by a Babylonian list of rations given to Jehoiachin. It shows the sliver of hope that such exiles found in the elevation of their king. Nevertheless, we never hear of Jehoiachin again, and Davidic kings never regained power. The sun had gone down on the Jerusalem monarchy and institutions linked directly with it. The people's future now lay in a life without their own monarch over them.

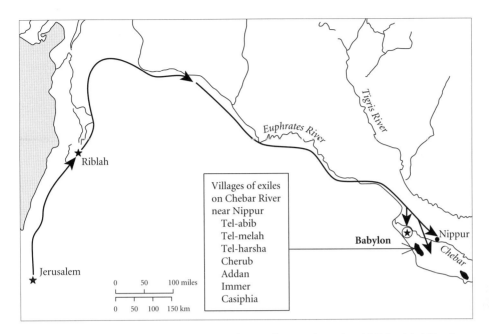

Map 9.1 The journey to Babylon. Redrawn from Yohanan Aharoni and Michael Avi-Yonah, *The Macmillan Bible Atlas* (revised edition). New York: Macmillan, 1977, map 163.

With no monarchy left to sponsor the writing of any history, we are in the dark about other specific events during the Babylonian exile. Biblical texts only provide indirect information about what life was like in exile. Certainly it was no picnic. The exiles were forcibly resettled into abandoned areas of central Babylonia where they worked and tried to form a viable communal life hundreds of miles from their homeland. Though the exiles were allowed to settle together and were not enslaved, exilic texts refer to Babylonian domination as a "yoke" (Ezek 34:27; Isa 47:6; also Jer 30:8) and Babylonia became a symbol of arch-evil throughout the rest of biblical tradition. Multiple traditions suggest that some exiles were in chains (Jer 40:1; the *Antiquities* [10.100–3] by the first-century CE Jewish historian Josephus; see also Nah 3:10), and exilic texts in

Forced Labor for Exiles Under Nebuchadnezzar

This is an excerpt from a building inscription by Nebuchadnezzar II about his use of peoples from across his empire to build "Etemenanki," the grand temple for Marduk in the heart of Babylon:

the whole of the races, peoples from far places, whom Marduk, my Lord, delivered to me, I put

them to work on the building of Etemenanki. I imposed on them the brick basket. (Translation: D. Smith, "The Politics of Ezra: Sociological Indicators of Postexilic Judaean Society." P. 79 of Philip Davies, ed., *Second Temple Studies, I*, JSOTSup 117. (Sheffield: Sheffield Academic Press, 1991)

Figure 9.2 Reproduction of part of the magnificent temple of Ishtar located in the heart of the empire of Babylon.

Isaiah speak of Jerusalem's time of "forced labor" (Isa 40:2), of being confined in prison (Isa 42:7; 49:9) and robbed (Isa 42:22). Meanwhile, one of Nebuchadnezzar's inscriptions boasts of how he forced people from Judah and elsewhere to rebuild the temple in Babylonia (see box on p. 169). Babylon had become their new Egypt (see Figure 9.2).

Laments and prophetic quotes from this period give a sense of the inner experience of this exile. Psalm 137 speaks of weeping by the rivers of Babylon where the captors of the Judeans mockingly asked them to "sing one of the songs of Zion." The exiles sing of how they will keep Jerusalem in their memory, though they are far from home.

> If I forget you, O Jerusalem,
>   let my right hand wither!
> Let my tongue cling to the roof of my mouth,
>   if I do not remember you,
>   if I do not set Jerusalem above my highest joy. (Ps 137:5–6 NRSV)

Lamentations 1 is an alphabet of suffering, where each stanza begins with a different letter of the Hebrew alphabet. After an initial lament over Zion, she cries forth her suffering herself:

> My crimes have been bound into a yoke,
>   my misdeeds braided together by [God's] hand.

They lie on my neck,
> They sap my strength.
The Lord has given me into the hands of
> Those I cannot overcome. (Lam 1:14)

Echoing pre-exilic prophets like Hosea and Jeremiah, this Zion figure says, "I called out to my lovers, but they betrayed me. My priests and elders died in the city while seeking food to survive" (Lam 1:19). Meanwhile, in a lament found in Isa 63:7–64:12, the ancient Judeans cry out to God, "your holy cities have become a wasteland, Zion has become a desert, Jerusalem a heap of ruins" (64:10) and assert to Yahweh, their "father" (64:8), that he has made them "stray from your paths and turn our hearts from fearing you" (64:7). Such laments are part of an ancient literary tradition in Israel of honest crying out to God, even accusing God of being responsible for the people's shortcomings. These laments will be discussed in Chapter 11. For now, it is important to recognize that this type of text, particularly the communal lament, voiced the exiles' mixed feelings of guilt, sadness, fear, and rage as they lived for decades under Neo-Babylonian oppression.

---

basics Book of Lamentations

Outline: **five-part (=Torah) cry for restoration of Jerusalem**	I	Four alphabet poems detailing the suffering of Jerusalem and its people	1–4
	II	Final communal plea for restoration	5

Theme and purpose Other ancient Near Eastern cultures had written and taught laments over the destruction of great cities. These chapters in Lamentations were composed to commemorate the destruction of Jerusalem in 586, particularly on the holiday remembering this event, the Ninth of Av. Over time, however, these poems in Lamentations have come to serve as a cry over Jewish suffering of many kinds, from the destruction of the Second Temple to the genocide of Jews under Hitler and other suffering up to today.

The dynamics of exile can be illuminated through **social-scientific analysis** of the Bible; that is, analysis that draws on contemporary sociological and anthropological studies to provide a more nuanced picture of ancient Israel. For example, Daniel Smith-Christopher's book *Religion of the Landless* (see this chapter's "Resources for Further Study") draws on ethnographic studies of contemporary groups who have experienced displacement from their homelands to try to reconstruct what the experience of Babylonian exile might have been like. He finds that separation from one's homeland inevitably involves major changes for the displaced group. Continuity is not the norm. Transformation is.

In addition, Smith-Christopher found that communities in exile change in similar ways, reflecting the similar challenges that many such diaspora communities face. Because they must now live as a minority in a majority culture, family and clan traditions often become more important, while other traditions connected with their old life either disappear or are transformed. For example, Judean traditions about the king's blessing may have been adapted in exile so that they now applied to an ancient ancestor's blessing or God's blessing of a foreign deliverer. Meanwhile, in place of the now defunct royal bureaucracy, the sole means of organization of Judean exiles were family units, "houses of the father," which were ruled by a group of "elders." These elders, along with the remnants of the priesthood, were the leaders in the exiled Judean community.

New practices became important for the Judeans in Babylonian exile, practices that preserved communal identity in a hostile cultural environment. It appears that circumcision (which was not practiced by Babylonians) and Sabbath observance grew in importance. Furthermore, exiles like them had to struggle against the tendency to assimilate into the broader culture, particularly through intermarriage. In the face of this, these exiles, like many contemporary communities in exile, sought ways to discourage their children from marrying foreigners. This is but one major way in which peoples in exile, both ancient and contemporary, change in order to survive culturally and build identity.

The violence of the exiles' departure may have been yet another factor leading to the transformation of their traditions. Though it is possible that Judean exiles took some scrolls of ancient texts with them into Babylon, it is also quite likely that many did not have a chance to pack much up while Jerusalem burned and the Temple – often a storage place for ancient scrolls – was destroyed. Yet the literate elite who went into exile had memorized ancient texts as part of their education. The Deuteronomic Torah, Proverbs, Song of Songs, and other texts were "written on the tablet of their hearts," as Proverbs would put it (Prov 3:3; 7:3). Once in Babylon, these people could call on their detailed memories of these texts as they produced new copies of them – copies that often reflected the new challenges and hopes of life in exile.

The Exilic Edition of the Deuteronomistic History (and Jeremiah)

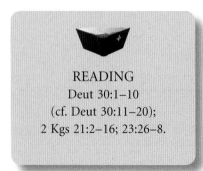

READING
Deut 30:1–10
(cf. Deut 30:11–20);
2 Kgs 21:2–16; 23:26–8.

One example of such preservation and change of ancient textual traditions is the exilic revision and extension of the Deuteronomistic history. In Chapter 7 we saw that the pre-exilic version of this history probably reached only as far as the final evaluation of Josiah's reign (2 Kgs 23:25). In this earlier form, this history was meant to provide a historical-theological rationale for Josiah's attempt to reunify northern and southern Israel under centralized worship of Yahweh. Josiah died, however, and Jerusalem, the one legitimate place for sacrificial worship in his kingdom, was destroyed. Later authors had to explain why this happened, and we see this explanation immediately after the positive comments about Josiah's righteousness. The exilic extenders of this history go on to say:

> [Despite Josiah's goodness] the Lord did not turn back from his great anger against Judah and all the awful things that Manasseh [Josiah's predecessor] had done to anger God. The Lord said, "As I banished Israel from my presence, so will I also banish Judah, and I will reject this city that I chose, Jerusalem, and the house where I said my name would live." (2 Kgs 23:26–7)

This is how one group of exiles, those extending the Deuteronomistic history, explained the greatest trauma of the exile: the destruction of the supposedly invulnerable city, Jerusalem, and its sanctuary. The reason they gave was that Manasseh's sin was so grievous that Josiah's virtue could not overcome it. One generation's guilt meant that another generation had to suffer. A proverb quoted by Ezekiel's audience puts it vividly: "the fathers have eaten sour grapes and the children's teeth are set on edge" (Ezek 18:2). As we will see, Ezekiel rejects this idea that a later generation must pay for the sins of their parents. Nevertheless, this passage from 2 Kgs 23:26–7 is a biblical affirmation of this concept. It asserts that later generations of Judah had to suffer the destruction of Judah and Jerusalem because of the sins of Manasseh. Sour grapes indeed.

This is only one example of a range of places where exilic authors seem to have revised or expanded on the pre-exilic edition of the Deuteronomistic history that they had. The readings for this section include one more example, taken from the beginning of the history in Deuteronomy. The speech in Deuteronomy 30:1–10 is shaped for people who have been "exiled to the ends of the world" (30:4), and it reassures them that the Lord will restore them and bring them back to the land if they follow the command of Deut 6:5, loving the Lord "with all your heart and life strength" (30:6). This is a contrast to the threats and promises in Deut 30:11–20, a probable pre-exilic portion of Deuteronomy. The more reassuring message in Deut 30:1–10 was probably added to Deuteronomy by Judean exiles to show a way forward amidst apparent total disaster. Through adding the promises in Deut 30:1–10, these exilic Deuteronomists offered their people hope, a hope based on return to the Lord and the Lord's Torah. Such revisions probably played a key role in insuring that the Deuteronomistic history, including and especially Deuteronomy, became an ever more important text in the exilic and post-exilic periods.

The same could be said for a variety of exilic Deuteronomistic additions in the book of Jeremiah and other prophetic books. Chapter 5 of this *Introduction* included discussion of how the books of Micah (especially chapters 4–5) and Isaiah (chapters 40–55) contain prophecies of hope for Jerusalem/Zion that probably were written to encourage exiles. The promise appended to the end of the book of Amos, Amos 9:11–15, is another place where exiles appear to have added a word of hope to earlier words of judgment. The book of Jeremiah was thoroughly revised during the exile through the addition of passages such as God's promise of a new covenant written on the heart (Jer 31:31–4) that was discussed in Chapter 8. We see our first close analogies to this idea of God actually changing the heart of God's people in the next prophet to be discussed, Ezekiel.

READING
Ezekiel 1–3, 8–11, 16, 36–7.

Ezekiel

Ezekiel is the only prophet in the Hebrew Bible whose prophecy can be dated with certainty to the exilic period. He was a priest who went into exile in Babylon with King Jehoiachin and thousands of other exiles in 597. There he lived in a Jewish settlement, Tel-abib, located just a few miles from the ancient Sumerian center of learning at Nippur. Though Zedekiah ruled in Jerusalem from 597 until its destruction in 586, all of Ezekiel's prophecies are dated by the years of Jehoiachin's exile. Apparently his career began six years before Jerusalem was destroyed and then continued another fourteen years after Jerusalem's destruction (see Ezek 1:2; 40:1). Many divide Ezekiel's book into two major parts, corresponding to the two major periods of his prophecy. Ezekiel 1–32 features oracles of judgment dated to the period before Jerusalem's destruction. These judgments by Ezekiel are roughly contemporary with the last phase of Jeremiah's prophecy but are delivered in exile to exiles. Then the tone shifts: once Jerusalem is destroyed and the exiles are in despair about their future with God, Ezekiel develops vivid images of hope, and these are stressed in chapters 33–48 of the book.

Like the other books of major prophets, the book of Ezekiel prominently features a story of his commissioning by God, in Ezekiel 1–3. Nevertheless, this commissioning is different in ways that mark the uniqueness of Ezekiel's prophecy. It begins, like Isaiah's, with a vision of God and God's attendants (1:4–28), but Ezekiel's vision is more elaborate: with four strange creatures (1:4–14), each associated with a chariot wheel (1:15–25), and a brilliant blue throne overhead on which God is seated, "an appearance of the likeness of the glory of the LORD" (1:28). Moreover, Ezekiel, unlike Isaiah, sees God outside the temple (1:2–28; 3:22–3), and the imagery of the wheels in his call narrative anticipates his later "Temple vision," where he sees God leave the Temple and go into exile (Ezekiel 8–11). This focus on God's presence outside the temple in both Ezekiel 1–3 and 8–11 is the first mark of the radically new, exilic context of Ezekiel's prophecy.

The message that Ezekiel is commissioned to speak, however, sounds like an extreme version of the message seen in Amos, Isaiah, and other prophets of judgment. God tells him to speak to God's people of "rebels," whether they listen or not (2:1–7). Indeed, God predicts that they will not listen, but will reject his message (3:4–9). Nevertheless, like a sentinel on a watchtower who sees an approaching army, Ezekiel must sound the alarm about God's oncoming judgment and let the people make the decision about whether to respond. Otherwise, the blood of his people will be on his hands (Ezek 3:16–21).

When other prophets faced rejection of their prophecy, they had their oracles written down for other generations (e.g. Isa 8:11–18; 30:8–14; Jeremiah 36), and this element of writing is yet more prominent in Ezekiel's call narrative. God offers him a scroll with words of doom written on it and tells Ezekiel to eat it. Ezekiel does eat it, an act signifying his obedient memorization of all that God has told him to prophecy (Ezek 2:8–3:3). Yet the scroll has not lost its purpose. Rather, this narrative implies that its words of doom were included in the book now found in the Hebrew Bible. Though his own generation did not listen, the writing down of his prophecy allowed it to endure and teach future generations.

One central element of Ezekiel's teaching was his proclamation that each generation stood on its own before God: a disobedient generation would be punished for its sins, but if the children of people in that generation were righteous, they would be rewarded. Not everyone agreed on this point. As we saw above, the exilic portions of the Deuteronomistic history blamed the suffering of Ezekiel's generation on the sins of an earlier one, especially the evil of Manasseh (2 Kgs 23:26–7). As we have seen, Ezekiel quotes people of his time saying "the fathers have eaten sour grapes, and the children's teeth are set on edge" (Ezek 18:2), but he decisively rejects that saying. On the contrary, he insists, the fathers will be punished or rewarded for their righteousness, and their children will stand or fall on the basis of their own righteousness as well (Ezek 18:3–24). Many who have read this chapter in the contemporary context of emphasis on the individual have seen here the first emergence in the Hebrew Bible of individual responsibility, but this is mistaken. At issue in every example in the chapter is whether or not

basics **Book of Ezekiel**

Outline: judgment and restoration of Jerusalem	I Sentinel announcement of judgment 1:1–33:20 II Restoration of Jerusalem and Temple 33:21–48:35
Date	Early to late exile.
Themes	The judgment and restoration theme is familiar from other prophets, but Ezekiel, a Zadokite priest, adds a different level of spectacle to his visions (e.g. Ezekiel 1–3 and 37) and a new emphasis on purity, and features a particular focus on the Temple (Ezekiel 9–11) and its restoration (Ezekiel 40–8).
More information	Ezekiel is also known for his weird symbolic actions, such as lying on his side for more than a year (Ezek 4:4–8) or not mourning the death of his wife (Ezek 24:15–27). Some in the past have explained these and other aspects of his prophecy as the result of a mental imbalance in Ezekiel. Nevertheless, such attempts to psychologically analyze the prophet on the basis of literature linked to him are extremely risky. Moreover, these approaches miss the emphasis throughout the book on the idea that Ezekiel's words and actions, however unusual, were a message from God for the exiles and later generations.

later generations must pay for the sins of their parents. The point is to get the exiles to stop saying how "unfair" God is for punishing them on the basis of an earlier generation's sins (18:25, 29). Instead, Ezekiel calls on them to repent of their own past crimes, get a "new heart and a new spirit," and live (Ezek 18:31–2).

Ezekiel's imagery for the people and description of their "crimes" sound somewhat like Hosea's, yet things have advanced a long way in the years that separate these prophets. Like Hosea, Ezekiel pictures God's disobedient people as female, and, as in Hosea, Ezekiel uses this image to stress the people's failure to be exclusively faithful to God, both in impure worship (16:15–27) and in playing power politics with other nations (16:28–9). Yet Ezekiel's use of female imagery for God's people(s) is more explicitly degrading and violent than Hosea's, and it is saturated with purity concerns typical of priests like Ezekiel. According to him, Jerusalem is the female offspring of Canaanite peoples and plagued by blood impurity from her birth (16:3–4, 22). Though God cleaned her up and eventually married her, she – and her sister Israel – engaged in the worst form of promiscuity. In response, God promises to offer her up for the stripping and beating that adulterous women receive (16:35–42). Even worse, another chapter that uses this metaphor, Ezekiel 23, promises that both sisters will be brutally killed (Ezek 23:22–49). The first part of the book concludes with God's command to Ezekiel not to mourn the death of his own wife as a sign of the numbness that the people will feel when their beloved city is destroyed (Ezek 24:15–27).

Nevertheless, Ezekiel, like other prophetic books, ends with hope, not judgment. After a series of oracles against foreign nations (Ezekiel 25–32), the book returns to a review of major themes from the first part of the book (33:1–20) before moving to prophecies dated to the destruction of the Jerusalem Temple (33:21) or later (40:1). Some of these are words of judgment, such as Ezekiel's oracle against people still in the land who claim Abraham as their ancestor (Ezek 33:23–9) or his condemnation of Judah and Israel's past kings, their "shepherds," for selfishness and injustice (Ezek 34:1–10). Yet these oracles of judgment introduce words of hope to exiles, promising that God will be their shepherd and rescue them from exile and resettle them under a new Davidic king (Ezek 34:11–31). Where Ezekiel prophesied against the mountains of the land in the first part of the book (Ezekiel 6), he offers them hope in this latter part (Ezekiel 36). Where he watched the glory of God leave the temple before (Ezek 11:22–5), he now sees it returning (Ezek 43:1–6). In one of the most powerful visions of all, he imagines Israel as a valley full of "dry bones," bones which symbolize exiles who are convinced that they are completely finished and hope is lost (Ezek 37:11). God calls on Ezekiel to prophesy to this valley of dry bones, this exiled people, and watch their miraculous resurrection (37:12–14).

The restoration imagined in Ezekiel does not depend on the people finding a way to change themselves. His earlier prophecies had already made clear that he thought the people incapable of this. Rather, in this part of the book, Ezekiel reiterates promises given earlier, that God will give the people a new heart and new spirit so that they can obey God's laws (Ezek 36:26–7; 37:14; cf. 11:14–21). Though the exiles might despair that God would ever have anything more to do with them after all that they had done wrong, Ezekiel reassures them that God will do all this "for the sake of [God's] holy name" (Ezek 36:22–3, 32). This idea of "holy name" refers to God's reputation. According to Ezekiel, God's reputation among the nations had suffered when they watched God's chosen people removed from their land (Ezek 36:20–1). Yet God promises to redeem God's name through bringing the Israelites back and settling them in the land so that the nations can see this too (36:28–36). In this way, Ezekiel describes a restoration that does not depend on any goodness in the exiles themselves. God's promises of restoration depend on God's wish to look good in front of the nations, not on the people suddenly changing their ways.

Second Isaiah (also called "Deutero-Isaiah")

Very similar themes appear in the other major prophet that is associated with the exile: the anonymous prophet that wrote chapters 40–55 of the book of Isaiah. Chapter 6 of this *Introduction* mentioned biblical scholarship that has identified this section of Isaiah as coming from a later period of Judah's history than the time of the original Isaiah. Here we examine how these chapters addressed the fears and hopes of exiles a few decades after the time of Ezekiel. By this point in the exile, this "**Second Isaiah**" (or **Deutero-Isaiah**) can proclaim that the LORD has anointed the Persian king Cyrus as God's shepherd, that is, God's king (Isa 44:28–45:1). We know from other historical documents that this Cyrus would eventually bring down the Neo-Babylonian empire in 539 BCE.

READING
Isaiah 40–55.

The Divine Council

The people of Israel and surrounding countries believed their god had a royal court of divine beings, a "divine council." Just as human kings had counselors and courtiers, so also the divine king had his. We see reflections of this idea of the divine council across the whole Hebrew Bible: Psalm 89:7 refers to Yahweh's "council of the holy ones." Isaiah 6:8, 40:1, and 40:3 feature commands addressed to an unspecified heavenly group. God debates with a group about whether Job is altruistic in Job 1–2. We may even see a pale reflection of this idea in Genesis where God decides to make humanity "in *our* image" (Gen 1:26) and later fears that humans will be "like *us*" (Gen 3:22 and 11:7).

This exilic portion of Isaiah opens with a commissioning scene in the **divine council** (Isa 40:1–8) that echoes the scene where the earlier prophet, eighth-century Isaiah, was commissioned (6:1–13). The original Hebrew of both texts, Isa 6:1–13 and 40:1–8, indicates that God speaks with other divine attendants, probably members of his divine council in the process of deciding who will take God's message to his people (Isa 6:8; 40:1–5). In Isa 6:8 God asks a group of people, "whom shall I send on our behalf?"

while Isa 40:1–2 calls a group to go and tell God's people that the exile, the "time of forced labor," is over:

> Comfort my people, comfort them,
>   Says your God.
> Speak tenderly to the heart of Jerusalem,
>   And call out to her.
> That her time of forced labor is now over,
>   That her bloodguilt has been paid for,
>   That she has received from Yahweh double for all her sins. (Isa 40:1–2)

Isaiah 6, the call narrative for Isaiah of the eighth century, stressed his confrontation with his and his people's "bloodguilt" (Isa 6:5). In contrast, this later exilic text emphasizes God's forgiveness. Isaiah 6 described Yahweh's "glory" as filling the whole earth (Isa 6:3), but this exilic text in Isa 40:5 now has the whole earth actually *seeing* Yahweh's "glory" (Isa 40:3–5). Just as Ezekiel had pictured God's reputation being restored through the nations' witnessing God's rescue of God's people (Ezek 36:28–36), so this exilic "Second Isaiah" imagines God's glory being revealed to the whole world in the exiles' departure from Babylon (Isa 40:3–5).

---

basics Second Isaiah/Deutero-Isaiah

Outline
I   Exhortation to second exodus out of Babylon   40–8
II   Announcement of hope and return to Jerusalem   49–55

Date Late exile.

Themes This part of Isaiah focuses on giving hope to the hopeless. Though possibly written as a separate prophetic collection, it now links in interesting ways with earlier parts of Isaiah (e.g. Isaiah 40:1–9//Isaiah 6). It is also the part of Isaiah that contains the famous "servant songs" (Isa 42:1–4; 49:1–6; 50:4–11; 52:13–53:12) that have been the subject of much religious and scholarly debate.

God's announcement of Jerusalem's liberation is followed by the prophet's call and his objection to the call (40:6), an exchange similar to ones in the call narratives for Isaiah (Isa 6:5) and Jeremiah (Jer 1:6). In this case, however, the exilic prophet is worried about despairing exiles, who wither "like grass" when "the breath of Yahweh blows upon it" (40:6–7). He knows that he must address a discouraged people who have heard many false hopes. Yet a divine presence answers his doubts, first by acknowledging their partial truth, "Yes, the grass withers, and the flower fades," then adding the reassurance that "the word of our God endures forever" (40:8). Though the exiles may feel weak and hopeless, God's word of hope and restoration persists and will prevail.

The rest of Isaiah 40–55 is divided into two main parts: Isaiah 40–8 and 49–55. The first part, Isaiah 40–8, is a passionate call for the exiles to embrace God's plan to take them out of Babylon. Central to this call is the prophet's reassurance that their God, who might have seemed defeated by other gods in the destruction of Jerusalem, is powerful enough to liberate them. Here "Second Isaiah" invokes creation traditions to affirm that the god who created the world can bring them out of Babylon (Isa 40:12–27). He reminds the exiles of God's care for their ancestors, both Abraham and Jacob and the people of the exodus generation (41:8–9; 44:1–2; also 51:1–2).

It is in the context of these arguments for Yahweh's power that Second Isaiah makes a monotheistic claim that is new in Israelite religion: he asserts that there is no other god anywhere but Yahweh. All other gods are false idols, worthless pieces of wood and metal (40:18–20; 41:7; 44:9–20). In this way Second Isaiah reassures the exiles that other nations' gods offer no contest whatsoever for the creator-liberator God of Israel. We have not seen this sort of argument for the non-existence of any other gods in Israelite traditions clearly datable to earlier periods. In Hosea and Deuteronomy we saw calls for Israel not to worship any other gods, yet those calls did not include the assumption that such gods did not exist. Yet here, in the context of Second Isaiah's reassurances to exiles, the prophet argues for just this point of view. Later traditions will take **monotheism** for granted.

Isaiah 40–8, the first half of Second Isaiah, concludes with an argument from prophecy, an argument that only works if it was directly addressed to exiles and not to an earlier audience. God reminds the exiles of earlier prophecies that have come true, "former things" declared through the prophets. Through seeing the past fulfillment of these prophecies, this text insists, God's "stubborn" people should now be able to trust God's announcement of "new things" (Isa 48:4–6), including God's plans to destroy the sixth-century Neo-Babylonian empire (48:14). Even though it is theoretically possible that an eighth-century prophet, Isaiah, could have accurately predicted the demise of the Babylonian empire, he would not have addressed his eighth-century audience as if his prophecies about Judah lay in the past. Nor would Isaiah of the eighth century have called on his audience, still in Judah, to "go out from Babylon, flee from Chaldea, declare with loud shouts . . . 'God has freed God's servant, Jacob'" (Isa 48:20). These are words addressed by an unknown exilic prophet to a later audience of exiles, an audience longing to go home.

The second major section of Second Isaiah, Isaiah 49–55, focuses on the task of resettling and restoring Jerusalem. Like 40–8, these chapters start with a commissioning (49:1–6; cf. 40:1–8). This time, God commissions a "**servant**" who is to gather the exiled Israelites back to the LORD and reveal God's glory to the end of the earth (49:5–6). The identity of the "servant" in this and other passages in Second Isaiah has puzzled readers for centuries (see other "**servant songs**" in Isa 42:1–8; 50:4–9; 52:13–53:12 that likewise focus on a distinctive "servant"). In most of Isaiah 40–8, God addresses the whole people of Israel/Jacob as God's servant (Isa 41:8–9; 43:10; 44:1; 48:20). In other cases, however, the "servant/suffering servant" seems to be separate from the people, serving them (e.g. 49:5–6). Early Christians insisted that the servant of these passages was Jesus Christ. It is highly doubtful, however, that an exilic Judean prophet originally understood himself to be prophesying Jesus Christ. Instead, scholars of the Bible usually conclude that the "servant" in Second Isaiah was either a now unknown individual in the community of the exiles or stood for the community of Israel as a whole. There are grounds for both positions in Isaiah 40–55.

The servant passage in Isa 49:1–6 is followed by a speech where God addresses Jerusalem, personified once again as a woman. Echoing the book of Lamentations, she cries out that "the LORD has abandoned me, my Lord has forgotten me" (Isa 49:14; compare Lam 5:20). God then answers this lament with a remarkable use of parental imagery:

> Can a woman forget her nursing child,
>> Or her compassion for the child of her womb?
> Even if these ones forget, I will never forget you. (Isa 49:15)

The exilic prophet uses mothers as the ultimate example of compassion and then says that God embodies such compassion and more toward the exiles.

MORE ON METHOD: (STUDY OF) INTERTEXTUALITY

Recent literary criticism has taught biblical scholars to be ever more aware of **intertextuality** in biblical texts. Intertextuality is a word used to refer to the myriad ways different texts can be related to each other. Literary-critical analysis of biblical intertextuality sometimes takes the form of analyzing ways in which biblical texts allude to or build on earlier texts, such as the echo of Lam 5:20 in the lament by Zion in Isa 49:14. Other times, however, such analysis highlights ways that any reading of a biblical text must now consider that text as part of a broader web of texts, many of which it was not originally connected to. For example, in the next section of this chapter we will look at later readings of the poem about the suffering servant in Isa 52:13–53:12 by Christians and Jews that have been influenced by earlier interpretations of the poem in each faith tradition. As Peter Miscall has put it (echoing John Donne), "no text is an island," whether in its original writing or its subsequent interpretation.

For more: Patricia K. Tull, "Rhetorical Criticism and Intertextuality," pp. 156–79 in S. McKenzie and S. Haynes, *To Each Its Own Meaning: An Introduction to Biblical Criticisms and Their Applications* (Louisville: Westminster, 1999).

Thus begins a series of speeches in Isaiah 49–55 that alternate between speeches of comfort to female Zion (50:1–3; 51:1–52:12; 54:1–17) and speeches by or about God's "servant" (50:4–11; 52:13–53:12). The climax of the songs about the servant is Isa

52:13–53:12, a poem about the shaming and exaltation of a "servant" who has borne the sicknesses of others. The climax of the songs about female Zion is Isaiah 54, a picture of God's eternal remarriage to Zion after abandoning her "for a brief moment" (54:7). This latter poem is a sharp contrast to Ezekiel's use of marriage imagery earlier in the exile to stress the people's wrongdoing and punishment (Ezekiel 16 and 23). The prophet in Isaiah 54 downplays any past troubles and uses the marriage metaphor to stress God's abiding love for God's beloved city.

The final chapter of Isaiah 40–55 features several distinctive promises to exiles in Babylon. Where once the Davidic monarchy was promised an eternal covenant (2 Sam 7:12–16; 23:5; Pss 89:3–4, 20–1), now – in the wake of the destruction of the monarchy – God promises an eternal, Davidic covenant with the people themselves (55:3). Echoing the earlier affirmation that "the word of our God endures forever" (40:8), this concluding chapter affirms that God's word "will not return to [God] empty" (55:11). As a result, the exiles should "go out in joy and be led back in peace," watching the mountains and hills break forth in song to greet them on their way home (55:12–13). These extravagant promises, made just on the eve of the destruction of the Babylonian empire, were on the minds of many exiles when they returned home with high hopes.

FOCUS TEXT

Isa 52:13–53:12

This text about the **suffering servant** is the fourth, longest, and most controversial servant song in Second Isaiah. Of all the texts about Yahweh's servant in Second Isaiah, this one most clearly seems to concern an individual. It starts with Yahweh's proclamation that many nations will be totally surprised by the rise and prosperity of God's "servant," who was once horribly disfigured.

> See my servant will be successful.
>> He will rise up, be lifted up, and be very exalted.
> Just as many were aghast at him,
>> As his looks were inhuman,
>> and his form unlike another mortal,
> So he will startle many nations,
>> Kings will shut their mouths because of him. (52:13–15a)

Looking at the sudden success of the servant, the Judean exiles finally will see "that which they had not been told" before and understand "that which they had not heard" (52:15b; compare with similar terms in Isa 48:6–8). The next part of the text and the heart of the passage, Isa 53:1–11a, is an imagined quoting of that community of exiles, starting with their own astonishment at the sudden rise of this disfigured servant. They say, "who can believe what we just heard? To whom has the arm of Yahweh been revealed?" (53:1). They then go on to describe their realization that the servant they once despised was actually suffering for their own sins (53:2–9), and they conclude that Yahweh both caused the servant's suffering and is now bringing the servant glory (53:10–11a). At this point, Yahweh speaks once again at the end of the passage, affirming that Yahweh will indeed glorify the servant because of his suffering, unto death, for the sins of his people (53:11b–12). This second divine speech echoes the initial divine speech in 52:13–15, enclosing the speech by the people in 53:1–11a in an envelope or **inclusio** structure – that is, a structure where a text begins and ends with similar elements (52:13–15 and 53:11b–12 – the envelope) that enclose a larger middle (53:1–11a). The effect of this envelope structure is to give divine authority to the thoughts of the people in 53:1–11a. There they realize that this disfigured person they thought to be rejected by Yahweh will soon be glorified by Yahweh for suffering on their behalf.

Though, if considered by itself, this text seems to focus on the fortunes of a particular individual known to the text's original audience, it can be read in a broader literary context as concerning the suffering and future glorification of God's servant people. As mentioned before, Yahweh addresses the whole people of Israel as his servant throughout much of Isaiah 40–8. And it appears that the word "Israel" has been added at one point in Isa 49:1–6, namely in Isa 49:3 (disturbing the poetic balance of this verse: "You are my servant, *Israel*, in whom I will be glorified"), so that this passage now describes the commissioning of God's people/servant, "Israel." Such descriptions of all of "Israel" as God's servant in Isaiah 40–8 provide a new context for understanding the speeches about God's servant in Isa 52:13–53:12. Read in light of them, this text can be reinterpreted to describe the suffering and future glorification of Yahweh's entire servant people.

These two levels of understanding the "servant" in Isaiah 52:13–53:12 – individual and collective – are reflected in the different Christian and Jewish understandings of the passage. Most Christian interpreters have asserted that the servant spoken of here is an individual – Jesus Christ. For them, the text predicts his crucifixion and resurrection. For example, in the biblical book of Acts, an Ethiopian eunuch reading the book of Isaiah asks the disciple Philip whether the description of the suffering servant in Isa 53:7–8 is about Isaiah or someone else. Philip then uses this text as the starting point for preaching about Jesus to the eunuch, who converts and becomes one of the first Christian missionaries (Acts 8:26–40). This illustrates a broader tendency in the New Testament and other early Christian writings to read the story of Jesus's crucifixion and resurrection in light of Isa 52:13–53:12. Apparently this text helped early Christians understand and cope with Jesus's humiliating death. Where most people of Jesus's time would have seen his life as a failure because of the crucifixion, the first Christians read Isa 52:13–53:12 and saw that such impressions could be deceiving: though Jesus was despised, humiliated, and seemingly rejected by God, he was actually God's faithful, suffering servant as described in Isa 52:13–53:12. With the help of this text they could affirm that his death was not the end but the prelude to his glorification by God for suffering on behalf of the sins of others.

Meanwhile, Isa 52:13–53:12 did not connect in such a clear way with major ideas or figures in Judaism, so early Jewish interpreters paid much less attention to it. When Jews did interpret this passage, they often understood it as describing all of Israel as

Yahweh's suffering servant. Thus the great twelfth-century Jewish interpreter Rashi watched Christian crusaders kill Jews on their way to the holy land and concluded that Isa 52:13–53:12 described Israel's suffering for the sins of others. Another Jewish commentator of the same time, Ibn Ezra, understood the speech in 53:1–11a as quoting what the shamed non-Jewish nations would say one day as they looked back on Israel's suffering at their hands.

Ironically, some Jewish suffering during the medieval period was connected with the reading in Christian churches of this very passage from Isaiah. For this passage – with its frequent use in Christian theology about Jesus's crucifixion – was the traditional scripture reading for the Christian holiday that commemorated the crucifixion: Good Friday. Throughout much of the medieval period Christians would hear this passage read, hear sermons blaming Jews for crucifying Jesus, and then go on a rampage through the Jewish quarter of their city terrorizing and even killing Jewish men, women, and children. In this way, the Jews of these medieval towns and villages were forced to bear the anti-Jewish iniquity of the Christian people hearing this text. Perhaps partly because such experiences may have led Jews to have bad associations with Isa 52:13–53:12, this passage is far less emphasized in Judaism than others in Second Isaiah. The Jewish holiday of the "Ninth of Av," which commemorates the destruction of the first and second Temples, for example, traditionally includes readings of comfort and hope from virtually every part of Second Isaiah *except* Isa 52:13–53:12.

Today it is impossible to approach this text without this web of associations built up by years of its history of interpretation. Even if Christians realize that the link of this text with Jesus is a later one, many are still preoccupied with finding out exactly who this ancient "suffering servant" of Isaiah was. A closer look, however, reveals that this text is not focused on helping the reader know who the servant is. Instead, it presupposes that the audience already knows this person, and it anticipates that this audience will soon realize that their prejudices about him were wrong. As we have seen, texts already in Isaiah 40–55 have reinterpreted this "servant" to be the people of Israel in exile, and later communities have further reinterpreted the "servant" of this passage, whether as Jesus or the Jewish people. It is too late to read this passage as the original audience would have. Instead, we must read it now in light of its sometimes painful history of interpretation. Christians can choose to continue the ancient tradition of Christological interpretation of the passage, though now knowing that this represents just one in a line of creative reinterpretations. Jews can continue to use this passage to understand the Jewish people's suffering and gain hope for future restoration. And it is possible to reinterpret this passage in relation to other contemporary situations where individuals or groups are despised and/or oppressed, yet might be God's servants bearing, unfairly, the wrongs of others.

CHAPTER NINE REVIEW

1. Know the meaning and significance of the following terms:
- Deutero-Isaiah
- divine council
- inclusio
- intertextuality
- monotheism
- Second Isaiah
- servant [in Second Isaiah]
- servant songs
- social-scientific analysis
- suffering servant

2. What were the differences in the exiles of 596, 587, and 582 and their significance for the destruction of the kingdom of Judah?

3. Where do the exilic edition of the Deuteronomistic history and the book of Ezekiel disagree? Why was this important in this period?

4. What insights can we gain into the experience of ancient Judeans in exile from survey of contemporary social-scientific studies of people living outside their homelands?

5. Make a list of the practices and beliefs that became especially prominent in the exile.

6. What elements of earlier prophecy are accentuated in Ezekiel? In which early prophet do they first appear and how are they different in Ezekiel?

7. How does Ezekiel 18 address the particular questions confronting the Judean exiles?

8. What can we learn about the unique characteristics of Ezekiel's and Second Isaiah's messages through the different emphases of their two major parts: Ezekiel 1–33/34–48 on the one hand and Isaiah 40–48/49–55 on the other?

9. Why would the "argument from prophecy" in Isaiah 48 not work as well if it were composed by eighth-century Isaiah?

10. Try reading Isa 49:1–6 without the word "Israel" in Isa 49:3. Does this seem to concern an individual or collective servant? How does this change if "Israel" is included in the passage?

11. What are two types of "intertextuality" studied by biblical scholars? Give two examples of such study from Second Isaiah. Can you think of other potential examples?

12. What would be contemporary analogies, whether individuals or groups, to the anonymous "suffering servant" of Isa 52:13–53:12? Do you see problems with applying this text's picture of "suffering for the sins of others" to these individuals and groups?

RESOURCES FOR FURTHER STUDY

Sociology of exile

Smith-Christopher, Daniel L. *Religion of the Landless: The Social Context of Babylonian Exile*. Bloomington, IN: Meyer-Stone Books, 1989.

Ezekiel

Blenkinsopp, J. *Ezekiel*. Interpretation. Atlanta: John Knox Press, 1990.

Greenberg, M. *Ezekiel 1–20*; *Ezekiel 21–37*. Anchor Bible. New York: Doubleday, 1983, 1997.

Second Isaiah

Blenkinsopp, Joseph. *Isaiah 40–55: A New Translation with Introduction and Commentary*. Anchor Bible. New York: Doubleday, 2002.

Muilenburg, James "Isaiah 40–66: Introduction and Exegesis." Pp. 381–783 in vol. 5 of *The Interpreter's Bible*. Nashville: Abingdon, 1956.

CHAPTER 10

THE PENTATEUCH

AND THE EXILE

Chapter Outline

CHAPTER OVERVIEW

In Chapter 9 we saw how the exilic prophecies of Ezekiel and Isaiah addressed the despair of the exiles through promise of Yahweh's salvation. This chapter traces similar themes in two major source strands spanning the present Pentateuch: an L Source (or Lay Source) created by lay scribes and leaders, and a slightly later P (Priestly) Source created by priests. In many ways, it is best to think of both of these sources, L and P, as expressions in narrative form of the exilic promise addressed to despairing exiles that we saw in prophetic form in the later prophecies of Ezekiel and Second Isaiah. Though the L and P narratives purport to be about ancient figures such as Abraham and Moses, they are stories and laws crafted to address the questions and concerns of exiles.

These sources built upon blocks of earlier material. For example, the L Source builds on *and includes* the J primeval history, Jacob story, and some form of the exodus–wilderness account. Nevertheless, both sources (L and P) reframed earlier traditions in light of exilic concerns. For example, where Ezekiel and Second Isaiah spoke the promise in words of prophecy addressed directly to Judeans, the L and the P sources added notes of promise to stories about Israel's patriarchs and matriarchs. Through so revising and combining older traditions about Israel's life before it had taken possession of the land, the authors of L and P reassured exiles separated from their land. The L and P sources implied that Yahweh would redeem them, just as Yahweh had redeemed their ancestors. The challenge of this chapter is twofold: to get a picture of these two, once-separate narrative strands embedded in the one Pentateuch that we have, and to consider how these two strands would have addressed or at least been heard by Judean exiles in Babylon.

The Lay Pentateuchal Source (L)

Our starting point is what will be termed here the "**Lay Source**" or "**L**." It is given this term because this source appears to have been composed by non-priestly scribes and features the "elders" as the main leadership group of the generation who lived during the time of Moses (indeed, many scholars would refer to this material with the more cumbersome term **non-Priestly** or **non-P**). Note: it is important to realize that though these "lay" leaders do not seem to have been priests, they were hardly everyday people either. On the contrary, they were members of the royal leadership (now out of power in exile) and/or other non-priestly elite scholars who drew on their knowledge of older compositions to write a new overall story of their people's life before they possessed the land.

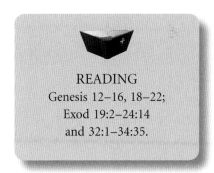

READING
Genesis 12–16, 18–22;
Exod 19:2–24:14
and 32:1–34:35.

The L Source that they produced included the older J primeval history (Gen 2:1–4:26; 6:1–4; a flood story starting with 6:5–8; 7:1–5, 10, 12 and concluding with Gen 8:20–2; 9:18–27) , a story about Abraham (Genesis 12–16, 18–22), a revised form of the northern Jacob and Joseph compositions (most of Genesis 25–50), and a transformed version of older stories about Moses leading Israel out of Egypt to the wilderness. This chapter focuses on the L Source story of Abraham (Genesis 12–16, 18–22) and the account of covenant making in the wilderness (Exodus 19–24, 32–4). Nevertheless, the source also included other stories about Moses and the Israelites such as the initial account of Israel's oppression in Egypt (Exod 1:8–12, 15–22), the story of Moses's early life and attempts to free Israel (Exod 2:1–22; 3:1–5:1), a strand of the story of the plagues on Egypt and deliverance at the Red Sea; and various stories about Israel in the wilderness (e.g. Exodus 17 and some form of the Sinai account in Exodus 19–24, 32–4). If you want to imagine this source, try to picture a text up through Numbers that included stories such as the J primeval history, Genesis 12–16, 18–22, etc., but did not have stories such as the Priestly creation story (Gen 1:1–2:3), the genealogy in Genesis 5, the covenant of circumcision in Genesis 17, etc. We have no manuscript of this separate L Source, but scholars have agreed on its basic contours for over one hundred years.

This L Source was a composite source, a combination of older building blocks and new material, probably created (as a whole) during the exile. In this sense, it was much like a conglomerate rock (see Figure 10.1) made out of a combination of older rocks (the pre-exilic sources) and rocky cement connecting them. Perhaps an even closer analogy can be seen in some ancient villages found in the hill country of Israel even today. Many buildings in such villages are a combination of old and new. The walls beginning at the ground may come from an older building, but then they are continued with

Figure 10.1 The exilic L Source or Lay Source is much like this conglomerate rock, with larger pre-exilic rocks (such as the J primeval history, Jacob–Joseph story) connected to each other by rocky cement (the exilic promise).

The L Source: Terms for It and Pictures of Its Formation

Many scholars would use other terminology for the L or Lay Source discussed here, terminology that reflects a different picture of the formation of this source than that which is presented in this textbook.

An older hypothesis: J ("Yahwistic Source") and E ("Elohistic Source")

Throughout the twentieth century, most bible specialists believed that the material discussed here as L contained two yet earlier sources: a **J Source** composed in Judah around the time of Solomon and an **E Source** composed in (northern) Israel sometime in the eighth century. The J Source or **Yahwistic Source** was so called because it frequently used the divine name "Yahweh," which, in the German language of those who pioneered this theory, is spelled with an initial "J." The E Source or **Elohistic Source** was so called because it more frequently preferred the divine name "Elohim," which means "god" in Hebrew. For example, earlier scholars maintained that the bulk of Genesis 12–16 and 18–19 came from the hypothesized J Source (note the predominance of "LORD" = Yahweh), while parallel stories about Abraham found in Genesis 20–2 were from E (note the predominance of "God" in these chapters).

Problems for the older hypothesis

Many scholars still find this idea of J and E persuasive. Nevertheless, many, if not most, specialists in the study of the Pentateuch have abandoned this approach, for several reasons. First, there are many elements of J and E that link conceptually with later periods of Israel's history, thus making it unlikely that they were early pre-exilic sources. Second, aside from the Abraham story and a handful of other texts, scholars have had a lot of trouble gaining consensus on what might have been the contents of J and E. Third, in cases such as the Abraham story, there are indicators that the hypothesized J texts were shaped in relation to the E texts and vice versa. This suggests that some parts of the Bible divided between J and E were not from separate (written) sources, but from diverse, possibly oral traditions.

Terminology

Scholars who still maintain this older approach would call the texts under discussion here "JE," a term for the combination of the hypothesized J and E documents. Those specialists who no longer believe in J and E often refer more neutrally to these texts in the **Tetrateuch** (Genesis–Numbers) as "non-P"; that is, the bulk of Tetrateuchal texts not assigned to the Priestly Source (to be discussed shortly). This textbook adopts the more positive term L Source or Lay Source to designate these texts, reflecting their links with non-priestly, lay leaders, probably of the exilic period.

newer materials that extend up to the roof. The yard walls may have an old Greek column built into them or another piece of ancient architecture embedded in newer mortar. So also the L Source was built in part around older literary building blocks such as the J primeval history (see Chapter 4 of this *Introduction*), the Covenant Code (see Chapter 4), revised forms of the Jacob and Joseph stories originally written in the northern kingdom (see Chapter 5), and a transformed version of the story of Moses written in the early northern kingdom (see Chapter 5). But such building blocks do not make a house. The major shape and emphases of the L Source came from those who used these older literary building blocks to create a broader story of Israel's existence before it had taken possession of the land, a story that extended from creation to Moses.

We gain insight into the broader values of the L Source by looking at themes that link its various parts together, binding the primeval history to the stories of the patriarchs and matriarchs and these stories to the Moses–exodus story. As was suggested above, the main theme that unites these various parts of the L Source is the theme of promise to the ancestors. This theme first appears in the Abraham story, when Abraham receives a promise of blessing from Yahweh (Gen 12:1–3) that contrasts with the theme of curse that frequently occurred across the older J primeval history (Gen 3:14, 17; 4:11; 5:29; 8:21; 9:25). The rest of the Abraham story is saturated with this theme of promise. Chapters 12–13 show that Abraham, not Lot, received the promise; chapter 15 stresses that Abraham will indeed have a child to inherit the promise of descendants and land; chapter 16 focuses on an attempt by Abraham to gain such a child through his wife's servant, Hagar; parallel hospitality scenes in Genesis 18–19 again demonstrate Yahweh's preference for Abraham over Lot; and other stories throughout the Abraham narrative show Yahweh's deliverance of family members connected to Abraham on account of the promise (Gen 12:10–20, 20, 21). Finally, in a strange story that has deeply moved Jewish, Christian, and Muslim interpreters (Genesis 22), Yahweh endangers Abraham's son, Isaac, in asking Abraham to burn him as a sacrifice (Gen 22:1–2). When Abraham shows a willingness to act on Yahweh's request (Gen 22:3–11), Yahweh stops him from sacrificing Isaac and reaffirms the promise to him (Gen 22:12–18).

There are many things that lead scholars to suppose that these stories about Abraham were shaped during the Babylonian exile (or later). The exile is the first time we see mention of Abraham as a major figure in datable prophecies – those of Ezekiel (33:24) and Second Isaiah (Isa 41:8; 51:2) – and both exilic prophets show exiles taking comfort from the idea of Yahweh's promise to Abraham. It was during the exile that Abraham became a symbol of Yahweh's promise to Yahweh's people, a symbol that could give hope to exiles who – like Abraham – were small in number and powerless in a country not their own. It was when the Judean exiles themselves lacked a land and felt themselves cursed that they talked about Abraham and referred ever more often to God's promise to him. They focused less on the history of the monarchy and, instead, emphasized stories about their history before entering the land – about their ancestors and Moses – that most closely approximated their current condition. As we will see at the conclusion of this chapter, the L version of the Abrahamic promise in Gen 12:1–3 even takes promises of blessing and fame that once were given to the Judean king and applies them to Abraham, the landless patriarch. This kind of transfer of themes from a past governmental context (in this case, the monarchy) to a new, non-governmental context (in this case, the life of an emigrant) is typical for people undergoing exile. It is one among many signs that these L stories about Abraham were shaped and written down by exiles seeking hope in this promise-centered picture of their ancestor, Abraham.

The Story of Jacob at Bethel as an Example of the Exilic Addition of Promise to an Older Story

Many scholars now think that the speech in which God gives Abraham's promise to Jacob in Gen 28:13–15 (along with his reaction in 28:16) was added secondarily into a story about Jacob at Bethel that once only focused on angels going up and down a stairway there. The material in **bold-face** probably was added to an original story about the "gate of heaven." Try reading the story without the boldface elements. How is it different?

And he [Jacob] dreamed, and, look!, a stairway founded on the earth with its top in heaven. And, behold, divine messengers were going up and down it.

And, look!, Yahweh was standing on it and said, "I am Yahweh, the god of Abraham, your father and the god of Isaac. The land on which you are lying I will give to you and your children ... all clans of the earth shall bless themselves by you and your descendents ...

And Jacob woke up from his sleep and said, "Look, Yahweh is in this place, and I did not know it."

And he [Jacob] was afraid and said, "how awesome this place is! It is nothing other than the house of God and the gate of heaven." ... He called that place Bethel [Hebrew: "house of God/El"]. (Gen 28:12–13, 14b, 16–17, 19a)

Before the exilic, Lay Source addition of the promise theme, the older Jacob Bethel story (in regular type) was addressed to Israelites of the north. It connected the northern kingdom's royal sanctuary at Bethel, "the house of God and gate of heaven," with Jacob, the hero of the Israelites. Now, with the L additions of the promise and Jacob's response to it (the indented, **boldface** section), the new story connects this Jacob to the promise of land and blessing to Abraham (Gen 12:2–3), assuring Judean exiles of God's promise ultimately to them.

Yet we have seen that these exiles also were sorely conscious of their shortcomings. They felt Yahweh's anger at them, and many wondered if Yahweh could still live with them after their misdeeds (in their view) had caused the destruction of the Temple and exile into Babylonia. As a result, both Ezekiel and Second Isaiah had to reassure the exiles, who doubted that Yahweh would redeem them, *despite their past and present shortcomings*. Similar themes run through the Lay Source version of the stories of the patriarchs. Like the exiles whom Ezekiel and Second Isaiah addressed, so also the Abraham character in Genesis – the ancestral model of an exile in the L Source – doubts God's promise of protection and lies about Sarah being his wife (Gen 12:10–20; 20:1–18). He also shows doubts concerning God's promise of a son by arranging to have a son through Hagar (Genesis 16). Later on, as a result of the addition of the promise theme to the older Jacob narrative (see box on p. 192), the stories about Jacob in L now depict him as receiving the promise (Gen 28:13–15) despite having cheated his brother and tricking his father (Genesis 25, 27). Yahweh's promise apparently does not depend on the absolute virtue of its recipients.

The L Source story of Yahweh's covenant with Israel at Sinai (Exodus 19–24, 32–4) provides the clearest illustration of this theme of Yahweh's steadfast love. It stresses Yahweh's forgiveness of Israel even in the wake of Israel's building of the golden calf. This is not an easy forgiveness. The building of the golden calf in Exod 32:1–6 is depicted in the L text as an awful act, one that point by point reverses the covenant that Yahweh just made with Israel. Where Yahweh had just led Israel out of Egypt (Exod 19:4), the people now think Moses did (Exod 32:1); where Yahweh specifically prohibited making "gods of gold and silver" (Exod 20:22–3), the people now feel the need to make a golden calf to lead them in the wilderness (Exod 32:1); and where the previous covenant with Yahweh was sealed with a feast, "whole offerings" and "shared offerings" (Exod 24:5), the very same things seal the new covenant that the Israelites, including Aaron, make with the golden calf (Exod 32:5–6). Faced with this golden calf anti-covenant, Yahweh of this L story is ready to destroy all of the Israelite people and start all over with Moses (Exod 32:7–10). It is only after Moses reminds Yahweh of the promises to the patriarchs and pleads with him to think about how the Egyptians would perceive such destruction (Exod 32:11–13) that Yahweh changes his mind (Exod 32:14). Punishment still comes. Moses recruits the Levites – who up until this point in the story are just another tribe – and their first act is to kill every Israelite that their sword can reach (Exod 32:26–9). In addition, Yahweh brings a plague on the people (Exod 32:35). Nevertheless, Yahweh eventually comes back near Israel via the "tent of meeting" (Exod 33:7–17), and makes a new covenant with Israel in which the essentials of the previous laws are summarized (Exodus 34).

Thus, like the more hopeful prophecies in Ezekiel and Second Isaiah, the L Source stresses Yahweh's ability to work with his people *no matter what they do*. To be sure, the L Source stories and exilic prophecies insist that God gets angry about disobedience and imposes consequences. Nevertheless, Yahweh's ultimate promise to the people does not depend on their virtue. Yahweh saves Israel for the sake of his reputation ("name") and/or his promise to their ancestors. On this basis, the exiles can trust that Yahweh will lead them out of Babylonian and back into their homeland, despite the fact that they have not always lived up to Yahweh's expectations for them, do not do so, and will not do so.

These affirmations of God's steadfast covenant with Israel in the Exodus L Source texts now stand at the outset of the Bible that Jews and Christians share, but, ironically, many Christians pay attention to only the judgment on Israel in these stories. For centuries, Christians have used these biblical stories of Israel's shortcomings as ammunition to show why God rejected the Jewish people and started over with the church instead. According to this approach, the shortcomings of Israel described in these Old Testament texts anticipate Judaism's later rejection of Jesus as the messiah, a rejection which supposedly resulted in God's termination of God's covenant with Jews. Yet

basics L Source

<table>
<tr>
<td>Outline:
Yahweh's
promise-based,
unbreakable
covenant</td>
<td>I   Gift of ancestral promise-covenant in the wake of
     repeated primeval problems
     A   Problems with creation and post-flood
     B   Gift of promise to Abraham and heirs
II Creation + preservation of Moses-led, covenant people</td>
<td>Genesis*

Genesis 1–11*
Genesis 12–50*
Exodus*, Numbers*</td>
</tr>
</table>

Date   Exile (building on earlier, pre-exilic compositions).

Themes   If we focus on the later L-Source materials and not their probable pre-exilic sources, the emphasis of the source seems to be on the gift of Yahweh's covenant despite any shortcomings in the recipients. We see this as early as Yahweh's gift and transmission of the covenant to Abraham, Isaac, and Jacob despite their misdeeds and occasional lack of trust. Then, in the Moses story, Yahweh perseveres in giving a covenant to Israel despite their making of the golden calf (Exodus 32) and lack of trust in the promise of conquest (Num 14:11–25), largely on the basis of the earlier promises to the patriarchs.

More information: the gap between ancestors and Moses   Scholars note that the L Source texts in the Pentateuch, aside from a few exceptions such as Genesis 15 or Exodus 32, do not explicitly link the time of the ancestors in Genesis with the time of Moses. This is an indicator to many that writings about the ancestors were not linked with those about Moses until a very late time. Before this time, the stories about Jacob–Joseph, and possibly even those about Abraham and Isaac, stood separately from the Moses story. They were an alternative account of how Israel became related to Yahweh and came into the land.

Thus the exilic link of the primeval, ancestral, and Moses traditions with each other was important. It took what were once competing traditions and put one (the ancestral traditions) before the other (the Moses traditions). Imagine: how would this kind of combination change the meaning of each block of tradition?

the point of the L Source story of the covenant at Sinai is that God has made an unbreakable covenant with Israel, one that can withstand absolutely anything that Israel might do to damage it. Certainly, these stories at the heart of the present Pentateuch decisively stand against any idea that God's covenant with Israel could be ended for any reason, including Israel's refusal to see Jesus as the messiah.

To be sure, there is a lot of judgment on Israel in these texts. Indeed, few other literatures in world history are so brutally self-critical about their people as Israel's is.

This may result from the fact that large parts of Israel's literature – both Pentateuchal narrative and prophecy – were shaped by exiles who believed that their exile had been caused by their, and their ancestors', disobedience. Yet the texts discussed here just as decisively affirm Yahweh's steadfast care for his people. In these stories, Yahweh knows full well that Israel is a "stubborn" and "stiff necked" people (Exod 32:9; 33:5), yet even after they build the golden calf, God proclaims (in a passage recited weekly in Jewish liturgy):

> Yahweh, Yahweh, a God merciful and gracious
> slow to anger, and abounding in steadfast love and faithfulness,
> keeping steadfast love for the thousandth generation,
> forgiving bloodguilt and transgression and sin,
> yet by no means clearing the guilty,
> but visiting the bloodguilt of the parents on children and the children's
> children, to the third and fourth generation. (Exod 34:6–7 NRSV modified)

This L Source affirmation of God's grace strikes a compromise between the exilic additions to the Deuteronomistic history and Ezekiel's prophecy. With exilic parts of Kings (e.g. 2 Kgs 23:26–7), it affirms that children, even grandchildren and great-grandchildren, can pay for the sins of their parents. Yet with Ezekiel (Ezek 18), this text gives despairing exiles and later generations hope by stressing that there is a limit to such intergenerational guilt. Yahweh's ultimate faithfulness to his people is far more permanent and dominant than his anger. This text, along with the L Source Abraham story and promise-related elements of other parts of the Pentateuch, would have given hope to despairing Judeans in Babylonian exile.

The Priestly Source (P)

Not everyone in the exile, however, would have appreciated the depiction of Israel's early history in the L Source. Alongside the elders, there was another prominent group of exilic leaders – the priests – and they do not come off well in the L Source, especially in the L Source story of the covenant at Sinai. In general, many lower-ranking priests traced their ancestry back to Jacob's son Levi, and the leading priests traced their descent to a particular Levite, Aaron. The L Source does not positively portray either Aaron or the descendants of Levi as a group. Within the L Source Aaron helps the people make the golden calf (Exod 32:1–6) and later challenges the authority of Moses (Numbers 12). Meanwhile, the L Source depicts the founding of the Levitical priesthood as a sad compromise. Yahweh had originally intended that *all* Israel would be a "nation of priests" (Exod 19:6), and this is shown in the fact that young men (not special priests) help Moses make the sacrifices that seal the first covenant (Exod 24:5). Only after Aaron had helped make a golden calf does Moses set aside the Levites as a special group, and their

READING
Gen 1:1–2:3, 17; and skim
Exodus 25–31 and 35–40.

first act is to kill every Israelite that they can reach (Exod 32:25–9). In sum, the L Source depicts the priesthood, particularly the Aaronide priesthood, as founded in idolatry and the shedding of Israelite blood – hardly the kind of picture the priests would want to paint of themselves.

These and other concerns probably led the leading Aaronide priests in exile to formulate their own story of Israel's history before it had taken possession of the land, a story aimed at replacing the L Source version of events with one more favorable to the priests and their concerns. Although the present Pentateuch now has texts from this **P Source** or **Priestly Source** intertwined with the L Source, P probably stood separately from L when it was originally composed in the exilic period. There are too many repeated narrations of events in L and P for one of them to have been created as a supplement to the other, and there are several instances where the original point of a Priestly text is only clear when it is read separately from its Lay Source counterpart. Consider, for example, the divergent accounts in L and P of the reasons for Jacob's

---

Which Texts Were Once Part of the P Source?

We have no separate copy of the hypothesized Priestly Source, but scholars have agreed for a long time on which parts of the Pentateuch probably were part of it. The following are some of them. Try reading them together.

P in the Genesis primeval history

Gen 1:1–2:3; 5:1–28, 30–32; major parts of the flood story (such as 6:9–22; 7:13–16a; 8:14–19; 9:1–17); the post-flood genealogy in 11:10–26 (and maybe parts of Genesis 10).

P in the Genesis ancestral history

Birth and journey of Abraham (11:27, 31–2; 12:4b–5; 13:6); birth of Ishmael (16:3, 15–16); covenant of circumcision (Genesis 17); birth of Isaac (21:3–5); death of Abraham and the transition to Isaac and his sons (25:7–21); Esau's marriages and Isaac's sending of Jacob to Padan-Aram for a better wife (26:34–5; 27:46–28:9); Jacob's encounter with God

at Bethel (35:9–15); death of Isaac and transition from family of Isaac to Jacob's family (35:22b–37:1); and possible fragments of a P Joseph story (e.g. Gen 37:2; 46:5–7 and 50:12–13).

P in the Moses story

The oppression in Egypt (Exod 1:1–5, 7, 13–14, 23–5); call of Moses and Aaron (Exod 6:2–7:7, also 7:8–13); plagues of blood, frogs, gnats, and boils (7:19–22; 8:5–7, 15–19; 9:8–12; 11:9–10); Passover and Red Sea crossing (12:1–20, 28, 40–51; 14:1–4, 8–10, 15–28, 21–3, 26, 28–9); departure for Sinai and giving of Mannah (15:22, 27; 16:1–3, 6–27); arrival at Sinai and Tabernacle building (Exod 19:1–2a; 24:15–31:18; 35:1–39:43; 40:1–38); all of Leviticus and Num 1:1–10:28; the spying of the land (Num 13:1–17a, 21, 25–6, 32–3; 14:1–3*, 5–10, 26–38); part of the rebellion of Korah story (Num 16:1–11*, 16–24, 27a, 35–50; all of Numbers 17–18); the rebellion at the rock (20:1–13); Aaron's death (20:22b–29).

departure from Canaan. The L Source version of this story is the old trickster tale about Jacob stealing his father's blessing and fleeing Esau's murderous wrath (Gen 27:1–45). The (later) P version of these events aimed to provide a different reason: Esau had married foreign wives (Gen 26:34–5), those wives had been awful to Rebekah (Gen 27:46), and so Isaac blessed Jacob (on purpose!) and sent him homeward to get a proper wife (Gen 28:1–6). Though they are now separated from one another by the older trickster story (Gen 27:1–45), the P texts that give this alternative explanation connect well together (Gen 26:34–5; 27:46–28:6). They probably originally stood apart from the trickster story in Gen 27:1–45 and were designed to replace it.

Thus, we can learn something about texts from this exilic Priestly Source when we consider them apart from the Lay Source texts with which they are now combined. When the P Source was separate from the L Source, it chronicled God's involvement with the world in three major stages: (1) creation, (2) the flood and following covenant with Noah, and (3) the covenant with Abraham and eventual creation at Sinai of Israel out of the heirs to Abraham's promise. The first stage, found in Gen 1:1–2:3 along with most of Genesis 5, is God's creation of an orderly and peaceful universe, a cosmos crowned by godlike humans who are made in God's image (Gen 1:26–31). The second stage, found in Priestly texts scattered across Genesis 6–9 (such as 6:9–22 and 9:1–17), describes God's actions after this creation was violated by violence: God's destruction of almost all life through a flood, God's rescue of Noah's family and other animals, and God's making of a covenant with Noah and the rest of life not to bring such a flood again. The third and most important stage in P is God's creation of the holy community of Israel. This starts with God's making of a special covenant of circumcision with Abraham (Genesis 17), a covenant in which God gives Abraham and his heirs a special version of the creation blessing given in Genesis 1 (Gen 17:6–8; compare Gen 1:27–8). Other Priestly texts in Genesis show the passing of this blessing on to Jacob (not Esau; Gen 26:34–5; 27:46–28:5; 35:9–15) and trace the genealogies of Abraham's offspring (Gen 25:7–18; 35:22–6; 36:1–43). Jacob in the P Source next goes to Egypt, where his descendants multiply into the people of Israel (Exod 1:1–7) and are oppressed by Pharaoh (Exod 1:13–14; 2:23–5). God then calls Moses and Aaron – in Priestly texts – to lead Israel out of Egypt through plagues and the dividing of the Red Sea (Exod 6:2–7:13; etc.). This prepares for the Priestly story of events and instructions given at Mount Sinai (most of Exodus 25 through Numbers 10). There God works through Moses to build a wilderness sanctuary, a "tabernacle," in which God can dwell (Exod 24:15–31:17; 35:1–40:33) and then instructs Israel (through Moses) on how it can become a holy community gathered round the tabernacle (Leviticus and Num 1:1–10:10). The other main narratives that were part of P focus on God's confirmation of Moses's and Aaron's leadership of this new, holy community.

This mass of Priestly material contains some of the oldest texts in the Pentateuch. One Priestly text, the priestly blessing in Num 6:24–6, has been found on an ancient, pre-exilic silver amulet, our earliest copy of a text now in the Bible, and scholars have found signs that other P laws and even some narratives may date from before the exile. Nevertheless, the overall sweep of the Priestly narrative shows several signs of being shaped in the exilic or early post-exilic periods:

basics (Hypothesized) P Source

Outline

I   Expanded genealogy: creation and promise
  A   Elohim: creation–re-creation   Gen 1:1–2:3; 5:1–9:28*;
     11:10–26
  B   El-Shaddai: the Abrahamic covenant   Gen 11:27–50:26*
II   Yahweh: Moses+Aaron-led pilgrimage
  A   Pilgrimage to Sinai   Exodus 1–19*
  B   Sinai indwelling and instruction   Exodus 20–Numbers 10*
  C   Pilgrimage from Sinai to the land   Numbers 11–36*

Date

Exile into post-exile (with short pre-exilic sources).

Themes: shifts in the divine name

As indicated in the outline above, some of the shifts in the Priestly Source correspond to shifts in the divine designation that it uses for God. In the primeval period God is known as *Elohim* (Hebrew for "God") and makes with Noah and all life a covenant that is marked by a rainbow. During the ancestral period God appears to Abraham as *El-Shaddai* (Hebrew for "God Almighty") and makes a covenant with him that is marked with circumcision and passed on by Abraham's heirs, Isaac and Jacob. In the final period, God appears to Moses and the rest of Israel as Yahweh (see the P version of Moses's call in Exod 6:2–8). The centerpoint of this period is Israel's stay at Sinai, where the tabernacle is built, the priesthood of Aaron and his sons is established, and Yahweh's glory comes down to dwell amidst Israel.

More information: P as "redaction" or separate "source"?

The bulk of past and present scholars believe that a shorter form of this Priestly narrative once existed as a separate source, independent of the L texts with which it is now combined. Others, however, believe that the Priestly texts of the Pentateuch were written from the outset as an expansion of the L texts and never existed separately. This alternative perspective – P as "redaction" –can make a difference in how one understands the structure and themes of the first Priestly Pentateuch. Can you imagine how the above survey of P would have to be rewritten if P were an expansion of the L Source?

- Where Deuteronomy and the rest of the Deuteronomistic history *argue* for the idea that sacrifice to Yahweh can only happen in one place, the Priestly narratives appear to presuppose this. P does not describe any sacrifice by Noah or the patriarchs before the establishment of the tabernacle at Mount Sinai.
- The P narrative focuses before Sinai on practices that could be carried out in exile and were particularly important then, such as circumcision (Genesis 17), an ancient

form of Passover celebration that was celebrated at home (Exod 12:1–20), and Sabbath (Exodus 16).

- Consistent with tendencies of exilic communities to focus on communal boundaries, the P document includes a prominent emphasis on the importance of ethnic purity and the problems with intermarriage, an emphasis seen particularly clearly in the story of Isaac's rejection of Esau because of intermarriage and his sending of Jacob to Haran to get a proper wife (Gen 26:34–5; 27:46–28:9).
- The P document as a whole leads up to the story of God's creation of the wilderness tabernacle with the priests of Aaron at its head. This points to an exilic time when the monarchy is no longer a living institution, and its accoutrements (e.g. a crown; Exod 28:36–8) are assumed by the priests.

The language and concerns of this Priestly document are closest to those of Ezekiel on the one hand and Second Isaiah on the other. Indeed, several scholars have shown that the author(s) of P seem(s) to know Second Isaiah and speak in a similar time period. Like Second Isaiah, the author of the P story encourages exiles to return to the land, in this case through stressing God's power in the exodus, the importance of the land in the promise (see Exod 6:2–8), and God's punishment of those who lack enough belief to embrace God's promise and return (Num 13:32; 14:36–7). In these ways and others, the narratives of P show the impact of the Babylonian exile, along with hopes of return, on the Priestly understanding of Israel's history before the conquest. Though the authors of this P document drew freely on pre-exilic texts of various kinds, the whole that they put together is a distinctively exilic story for exiles about ancient Israel before the people had a land.

We can see the distinctive mix of older and later materials in the seven-day creation account with which the Bible opens: Gen 1:1–2:3. On the one hand, scholars have found some signs that this chapter was formed out of older materials, and Jeremiah may show knowledge of an older form of this story when he refers to earth as "formless and void" and heaven as "having no light" (Jer 4:23; see Gen 1:1–3). On the other hand, like other texts in P, this story as we have it now links with issues and themes that became particularly prominent in the exile. For example, the whole structure of the text is oriented around a seven-day scheme that climaxes in God's observance of the Sabbath (Gen 2:1–3). We see a similar emphasis on the Sabbath in Ezekiel (Ezek 20:12–24; 22:8, 26; 23:38).

In addition, the text transfers royal traits to non-royal figures, much as in Second Isaiah. In this case, the text builds on ancient ideas in

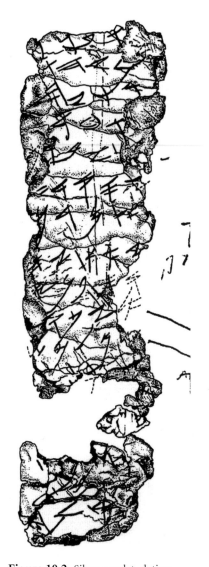

Figure 10.2 Silver amulet, dating to just before the fall of Jerusalem. It contained a version of the priestly blessing found in Num 6:24–6. The inscription proves that some texts now found in the Priestly layer of Genesis (e.g. Num 6:24–6) date to the pre-exilic period. This does not mean, however, that all of the Priestly layer can be dated to that period.

basics | Book of Leviticus

Outline	I	Establishment of the tabernacle cult	1–10
		A Instructions for sacrifices	1–7
		B Establishment of priesthood subject to instructions	8–10
	II	Establishment of holy people	11–26
		A Purity rules	11–15
		B Holiness Code	16–26

Date Exilic to early post-exilic (building on pre-exilic sources).

Themes Leviticus now stands at the center of the Pentateuch, and it represents the center of Priestly teaching. Though the book starts with specific instructions for priestly sacrifice (Leviticus 1–7), it concludes with rules for creating a holy, priest-like people (Leviticus 16–26). Many eating and purity rules, once meant only for priests, are extended in Leviticus to the whole people of Israel. These cultic rules are not seen as a burden in the book or difficult to follow. Instead, they are an affirmation of the special, particularly holy character of Yahweh's beloved people.

More information: the "Holiness Code" Some past scholars identified Leviticus 17–26 as a "**Holiness Code**" (**H**) that contains distinctive laws, close in perspective to the prophet Ezekiel. This code may have existed before P and been inserted into its present context by a Priestly or later author. Like both the Covenant Code and Deuteronomy, this Holiness Code started with a law about where to sacrifice (Leviticus 17).

Other scholars, such as Israel Knohl (*The Sanctuary of Silence: The Priestly Torah and the Holiness School* [Minneapolis: Fortress, 1995]), see the bulk of Leviticus 17–26 as part of a broader H layer of texts found throughout the Pentateuch. According to Knohl and others, the texts in this H layer are distinguished in language and thought from *earlier*, originally separate Priestly traditions, such as those found in Gen 1:1–2:3 or Exodus 19–25, 35–40.

Egyptian and Mesopotamian royal theology that the king was made in the image of God; he bore in his body a sign of his divine commission to rule others. The description of the creation of humanity in Gen 1:26–7 takes these ideas and applies them to humanity in general, both men and women. Indeed, many translations overlook the fact that the Hebrew of this passage explicitly connects the creation of humanity in God's image with their destiny to rule creation. God's speech to the divine council (note the plural address) makes this clear:

MORE ON METHOD: INSIGHTS FROM HISTORY OF RELIGIONS

Often we can learn more about the ancient images, metaphors, and ideas in the Bible through looking at other ancient religious ideas and practices studied as part of what is sometimes termed "**history of religions**." An example is the tantalizing reference to being made "in the image of God" in Gen 1:26–7.

The king as the image of god in the ancient Near East
Texts in both Mesopotamia and Egypt depict the king as an image of god, representing that god on earth much as a divine statue would. For example, one Mesopotamian letter to the king says:
The father of the king, my lord, was the image of [the god] Bel, and the king, my lord, is likewise the image of Bel.

Similarly, an Egyptian text has the god Amun proclaim about the king:
You are my beloved son, who came forth out of my love, my image that I set on earth. I let you rule the land in peace.

How this might inform a reading of Gen 1:26–7
These royal ideas are applied to all of humanity in Gen 1:26–7, both the idea of being made in god's image and the idea of this divine image being a mark of authority to rule others.

Then God said, "let us make humanity in our image and like our form, *so that* they may rule the fish of the sea, the birds of the heavens, the cattle and all the earth, and all the creatures creeping on the earth." (Gen 1:26)

According to this radical reapplication of ancient royal theology, there is a reason for the agreement between the human form and human pictures of God in human terms. God had the "human" form first and gave it to humans as a mark of the human destiny to rule creation. According to this text, we are like little god statues walking around the earth, and all the animals of the earth can see in our divine bodily form the stamp of our authority to rule them.

Later interpreters of this text often have been reluctant to see it as affirming an actual bodily similarity between God and humans. Though the text is quite explicit in using multiple terms for physical similarity, both "image" and "likeness," these interpreters have argued that the chapter really means to assert that humans bear a spiritual or intellectual likeness to God. Being "made in the image of God" thus means that humans share God's capacity for relationship or rational thought or the like. Later historical critics have buttressed this approach by arguing that the Priestly narrative has too elevated a picture of God to imagine that God might have a body that humans could resemble. Nevertheless, Ezekiel, a prophet with many affinities to the Priestly narrative, has a vision in his call narrative of the divine throne with "something like the appearance of a human" upon it (Ezek 1:26). Apparently Priestly exiles such as Ezekiel *could* imagine that God had a form that humans could resemble. It is later Biblical interpreters, including historical critics, who have struggled with seeing humans as having a bodily similarity to God.

Read in this way, Gen 1:1–2:3 would have helped Judean exiles understand their situation in a new way. Though they might be relatively powerless vis-à-vis their Babylonian overlords, they shared with the rest of humanity a likeness to God that was seen in their bodies, a likeness that made them "kings" of creation. Moreover, unlike the rest of humanity, the Judean exiles acted out this similarity to God in a particular way: just as God observed a Sabbath after creating the universe, they likewise observed a Sabbath every week. Thus this text takes an ancient practice that became more important during the exile, the Sabbath, and makes it a sign of the exiles' likeness to God.

History and Fiction

By this point many readers may be wondering, "But what about what actually happened with Abraham or at Sinai? Does all this just mean that the exiles made all these stories up?" To this, the answer is both "no" and "yes." The answer is "no," because ancient peoples, including ancient Israel, almost always built new stories out of older ones. Especially with respect to stories about people (rather than gods), ancient authors almost always started with a tradition – whether oral or written – about a given person and then built on that tradition. They did not "make them all up." Yet there is also a sense in which the answer to the question is "yes." Ancient authors did make up certain things. Unlike many contemporary historians, these ancient authors felt free to embellish, modify, and extend the traditions given to them. In light of their experience of exile, for example, exilic authors found new, promise-centered ways to tell stories about Jacob and Moses, ways that would never have occurred to them before. They saw these stories through the lens of truths they had learned in exile. As a result, they retold, extended, and connected these stories in light of these truths, in light of what they believed "must have happened."

Now we no longer can untangle later "truths" learned in exile or other periods from the kinds of "historical truth" about Israel's early history that contemporary readers often want to know. Through using both data from archaeology and analysis of non-biblical literature, we can affirm that the traditions in the Pentateuch, both L and P, probably have some kind of historical core. Later storytellers would not have made up characters such as Abraham and Sarah. Certainly, exiles would not have created a deliverer figure like Moses with an Egyptian name and foreign wives. Nevertheless, it appears that the stories as we have them now, including almost all their dialogue and other details, reflect their settings in later periods of Israel's history. As a result, they are more useful as sources for the "truths" learned by Israelites in these later periods than in reconstructing historical "truths" about the times of Abraham and/or Moses. We might wish we knew exactly what Sarah said to God or Moses said to Pharaoh, but the biblical texts about them are not good sources for this. They *can* tell us, however, what later Israelites had to say to each other about their identity as a people and God's intentions toward them.

Let us consider this in relation to a concrete example: the L Source story of covenant at Sinai discussed above (Exodus 19–24, 32–4). Contemporary readers of this story could argue endlessly about whether or not it actually happened. Yet in the end, such arguments miss the larger point of the story. The story that we now have is addressed to Israel of the "thousandth" generation, long after Sinai, an Israel who wonders – as in the laments discussed above – whether God will be eternally angry for past disobedience or will turn and save God's people. The answer given in this story is a decisive affirmation of God's intent to save the people no matter what. This text, with its "yes" to God's mercy, has been absolutely central to Jewish worship and thought, and this affirmation of God's unconditional relationship with Israel can be read by Christians as an anticipation of God's broader unconditional grace toward the world as seen through Jesus Christ. Ultimately, such "truths" about God in Judaism and Christianity are much more central to the ongoing significance of the Bible than specific historical "truths" that could be affirmed or uncovered using modern historical methods. Moreover, these important ideas in ancient biblical texts can be missed if the debates about them all focus on whether or not the events described in them actually happened.

Gen 12:1–3

FOCUS TEXT

Let us conclude by taking a brief look at God's first speech to Abraham, still called "Abram" at this point, in Gen 12:1–3. This text has two main parts: Yahweh's command to Abram to "go now from your country, your kindred, and your father's house to the land that I will show you" (Gen 12:1), and the following promises that Yahweh will make Abram into "a great nation," make his "name great," and grant him abundant blessing (Gen 12:2–3). These promises echo a more ancient prayer for kings, seen in Ps 72:17, that the king be blessed, have his "name" (reputation) endure forever, and be so fortunate that others "bless themselves by him." This means that the king will be such a paradigm of good luck that others wish on themselves the kind of blessing that the king enjoys (for example, "may God make me as blessed and fortunate as king David of Israel"). Now, in the climactic promise in Gen 12:3, Abram is promised that he, like such kings, will be such an example of blessing that all "clans of the earth" will look to him and bless themselves by him, so that people in other nations might say something like, "may God bless me like Abram and more so."

This promise is echoed in various forms throughout other parts of Genesis (Gen 22:15–18; 26:2–5; 28:13–15), yet Christians and Jews disagree in a basic way on how to interpret the final part about Abram's blessing and other nations: "all the clans of the earth shall . . ." Many Jews follow the lead of Rashi, one of the greatest Jewish commentators on the Bible, who followed a translation much like that given above: that all clans of the earth shall "bless themselves by" Abram; that is, wish on themselves a blessing as good as the one he has. Understood this way, the rest of the Pentateuch following Gen 12:1–3 is a story of God's (partial) fulfillment of the special promises of blessing on Abraham and his offspring, especially God's blessing and protection of God's chosen people, Israel. In contrast, many Christians follow the lead of Paul in understanding this text as a promise to Abram that "all the gentiles shall be blessed through you" (Gal 3:8), that blessing will flow through Abram – by way of Jesus Christ – to the other nations of the earth. Understood this way, the rest of the Pentateuch following Gen 12:1–3 is focused not on God's blessing and protection of Israel per se, but on the way the people of Israel, Abram's offspring, are a medium of blessing for the other nations of the earth. Thus, these two options for translating the promise in Gen 12:3, both of which are possible in Hebrew, lead to very different understandings of the whole Pentateuch. Rashi's reading remains closest to the emphasis on the people of Israel in the rest of the Hebrew Torah. Paul's reading – reflected in many contemporary translations of Gen 12:3 – reinterprets Abraham's promise in the context of a broader Christian Bible that includes Jesus Christ.

Turning to historical interpretation, Gen 12:1–3 looks quite different depending on whether one thinks it was written by Solomon's scribes or by exilic authors. Some would see Gen 12:1–3 as part of an early continuation of the J primeval history, a continuation written to support and endorse Solomon's kingdom. Read this way, God's promises of greatness and blessing to Abram in Gen 12:1–3 anticipate the time when Israel will "become a great nation" under Solomon, and Solomon will enjoy an immense reputation and fabled blessing. If this is correct, Gen 12:1–3 and the rest of the extended J/Yahwistic document thus provide divine sanction to Solomon's mini-empire. This has led some, such as Walter Brueggemann in his influential book *The Prophetic Imagination* (Minneapolis: Fortress, 2001), to criticize texts such as Gen 12:1–3 because they see them as J texts endorsing an oppressive empire.

Things look quite different, however, if one understands Gen 12:1–3 and other promise texts to be words of hope to despairing exiles in the wake of the destruction of Jerusalem and loss of the monarchy. Put in this context, Gen 12:1–3 (like Gen 1:1–2:3) is a story where a non-royal figure, Abram, receives promises that were once given to kings. We have seen similar exilic gifts of royal promises to other figures in Second Isaiah – to the Persian Cyrus in Isa 44:28–45:1 and to the people in Isa 55:3. Yet the author of Gen 12:1–3 and surrounding texts tells the Abram/Abraham story in a special way, so that Abraham almost sounds like an exile living long before the Babylonian exile. He is made into someone to whom the exiles can relate. Like them, he lives in Babylon, "Ur of the Chaldees" (Gen 11:28), and, like them, he has been called to go and live as a stranger in a land he does not know (Gen 12:1). In light of this, the promises to Abram become promises of hope to the exiles, much like the prophecies of hope to exiles that we saw in the exilic portions of Isaiah (40–55), Jeremiah, and Ezekiel. Where the exiles longed for a restoration of their nation, they hear in Gen 12:2 that their ancestor Abram, also an exile, was promised that he would "become a great nation."

Where we know that the exiles felt "cursed" because of their exile, this text asserts the opposite: they will be so blessed that they will become an example of blessing to other peoples on earth (Gen 12:3). Moreover, there is an additional promise in Gen 12:2–3 that relates specifically to the vulnerability that exiles faced when living as a minority in a larger culture. God reassures Abram of his protection. God will bless those who bless him, and God will curse those who so much as "treat [him] lightly" (Gen 12:3). Exiles would have heard this as a promise that God will provide similar protection to them, as Abraham's children, while living in Babylon.

Conclusion on the Torah (Pentateuch) and Exile

In sum, it makes a big difference whether you read Gen 12:1–3 and related texts as endorsing Solomon's mini-empire or as reassuring exiles who had been crushed by the Neo-Babylonian empire. This book has followed recent scholarship that dates Gen 12:1–3 and other L promise texts to the exilic period. Yet whatever the date of the L and P texts, it was during the Babylonian exile, when Judean exiles most desperately needed words of hope, that these writings about God's promises to Abraham's children and God's formation of Israel in the wilderness moved to the center of the Hebrew Bible. It was during exile that stories of Israel's history before conquest and monarchy started to become the literary foundation on which everything else in the Bible was based.

Up through the exile, however, this literary foundation, this "Torah of Moses," was split in two: an L narrative and a quite different P narrative. Each text features different groups, groups probably responsible for preserving each narrative and expanding it. The L narrative features the "elders," a major group of lay leaders in the exilic and post-exilic periods. The P narrative features the Aaronide priests, a priestly group that first achieves dominance in the late exile and post-exilic periods. These groups, and their texts, remained independent throughout the exile. There was no unifying political structure in this period to bring them together; the monarchy was gone. We will not see conditions for unifying these L and P stories until the Persians sponsor the rebuilding of a community of returnee exiles in Jerusalem. We turn next to that important event.

CHAPTER TEN REVIEW

1. Know the meaning and significance of the following terms discussed in this chapter:
- E (or Elohistic) Source
- H
- history of religions
- Holiness Code.
- J (or Yahwistic) Source
- JE
- L (or Lay) Source
- non-Priestly (or non-P) Source
- P (or Priestly) Source
- Tetrateuch

2. What is one major reason that scholars now doubt whether separate and yet parallel J and E documents once existed and stand behind the non-Priestly materials of the Pentateuch? (Hint: it's *not* because we lack copies of those sources.)

3. What are three sorts of problems that have arisen for the early dating of non-Priestly, L traditions?

4. What sorts of "history" are best discussed in relation to the Pentateuch? How?

5. Who are the two groups, newly prominent in the exilic period, that may have preserved the separate L and P traditions before they were combined?

RESOURCES FOR FURTHER STUDY

More on the formation of the Pentateuch

Carr, David. *Reading the Fractures of Genesis*. Louisville, KY: Westminster John Knox Press, 1996.

Genesis

Brueggemann, Walter. *Genesis*. Interpretation. Atlanta: John Knox Press, 1982.

Sarna, N. M. *Genesis*. Jewish Publication Society Torah Commentary. Philadelphia: Jewish Publication Society, 1989.

Westermann, Claus. *Genesis: A Practical Commentary*, trans. David Green. Grand Rapids: Eerdmans, 1987.

Exodus

Childs, Brevard. *The Book of Exodus: A Critical Theological Commentary*. Old Testament Library. Philadelphia: Westminster Press, 1974.

Johnstone, William. *Exodus*. Old Testament Guides. Sheffield: Sheffield Academic Press, 1990.

Sarna, Nahum. *Exodus*. JPS Torah Commentary. Philadelphia: Jewish Publication Society, 1991.

Leviticus

Gerstenberger, Erhard S. *Leviticus: A Commentary*. Old Testament Library. Louisville, KY: Westminster John Knox Press, 1996.

Gorman, Frank H. *Divine Presence and Community: A Commentary on the Book of Leviticus*. International Theological Commentary. Grand Rapids: Eerdmans, 1997.

Numbers

Budd, Philip J. *Numbers*. Word Biblical Commentary. Waco, TX: Word, 1984.

Olson, Dennis. *Numbers*. Interpretation. Louisville, KY: Westminster John Knox Press, 1996.

Wenham, Gordon J. *Numbers*. Old Testament Guides. Sheffield: Sheffield Academic Press, 1997.

CHAPTER 11

THE TORAH, THE PSALMS, AND THE PERSIAN-SPONSORED REBUILDING OF JUDAH

Chapter Outline

CHAPTER OVERVIEW

This chapter traces how central parts of the Hebrew Bible subtly reflect a *positive* relationship between Judeans and the Persian empire inaugurated by Cyrus. We will see how the Persians played a supportive role at several stages in the restoration of Judah, allowing many exiles to return and helping establish a Temple-centered community of returnees in Jerusalem. In significant ways, the present Hebrew Bible is a collection of Hebrew texts made by former exiles sponsored by the Persian government. This helps explain why so many biblical texts sharply criticize the Assyrian and Babylonian empires but adopt a generally positive tone the few times they mention Persia.

The crowning achievement of this period was the elevation of a combined Pentateuch, a new "Torah of Moses," as a central authority to the community of returnees in Jerusalem. As we will see, there is even some evidence that the relationship with the Persians may have played some role in occasioning the dramatic, artful interweaving of L and P that characterizes Genesis–Deuteronomy. Not immediately, but over time, this combined Pentateuch came to play a central and unifying role for Judeans everywhere. One sign of its decisive importance is the way the book of Psalms, a collection of collections of ancient prayer texts used in worship and education, is now introduced by a Torah psalm and divided into five parts that correspond to the five books of the Torah.

Figure 11.1 Relief from the Persian capital of Persepolis. It depicts the many subjects of the Persian empire, dressed in the distinctive dress of each country, bearing tribute to the Persian king. The image well illustrates ways that the Persian empire cultivated the support of diverse cultures for its far-flung empire.

History: Persian-Sponsored Building of a Temple and Torah-Centered Judaism

READING
The Nehemiah memoir (Neh 1:1–7:4; 13:10–14, 30b–31) and Ezra narrative (Ezra 1–10 and Neh 8; compare this with 1 Esdras in the Apocrypha).

EXERCISE
Using the parallel below, compare and contrast the Persian king Cyrus's edict about his anointing by the Babylonian gods (Marduk, Bel, and Nabu) with Ezra 1:1–4.

Cyrus cylinder	Ezra 1:1–4
"I am Cyrus, king of the world, great king, mighty king, king of Babylon, king of the land of Sumer and Akkad, king of the four quarters, son of Cambyses . . . whose rule Bel and Nabu cherish, whose kingship they desire for their hearts' pleasures. . . . I did not allow any to terrorize the land of Sumer and Akkad. I kept in view the needs of Babylon and all its sanctuaries to promote their well being. The citizens of Babylon . . . I lifted their unbecoming yoke . . .	1:2 Thus says King Cyrus of Persia:
At my deeds Marduk, the great Lord, rejoiced, and to me, Cyrus, the king who worshipped, and to Cambyses, my son, the offspring of my loins, and to all my troops he graciously gave his blessing, and in good spirit before him we glorified exceedingly his high divinity.	"Yahweh, the God of heaven, has given me
All the kings who sat in the throne rooms, throughout the four quarters, from the Upper to the Lower Sea, those who dwelt in . . . all the kings of the West Country who dwelt in tents, brought me their heavy tribute and kissed my feet in Babylon.	all the kingdoms of the earth,
From . . . to the cities of Ashur and Susa, Agade, Eshnuna, the cities of Zamban, Meurnu, Der, as far as the region of the land of Gutium, the holy cities beyond the Tigris whose sanctuaries had been in ruins over a long period, the gods whose abode is in the midst of them I returned to the places and housed them in lasting abodes. I (also) gathered together all their inhabitants and restored to them their dwellings.	and he has commanded me to build a house for him in Jerusalem which is in Judah. 1:3 Any of you who are from his people – may his God be with him! – are now allowed to go to Jerusalem in Judah, and rebuild the house of Yahweh, the God of Israel – he is the God who is in Jerusalem;
The Gods of Sumer and Akkad whom Nabonidus had, to the anger of the Lord of the Gods, brought into Babylon, I, at the bidding of Marduk, the great Lord, made to dwell in peace in their habitations, delightful abodes." (Translation: ANET 316)	1:4 and let all who remain, wherever they live, be supported by the people of their place with silver and gold, with goods and with animals, besides freewill offerings for the house of God in Jerusalem."

Figure 11.2 The Cyrus cylinder.

The **Cyrus cylinder** quoted above (see Figure 11.2) marks another major shift of empires in the Near Eastern world. The Persian king, Cyrus, had just conquered Babylon without a fight, aided in part by disgruntled priests in Babylon who violently disagreed with the religious policies of Nabonidus, the last king of Babylon. Nabonidus had elevated the status of the moon god, Sin, over that of traditional Babylonian gods, and he had removed the divine statues of those gods from their sanctuaries across Babylon. In the Cyrus cylinder, Cyrus uses the Akkadian language and the form of an Akkadian inscription to describe how the Babylonian gods chose him to be king over Babylon and restore the divine statues to their proper places. Apparently, Cyrus's self-promotion was at least partially successful. A Babylonian priest wrote another text around the same time, called "the verse account of Nabonidus," that chronicles the religious crimes of Nabonidus, praises Cyrus's restoration of Babylon's sanctuaries, and concludes by saying that the people of Babylon now have "a joyful heart" and rejoice "to look upon Cyrus as king."

Though Cyrus never mentions Judah in his cylinder, we know from the Bible that the Judean exiles also celebrated this shift in power. Even before Cyrus had conquered Babylon, Second Isaiah had seen him on the horizon and quoted Yahweh as anointing Cyrus to subdue nations and rebuild Jerusalem (Isa 44:28–45:1). Furthermore, similar texts at the end of the books of Chronicles (2 Chr 36:22–3) and beginning of Ezra (Ezra 1:1–4) give a Judean version of Cyrus's proclamation, this time proclaiming that Yahweh has given him rule over all the earth and appointed him to rebuild Jerusalem. Since there is no Persian copy of such an inscription, we do not know if something like this was issued by the Persian government or whether it was created by Judean scribes on analogy with inscriptions like the Cyrus cylinder. In either case, these texts from Second Isaiah and the beginning of Ezra show an important development among the exiles. Where they hated Babylon, many fully supported the Persian empire and endorsed the idea that the Persian king, Cyrus, had been appointed by God to save and restore them.

The biblical texts show in turn that the Persians did much to support the Judean exiles, supporting their return and rebuilding efforts and thus insuring that there was pro-Persian local leadership in Judah and Jerusalem, a somewhat strategic area for the Persians as they struggled with Greece for control of the Eastern Mediterranean. In supporting such local leadership, the Persians were not doing something entirely new, since Mesopotamian empires such as Assyria had used similar tactics to cultivate sympathetic local leaders in areas that were important to them. The difference is that the Hebrew Bible was shaped by former exiles who had been supported by Persia, while it appears that earlier biblical authors did not enjoy such sponsorship by imperial powers.

Our main source for history of Judah in this period, Ezra–Nehemiah, appears to be another example of combination of separate sources, one that ends up focusing on Ezra and another on Nehemiah. Ezra–Nehemiah treats these figures separately, and several early Jewish sources seem to know their stories separately (including, in this case, an old Greek translation of the Ezra source, 1 Esdras). For these reasons, many scholars believe there are two main sources behind the present book of Ezra–Nehemiah: a first person account by Nehemiah of how he rebuilt Jerusalem and provided for the Levites (Neh 1:1–7:4; parts of Nehemiah 13 and possibly 12), and a mostly third person account of the rebuilding of Jerusalem and then Ezra's leading of the community to divorce foreign wives and obey the Torah (Ezra 1–10 and Nehemiah 8//1 Esdras). Only later, probably centuries later in the Hellenistic period, did an author interweave these two sources and add new materials, forming a new book where Ezra and Nehemiah overlapped. In the process, this much later author appears to have confused the order of the two figures, not knowing that there were two different Persian kings named "Artaxerxes." He mistakenly placed Nehemiah, who arrived and rebuilt Jerusalem's walls in the twentieth year of Artaxerxes *the first* (445 BCE), *after* Ezra, who found those walls rebuilt and probably arrived in the seventh year of Artaxerxes *the second* (397 BCE).

Along with these two main narratives – the Nehemiah memoir and the Temple rebuilding/Ezra story – we also have the words of several prophets dated to this time as sources for learning about the period of the post-exilic restoration of the Jerusalem community. These include Haggai, Zechariah (particularly Zechariah 1–8), and post-exilic portions of Isaiah such as "Third Isaiah" in Isaiah 56–66 (see Chapter 12). Using these sources, scholars have identified four main stages of the restoration, each of which seems to have featured some sort of Persian sponsorship: the return of some exiles to Judah, Zerubbabel and Joshua's rebuilding of the Jerusalem Temple, Nehemiah's rebuilding of the walls of Jerusalem, and Ezra's elevation of the Torah of Moses to the center of a Jerusalem community who had just expelled foreign wives and their children. The following paragraphs discuss each stage in turn before briefly considering the situation of Judeans still living abroad in Egypt and Mesopotamia.

The biblical account of Cyrus's decree gives permission to exiles to "go up to Jerusalem which is in Judah and build the house of Yahweh, god of Israel, the god who is in Jerusalem" (Ezra 1:3). This introduces the first of a series of returns of exiles from Babylon to Jerusalem. The first wave, probably a tiny fraction of the exiles, returned under Sheshbazzar, a son of the exiled king Jehoiachin, shortly after Cyrus's defeat of the Babylonians in 539 BCE. The book of Ezra asserts that Cyrus even gave Sheshbazzar the Temple implements stolen by the Babylonians so that he could take them back to Jerusalem (Ezra 1:7–11), and Sheshbazzar is reported to have rebuilt the foundation of the Temple (Ezra 5:16). A few years later, around 520 BCE, one of Jehoiachin's grandsons, Zerubbabel, led another group of exiles back to Jerusalem. Still other exiles appear to have returned to Jerusalem under Ezra 120 years later (397 BCE; Ezra 7:1–7). In sum, not all exiles came back to Jerusalem, and those that did return came back in several waves. Many, if not most, exiles probably did not want to leave Babylonia. Some, such as Sheshbazzar and Zerubbabel, had assimilated enough to Babylonian culture to have Babylonian names, and we know from later documents of a Jewish family in Babylonia (in the Murashu archive) that some exiles remained there in subsequent centuries. This means that the expression "**post-exilic period**" is only accurate in indicating the end of *forced* exile, since many Judeans never stopped living away from their homeland.

In addition to allowing some Judeans to return to Judah, the Persians played a major role in the **rebuilding of the Jerusalem Temple** that had been destroyed by the Babylonians. This rebuilding, a centerpiece of Cyrus's decree in Ezra 1:1–4, happened in at least two stages. The first, mentioned above, was Cyrus's giving of the Temple vessels to Sheshbazzar, and Sheshbazzar's delivery of these vessels to Jerusalem and laying of the foundations for this **Second Temple** there. This probably occurred shortly after Cyrus's victory over Babylon, around 538 BCE. This initial rebuilding work was not completed, however, until about twenty years later, from 520 to 515 BCE. By this point, Cyrus had died (in 530), his son Cambyses had reigned for eight years (530–522), and Darius, a more distant member of the royal family, had seized power in the wake of Cambyses's death. Darius gained support among peoples of his empire by reversing the harsh policies of Cambyses and rebuilding temples and priesthoods, especially in Egypt (which Cambyses had conquered and subdued). The rebuilding of the Temple in Jerusalem early in Darius's reign probably was part of this broader project. Yet an important shift in Judean leadership seems to have occurred sometime before the Jerusalem Temple was finished. Its rebuilding had begun under both the Davidic leadership of Zerubbabel and the priestly leadership of Joshua. Indeed, certain prophecies by Haggai (2:20–3) and Zechariah (the "branch" in 3:6–10; 4:6–10; 6:9–14) indicate that some hoped that Zerubbabel would re-establish the monarchy in Jerusalem, working alongside Joshua. Yet we hear no more of Zerubbabel in traditions after the Temple was completed. No one knows why. From that point forward the Davidic monarchy was completely finished, and the time of Temple-centered Judaism had begun, the time of the Second Temple (515 BCE–70 CE).

The next major step in the restoration that we know much about is Nehemiah's rebuilding of the walls of Jerusalem seventy years later in 445 BCE. According to his memoir, Nehemiah was a cupbearer in the court of Artaxerxes, probably Artaxerxes I, who reigned from 464 to 423 BCE. Having heard reports of the dilapidated state of Jerusalem, Nehemiah convinced Artaxerxes to send him back to Jerusalem to rebuild the city (Neh 1:1–2:8). There he organized the Judean community to rebuild Jerusalem's walls, despite the opposition of neighboring peoples and internal dissenters (Neh 2:17–6:19). His role was that of Persian-appointed "governor" of Judah (Neh 5:14–19), a lay leader alongside the holy leadership of the priests. His biggest achievement was the re-establishment of Jerusalem as a walled city, an independent political entity. Sometime later, perhaps in a second term as governor, Nehemiah may have taken additional measures, such as the purging of the Jerusalem temple of foreign priests (see Nehemiah 12–13). If so, this was an anticipation of more major purges that were to happen under Ezra.

Ezra took this purging to a new level as part of a more general program of centering Judaism on observance of the Torah of Moses. Like Nehemiah, Ezra was a highly placed Persian official – some sort of secretary in the Persian court. According to Ezra 7, he was commissioned by king Artaxerxes to bring offerings to the Jerusalem Temple and evaluate the extent to which people in the province were obeying "the law of god and the law of the king" (Ezra 7:26). There has been endless debate about what each of these laws contained, but the subsequent narrative of the reading of the "Torah of Moses" in Nehemiah 8 makes clear that something like the present Pentateuch is understood in this narrative to be "the law of god." Nevertheless, on his way to publicly reading and enforcing this holy law, Ezra comes to learn that earlier returnee Judean men have intermarried with foreign women and thus – in his mind – put at risk the whole project of the restoration of the people (Ezra 9:1–3). Many exiles such as Ezra perceived intermarriage with foreigners as a primary reason why Judah had gone into exile in the first place. Seeing this intermarriage among the returnee exiles, Ezra cries out to God:

> God has not forsaken us in our slavery, but has extended to us his steadfast love before the kings of Persia, to give us new life to set up the house of our God, to repair its ruins, and to give us a wall in Judea and Jerusalem.
>
> And now, our God, what shall we say after this? For we have forsaken your commandments, which you commanded by your servants the prophets, saying, . . . do not give your daughters to their sons, neither take their daughters for your sons, and never seek their peace or prosperity, so that you may be strong and eat the good of the land and leave it for an inheritance to your children forever. (Ezra 9:9–12 NRSV)

Ezra sees the whole Persian-sponsored process of the rebuilding of Jerusalem put into question by intermarriage of exile men with "foreign women," probably a mix of actual non-Israelites and some Judeans who had not gone into exile. In response, Ezra gets all men to divorce their foreign wives and expel them and their children. This "purification" of Judah is the prelude to his climactic reading of the "Torah of Moses" before all of Judah (Nehemiah 8), a Torah that seems to be much like the present Pentateuch,

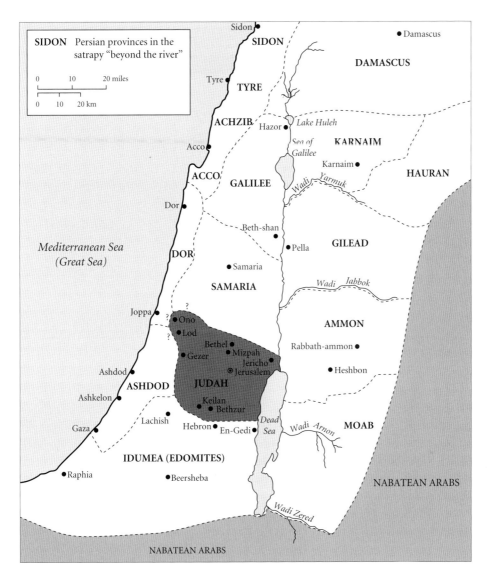

Map 11.1 Judah as a province of the Persian empire. Redrawn from Norman Gottwald, *The Hebrew Bible: A Socio-Literary Introduction*. Minneapolis: Fortress, 1985, page 406.

with P and L sources combined into a single whole. We will return to the issue of intermarriage and the post-exile in the next chapter.

This enactment of the "Torah of Moses" by Ezra is a major step in the formation of a Torah-centered Judaism. After this, virtually all groups in Judaism, whatever else they may disagree about, agree on at least one thing: the importance of the Torah of Moses. This makes the reported Persian role in authorizing Ezra's mission all the more interesting. Elsewhere, the Persians are known to have worked with local leaders to authorize local laws as official Persian legislation (**Persian governmental authorization**). The

Significant Dates: The Persian-Sponsored Restoration of Judah	
Cyrus's defeat of Babylon	539 BCE
Wave 1 of returnees to Judah	538 BCE
Another wave of returnees with Sheshbazzar	532 BCE
Return of Temple implements, laying Temple foundation	
Another wave of returnees with Zerubbabel	520 BCE
Rebuilding of Second Temple	520–515 BCE
Nehemiah's return and governorships	445–425 BCE
Rebuilding wall, purification of priesthood	
Another wave of returnees with Ezra	397 BCE
Divorce of foreign wives	
(Combination of L+P?) Elevation of Torah	

Persians sponsored an Egyptian priest, Udjahorresnet, to collect and publish Egyptian priestly texts, and an inscription found in what is now Turkey shows that indigenous elites secured Persian endorsement of their local sacrificial laws as well. Apparently such local leaders could seek Persian governmental support for their texts, while the Persians' offering such support strengthened the hand of their local allies and thereby reinforced Persian control over diverse parts of their empire. So why would Ezra have been interested in Persian support? His leadership status in Jerusalem (beginning around 397 BCE) probably was shaky vis-à-vis the several waves of exiles who had already returned over a century earlier under Sheshbazzar (538 BCE) and Zerubbabel (520 BCE). We know from sociological studies that later returnees like Ezra often must fight hard against the entrenched positions of people already in the land. How was he to prevail? Apparently, he was able to present a "Torah of Moses," made up of L and P texts together, as the Hebrew law authorized by king Artaxerxes, which others in the province had to follow. The Ezra traditions present him as having such governmental authorization to bring this law to the people (Ezra 7). After him, this law is valid across virtually all stretches of Judaism.

Much of the significance of all these changes can be seen when comparing Jerusalem of Ezra's time with the situation around the time of Ezra in **Elephantine**, a Jewish colony of mercenaries settled in the southern Nile area of Egypt. This colony had its own temple, dating from before the rebuilding of the Jerusalem Temple. The members of the community did correspond with leaders in Jerusalem and Samaria about various cultic matters, such as the celebration of Passover and rebuilding of their local temple, but they do not seem to have known the Torah of Moses advocated by Ezra, or to have followed the more stringent rules against foreign religions seen in the book of Deuteronomy. Only after many years did communities like this either die out or conform to the Torah-centered form of Judaism that arose in Jerusalem. Documents such as the Elephantine archives give us a small taste of the broad diversity of Jewish religion and life in the Persian period which supplements the biblical accounts given by Jewish returnees to Jerusalem.

The Formation of the Torah

The major literary event of this period was the completion of the Torah and its elevation to the center of post-exilic Judaism. This was a work as much or more about combining older texts as it was about the writing of new ones. Building on earlier traditions, Judeans in exile had already written larger stories of Israel's pre-land history in L (including Deuteronomy) and then P. These larger histories probably were separate from one another and cherished by the two major leadership groups in the exile and afterwards: the priesthood descending from Aaron (celebrated in P) and the elders (featured in L). Yet at some point an author combined these L and P sources into one,

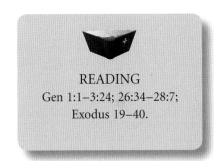

READING
Gen 1:1–3:24; 26:34–28:7;
Exodus 19–40.

producing a Pentateuch much like the one we have now. The process of Persian governmental authorization described above may have played some role in this, since it would not have helped someone like Ezra to have the Persians authenticate *two* competing local narrative laws, L and P. Nevertheless, it would be a mistake to see this joining of traditions as a purely political process. Rather, whatever occasion prompted this creation of the combined Lay and Priestly Torah, there is evidence of considerable theological-literary genius in its execution.

One example of this is the combination of the L and P primeval narratives so that both human possibilities and human limitations are more fully expressed. Genesis starts with the Priestly narrative of creation, where God crowns the cosmos with the creation of humans "in our own image and likeness" (Gen 1:26–7), blesses humanity, and says that the whole creation is "very good." In our present Pentateuch this is now balanced by the garden of Eden story (Gen 2:4–3:24; originally part of the J primeval history and included in L). Now placed after the P creation story (Gen 1:1–2:3), this ancient text tells us more about the sixth "day" on which God created animal and human life (Gen 2:4; cf. 1:24–31). The Eden story ends with curses (Gen 3:14, 17–19) and stresses all of the problems that come from humans' eating the fruit of knowledge and seeking to be "like God" (Gen 3:1–19). In contrast to the P creation story, in which God made humans godlike from the beginning, in this L story God is anxious about humans becoming ever more godlike and expels them from the garden so that they will not gain divine immortality (Gen 3:23–4). So goes the beginning of the L/P creation and *basics* **Book of Genesis**

Outline: the transmission of the Abrahamic promise to Jacob as an answer to the problems of creation

I	Story of creation and re-creation of humanity		1–11:26
II	Yahweh's response: promise to ancestors		11:27–50:26
	A	Abraham (and Lot)	11:27–25:11
	B	The next generation: non-heir and heir	25:12–35:39
		1 Genealogy of Ishmael, the non-heir	25:12–18
		2 Stories of Isaac's family, the heir	25:19–35:29
	C	The next generation: non-heir and heir	36:1–50:26
		1 Genealogy of Esau, the non-heir	36:1–37:1
		2 Stories of Jacob's family, the heir	37:2–50:26

Note: though the above outline focuses on men who inherit or do not inherit the promise, it is women such as Sarah and Rebekkah who play a prominent role in determining who inherits the promise (Isaac, Jacob) and who does not.

Date   Post-exilic (building on earlier sources).

Themes   Genesis is a grand synthesis of Priestly and non-Priestly, Lay texts. The introduction and structure of Genesis come from the Priestly Source. The book starts with the Priestly vision of creation in Genesis 1:1–2:3, and the rest of the book is punctuated with Priestly genealogical headings that now structure the whole (Gen 2:4; 5:1; 6:9; 10:1; 11:10, 27; 25:12, 19; 36:1; 37:2). Much of the substance of Genesis, however, is L, detailing Yahweh's struggles to interact with fallible humans, from Adam and Eve (Gen 2:4–3:24) to Joseph and his brothers (Genesis 37–50). The result of this combination is a book that presents both Yahweh's power to produce order and his struggles to effect his designs with humanity in general and Abraham's family in particular.

flood story, a story that balances affirmation of human godlikeness (Gen 1:26–7; 5:1–3) with stress on God's care to preserve the divine–human boundary (Gen 6:1–4; 11:1–9). In this way and others, the L and P perspectives are put in a creative tension that is more theologically evocative than either one alone would have been.

We see a similarly majestic combination of sources in the Sinai narrative, where the combined L and P narrative describes God's overcoming of the divine–human boundary that was so carefully protected in the primeval history. As we saw in the Chapter 10, the separate L and P sources described events at Sinai quite differently. The L Sinai story stressed God's forgiveness in the face of Israel's building of the golden calf, an act

basics

Book of Exodus

Outline: pilgrimage of Moses and of Israel from Egypt to Sinai

(See M. Smith, *The Pilgrimage Pattern in Exodus*, Sheffield: Sheffield Academic Press, 1997.)

I	From Egypt		
	A	Oppression and journey of Moses to Midian	1:1–2:25
	B	Two calls and two confrontations	3:1–15:21
II	To Sinai		
	A	Provision on wilderness journey to Sinai	15:22–18:27
	B	Two covenants and two sets of tablets	19:1–40:38

Date

Post-exilic (building on earlier sources).

Themes

Many think of the book of Exodus solely in terms of its initial story of Israel's escape from slavery in Egypt. But the climax of the book is Israel's entry into service to a new lord, Yahweh, as a cultic community centered on the wilderness tabernacle (Exodus 19–40). Thus, Exodus is not just a story of getting away. Instead, it is a pilgrimage from painful service to Pharaoh to life-giving service to Yahweh. This Exodus journey by Israel now occurs across the Jewish liturgical year, starting at Passover (Exod 12:2, 39–42), with arrival at Sinai at the feast of weeks (Exod 19:1) and building of the tabernacle at the New Year (Exod 40:2, 17).

More information: whose exodus?

Jon Levenson has criticized some liberationist Christians, such as George Pixley, for their claim that the people of Israel was not the actual historical group to leave Egypt in the exodus. Instead, according to Pixley, the actual exodus group was an impoverished group of slaves that would only later join "Israel." For Levenson, this approach is one more example of an all-too-familiar Christian tendency to try to separate the Old Testament from the Jewish people. He argues that the present, canonical form of the book of Exodus emphasizes the idea that Yahweh rescued Israel not because it was poor, but because it was special to Yahweh. Moreover, this exodus did not mean a rejection of slavery in general, but of Israel's slavery to Pharaoh rather than Yahweh. The *Bible's* story of exodus is *Israel*-centered, not a general endorsement of liberation of the poor.

In response, Pixley and others question whether Christians must focus only on the final form of a book like Exodus. They argue that their historical reconstruction should be evaluated on its historical merits, rather than on its theological implications. For these perspectives, see: Alice Ogden Bellis and Joel Kaminsky (eds.), *Jews, Christians, and the Theology of the Hebrew Scriptures* (Atlanta: Society of Biblical Literature, 2000).

basics   Book of Numbers

(For basics on Leviticus, see box on p. 200.)

Outline

I	Dissolution of the exodus generation	1–25
	A Preparations for departure from Sinai	1:1–10:10
	B Disobedience, death in the wake of Sinai	10:11–25:18
II	Beginning of the conquest generation	26–36

Date   Post-exilic (building on earlier sources).

Themes   Priestly material again provides the introduction (1:1–10:10) and general structure, with the overall book moving from the Priestly counting of the exodus generation (Numbers 1–4) to another Priestly counting of the next generation after their parents have died in the wilderness (Numbers 26). In between, we have P and L stories about rebellion against the authority of Moses and Aaron (11–12, 16–17), the failed expedition to spy out the land (13–14), and a final catastrophic rebellion at Baal Peor (25). These stories help explain the destruction of this exodus generation before their children can enter the land. In the post-exile, this form of the book would have mirrored the experience of most exiled families, in which the vast majority of parents who went into exile did not survive to take their children back to the promised land.

More information: the book of Numbers in context   The focus of Numbers on the transition between generations provides a context for the book of Deuteronomy that follows. Read after Numbers, Deuteronomy is the story of Moses's review of history and law for a generation that did not experience all these events themselves.

of idolatry that signaled the ultimate rejection of the covenant God had just made with them to make them a kingdom of priests (Exod 19:1–24:14; 32:1–34:35). The "elders" stand at the center of this L narrative (Exod 19:7; 24:1, 9), and God only appoints a special priesthood, the Levites, as a measure to punish the disobedient Israelites (Exod 32:26–8). In contrast, the Priestly story says nothing about any disobedience and focuses instead on God's founding of a wilderness sanctuary run by an Aaronide priesthood (Exod 24:15–31:18; 35:1–40:38; Leviticus; Numbers 1:1–10:10). The emphasis in P is on the creation of a holy people with a sanctuary and proper priesthood to atone for the people's sins.

When these two narratives were combined, the Priestly emphasis on the sanctuary for atonement became part of God's answer to the people's sin that was emphasized in the Lay narrative. Thus, our present combined (L/P) story in Exodus has two simultaneous scenes follow the L story of Yahweh's covenant with the people of Israel (Exod 19:1–24:14). On the mountain (here P material), God gives Moses instructions for creating the sanctuary through which the people can atone for their sin (Exod 24:15–31:18). At the very same time, down below (L material), the people build the golden calf and thus prove their desperate need for such a means of atonement (Exod 32:1–6). In the rest of the L/P Sinai account, the Priestly story of the building of the tabernacle sanctuary (Exod 35:1–40:38) becomes the crowning moment of the L Source story of Yahweh's gradual forgiveness of Israel and willingness to make a new covenant with them (Exod 32:7–34:35). The original L text describes God's new covenant with God's "stiff-necked" people (Exod 34:1–28; L) before the P text tells of how Moses led that people in building a tabernacle sanctuary through which they could atone for their sins (35:1–40:33; P).

This event is a high point of the present Pentateuch, and we see this through parallels between the conclusion of the Priestly creation narrative (Gen 1:1–2:3) and the conclusion of the Priestly tabernacle narrative (Exod 39:42–40:33).

Creation of the cosmos	Construction of the tabernacle
Gen 1:31	*Exod 39:43*
God saw all which God had done And indeed it was very good (Gen 1:31a)	And Moses saw all the work and indeed it was done just as YHWH had commanded (Exod 39:43a)
And the heavens and earth were finished (2:1) And God finished on the seventh day God's work (2:2a) And God blessed the seventh day (2:3a)	And all the work on the tabernacle of the tent of meeting was finished (39:32a) And Moses finished the work (40:33b) And Moses blessed them (39:43b)

These parallels are between parts of the Priestly narrative, but the completion of the tabernacle means yet more in the combined L/P narrative we now have. The story of God coming down to the tabernacle follows L stories in Genesis about how God once worked to preserve the divine–human boundary, expelling humans from the garden (Gen 3:22–4), limiting their lifespan after they intermarried with divine beings (6:1–4), and ending their attempt to build a tower up toward heaven in Babel (11:1–9). Within this broader stretch, the Priestly description of the descent of God's glory to dwell in Israel is a crossing of the divine–human boundary described in the J primeval narratives now in L, and a climax of earlier, Lay Source promises that God would "be with" the patriarchs and their descendants (Gen 26:3; 28:15; 46:4; Exod 4:12 L).

Though later authors and editors made some additional changes to the Pentateuch, this combination of L and P narratives was the most significant stage in the formation of the Pentateuch. It was a daring move, taking one narrative (L) and combining it with a narrative (P) that was originally designed to replace it. Turning back to the example of the L and P stories of Jacob's gaining his father's blessing, we see that parts of the P story are placed before (26:34–5 P) and after (27:46–28:7 P) the trickster story they were meant to replace (27:1–45 L). As a result, the P materials provide a new context for Jacob and Rebekkah's deceitful actions. In the combined text now in Genesis, Esau marries foreign wives (Gen 26:34–5; P), which provides some justification for Jacob's theft of his father's blessing (Gen 27:1–45; L), which in turn provides a context for Isaac's repeated blessing of Jacob and sending him abroad to get a proper wife (Gen 28:1–5; P). Thus, at this place and others, the post-exilic author who combined L and P balanced the perspectives of both sources without hiding or homogenizing the contrasts. Enough traces of his work were left that scholars could achieve consensus on the basic contents of the L and P sources despite the fact that we have no separate manuscript of either.

The Book of Psalms as a Torah-Centered Collection of More Ancient Psalms

READING

Pss 13, 22, 57, 74, 88 (lament psalms); Pss 8, 29, 33, 104, 117, 145, 150 (hymns); Pss 32, 116, 138 (thanksgiving songs); Ps 1 (a wisdom psalm); Ps 23 (psalm of trust). Read and compare Pss 41:13; 72:18–19; 89:52; 106:48; 150.

As we have seen, Israelites wrote, read, and learned psalm texts from the earliest point of Israelite history onward. Chapter 3 of this textbook discussed royal and Zion psalms in connection with David and Solomon's monarchy. We saw traces of an ancient lament tradition in Jeremiah's complaints to God about his task. In Chapter 9, we studied communal lament psalms, such as Psalm 137 and Lamentations, as a window into the suffering of the exiles. And there are many more texts across the book of Psalms (also known as the **Psalter**) that probably date from the pre-exilic and exilic periods. One sign of the antiquity of this book is the fact that it is made up of yet older collections of psalms, such as a series of psalms used in pilgrimages (Psalms 120–34), or an "Elohistic" collection of psalms in 42–83 which predominantly uses "Elohim" for God and occasionally duplicates psalms found elsewhere (such as Psalm 53//Psalm 14).

The book of Psalms as a whole, however, is later, and it shows some special emphases that are connected to the post-exilic period. First and foremost, it is a collection oriented toward Torah instruction. It opens with a psalm encouraging its readers to "meditate" day and night on the "Torah of Yahweh" (Psalm 1), and its longest psalm is a praise of God's Torah that is 176 verses long, organized into alphabetic stanzas (Psalm 119). The book of Psalms is divided into five parts by a set of similar calls to praise found at Pss 41:13; 72:18–19; 89:52; 106:48; and a concluding psalm of praise in Psalm 150. The focus on praise in these sections helps explain the name of the book of Psalms in Hebrew, *tehillim* – (book of) praises. At the same time, the fivefold division of the book of Psalms (Psalms 3–41, 42–72, 73–89,

90–106, 107–50) mirrors the fivefold division of the Pentateuch (Pentateuch is Greek for "five scrolls"). The focus of the present, five-part book of Psalms is on praises that are grounded in and flow from meditation on and study of God's Torah.

More on Method: Form Criticism and Genre

Biblical **form criticism** looks at the characteristics, intention, and social setting of typical categories of psalms; that is, it looks at **genres** in biblical texts. For example, the **lament psalm** discussed here is a genre characterized by some or all of the following elements: complaint, plea for help, vow, statement of trust in God's help, and thanksgiving for God's help. One typical intention of such psalms is to gain God's help in a desperate situation. The original social setting for the lament psalm was worship, whether at home, at a local sanctuary, or at the Jerusalem Temple.

Form criticism has achieved many of its greatest results in the study of psalm genres and their social settings, but there have been form-critical studies of many other genres in the Bible as well. Some genres already discussed in this textbook include call narratives (Chapter 6), and proverbs and instructions (Chapter 5).

As study of form criticism has progressed, scholars have seen more and more complexity, both in the genres and in their links to particular social settings. Many biblical texts are a mix of genres. Moreover, genres can be inverted, as in Amos's use of the lament form to pronounce doom on the nation of Israel. Finally, some genres, such as the Hebrew short story, may be linked to a set of cultural conventions rather than a particular social setting like worship.

For more: Marvin Sweeney, "Form Criticism." Pp. 58–89 in S. McKenzie and S. Haynes (eds.), *To Each Its Own Meaning* (Louisville, KY: Westminster John Knox Press, 1999).

The study of Psalms, however, need not focus only on the shape of the book in its final form. Scholars have found in the psalms a rich source of knowledge about the piety and worship of ancient Israel. In particular, a discipline called "form criticism" (see box above) has uncovered several categories of psalms that were used for different purposes in ancient Israelite worship.

The most common type found in the Psalter is often termed a "lament psalm," sometimes called a "**complaint**" or "**supplication**" as well. The word "**lament**" by itself refers to mourning over an irreversible bad event, such as a death (2 Sam 1:18–27) or destruction of a city (Lamentations). In contrast, a lament psalm is a plea for divine help in the midst of dire distress. Indeed, lament psalms such as Psalm 22 go on to include praise for God's help as if it has already arrived. For example, the psalmist in Psalm 22 starts out by saying "my God, my God, why have you abandoned me? . . . I cry by day, but you do not answer; by night and find no rest" (22:1–2). Later in the same Psalm, however, the psalmist is thanking God for God's response, saying "God *basics*   **Book of Psalms: Part 2**

(For basics on "Book of Psalms: Part 1," see box on p. 68.)

Outline:
Torah-centered
praise of
Yahweh's
kingship

I	Torah and king introduction		1–2
II	Five-part collection		3–145
	A	Book 1: final individual praise by king	3–41
	B	Book 2: concluding in prayer for king	42–72
	C	Book 3: concluding with lament about destruction of the Judean monarchy (Psalm 89)	73–89
	D	Book 4: moving toward exile (Psalm 106) and stressing Yahweh's kingship (Pss 93, 95–9)	90–106
	E	Book 5: moving toward restoration	107–45
III	Fivefold concluding praise of Yahweh		146–50

Date   Post-exilic (building on earlier sources).

Themes   In addition to the Torah focus mentioned in the main text, scholars have observed ways that the complex collection of psalms now reflects Israel's journey through history, from monarchy to exile and then post-exilic restoration. As indicated in the outline, the concluding psalms in the first four books show a movement from focus on the king (Psalms *3–41*) and his role vis-à-vis the people (Psalms *42–72*), to the collapse of the monarchy (Psalms *73–89*) and rise of Yahweh's kingship in exile (Psalms *90–106*). This prepares for the final book, which starts with a psalm focusing on return from exile (Psalms *107*–45).

More
information:
another edition
of the book
of Psalms   Several psalm scrolls found among the Dead Sea Scrolls at Qumran contain an edition of the book of Psalms that is quite different from the Masoretic edition of Psalms that is used in Jewish tradition and surveyed above. The divergences are particularly striking after Psalm 89. This suggests to some scholars that that Psalms 1–89 (books 1–3 of the Psalter) may have reached their form earlier, while the following Psalms (90–150) may have been organized later into the form we now see them.

did not despise or detest the suffering of the oppressed. God did not hide God's face from me, but heard when I cried to God" (22:24). Scholars have developed many theories to explain the abrupt change in tone in such lament psalms, but have not reached agreement. Whatever their original function, such literary lament psalms provided a template for ancient Israelites to voice their deepest pain and anger and move toward hope. Some contemporary readers of such lament psalms are put off by their harsh language about enemies and their bargaining with God (see Ps 22:16–21a and 25). Others find that such psalms are a refreshing alternative to highly censored and sanitized prayers that do not really plumb the depths of human suffering and isolation. In the end, these biblical psalms do not encourage the reader to go out and exact vengeance themselves. Instead, through giving speech to suffering and including invitations for others to join in praise, these lament psalms ultimately move toward reintegration into the community. Even now, they give many contemporary readers a more general language to express their deepest and most personal suffering.

There are many other psalm types in the Psalter as well. One is the "**thanksgiving song**," such as Psalm 32, where an individual praises God for deliverance from suffering and calls on others to join in that praise. Another is the **hymn of trust**, such as Psalm 23 ("The Lord is my shepherd"), that expresses trust in God's protection and sustenance. Yet another psalm form is the **hymn of praise**, a praise of God often punctuated by short refrains, such as the praise of creation in Psalm 8 or the praise of God's acts in history in Psalm 136.

Several of these psalm types appear in association with the king, such as the prayer for royal victory in Psalm 20 or the thanksgiving for such victory in Psalm 21 (royal psalms; see Chapter 3). Overall, it appears that the authors of biblical psalms drew freely on these and other psalm genres. They were obviously well versed in the poetic possibilities of such typical psalm patterns. Nevertheless, they did not rigidly adhere to a single template. The psalm patterns were the melodies on which psalm writers could improvise.

Contemporary readers of psalms now can work with them on multiple levels, depending on their interests and their community. Study of the psalms in relation to their original historical contexts has illuminated their diverse types and possible settings in worship, their roots in older pre-Israelite traditions, and their rich imagery (among other topics). Yet, as in the case of biblical prophets whose words were preserved for later generations, the book of Psalms has survived because the texts in it have transcended their original contexts. Many psalms probably originated in some form during the time of Solomon's first Temple, but that Temple was destroyed and these older psalms (along with newer ones) came down to us as part of a post-exilic, Torah-centered collection. Now, thousands of years later, the book of Psalms is used more consistently in Jewish and Christian worship than almost any other biblical book. Each community places the psalms in a different context. Jews use Psalms in a cycle of Torah-oriented worship, while Christians often reread psalms as Christological prophecies. The use and re-use of these ancient, evocative texts, a process already begun in the formation of the book itself, continues even today.

The Introduction to Psalms in Psalms 1–2

Psalms 1–2, the introduction to the book of Psalms, illustrate the mix of emphases and materials in the book. They are marked as an introduction by the fact that these two Psalms lack any kind of superscription and by the ways in which they introduce major themes that occur across the rest of the book of Psalms. The superscriptions of Psalms start in Psalm 3 with a label that places this lament in the context of David's flight from Absalom (see 2 Sam 15:14–17). As discussed in Chapter 3 (box on p. 66), these labels are not historical, but represent an early Jewish attempt to place various "Psalms of David" in the context of his life. Psalms 1–2 lack such a label – not even an attribution to David or another figure. Their function lies not in themselves, but in the way they set the other Psalms in context. One might view these two psalms as an extended "superscription" to the Psalter as a whole.

Psalm 1 sets the tone for the whole by calling on the readers of Psalms to devotion to Torah. It is a teaching psalm – often called a "**wisdom psalm**" – but one focused particularly on Torah teaching. The expression that begins the psalm, "happy is the one," is a teaching expression typical of Proverbs, and, like the sayings in Proverbs, this psalm features a sharp contrast between the "way of the wicked" and the "way of the righteous" (Ps 1:1, 6). Unlike Proverbs, however, the thing that distinguishes these two ways is not "fear of Yahweh" in general, but meditation on the Torah day and night (Ps 1:2). The psalm draws on the ancient tree imagery central to Proverbs and ancient Israelite religion (the tree associated with the goddess Asherah) to describe the benefits that the Torah devotee will enjoy: that person will be "like a tree planted by the water . . . everything that person does will succeed" (Ps 1:3). In contrast, the wicked, who lack such devotion to Torah, will perish (Ps 1:4–6).

In this way the opening of Psalms links both to the Torah itself and to its immediate aftermath as described in the book of Joshua. At the outset of Joshua, just after Moses has died, Joshua is commanded to do exactly what this Psalm calls for: recite Torah constantly and "meditate on it day and night" (Josh 1:8). Through echoing that call here, this psalm calls on its readers to emulate Joshua, the successor to Moses, in constantly keeping before them the teaching of Moses that became ever more central in the post-exilic period.

The introduction to the Psalms does not stop here, however. It also includes Psalm 2. Chapter 3 discussed how parts of this psalm – among several other royal psalms in the Psalter – are good candidates for being among Israel's earliest texts. Royal and Zion psalms like these helped early Israelite people understand how Yahweh was involved in setting up a king in the new capital city, Jerusalem. Now, however, this psalm is linked to Psalm 1 as part of a common introduction to what is a post-exilic Psalter. The rebellious "conspiring" of the peoples at the beginning of Psalm 2 (2:1 NRSV; Hebrew *hagah*) is the opposite of constant "meditating" on Torah at the outset of Psalm 1 (1:2; again Hebrew *hagah*). Psalm 2 then describes how Yahweh's anointed king at Mount Zion will destroy his opponents (2:4–9) before echoing Psalm 1 again through proclaiming, "*happy are* those who take refuge in Yahweh" (2:12; see 1:1). In sum, within Psalms 1–2 as a whole there are two groups: (1) the "happy" righteous ones who meditate on

Torah and take refuge in Yahweh, and (2) "the wicked" – a.k.a. the rebellious nations of Psalm 2 – who meditate or conspire for nothing and will be destroyed by Yahweh's anointed king.

The emphasis both on Torah and on Yahweh's anointed king had a special significance in the Torah-focused, post-monarchic context of the Persian period. After all, there was no anointed Davidic king in this time. Rather, Temple and Torah had risen to take the central place in the existing community that the Davidic monarchy once had. As a result, the returnees in Judah now placed their *hope* in ancient royal traditions. They reread royal Psalms such as Psalm 2 not as endorsements of existing power structures but as *promises* that God, the cosmic king, would anoint an earthly king who would put the empires of the world in their place. This is the expectation of a royal **messiah**, the Hebrew word for "anointed" (Ps 2:2). It is a late, post-exilic hope that the empire of God, with a Davidic monarch at its head, would destroy the foreign empires dominating the people of Israel.

In this way the introduction to the Psalter embraces both elements that have been important to centuries of Jewish and Christian interpretation of the Psalms. Psalm 1 anticipates the focus of the rest of the Psalter on the Mosaic Torah. This is a major feature in Jewish exegesis of the Psalms. Psalm 2 anticipates the focus of other parts of the Psalter on kingship – both human and divine – and the expectation that God would establish God's kingship and destroy foreign oppressors. Such hope is still found in Judaism, but the emphasis on God's anointed king in the Psalter has been particularly strong in Christianity, a religion whose name is formed from the Greek word for "anointed" – *Christ*. Psalms 1–2, the introduction to the Psalter, show how such hope for God's *messiah* during the post-exilic period was integrally connected to devotion to the Torah of Moses.

CHAPTER ELEVEN REVIEW

1. Know the meaning and significance of the following terms discussed in this chapter:
- Cyrus cylinder [know similarities to and differences from Ezra 1:1–4]
- form criticism
- genre
- hymn of praise
- hymn of trust
- lament
- lament psalm
- messiah
- Persian governmental authorization
- Psalter
- rebuilding of the Jerusalem Temple [know the date and circumstances]
- Second Temple
- thanksgiving song
- wisdom psalm

2. Know the four major stages in the post-exilic rebuilding of the Judean community:
- several waves of return;
- rebuilding of the Temple;
- rebuilding of the wall around Jerusalem;
- centering on the Torah.
- Be able to summarize the Persian role in each and other associated circumstances.

3. Why is the Bible's depiction of the Persians so different from its depiction of the Assyrians and Babylonians?

4. What are some problems in using Ezra–Nehemiah as a historical source for this period?

5. What two major sources seem to stand behind Ezra–Nehemiah and where can we find parts of each?

6. The expulsion of foreign wives is one of the most difficult events for contemporary readers to deal with. Are there circumstances in which you can imagine supporting a community's wish to insure that their children only marry other members of that community? Or are there other circumstances where you can imagine a community legitimately needing to protect its identity in other ways? Conversely, in what kinds of circumstances can such tendencies be particularly dangerous?

7. What is a way that the documents from the post-exilic Jewish colony at Elephantine are significant?

8. How are the L and P creation stories different and what is the significance of their combination?

9. What is the significance of the combination of the L and P stories of the Sinai covenant?

10. What are two things that the praises of God at Pss 41:13; 72:18–19; 89:52; 106:48; and 150 tell us about the overall emphases of the book of Psalms?

11. What are the main characteristics of the lament psalm? What other terms have scholars used to better characterize this type of psalm?

RESOURCES FOR FURTHER STUDY

(Resources for study of Ezra–Nehemiah are listed at the end of Chapter 12.)

Psalms

Brown, William. *Seeing the Psalms: A Theology of Metaphor*. Louisville, KY: Westminster John Knox Press, 2002.

Brueggemann, Walter. *Praying the Psalms* (revised edition). Winona, MN: St. Mary's, 1993.

Holladay, William. *The Psalms Through Three Thousand Years: Prayerbook of a Cloud of Witnesses*. Minneapolis: Fortress, 1993. History of interpretation of Psalm.

Mays, James L. *Psalms*. Interpretation. Louisville, KY: Westminster John Knox Press, 1994.

CHAPTER 12

OTHER TEXTS FORMED

IN THE CRUCIBLE OF

POST-EXILIC REBUILDING

Chapter Outline

CHAPTER OVERVIEW

Though Chapter 11 stressed support provided by the Persians for several stages of restoration of Jerusalem, the returnees to Jerusalem faced significant disappointments in the process of rebuilding. Second Isaiah, a pro-Persian exilic prophet, had promised that the exiles would return in joy and Jerusalem would be grandly rebuilt (e.g. Isa 49:7–26). Yet things were much more difficult. For example, the prophet Haggai has to reassure returnees that the sad, small Temple that they have rebuilt will be much greater (Hag 2:2–9). In the wake of such disappointments, biblical writers of this time had different explanations for why things were not better and what needed to change.

In addition, the memory of exile was deep and painful for these returnees, and they disagreed over what needed to be done to prevent another one. As we saw in Chapter 11, worries about incurring another exile were so intense that Ezra is reported to have led all the returnees in Judah to divorce their "foreign" wives to prevent another exile, with "foreign" now defined as any woman not among the returnees from Babylon (including some Judean women). Meanwhile, in this chapter, we will discuss other biblical texts probably dating from around this period, such as "Third Isaiah" (Isaiah 56–66) and the story of Ruth, that offer a positive assessment of the benefits of inclusion of foreigners – that is, Torah-observant foreigners – in the community. These texts, along with other, probably late positive depictions of foreigners in books such as Jonah and Job, form an important counter-balance to difficult stories such as the divorce under Ezra. Read this chapter with a particular focus on uncovering the full diversity of post-exilic perspectives preserved in different parts of the Hebrew Bible.

Texts Closely Associated with the Rebuilding of the Judean Community

READING
Zechariah 1 and 4;
Haggai 1:1–2:9;
Job 1–5 and 38–42
(for excursus).

REVIEWING
The Nehemiah memoir (Neh 1:1–7:4; 13:10–14, 30b–31) and Temple/Ezra narrative (Ezra 1–10 and Neh 8; cf. 1 Esdras in the Apocrypha).

basics   Book of Haggai

Outline:
blessing + new
rulership after
Temple
rebuilding

I   Oracles around the start of Temple rebuilding
   A   Prophetic-inspired beginning of rebuilding   1:1–14
      (including promise of blessing for rebuilding 1:2–11)
   B   Encouragement: Zerubbabel's future riches   2:1–9
II   Oracles following up on start of rebuilding
   A   Renewed promise of blessing   2:10–19
   B   Encouragement: Zerubbabel's future rule   2:20–3

Date   Fifth century BCE (400s, building on prophecies from 520 BCE).

Themes   In his original setting, Haggai promised his discouraged post-exilic community that investing now in rebuilding the Temple would yield returns of agricultural plenty and political independence under Zerubbabel. Amidst the turmoil of Darius's seizure of the throne of Persia in 522 BCE, Haggai may have hoped that Zerubbabel, a descendant of David, would re-establish the Davidic monarchy (2:23). Though this did not happen and the rebuilt Temple was later destroyed by the Romans (70 CE), the book of Haggai still preserves Jewish hope for renewal and restoration on the other side of another Temple rebuilding.

This review of post-exilic writings (outside the Pentateuch and Psalms) starts with the prophecies of Haggai and Zechariah. In Ezra 5:1 these two figures provide the impetus for Zerubbabel and Joshua to restart the Temple rebuilding process. And indeed, aside from a later set of prophecies now found in Zechariah 9–14, much of Haggai and Zechariah's prophecy focuses on Zerubbabel and Joshua and on questions surrounding Temple rebuilding. Haggai blames the economic hardship of the returnees on their failure to rebuild the Temple (Hag 1:1–11; 2:10–19). He reassures them that the small Temple that they have built will one day be much greater (Hag 1:12–2:9), and he announces that God chose Zerubbabel and made him "like a signet ring," an apparent prediction of Zerubbabel's future glorification and possible anointing as king (Hag 2:23). Zechariah 1–8, sometimes referred to as "First Zechariah," includes prophecies about the rebuilding of the Temple along with Zion (1:7–2:17) and God's future glorification of Zerubbabel and Joshua, the Temple builders (3:1–10; 4:1–15; 6:9–15). Together, these two blocks of prophecy are valuable witnesses to events surrounding the Temple rebuilding, since at least some of these prophecies seem to come from that time.

---

basics   Book of Zechariah

Outline: from Temple restoration to Yahweh's rule

I	Zechariah's visions surrounding Temple rebuilding	1–8
II	Later visions of Yahweh's establishment of rule	9–14

Date

Fifth century BCE (400s) for a form of Zechariah 1–8 (earlier oracles). Fourth century BCE (300s) for whole book (note Greeks in Zech 9:13).

Themes

The book of Zechariah is a combination of an earlier book surrounding eight visions attributed to Zechariah (Zechariah 1–8) and so-called "Deutero-Zechariah" (Zechariah 9–14). The earlier book, like Haggai, was associated with Temple rebuilding and the future rule of Zerubbabel and Joshua. Zechariah 9–14, however, lacks the superscriptions and dates of the earlier chapters that link them to Zechariah and the Temple-building process. Divided into two "oracles" (9–11 and 12–14), this latter part of the book envisions Yahweh's dramatic punishment of all Judah's enemies and the lifting up of Jerusalem to be the center of the world.

In contrast, the Temple-rebuilding/Ezra narrative standing behind Ezra 1–10 and Nehemiah 8 is much further removed from the events it describes. It divides the rebuilding of the community into two major parallel phases, each of which starts with an act by a Persian king, proceeds to separation from foreigners, and climaxes in the celebration of a major festival. The first phase, Temple rebuilding, moves from the departure from Babylon to the rebuilding of the Temple and celebration of Passover. The second phase, Torah centering, moves from Ezra's commission by Artaxerxes for Torah enforcement to his climactic reading of the Torah to the assembled people.

Phase 1: Temple rebuilding	*Phase 2: Torah centering*
Cyrus's edict to rebuild the Temple (Ezra 1:1–4)	Artaxerxes' commission of Ezra – Torah (Ezra 7)
Exiles' leaving of foreigners in Babylon (Ezra 1–2)	Returnees' divorce of foreign wives (Ezra 9–10)
Rebuilding of the Temple (Ezra 3–6)	Reading of the Torah (Nehemiah 8)
Celebration of Passover (Ezra 6:19–22)	Celebration of Sukkoth – Feast of Booths (Neh 8)

The parallels between these phases reveal a striking combination of pro-Persian and anti-foreign sentiment. On the one hand, the narrative prominently describes Persian sponsorship at the start of each phase of community rebuilding, and Ezra's prayer in Ezra 9 reinforces this by saying that God has "extended to us his steadfast love before the kings of Persia, to give us new life to set up the house of our God, to repair its ruins, and to give us a wall in Judea and Jerusalem" (Ezra 9:9). On the other hand, this narrative stresses that each stage of rebuilding was preceded by an act where Judeans separated themselves from foreigners: (1) leaving exile among foreigners in Babylonia (before rebuilding the Temple) and (2) divorcing foreign wives and expelling them and their children (before centering on the Torah).

The writers of this narrative probably saw no contradiction here. They believed that the exile had been caused by God's people forsaking God's Torah and falling under the influence of foreigners around and among them. Like contemporary Jews deeply committed to preventing another genocide of Jews like that which happened in twentieth-century Germany, these ancient Judean returnees wanted to do everything possible to make sure that such foreign influence did not send them into exile again. They had no trouble with Persian sponsors who would help them in this project. Their problem, building on their experience of exile, was with foreigners *in their midst*. Therefore much in the Temple/Ezra narrative is organized around these theological themes.

Nehemiah's memoir is a bit more difficult to discuss, since it is less completely preserved than the Temple-rebuilding/Ezra narrative. Nevertheless, it too tells a story of rebuilding in the face of foreign opposition. When Nehemiah starts the process of rebuilding the wall, he is opposed at several stages by leaders in the local area, including and especially the Tobiad family, who were leaders in Samaria (Neh 2:19–20; 4:1–17; 6:1–13). When the wall is finished, he appoints Levites to guard the gates, and he works to repopulate the city with those who had returned from exile (Neh 6:15–7:5). Later on, after another period of service to Artaxerxes (13:6), Nehemiah narrates his confrontation with returnees over their intermarriages with foreigners (13:23–7). He even expels one of the high priest's sons from the Temple because of his intermarriage with a "foreign" woman – a daughter of the Tobiad family of Samaria (13:28). At first glance this would seem close to stories about the divorce of foreign wives in the Ezra narratives

basics   Book of Job

The book of Job is a post-exilic book that features a foreign sage, but its riches are not to be found in its message about foreigners, but in its reflections on unjust suffering. The book, particularly the poetry at its center, presents different perspectives on this timeless issue, alluding in subtle ways to a wide range of Israel's literature up through the Persian period: proverbs (in the friends' speeches), psalm laments (in Job's speeches), hymns of praise (in God's reply), and much more. Eventually, God appears, rejects the friends' words, and affirms and rewards Job (see Job 42:7–17). Yet this resolution at the end of the book does not do justice to the profundity of the preceding poetic dialogue. Instead, the book has an unresolved quality about it. It is a symphony of voices and perspectives from Israelite tradition up through the Persian period, all marshaled to address a problem of suffering that was as acute as ever then and has never gone away.

Outline: dialogue on disinterested virtue and divine justice

I	Dialogue setting: Job's suffering as a test of whether he is altruistic	1:1–2:13
II	Dialogue between Job, his friends, and God	3:1–42:6
III	Divine affirmation and restoration of Job	42:7–17

Date

Fifth century BCE (400s, possibly building on an earlier prose narrative reflected in Job 1–2).

Important information: the "accuser" not Satan in Job

Many interpreters have believed that the evil figure of Satan is God's dialogue partner in Job. Nevertheless, this interpretation rests on a mistranslation of the Hebrew word *satan* found in Job 1:6–12; 2:1–7. Throughout this text (and also in Zechariah 3), the word *satan* is not a proper name (as in 1 Chr 21:1) but appears with the Hebrew definite article, "the," and thus is equivalent to "the *satan*." Judging from both Job 1–2 and Zechariah 3–4, this *satan* figure is a roaming spy (the word *satan* comes from the Hebrew word "to roam"). This is a formal position in Yahweh's divine council (see 1 Kings 22; Isaiah 6); the figure who fills it is responsible for finding out the misdeeds of Yahweh's people.

More information

The figure of Job is found elsewhere in the Bible and non-biblical literature, but this depiction of him is unique. The book centers on Job's passionate dispute with his friends and God about his unjust suffering. There are other examples of such dialogues about unjust suffering in the Near East, such as the "Babylonian Theodicy" or the Egyptian "Dispute Between a Man and His Ba." This biblical teaching dialogue is prompted by an unusual and disturbing narrative prelude: Yahweh's decision to remove Job's riches, health, and children as part of a test to see whether he is only being good in order to receive divine reward (Job 1:6–12; 2:1–6).

(compare especially Neh 13:25 to Ezra 9:2). Yet Nehemiah does not seem to know of Ezra's work, and he focuses in his memoir on purifying the priesthood of those with foreign wives rather than on encouraging any general divorce of such wives (13:28–30). Nehemiah discourages the Judeans from *future* intermarriages but holds the priests to a higher standard because of their holy vocation.

Both of these stories contrast with the material added to join them (Nehemiah 9–11) in their generally positive attitude toward the Persians. Both feature Judean exiles who have achieved high status in the Persian court, and both describe how they are able to convert their connections into substantial and helpful Persian sponsorship of Judean rebuilding: the Temple, the Torah, the walls of Jerusalem. In his prayer, Ezra contrasts the past captivity and utter shame of his people with the opportunities they now have to rebuild under the Persians (Ezra 9:7–9). In contrast, Nehemiah's prayer in Neh 9:6–37, a probable later addition to the Nehemiah story, concludes with the following complaint to God about foreign rulers:

> Today we are slaves, and the land that you gave our fathers to enjoy its fruit and bounty – here we are slaves on it. On account of our sins it yields its abundant crops to kings whom you have set over us. They rule over our bodies and our beasts as they please, and we are in great distress. (Neh 9:36–7 NJPS)

These hardly seem the words of the Nehemiah who was cupbearer to Artaxerxes (Neh 1:11) and later returns to work yet further for the king (Neh 13:6). These words and the prayer of which they are a part come from another time and a perspective different from the generally pro-Persian sentiments of both the earlier Ezra and Nehemiah narratives. They will be discussed in the next chapter in connection with a different empire (the Hellenistic empire).

Texts Emphasizing God's Favor Toward Foreigners

History may be written by the winners, but, in the case of post-exilic Judah, the prophets and others got a chance to write a rejoinder. Indeed, several texts in the Hebrew Bible appear to respond to the hostility toward foreigners found in post-exilic traditions such as the Ezra stories. Sometimes the response to the issue takes the form of narrative, as in the story of God's grace toward Assyrians in the book of Jonah, Naomi's evolving attitude toward her Moabite daughter-in-law in the book of Ruth, or the story of an Edomite's unjust suffering in the book of Job. Sometimes, however, the response takes the form of direct prophetic engagement, as in the call in Isaiah 56:3 that the foreigner might not say "Yahweh will separate me from his people," an apparent response to post-exilic efforts to purify Israel through expelling foreigners. Though it is not certain that each of these texts dates from the post-exilic period, they address concerns about foreigners and foreign influence that became prominent in that time. The

READING
Jonah, Ruth, and
Job 1–5, 38–42.
Isaiah 56, 58, 61, 65–6.

basics | Book of Jonah

Outline: satire of xenophobic prophet	I	Initial call, prophetic flight, and mission of Jonah	1–2
	II	Renewed call, prophecy, and anger at repentance	3–4

Date   Whatever the date of this fable, it is far removed from the Neo-Assyrian period that it describes. The Assyrian king is not named.

Themes   The book of Jonah satirically contrasts Jonah with foreigners like the sailors and Assyrians. Jonah repeatedly opposes Yahweh's wishes, fleeing from Assyria when called to prophesy to it (Jonah 1:3) and angrily rejecting Yahweh's decision to have mercy on Assyria (4:1–5). In contrast, the foreign sailors and the Assyrians respond piously to Yahweh's actions (1:7–16; 3:5–9). Whether or not the book was originally intended to speak to issues of foreigners in the post-exilic period, its satiric portrait of Jonah and foreigners now balances the perspective of several other biblical books.

following section looks at what each of these texts might have said to Judeans of the time of Nehemiah and Ezra.

At first glance, the book of Jonah appears to take us back several centuries to the time of Assyria (the eighth to seventh centuries), but a closer look reveals that it is actually a teaching parable from much later. The book tells a story about God's call of a prophet, Jonah, to preach an Amos-like message of total destruction to the mighty nation of Assyria. Given Assyria's reputation for merciless brutality, the reader is not surprised to hear that Jonah runs in the opposite direction (Jonah 1). This is where God introduces the famous whale to bring Jonah back on track (Jonah 2). He preaches destruction, the Assyrians repent, and Jonah gets very angry with God about God's decision not to destroy the Assyrians after all (Jonah 3–4). The narrative ends with God gently reproving Jonah for his persistent wish to see the destruction of foreigners. God asks Jonah, "should I not care about Nineveh, that great city, in which there are more than a hundred and twenty thousand persons . . . and many animals besides?" (Jonah 4:11). This rhetorical question is but one pointer to the teaching function of the whole. Jonah is not a historical record, set in a specific time of a particular Assyrian king. Rather it is a fable telling of God's ability to have mercy even on such a brutal empire as the Assyrians. The question addressed to Jonah at the end of the book is also a question addressed to the readers: should God care about foreigners like the Assyrians and their animals? In contrast to biblical books such as Nahum or anti-foreign attitudes reflected in Ezra, the book of Jonah implies that the answer to this question about God's care for foreigners is "yes."

basics	**Book of Ruth**		
Outline: loyalty of all leading to David's line	I	Potential problem: widowed foreign wife in Judah	1
	II	Problem into solution: foreign wife produces ancestor of David	2–4
Date	Fifth century BCE (400s, for the present form of the book).		
Themes	See the discussion of Ruth in the main text.		

The book of Ruth is another narrative that subtly addresses the issue of foreigners, especially the issue of foreign intermarriage. The book opens with the death in Moab of two Judeans, Mahlon and Chilion, about ten years after they married Moabite wives, Orpah and Ruth (1:4–5). Seen through the lens of post-exilic concerns about intermarriage with foreigners, their deaths could be seen as a possible consequence of their intermarriages with foreign women. The character of Naomi, the mother-in-law of these Moabite women, seems to embody such concerns when she urges Orpah and Ruth not to follow her back to Judah (1:8–9). Certainly later post-exilic readers would be able to relate to Naomi when she is silent, rather than thrilled and grateful, when Ruth, the "Moabite" (1:22), passionately declares her intention to follow Naomi to her grave (1:16–18). The rest of the book can be viewed as the education of Naomi in Ruth's importance to her. By the end of the book, Ruth bears a child by Boaz, which Naomi recognizes as her own, and this child becomes one of the ancestors of the great king David (4:13–20). This story, especially the genealogy linking David to a Judean's intermarriage with a Moabite, would have had radical implications in the time of Ezra. Some parts of it may have been written in an earlier time, but the present form of the book would have educated post-exilic Judeans opposed to intermarriage. It would have told them about how Naomi overcame her initial concerns about a Moabite daughter-in-law and ended up becoming the grandmother of an ancestor of Israel's founding king.

Finally, we turn to post-exilic prophecy in Isaiah, particularly the post-exilic prophecies concentrated in chapters 56–66 of the book. Previous chapters of Isaiah also feature texts that are characterized by their positive attitudes toward foreigners. These include the proclamation that peoples of the earth will stream toward Zion to learn Torah (Isa 2:1–4) and the prophecy in Isa 19:19–25 that concludes with Yahweh's blessing on "my people Egypt, my handiwork Assyria, and my very own Israel." Many scholars now think that these and many other parts of Isaiah 1–35 were written in the Persian period or later. When we come to Isaiah 56–66, however, the vast majority of texts come from this period (aside from the possible exilic lament in 63:7–64:12). This section is often called "**Third Isaiah**," and it is distinguished from other parts of Isaiah by the way it applies the prophecies of both Second Isaiah and the eighth-century prophet Isaiah ("First Isaiah") to delays in Jerusalem's rebuilding and other problems of the post-exile.

Second Isaiah contained grand promises that God would "light" the way for the returning exiles (Isa 42:16) and rebuild Jerusalem, but texts in Third Isaiah show that things did not go as well as expected. In Isaiah 59:9 a group cries, "we wait for light and it does not reach us, for brightness, but we walk in gloom," and Isa 58:3 quotes people complaining to God, "why do we fast, but you do not see?" The rest of Isaiah 58 provides a powerful answer to this question: the promises of Second Isaiah have not come true because the fasting and sacrifice of the returnees have not been combined with acts of justice (Isa 58:2–5; also 66:1–4). Like the people of the time of eighth-century Isaiah (1:10–17), they have corrupted their worship practices with oppression of others. Third Isaiah goes on in Isaiah 58 to promise that acts of justice and Sabbath keeping will turn things around. When the returnees share their homes with the poor and stop abusing the Sabbath for profit, the promises of Second Isaiah will come true: God's light will break forth on them like the dawn (58:8, 10) and Jerusalem will be rebuilt from its ruins (58:12). Similar themes arise again at the heart of Third Isaiah, where a speaker – the prophet himself? – proclaims that he was commissioned by God to "bring good news to the poor" and "comfort all who mourn in Zion" (Isa 61:1–3). These words of comfort and liberation to the poor will lead to the rebuilding of Jerusalem (61:4).

---

basics   Book of Isaiah

Outline: exhortation to repentance

I	Introduction: initial exhortation to repentance	1:1–31
II	Elaboration: restoration of Zion after purging judgment on it and the nations	2:1–64:12
III	Concluding paired oracles: consequences for the disobedient (65:1–66:4) and obedient (66:5–24)	

The above outline builds on scholars' observations of an inclusio in Isaiah, where themes appearing together in the exhortation to repentance in Isa 1:1–31 reappear again in the paired divine speeches to the disobedient and obedient in 65:1–66:24. See the list of parallels between the two halves of the book on the opposite page. There are other patterns to be observed as well in Isaiah. In this and other cases, books like Isaiah are too complex to be tamed by one outline.

Date   Fifth century BCE (400s, building on earlier materials).

Themes   See the discussion in the main text and in Chapters 7 and 10.

For Third Isaiah, the fulfillment of the promises of restoration in Second Isaiah is dependent on people listening to First Isaiah's call for justice and righteousness. This is clear once again in the last four chapters of the book, which include a quotation from an exilic lament (63:7–64:12) and God's response (Isaiah 65–6). The lament concludes with an anguished cry to God that "Zion has become a wilderness" and a following question: "after all this, will you restrain yourself, oh Yahweh? Will you keep silent?" (64:10–12). Yahweh is not silent, but gives conditional words of hope: God will restore Zion for God's righteous "servants," but God will destroy those in Zion who worship in gardens and tombs and then say, "keep to yourself, do not come near me, for I am holy" (Isa 65:3–5; cf. Isa 1:29–31). In this and other ways, the conclusion of Third Isaiah echoes the prophecy in First Isaiah that Yahweh would purge Jerusalem of its corrupt leadership and restore it to its former glory (Isa 1:21–31).

Scholars have found numerous ways in which the book of Isaiah as a whole, though written over centuries, is organized by broader patterns that span its various layers. For example, Isaiah 1:1–2:3 has been seen by many as an introduction to the whole book, introducing themes of judgment and restoration that extend to its end. Isaiah 65–6 serves as a conclusion, echoing many parts of Isaiah 1 in particular. In addition, several parts of the first half of the book, Isaiah 1–33, parallel portions of the second half, Isaiah 34–66:

Isaiah 1–33 (plan for Yahweh's rule from Zion)	Isaiah 34–66 (initial realization of plan)
Introduction: call to hear (Isaiah 1)	Call to hear revenge and restoration (Isa 34–5)
Commission of eight-century Isaiah (Isaiah 6)	
Isaiah-Ahaz materials (Isaiah 7–8)	Isaiah–Hezekiah narratives (Isaiah 36–9)
	Commission of exilic prophet (40:1–11)
Anti-nations/Babylon (Isaiah 13–27)	Oracle against Babylon (Isaiah 47)
Oracles focused on Zion (Isaiah 28–32)	Oracles on Zion's restoration (49–66)

There is some evidence in the Dead Sea scrolls that early Jewish communities sometimes copied these two halves of Isaiah on separate scrolls (thus 1 and 2 Isaiah, like 1 and 2 Samuel or Kings), but these and other patterns also bind the book together into a complex unity. It is a chorale of prophetic voices from different centuries, joining in witness to Yahweh, "the holy one of Israel," and his plans for Zion and the nations around it. Let us now focus on one text from Third Isaiah that speaks particularly directly to the issue of Zion and foreigners from "the nations": Isa 56:1–8.

Isa 56:1–8

FOCUS TEXT

Isa 56:1–8 opens the collection of post-exilic prophecies in Isaiah 56–66, prophecies that immediately follow Second Isaiah's words of "comfort" to exiles in 40–55. Second

Isaiah had promised that Yahweh would soon bring his salvation and deliverance. This "Third Isaiah" asserts that the fulfillment of these promises requires a prior act by the people themselves: that they "bring about justice and act with social solidarity" (Isa 56:1). The post-exilic prophet adds that only those who "observe the Sabbath" and "keep away from evil" will be "happy" (56:2). These two verses encapsulate Third Isaiah's addition of moral conditions to the promises of Second Isaiah.

Nevertheless, the balance of the passage goes on to address a particular moral concern of the post-exilic community: the status of foreigners and people considered to be cultically impure. A passage in Deuteronomy insists that neither eunuchs (men whose testicles have been removed or damaged) nor Ammonites and Moabites (both neighboring foreign peoples) should be allowed to enter the worshipping community of Yahweh (Deut 23:1, 3). In Isa 56:3–8, Yahweh addresses the matter of eunuchs and foreigners who are being excluded from the Temple on this basis, despite their observing the Sabbath and keeping Yahweh's covenant:

> Let not a foreigner say,
>   who has joined himself to Yahweh,
>   "Yahweh will surely separate me from his people,"
> And let not a eunuch say,
>   "I am a dried up tree." (56:3)

To these people, the prophet gives a direct word from Yahweh that contradicts the law in Deuteronomy:

> For thus says Yahweh,
>   To the eunuchs who keep my Sabbaths,
> who have chosen that which I desire,
>   And hold fast to my covenant,
> I will give them a monument and name in my house and my walls
>   better than sons or daughters . . .
> And to the foreigners joined to Yahweh,
>   to serve him and love the name of Yahweh . . .
> I will bring them into my holy mountain,
>   And help them celebrate in my house of prayer;
>   Their burnt offerings and sacrifices will be pleasing on my altar.
> For my house shall be called a house of prayer
>   for all peoples. (56:4–7)

Thus the prophet offers a direct quotation from Yahweh that contradicts a part of the Mosaic Torah. As we know, the Mosaic Torah was ever more prominent in the post-exilic period, and there was an increasing concern to avoid a future exile by "separating" from foreign peoples, as in Nehemiah's and Ezra's initiatives against intermarriage with foreign women. In this case, the focus is not on intermarriage but on foreigners (and eunuchs) who are faithful to Yahweh but find themselves excluded, on the basis of the

Mosaic Torah, from the Temple because of their foreign status. Yahweh in this passage contradicts that Torah, assuring them that all who keep his Sabbaths and hold fast to the covenant are welcome in his house.

The basis for this radical contradiction of Mosaic Torah is the message of Second Isaiah. There the exilic prophet described Yahweh as appointing a "servant" for a task that went beyond just bringing Judeans back from exile:

> It is too light a thing that you should be my servant,
>> To establish the tribes of Jacob
>> And bring back the survivors of Israel.
> I will make you a light to the nations,
>> To be my salvation to the end of the earth. (49:6)

In this passage in Third Isaiah, a post-exilic prophet echoes this message, saying:

> Thus says Yahweh,
>> Who gathers the scattered of Israel,
> I soon will gather yet others to them,
>> Besides those already gathered. (56:8)

By this point the prophet can look back on an in-gathering of exiles that has already occurred. Both he and the rest of his post-exilic audience know Yahweh now as a God who has proven true to promises to bring back the exiles. Building on this and on Second Isaiah's message, he extends this idea to foreigners, saying that Second Isaiah's message about being a "light to the nations" also holds. Yahweh is about a larger project of in-gathering, one that means that foreigners joined to Yahweh, Yahweh's "servants" (56:6), will have a full place in worship at Yahweh's mountain. This proclamation of including foreigners is later echoed toward the very end of (Third) Isaiah with a prophecy that some foreigners will even become priests and Levites (66:18–23).

These prophecies stand in sharp contrast to the application in the Ezra traditions of messages from the Pentateuch and Second Isaiah. Ezra seems to have modeled his procession from Babylon to Judah on the exodus from Egypt, departing on the first day of the year (Ezra 7:9; cf. Exod 12:2) and then making sure that his caravan corresponded to Moses's in having Levitical priests and 12 lay leaders (Ezra 8:1–20). Yet he also seems to have understood this second exodus in terms taken from Second Isaiah, praying, for example, that Yahweh would "make [their] way straight" on the way home to Judah (Ezra 8:21; see Isa 40:3). Ezra soon finds out that the people already in Judah have failed to "separate themselves" from foreign peoples, intermarrying with them (Ezra 9:1), and he moves to expel foreign wives as a precondition for leading the people in devoting themselves to the Torah of Moses (Ezra 9–10; Nehemiah 8).

Third Isaiah is not focused on exactly the same issues, but still represents a sharp contrast to Ezra. Ezra aimed for "separation" from foreign peoples (Ezra 9:1–3; 10:11), while Third Isaiah proclaimed Yahweh's reassurance to foreigners who were concerned – perhaps on the basis of initiatives like Ezra's – that "Yahweh will surely separate me from his people" (56:3). Ezra focused on Second Isaiah's message that Yahweh would bring the exiles home in a second exodus. Third Isaiah added an emphasis on the other half of Second Isaiah's message: that this homecoming of exiles was part of a broader plan in which Yahweh's servant would be a light to "the nations." Ezra's narrative climaxes with the reading of the Torah and the people's rededication of themselves to it (Nehemiah 8). Third Isaiah contradicts a part of that Torah that excludes foreigners and eunuchs from God's temple (Deut 23:1, 3), quoting Yahweh as saying, "my house shall be a house of prayer for all peoples" (56:7). Thus, Third Isaiah stands alongside other traditions discussed above, such as Ruth and Jonah, as an important witness to the ongoing diversity of perspectives in Persian-period Judah. Seeing the period purely through the lens of the Ezra and Nehemiah narratives misses an important part of the picture.

Scriptures in the Post-Exile

Ultimately, both the Mosaic Torah and book of Isaiah were included in the broader scriptural corpus of post-exilic Judaism. But the Mosaic Torah, now in combined L and P form, increasingly became the foundation of everything else. Other holy texts were increasingly understood in light of the Torah. For example, ancient collections of psalms were organized into what is now a five-part, Torah- and praise-oriented whole. Shorter prophetic books such as Hosea and Zechariah were combined into a collection of 12 books that concludes with a passage that urges constant memory of the "Torah of my servant Moses" (Mal 4:4). And readers of other texts would have seen this combined L/P Torah in other references to God's "Torah" in Isaiah, Jeremiah, and Ezekiel.

In these ways, the Torah that first started to emerge under Josiah and was affirmed – in L and P forms – in the exile became ever more central in the post-exilic Persian period, possibly with help from the Persians themselves. But this process took time. Some early post-exilic texts, such as Third Isaiah and Job, do not yet reflect the dominance of the Mosaic Torah that we see later. The community of Judah evolved significantly from the initial returns of exiles under Davidic descendants (Sheshbazzar, Zerubbabel) to its consolidation around the Torah under Ezra the priest. Only toward the end of this period do we see the clear outlines of a Temple- and Torah-centered Judaism that would persist for several centuries of Hellenistic rule. Next we shall look at that chapter in the history of the people and development of the Bible.

CHAPTER TWELVE REVIEW

1. Know the meaning and significance of the following terms:
   - *satan* (not Satan!)
   - Third Isaiah

2. How did the authors of the Ezra and Nehemiah traditions reconcile pro-Persian sympathies with their concern about foreign influence?

3. The book of Job can be seen as a staged dialogue between different parts of Israelite tradition up through the early post-exile. Which parts of Job represent what types of literature? Which type of literature does not seem prominently represented in Job?

4. What is "Third Isaiah" and how is it related to earlier parts of Isaiah?

5. What emphases does the Temple-rebuilding/Ezra narrative now included in Ezra–Nehemiah have in common with Third Isaiah and where do these two writings diverge?

6. Are there contemporary analogies to the need for a marginalized group to reinforce its boundaries? Where would such initiatives be dangerous or wrong and why?

7. If a prophet like Third Isaiah were to speak today, to what situation would she or he need to address her or his prophecy? The author of Third Isaiah built on earlier Isaiah (and other) traditions. What traditions would this contemporary prophet build on?

8. Try rewriting Isa 56:1–8 for a contemporary audience, matching sentence for sentence, metaphor for metaphor, etc.

RESOURCES FOR FURTHER STUDY

Haggai and Zechariah 1–8

Petersen, David. *Haggai and Zechariah 1–8: A Commentary*. Old Testament Library. Philadelphia: Westminster Press, 1984.

Ezra, Nehemiah, and Esther

Blenkinsopp, Joseph. *Ezra–Nehemiah: A Commentary*. Old Testament Library. Philadelphia: Westminster Press, 1988.

Clines, David. *Ezra, Nehemiah, Esther*. New Century Bible Commentary. Grand Rapids: Eerdmans, 1984.

Williamson, H. G. M. *Ezra, Nehemiah*. Word Biblical Commentary 16. Waco, TX: Word Books, 1985.

Jonah

Lacocque, Andre, and Lacocque, Pierre-Emmanuel. *The Jonah Complex*. Atlanta: John Knox Press, 1981.

Trible, Phyllis. *Rhetorical Criticism: Context, Method, and the Book of Jonah*. Minneapolis: Fortress, 1994.

Ruth

Fewell, Danna Nolan, and Gunn, David Miller. *Compromising Redemption: Relating Characters in the Book of Ruth*. Literary Currents in Biblical Interpretation. Philadelphia: Westminster John Knox Press, 1990.

Kates, Gail Twersky, and Reimer, Judith. *Reading Ruth*. New York: Ballentine Books, 1994, 1996. Excellent collection of contemporary interpretations by Jewish women.

Job

Janzen, J. Gerald. *Job*. Interpretation. Atlanta: John Knox Press, 1985.

Newsom, Carol. "Job." Pp. 319–637 of vol. 4 of the New *Interpreters Bible*. Nashville: Abingdon, 1996.

Isaiah 56–66

Blenkinsopp, Joseph. *Isaiah 56–66: A New Translation with Introduction and Commentary*. Anchor Bible. New York: Doubleday, 2005.

(See also the end of Chapter 9 for commentaries on Isaiah 40–66.)

CHAPTER 13

HELLENISTIC EMPIRES

AND THE FORMATION OF

THE HEBREW BIBLE

Chapter Outline

CHAPTER OVERVIEW

It is hard to come up with a sharper contrast in the experience of empire than that between the Judeans' experience of Persian support and their later near annihilation by the Hellenistic (Greek) king Antiochus Epiphanes IV. Though Hellenistic rule was not a serious problem in the first 157 years after Alexander the Great's conquest of the area (in 332 BCE), a major confrontation occurred in Judah in 174 BCE when Hellenizers sought to take control of Jerusalem and turn it into a Greek city. This led to an attempt to eradicate Judaism by the Hellenistic king Antiochus IV, successful rebellion led by a family of provincial priests (the Hasmoneans), and their establishment of a priest-ruled kingdom in Jerusalem that lasted eighty years.

This chapter examines writings composed before and after this confrontation, along with probable finalization of the Hebrew Bible under the Hasmonean rulers. Some writings composed earlier in the Hellenistic period, such as the wisdom of Ben Sira or some apocalypses now in Enoch, were included in the Old Testament collections of the Roman Catholic and/or Orthodox churches, but excluded from the Jewish Tanach (and, as a result, the later Protestant Old Testament). Some later writings composed during or after the Hellenistic confrontation, such as the book of Daniel, were included in the Jewish Tanach (as well as the Old Testament of all churches). Toward its conclusion, this chapter explores the important question of why some texts were included in the Hebrew Bible, while others were left out.

Judaism and Hellenism before the Hellenizing Crisis

Though early Hellenistic rule was not benign, it was not antagonistic toward the religion and culture of peoples such as the Judeans. From the time of Alexander's conquest (332 BCE) up to initial efforts to Hellenize Jerusalem (174 BCE), Judah was ruled by a succession of Hellenistic rulers without major incident. After Alexander's death in 323 BCE, his kingdom was split among his generals, including Ptolemy in Egypt and Seleucus in Mesopotamia. Judah was ruled first from Egypt by heirs of Ptolemy (323–198 BCE). Then, after a series of major battles, the Seleucids (heirs of Seleucus) took over in 198 BCE and ruled Judah much of the following century. Things were difficult as

READING
Sirach/Ben Sira 1:1–10;
24:1–34; 44–50.

the two Hellenistic empires struggled for control of the area, but there is no evidence (prior to the ruler Antiochus IV: more on him below) that either the Ptolemaic or Seleucid rulers interfered with the religion of those they ruled or otherwise tried to Hellenize them.

Nevertheless, Greek cities and people who had Greek education received privileges in these kingdoms, while those lacking Greek culture sometimes faced prejudice. For example, a non-Greek camel driver complains in an inscription that he was treated poorly because "I am a barbarian" and "I do not know how to behave like a Greek." An Egyptian priest complains in another inscription that a person whom he is suing "despises me because I am an Egyptian." Within Hellenistic cultures, Greek-educated children of Greek parents were at the top of the social pyramid, followed by Greek-educated children of non-Greek parents. Those who lacked any Greek education were disadvantaged even if they – like the Egyptian priest mentioned above – had extensive education in local, non-Greek texts, such as Egyptian classics or Hebrew books.

The solution for more and more people was to get a Greek education. Families would either have an in-house teacher for their children or pay someone else to educate them in a small group of private students. Students would start by learning the Greek alphabet and go on to learn practical wisdom such as Aesop's fables. Later they would progress to writings by a select list of authors from the classical period of Greek culture: Euripides, Thucydides, Plato, and others. The focal point of Greek education, however, was to learn the writings of Homer, whose epics were the classics among classics of Greek literature. Students started memorizing selections from the *Iliad* and *Odyssey* early in their education, and they returned to these texts again and again. Of course, some students did not progress very far, especially if they came from families where no Greek was spoken or read. Often a student would learn only enough Greek to do the simplest of scribal tasks. Some non-Greeks, however, achieved very high levels of Greek learning and obtained high positions in Greek government and/or society. Their education made them culturally "Greek," and they were treated differently than others who lacked such education.

This meant that societies under Hellenistic rule had a growing cultural divide. On the one side stood Greek culture, the knowledge of which gave students access to government positions and/or business contacts across the Greek world. On the other side stood the cultures and native texts of peoples in Judah, Egypt, and Mesopotamia. The knowledge of ancient Near Eastern texts was less and less important in the broader Hellenistic culture but was still valued in temple–priestly circles. Therefore, within Judah, the Temple and various priesthoods connected to it became the primary place where people still learned and wrote texts in Hebrew. Otherwise, priests found themselves and their knowledge of ancient texts increasingly marginalized. In earlier times, knowledge of ancient Hebrew texts gave a person privileges in the Hebrew monarchy or Persian empire, but things were different under Hellenism. Now primary political and economic power belonged increasingly to those who could claim on some level to be "Greek."

Judeans and others dealt with this divide in different ways. Some priestly groups in both Egypt and Judah wrote esoteric visionary texts, called "**apocalypses**" after the Greek word for "uncovering." Some of these texts featured detailed tours of heaven ("**heavenly apocalypses**"), while others reviewed past history and then predicted divine intervention to remove Hellenistic rulers and restore native leaders ("**historical apocalypses**"). These apocalypses reflected both the broad scholarship of their priestly authors and their alienation from the surrounding Greek-dominated culture. The book of (first) Enoch, revered as scripture in the Ethiopic church, contains some of Judaism's oldest apocalyptic texts, such as the story of God's imminent destruction of bad angels (Enoch 6–11) and Enoch's sermon to the rebellious angels (Enoch 12–16). The meaning of these often obscure apocalyptic texts is unclear initially to most readers. On one level, they elaborate on biblical narratives and feature many unfamiliar characters and scenes, battles between angels and the like. Yet on another level, these apocalypses in Enoch are coded descriptions of battles between Hellenistic rulers (Enoch 6–11) or crises in the Jerusalem priesthood (Enoch 12–16) and God's plan to intervene and set things right. These texts speak to concerns that were present in the third century BCE about Hellenistic domination and the corruption of the Temple, but they claim as their author an ancient, pre-Hellenistic sage, Enoch (see Gen 5:21–4). Such attribution of a later text to an ancient author, termed "**pseudepigraphy**," was particularly common in the Hellenistic age, when ancient authorship determined whether or not a given text would

Figure 13.1 Copy of the Hebrew book of Ben Sira found near the Dead Sea.

be studied in schools. In this case, however, Hellenistic-style pseudepigraphy was used by Jewish authors to provide extra authority to their predictions of liberation from Hellenistic kings and corrupt leaders.

The book of **Ben Sira** (also known as **Sirach**, its Greek name), originally written in Hebrew by Joshua ben Sira around 200–180 BCE, shows a different way to respond to the divide between local and Hellenistic culture (see Figure 13.1). In a possible critique of esoteric apocalypses such as those in Enoch, Ben Sira discourages speculation about heavenly realms (3:21–4) and rejects dreams as generally misleading (34:1–8). Instead, he writes a wisdom instruction to fit (both) the Torah focus and Hellenistic tenor of his present time. Like older instructions in Proverbs, Ben Sira directly addresses his students, encouraging them to live prudently and put wisdom above other values. Like more recent works from the exile and post-exile, Ben Sira portrays the Torah as the ultimate wisdom, now going so far as to identify the Torah of Moses with the female personified wisdom seen in Proverbs and elsewhere (Ben Sira 24; see Proverbs 8).

Yet Ben Sira also shows influence from Hellenistic culture. At various points, his sayings resemble Greek sayings by the sixth-century BCE Greek poet Theognis that were commonly used early in the process of Greek education. Moreover, the Torah takes on a role in Ben Sira that is similar to that of Homer's epics in Greek education. It, like Homer, is the foundation and end point of the rest of the process of education and study. Finally, the book of Ben Sira concludes with a set of praises that have much in common with the Hellenistic genre of *encomium* (work of praise): a praise of "great fathers" that is divided between figures in the Pentateuch (Ben Sira 44–5) and figures found in all of the rest of the Hebrew Bible (46–9), followed by an extended praise of the high priest in Ben Sira's own time, Simon (50:1–21).

Many scholars rightly have seen in this "praise of great fathers" evidence that virtually all of the books in the Hebrew Bible were known and revered by Ben Sira's time (200–180 BCE). Nevertheless, other parts of the book of Ben Sira show that its author was not yet working with an idea of a closed collection of scriptural books. His own description of what a scribe studies includes "the law of the most high" (probably the Torah), wisdom of the ancients, prophecies, sayings of the famous, parables and proverbs (Sir 39:1–3) as well as foreign wisdom (39:4). The book of Ben Sira, explicitly written in the late second century by a sage of that time, aims to be a new addition to that broader scribal curriculum.

Ben Sira is just one example of a book written in a local language (Hebrew) that reflects Greek learning. But Jews also wrote Greek works and translated originally Hebrew works into Greek. Sometime in the third century the Pentateuch was translated into Greek (the "Septuagint"), and other Hebrew scriptures (including Ben Sira) were translated later on (sometimes the group of these Greek translation is referred to with the term "Septuagint"). New works written by Judeans in Greek often drew deeply on models and values seen in the Greek literature that they had learned. Some of these are found in the deutero-canonical books of the Roman Catholic and other churches, books such as 2 Maccabees, Judith, and the Wisdom of Solomon. For example, the Wisdom of Solomon is a work in Greek that draws deeply and broadly on Stoicism and other parts of Greek philosophy in the process of retelling the story of Solomon's search for wisdom.

Because of the high prestige of Greek culture, many Jews wrote books in Greek to improve the image of Judaism both among their own people and in the broader Hellenistic world. A second-century Jewish philosopher, Aristobolus, wrote a work attempting to show how Moses was the true source of the best of Greek learning. Another author, Ezekiel the tragic poet, rewrote the story of the exodus in the form of a Greek tragedy. Still others wrote texts with a positive picture of Judaism that they attempted to present as long-lost lines of famous Greek works or as missing works by famous gentile authors. Such works reveal both a respect for Greek culture and a defensiveness about the place of Judaism vis-à-vis that culture.

When we look across the full range of Jewish texts of this time, it becomes clear that all parts of Judaism were deeply affected by Hellenism and Hellenistic culture, even when they opposed elements of that culture. The apocalypses undergird their messages with Hellenistic-style pseudepigraphy. Ben Sira writes in Hebrew, but draws on sayings, ideas, and forms from Greek education. And the author of the Wisdom of Solomon draws on multiple strands of Greek philosophy in its depictions of wisdom. As a result, there is no clear distinction between "Hellenistic Judaism" and other forms, since all of Judaism was touched by Hellenistic culture and ideas. The main distinction that does appear is between forms of Hellenistic Judaism that were neutral or positive about Hellenism and forms of Hellenistic Judaism that were opposed to it. This distinction emerges particularly in the crisis around the attempt to Hellenize Jerusalem, to which we turn next.

The Crisis over Hellenizing Jerusalem and the Book of Daniel

READING

Narratives about the
Maccabean crisis:
2 Maccabees 4–8.
Apocalyptic writing:
Daniel 7–12.

EXERCISE

After reading this section, try writing a brief historical apocalypse that would empower a contemporary oppressed group. Try to incorporate in your apocalypse the kinds of features (pseudepigraphy, historical review, and projection of divine triumph) that are seen in texts such as Daniel 7 and 10–12, but develop your own coded imagery and attribute the apocalypse to someone other than Daniel. Have a friend read and try to decode it. What is similar and different about your twenty-first-century apocalypse and the one found in Daniel 10–12?

The Seleucids under Antiochus III were initially quite friendly to Jews and Judaism. When Antiochus III took control of Judah from the Ptolemies in 198 BCE, he affirmed more ancient Persian policies toward Judah. He gave tax relief to the city and money for the Temple, and affirmed by royal decree the right of Jews to live "according to [their] ancestral laws." Later on, however, he suffered defeat by the Romans and started to pay heavy tribute to them. He died in the process of trying to raid one of the temples in his kingdom for money, and a similar attempt apparently was made during the reign of his successor, Seleucus IV (see 2 Maccabees 3). By the time Antiochus Epiphanes IV seized the throne from Seleucus in 175 BCE, his kingdom had been humiliated by the Romans, and he needed money to pay them a large annual tribute. At this point, Judah was one of the few Seleucid territories remaining on the Western Mediterranean.

It was under these circumstances that Antiochus IV started to sell the high priesthood in Jerusalem to the highest bidder, a significant move, since the high priest of Jerusalem's Temple functioned at this time as the local ruler and tax-collector for the region. First, Jason, who was a brother of the existing high priest, paid money to Antiochus on the occasion of the latter's accession to the throne for two privileges: (1) the office of high priest and (2) the right to turn Jerusalem into a Greek city, complete with its own gymnasium within sight of the temple (174 BCE). Three years later, Menaleus, a member of the Tobiad family that once had opposed Nehemiah, outbid Jason, seized the high priesthood, and forced Jason to flee (171 BCE). Menaleus's rule proved highly unpopular, however, and the Seleucids had to intervene twice to restore him to power. The second time, fed up with revolts, Antiochus IV enacted harsh measures aimed at crushing any trace of Jewish culture (in 167 BCE). He imposed the death penalty on Jews for continuing to follow Torah laws such as eating regulations and circumcision, and he set up an altar to Zeus Olympius over the altar to Yahweh in the Jerusalem Temple. What had started as a mild attempt by Jason and other Jerusalemites to gain Greek privileges for Jerusalem and its citizens had turned into a life-and-death struggle for the continuance of Torah observance.

The visions in Daniel 7–12 were written to give Judeans hope in this crisis. Like the apocalyptic visions in Enoch, these chapters of Daniel are attributed to an earlier figure, this time the exilic figure of Daniel who is featured in the tales of Daniel 1–6. More-over, like other historical apocalypses, these visions in Daniel give a coded overview of past history before predicting God's intervention to make things right. We can see an example of this in the vision of four beasts coming out of the sea in Daniel 7. These four beasts correspond to four major world empires leading up to the time of Antiochus IV: the Babylonians who destroyed the Jerusalem temple (7:4), the Medes who dominated lands east of Babylonia (7:5), the Persians (7:6), and the Greeks, particularly the 10 rulers – "horns" – of the Seleucid dynasty (7:7), from which a "little horn," Antiochus IV, sprouts (7:8).

---

basics **Book of Daniel**

Outline:	I Stories about Daniel and other exiles	1–6
apocalyptic	II Daniel's four visions	7–12
visions with		
prologue of		
stories of		
deliverance		

Language   Several chapters of Daniel are in Aramaic (2–7), others in Hebrew (1, 8–12).

Date   The Aramaic legends in Daniel 2–6 probably date from the late Persian or early Hellenistic period. The book as a whole, including the Hebrew chapters, dates from just before 164 BCE and reflects the crisis of that time.

More information   The Greek translation of Daniel preserves yet other traditions about Daniel and other figures (e.g. Susanna in Daniel 13). In addition, an Aramaic story about Nabonidus was found in the Dead Sea Scrolls at Qumran and represents a different form of the tradition seen in Daniel 4.

After surveying these four empires, the vision moves to the future, predicting the destruction of the fourth, Greek beast and God's gift of eternal dominion to a mysteri-ous "one like a human being" (7:9–14). Many Christians have read this text in light of gospel accounts where Jesus refers to himself as the "son of man," and have understood Daniel 7 as a prediction of the coming of Jesus. Nevertheless, the details of the text, especially the "interpretation" given to Daniel in 7:15–27, indicate that this chapter was originally intended to give hope to Torah-observant Jews under threat from Antiochus. Antiochus is the one who attempted to end sacrifice and forbid Torah observance, to "change the sacred times and the law" (7:25). In his vision, Daniel is told that God will destroy the kingdom of Antiochus and grant eternal rule to those who have remained faithful to the Torah, "the holy ones of the most High" (7:27).

Things did not work out exactly as this or other visions in Daniel 7–12 predicted, but these visions have continued to give hope to generations of Jews and Christians. Jews have read the text as a prediction of God's establishment of his rule with the future arrival of the messiah. Christians have read it as a prediction of God's transformation of the world with the second coming of Jesus Christ. In each case, people have found numerous ways to coordinate the obscure symbols of Daniel 7–12 with groups and events of their own time. At their best, such interpretations have given much-needed hope to communities facing oppressors as bad as or worse than Antiochus IV. At their worst, these reinterpretations of Daniel have encouraged people to withdraw from the world and wait for God's imminent intervention on their behalf. Certainly it would be a mistake for any community to suppose that their own understanding of the visions in Daniel is the one and only true way to unlock the code of the book. The persistently strange imagery of the book resists this kind of certainty and is part of what has allowed Daniel to be revered and reinterpreted by communities long after the time of the Hellenistic crisis.

The Hasmonean Kingdom and the Formation of the Hebrew Bible

Ultimately, Antiochus IV was unsuccessful, though not in the ways envisioned in Daniel 7–12. Members of a marginal priestly family in rural Judah, the **Hasmoneans** or **Maccabees**, launched a guerilla war against the Seleucids. They started by destroying pagan altars, killing Jewish collaborators with the Seleucids, and forcibly circumcising males who had been left uncircumcised under Seleucid order. Their effort culminated with the recapture of Jerusalem and purification of the Temple (164 BCE). (Note: **Hanukkah** is the Jewish holiday celebrating this triumph and the purification of the Temple.) In addition, the Hasmoneans were able to negotiate an end to the edict of Antiochus IV against Judaism. Jews were free to observe Torah regulations again, and we hear no more of any attempts to reverse this policy.

All this did not, however, mean an end to Greek domination. Though Antiochus IV died around this time, the Seleucids soon regained control over Judah, killing the leader of the Hasmonean family, Judas Maccabeus ("the hammer"), in battle and forcing the other Hasmoneans and their supporters to flee. Around 152 BCE, however, the Hasmoneans played their cards right in a power struggle over the Seleucid throne, choosing to back the winner of that struggle, Demetrius. In return, Demetrius appointed the Hasmonean Jonathan as high priest and thus ruler of the province of Judah. When Jonathan was murdered a decade later, his brother Simon declared independence from the Seleucid

Significant Dates: The Rise of the Hasmonean Kingdom

Antiochus IV seizes power over Seleucid empire	175 BCE
Jason buys high priesthood and initiates Hellenizing	174 BCE
Menelaus purchases priesthood	171 BCE
Unpopular rule, uprisings	
Harsh measures by Antiochus IV to eradicate Judaism	167 BCE
Beginning of Maccabean rebellion under Hasmoneans	
Purification/rededication of Temple	164 BCE
End of harsh edicts against Judaism	
Independent Hasmonean rule	142–63 BCE
Beginning of Roman rule of Palestine	63 BCE

empire (142 BCE). By then the Seleucids did not have the power to bring Judah back under their control.

Thus Judah was free of direct foreign rule for the first time in hundreds of years. For approximately seven decades (142–63 BCE), the Hasmoneans controlled Jerusalem and the high priesthood. Moreover, they gradually expanded their realm to include not only the old heartland of Judah and Israel but also areas that had few Jews and had not been dominated by Jerusalem for centuries: the Phoenician coastland, Edom and the rest of the Transjordan, and Galilee (see Map 13.1). At the beginning of their activity the Hasmoneans fought for Jewish rights to observe the Torah. Now, as rulers, they expelled gentiles from some of the areas they conquered, converted others, and imposed (male) circumcision on their subject populations. Their passion for ancient ways is seen in their promotion of the Torah, their advocacy for the Hebrew language in a now Aramaic-speaking populace, and their use of ancient Hebrew script on the new coins that they minted. The book of 1 Maccabees was originally written in Hebrew to celebrate and support the Hasmonean kingdom. It presents the Hasmoneans as true heirs of the Israelite judges, proponents of Hebrew heritage, and righteous opponents of the forces of Hellenism.

Nevertheless, the Hasmonean rulers were also influenced in multiple ways by the Hellenistic culture they purported to oppose. The whole practice of issuing coins was a Greek one, and the Hasmonean coins with ancient Hebrew letters also featured images and symbols drawn from older Greek coins of the Ptolemies and Seleucids. In this way, coins, such as the one pictured in Figure 13.2, vividly illustrate the kind of cultural **hybridity** we have seen at other points in Israelite history: the blending of self-determination with elements drawn from the culture of the past oppressor. We see similar hybridity in other cultural products of the Hasmonean period: The Hasmoneans

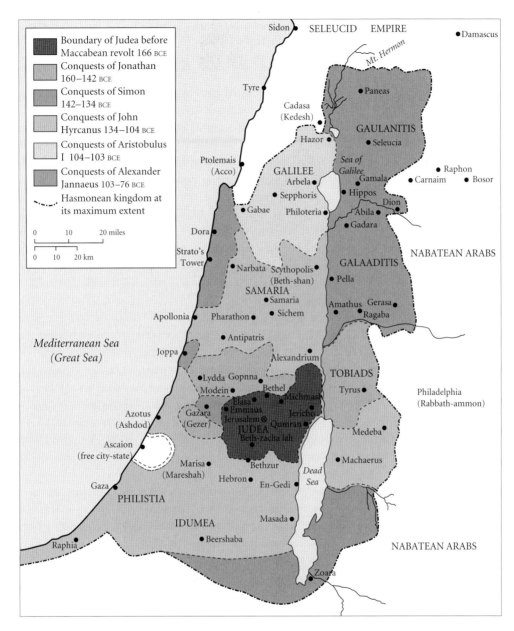

Map 13.1 The expanding kingdom of the Hasmoneans. Redrawn from Norman Gottwald, *The Hebrew Bible: A Socio-Literary Introduction*. Minneapolis: Fortress, 1985, page 407.

Figure 13.2 Coin from the time of the Hasmoneans, combining the Greek practice of coinage (with an image!) with an inscription on the other side in archaic Hebrew lettering.

built palaces with Greek columns and friezes but were careful to equip them with baths to preserve ritual purity. Jewish burial tombs from this time are virtually identical with their Greek-pagan counterparts in other countries except for their avoidance of pictorial representation, in obedience to dictates found in Deuteronomy (Deut 4:15–19). The book of 2 Maccabees celebrates heroes who fought for the Torah, using Greek models of heroic martyrs. In these and other ways the Hasmoneans developed a hybrid culture that promoted anti-Hellenism while adapting Hellenistic features.

There are several signs that it was the Hasmoneans who finalized the contents of what we now know as the Hebrew Bible. For example, it is during the time of the Hasmoneans that we first see manuscripts that are close to the later Jewish "Masoretic text" tradition. Moreover, across the whole range of Jewish history after the destruction of Jerusalem and its temple in 587 BCE, it is the Hasmonean monarchy that most had the power and motivation to establish and promote a standardized set of Jewish texts that could compete with the similarly standardized set of Greek texts valued in the Hellenistic world. These texts then could help unify the Hasmoneans' mini-empire, which expanded into neighboring areas in the late second and early first centuries.

This is most likely the time when it was decided which books were in the Hebrew Bible and which ones were out. Before the Hasmoneans, authors such as Ben Sira knew these texts as a looser collection to which one could still add a book or two. During the Hasmonean period, however, we start to see references in early Jewish texts to a defined collection of scriptures termed the "Torah and Prophets." In addition, the books of Maccabees introduce a new idea of the "end of prophecy," which served to limit which books were understood to be "prophets" (1 Macc 9:27). This boundary included books such as Samuel, Isaiah, or Daniel, since they were attributed to prophets. It even included books such as Psalms and Proverbs, since they were seen as written under the prophetic inspiration of David and Solomon. But the idea of an "end to prophecy" excluded books such as Ben Sira and all Jewish Greek works, since they quite clearly were written in the Hellenistic period. This explains why Ben Sira's grandson felt the need to assert in his prologue to his Greek translation of his grandfather's book that Ben Sira had not only studied and benefited from the "Torah and Prophets," but also studied "other books of our fathers." He was arguing for the ongoing importance of these "other books of our fathers," such as the book of Ben Sira itself, in an environment where many believed that only the "Torah and Prophets" were worth studying.

This does not mean that all Jews everywhere instantly agreed on which books they would consider to be authoritative. The Jews at Qumran who collected the Dead Sea scrolls recognized a broader set of Hebrew texts as scripture, as did the first Christians (who were also Jewish), and even the book of Ben Sira is cited as authoritative in a few rabbinic writings. Nevertheless, the Hasmoneans are the best candidates for producing and initially promoting a clearly defined set of Hebrew scriptures. They had the political authority to establish such a collection and anti-Hellenistic, pro-Hebrew (pro-Judean) motives for doing so. For them a clearly defined collection of the "Torah and Prophets" would have served as an authentic Hebrew substitution for the Greek literary texts used in Hellenistic kingdoms like that of the Seleucids. Where youths preparing to work in the Seleucid government once were required to study the Greek curriculum, the Hasmoneans now could have such youths prepare to work in their mini-empire by learning a clearly defined corpus of Hebrew scriptures. These were the texts that the Hasmonean priest-kings preserved and promoted even if other Jewish groups did not agree, and these are the texts that later rabbinic Judaism took as the authoritative Hebrew Bible.

The Hellenistic Period as the Setting for Other Hebrew Bible Texts

Though the Hasmoneans may have intended to create a collection of pre-Hellenistic books, the Hebrew Bible contains several books that probably were written sometime during this Hellenistic period. We have already discussed the visions of Daniel, which show clear signs of having been written sometime during the Hellenistic crisis of 169–164 BCE. But other books of the Bible also were either written or modified in the years after Alexander conquered the area.

READING
Writings about life in the diaspora: Esther, Daniel 3.

One example is the books of Chronicles, at least in their present form. The genealogies at the outset of the book (1 Chronicles 1–9), for example, include figures who lived during the Hellenistic period (1 Chr 3:17–24). To be sure, parts of the historical overview in 1 Chronicles 10 through 2 Chronicles 36 are parallel to parts of Samuel and Kings, which means that these sections come from the exilic or pre-exilic periods. Indeed, some parts of Chronicles may be earlier than their counterparts in Samuel and Kings, preserving some historical records from the eighth or early seventh century. Nevertheless, the bulk of texts that are unique to Chronicles, both the genealogies in 1 Chronicles 1–9 and portions of the following historical sections, show linguistic and other signs of having been written in the Persian or Hellenistic periods. As such, the books of Chronicles are another witness to the theology and values of late post-exilic priestly groups, particularly the Levites, who are promoted in the book and were responsible for singing and teaching in post-exilic Judah.

The Hellenistic period is also the most likely time for the composition of the books of Ezra–Nehemiah. As discussed in Chapter 12, this set of books was formed through the combination of separate Ezra and Nehemiah traditions probably written in the Persian period. Nevertheless, these older traditions are combined in a very particular way in Ezra–Nehemiah, as seen in the following chart:

basics	Books of Chronicles
Outline: Temple and priest-centered history of Judah's kings	I Genealogy: Adam to exile 1 Chr 1–9 II Reign of David 1 Chr 10–29 III Reign of Solomon 2 Chr 1–9 IV Judean kingship until exile 2 Chr 10–36
Date	Fourth century BCE (300s).
More information	Though most of the material special to Chronicles is very late, isolated parts may preserve historical materials that are earlier than Samuel–Kings.

Rebuilding/Ezra narrative	Nehemiah memoir	Combined text
Temple rebuilding Expulsion of foreign wives Centering on Torah	*Rebuilding of wall* *Opposition to Tobiads*	Temple rebuilding Expulsion of foreign wives *Rebuilding of wall* Centering on Torah *Opposition to Tobiads*

Setting the narrative up this way corresponds to the later effort by the Hasmoneans to protect Torah obedience by gaining political power. In this combined Ezra–Nehemiah narrative, Nehemiah builds the wall and thus protects Jerusalem *before* Ezra leads the people in committing themselves to the Mosaic Torah. In addition, the combined Ezra–Nehemiah narrative would have discredited opponents of the Hasmoneans, specifically the Tobiad family, which supported Hellenization and was sponsored by Antiochus IV. This family is prominent among those who opposed Nehemiah's wall building (Neh 2:10, 19–20; 4:1–9; 6:1–19), and the concluding chapter of Ezra–Nehemiah narrates Nehemiah's expulsion of Tobiah from the temple (13:4–9). Finally, the authors who combined the older Ezra and Nehemiah materials also wrote new texts of their own. One major example is the prayer of Ezra in Nehemiah 9, which describes the people as suffering from slavery to the Persians and "in great distress" (Neh 9:36–7). This negative attitude toward the Persian empire is alien to the older Ezra and Nehemiah traditions, but it is right at home in the Hellenistic period. We see similar negative pictures of the Persians in the visions of Daniel and other Hellenistic-period texts. For example, most scholars would agree that the book of Esther dates from this time, mostly on the basis of its late language. The Hasmoneans and their supporters would have liked the book's celebration of successful Jewish resistance to an attempt by a corrupt Persian official to kill all of the Jews in the empire.

A yet better case can be made for dating the book of Esther to the Hellenistic period, on the basis of both late language and its unflattering portrayal of Persian rule.

basics Books of Ezra–Nehemiah

Outline: the cultic and political establishment of Torah-centered Judean community

I	Return and rebuilding of Temple	Ezra 1–6
II	Torah+Temple-centered community	
	A Preparations	
	1 Ezra's commission and divorce of foreign wives	Ezra 7–10
	2 Nehemiah's building of politically independent Jerusalem	Nehemiah 1–7
	B Ezra and Nehemiah's creation of Torah-centered community	Nehemiah 8–13

Language Ezra 4:8–6:18 and 7:12–26 are in Aramaic, while the rest is in Hebrew.

Date The present form of the book may date as late as the mid-second century (160–150s BCE).

More information The bulk of the book is probably earlier, particularly the sources for Ezra (Ezra 7–10; Nehemiah 8) and Nehemiah (Neh 1:1–7:4; 13:10–14, 30b–31) that were discussed in Chapter 12.

The apocryphal/deutero-canonical book of 1 Esdras is a Greek narrative that parallels Ezra 1–10 and Nehemiah 8 but lacks any of the Nehemiah materials found in Nehemiah 1–7, 9–13. Many scholars think this book is a Greek translation of an earlier form of the Temple-rebuilding/Ezra account (preceded by a fragment from 2 Chronicles 35–6) before it was combined with the Nehemiah memoir. 1 Esdras also includes a late court tale about a debate between three bodyguards concerning whether wine, the king, women, or truth are more powerful (1 Esdras 3:1–5:6).

Finally, the Aramaic court tales found in Daniel 2–6, though earlier than the visions of 7–12, probably date from the late Persian or early Hellenistic periods. They celebrate the survival and triumph of Daniel and other exiles in the hostile environment of the Neo-Babylonian empire.

Overall, many parts of the Hebrew Bible probably reached their present form in the Hellenistic period. This seems to be the case with books such as the Song of Songs and Ecclesiastes, both of which feature late forms of Hebrew typical of Hellenistic-period texts. Though earlier in this textbook we suggested that parts of these books may have been written during the early monarchy (see Chapter 4), they certainly were modified later on. For example, a Hellenistic-period scribe appears to have added the following orthodox conclusion to the book of Ecclesiastes:

basics | **Book of Esther**

Outline | story of victory behind the holiday of Purim

I   Esther's rise and saving of her people   1–8
II   Revenge of Jews and beginning of Purim   9–10

Date | Third century BCE (200s).

More information | The book of Esther in Hebrew is distinguished by its lack of mention of God or traditional piety. The Greek translations of Esther include additions which solve this problem by inserting prayers, references to God, etc. These more pious forms of Esther were preserved in the Christian church.

Meanwhile, Esther has become the central reading within Judaism for the raucous holiday of Purim. This holiday, which happens in late February or early March, features dressing up, candy, gifts for the poor, and audience response during the reading of the Esther scroll.

The conclusion of the matter:
All has been heard,
Fear God and keep God's commandments
This is the duty of every human.
For God will bring every deed to judgment
Even every secret thing, whether good or bad. (Eccl 12:13–14)

This conclusion shows ideas of Torah obedience and final judgment that are common in the Hellenistic period. They contrast strongly with the skepticism of most of the rest of Ecclesiastes, such as "Do not be too righteous and do not be too evil, for why should you be ruined? (Eccl 7:16). In this way and many others, the present Hebrew Bible/Old Testament, in Ecclesiastes and many other books, is an intricate blend of old and new.

FOCUS TEXT

Daniel 10–12

The report of a vision in Daniel 10–12 is one of the best examples of a text that is presented as old, but is manifestly new. At the outset we hear that the exilic figure Daniel received this vision in "the third year of king Cyrus of Persia" (Dan 10:1). Nevertheless, the following two chapters make clear that the author knew world history up to the time of the Hellenistic crisis, but not events afterwards. The vision starts with an angelic figure, perhaps Gabriel, appearing to Daniel and anticipating future events in the Hellenistic and Persian periods: the defeat of the Persian empire by Alexander ("the warrior king," 11:3), the division of his kingdom among his four generals (11:4), various specific events in the history of the Ptolemies of Egypt ("the king[s] of the south," 11:5–12), the conquest of Judah and Egypt by the Seleucid Antiochus III (11:13–16), the attempt to rob the Jerusalem Temple under his successor, Seleucus IV (11:20), the rise and initial conquests of Antiochus IV (11:21–8), and his profaning of the Temple and persecution of observant Jews (11:29–39). At this point, however, the text diverges from history, inaccurately predicting further conquests by Antiochus IV (11:40–5) and the time when the Temple would be purified and rededicated (12:11–12). Clearly this vision was written after the onset of the Hellenistic crisis in 169 BCE but before its end and the death of Antiochus IV.

This text is particularly important, however, because it concludes with a vision of resurrection that is unique in the Hebrew Bible. Elsewhere, the Hebrew Bible has little place for an idea of afterlife. There is no belief in heaven and hell. Instead, all who died were thought to go to a shadowy existence in "Sheol" that involved neither reward nor punishment. As Proverbs indicates, the main hope for virtuous reward was prosperity in this life, along with children and a good name to continue after death (e.g. Prov 10:4, 7, 27–8; 12:28). This perspective, however, did not provide much comfort amidst a situation like the Hellenistic crisis. There people (and their children) were being killed for staying faithful to the Torah. This text in Daniel promises that this is not the end for them. Instead, those that have been faithful – that is, "the wise ones" – will be resurrected after the death of Antiochus IV and "shine like the brightness of heaven." Meanwhile, those of their persecutors who have died will also be resurrected, but to shame and continual punishment (Dan 12:1–3).

The Greeks had long believed in some kind of individual afterlife (e.g. the kingdom of Hades), but this Hebrew idea of collective afterlife in Daniel now empowered resistance to Greek oppression. It gave people hope to resist Antiochus IV even if opposition to his decree would cost them their lives. Here again we can see how the cultural traditions of the oppressor could be used by the oppressed to enable resistance. Moreover, this idea of afterlife has continued to empower resistance by people facing difficult odds. The belief in a reward during God's final judgment has helped generations of Jews and Christians remain faithful even when facing powerful oppressors capable of killing them.

Two centuries later, these kinds of beliefs in God's (coming) transformation of the world would be common among the Jews of the first century, among whom Jesus and the earliest Christians should be numbered. By then a new powerful empire, that of the Romans, had taken control of Judah. Soon Judah was hammered by crises at least as severe as, if not more so than, the Hellenistic crisis of the second century BCE. Within this context, visions such as Daniel 10–12 gave Jews hope that death at the hands of the Romans was not the final chapter in their lives. Though it might seem to them as if the political powers of evil were triumphing, texts such as Daniel reassured them that God soon would intervene, destroy evil empires, and resurrect the faithful ones to everlasting glory.

Conclusion

This chapter has focused on biblical texts written (or revised) during the Hellenistic period, but we must remember again that these texts soon transcended their original historical contexts. The tales of Daniel 1–6 and Esther gave hope to Jewish exiles of later centuries. The visions of Daniel 7–12 reassured Jews and Christians facing persecution. The histories in Chronicles and Ezra–Nehemiah communicated a vision of Temple- and Torah-centered Judaism to later generations.

In addition, the Hebrew Bible as a whole, the "Torah and Prophets," underwent transformations as it became the foundation of two religious movements: Judaism and Christianity. In each case, it was further shaped by its use in the given community. Within Judaism, certain books in the "Prophets," such as the books of Psalms and Proverbs, were eventually sorted into a third category of scripture called "writings," perhaps partly because these "writings" were not regularly "read" in synagogue worship. Within Christianity, the Jewish collection of the "Torah and Prophets" was eventually complemented by a distinctively Christian corpus of "Gospels and Epistles," and the two were given the labels "Old Testament" and "New Testament." People of these times valued what was old, so this labeling of Hebrew scriptures as "*Old* Testament" reflected an ongoing reverence for these texts. Yet the naming of specifically Christian scriptures as "*New* Testament" also showed an emphasis within Christianity on the special importance – both in theology and in worship – of Christian writings such as the gospels and Pauline letters.

CHAPTER THIRTEEN REVIEW

1. Know the meaning and significance of the following terms discussed in this chapter:
- apocalypse
- Ben Sira/Sirach
- Hanukkah
- Hasmoneans (Maccabees)
- heavenly apocalypse
- historical apocalypse
- hybridity
- pseudepigraphy

2. Even before the Hellenistic crisis, what was unique about the Jewish encounter with Hellenistic education and literature in comparison to older literary systems that Judah and Israel had experience with?

3. What major empires are reflected in the coded visions of Daniel 7 and 10–12? How is the Persian empire viewed in these visions in comparison with the Nehemiah memoir and Temple-rebuilding/Ezra narrative?

4. How was the Hasmonean kingdom different from the ancient Davidic monarchy?

5. How is the phenomenon of hybridity reflected in the works of the Hasmoneans? How might it be reflected in the final formation of the Hebrew Bible?

6. What are examples of Jewish groups in the Hellenistic period that did not yet recognize a clearly closed group of Hebrew scriptures?

7. What is older and what is newer in the books of Chronicles? And in Ezra–Nehemiah?

8. What are other major candidates in the Hebrew Bible to be writings from the Hellenistic period, and why?

Should there be a place in the present day and age for the kind of "historical apocalypse" seen in Daniel? If so, why and where? If it should not be reapplied (yet again), why not?

RESOURCES FOR FURTHER STUDY

Jewish writings from the Hellenistic and early Roman periods

Collins, John J. *Jewish Wisdom in the Hellenistic Age.* Old Testament Library. Louisville, KY: Westminster John Knox Press, 1997.
Nickelsburg, George. *Jewish Literature Between the Bible and the Mishnah* (revised edition). Minneapolis: Fortress, 2005.

Daniel

Collins, John J. *Daniel.* Hermeneia. Minneapolis: Fortress, 1993.

Chronicles

Japhet, Sara. *1 an*

Esther

Beal, Timothy. *The Book of Hiding: Gender, Ethnicity, Annihilation, and Esther.* London: Routledge, 1997.
Berlin, Adele. *Esther.* Philadelphia: Jewish Publication Society, 2001.

The formation of the Hebrew Bible

Carr, David. *Writing on the Tablet of the Heart: Origins of Scripture and Literature.* New York: Oxford University Press, 2005.

GLOSSARY

Each entry includes (in parentheses) reference to the first location where a term is discussed, whether Prologue or chapter number, along with other major location(s). **Boldface** indicates terms that occur elsewhere in this Glossary.

act-consequence (4) – see **moral act-consequence**.

apocalypse (13) – a text commonly attested in the Hellenistic and later periods that describes a heavenly revelation to a human recipient, often a human recipient from Israel's distant past (e.g. Enoch, Levi, etc.; see **pseudepigraphy**). Such apocalypses appear in two main types, the **heavenly apocalypse** and the **historical apocalypse**, frequently show priestly connections, and feature much focus on esoteric knowledge.

apocrypha (Prologue) – Protestant term for **deuterocanonical books**, in this case designating books that are not viewed in the Protestant tradition as fully **canonical**.

Asherah (2) – the mother goddess of the Canaanite pantheon, consort of the chief god, **El**.

Assyria (5) – a Mesopotamian state based in what is now northern Iraq.

Baal (2) – a storm god in the Canaanite pantheon.

Babylonian exile (1) – 586–538 BCE, a time when most of the elite living in Judah (especially Jerusalem) were forced to live outside the land in Babylon (with many never having the chance to return).

beginning of the Roman period (1) – 63 BCE: the end of the **Hasmonean monarchy** and the beginning of rule of Palestine by rulers appointed by Rome.

Ben Sira (13) – a collection of instructional texts authored in the early second century BCE (approx. 200–180 BCE). It is one example of a **deuterocanonical** book included (under its Greek name **Sirach**) in the Old Testament of the Roman Catholic and Orthodox churches, but excluded from the Jewish Tanach and Protestant Old Testament.

book of the Twelve Prophets (5) – a book in the Jewish Tanach that includes the 12 **minor prophets** (Hosea through Malachi).

books of the former prophets (7) – the historical books of Joshua, Judges, 1–2 Samuel, and 1–2 Kings.

canon and **canonical** (Prologue) – "canon" is a collection of books that are recognized as divinely inspired scripture by a given religious community. Those books are recognized as "canonical."

chiasm (2) – a circular literary form that moves through a set of themes to the center (e.g. A, B, C, D) and then goes through similar themes in reverse order after the center (e.g. D′, C′, B′, A′). Major emphasis is often put on the texts that occur at the center of a chiasm.

complaint (11) – for discussion see **lament psalm**.

conjectural emendation (Prologue) – a correction of the biblical text proposed by scholars that is not based on any **manuscript witness**.

couplet (3) – along with the less common **triplet**, a basic unit in Hebrew poetry, where the first line is paralleled, contrasted, or otherwise **seconded** by the climactic second line. Many translations identify the second line of a couplet by indenting the beginning of the line a few spaces.

covenant (5) – a solemn agreement between two parties, sealed, in the ancient Near East, by oaths and sometimes by ritual acts calling down curses on the parties if one of them broke the agreement.

Covenant Code (4) – a set of early laws embedded in Exod 20:22–23:33 that (apart from some late additions) seem to predate later regulations asserting the requirement to worship Yahweh in just one place (e.g. Deut 12; cf. 2 Kings 22–3). The parallels between the topics of these laws and large portions of the Code of Hammurabi are an indicator that some form of this collection may have been composed already in the early monarchal period, e.g. tenth or ninth century BCE.

cultural criticism (1) – when applied to the Bible, study of the myriad ways in which biblical texts are reflected or used in popular culture. The focus on popular culture distinguishes the emphasis of cultural critical study of a biblical text from study of its **history of interpretation**.

cultural memory (2) – a common set of memories, taught to each generation and celebrated in common rituals, that help define a group by its shared past.

Cyrus cylinder (11) – a proclamation by the Persian king Cyrus that he was appointed by the Babylonian gods to liberate the Babylonians and rebuild their temples. It shows many parallels to the Cyrus proclamation quoted in Ezra 1:1–4 that Yahweh had appointed him to rebuild the temple and allow the Judeans to return home.

Day of Yahweh (8) – a term seen in biblical literature that generally seems to have meant a day when Yahweh would rescue his chosen people (thus part of **election theology**), but is often reinterpreted by prophets (e.g. Amos, Zephaniah) as a day when Yahweh will judge that people.

destruction of Jerusalem (1) – 586 BCE: a climactic event in the history of Judah, including the destruction of Solomon's Temple and the end of the holy city many thought to be invulnerable.

destruction of the Second Temple (1) – 70 CE: occurred in the wake of a Jewish revolt against Rome and – along with the total destruction of Jerusalem in 135 CE after another revolt – represented the end of the local Jewish temple-state and the recentering of much Jewish life in the communities outside the land.

deutero-canonical (Prologue) – books recognized as **canonical** by the Roman Catholic church, but not part of the Jewish Tanach or Protestant Old Testament.

Deutero-Isaiah (9) – see **Second Isaiah**.

Deuteronomistic (7) – adjective describing biblical texts that feature terminology and/or theology similar to that permeating the book of Deuteronomy.

Deuteronomistic history (7) – a history extending from Moses's speech to Israel on the edge of the land (Deuteronomy) through the books of Joshua, Judges, 1–2 Samuel, and 1–2 Kings to Judah's eventual exile from the land at the end of the books of Kings. Though incorporating potential earlier blocks of tradition (e.g. a possible early "**succession narrative**"), this broader history of Israel in the land is dominated by the later theology articulated most clearly in Deuteronomy, and is thought by most scholars to have been composed partly in the late seventh century and completed during the exile.

divided monarchy (1) – 930–722 BCE: a time when there were separate monarchies in the south (based in Jerusalem and ruled by descendants of David) and the north (ultimately based in Samaria and ruled by a variety of royal dynasties).

divine council (9) – the idea that the divine world is organized on analogy with a human monarchal court, with a divine king, his consort, his officials, and other parts of his administration. This idea is reflected in many non-biblical texts as well as in the Bible itself.

dynamic equivalence (Prologue) – a term for a translation that aims to produce a meaning-for-meaning translation of a (biblical) text, as necessary diverging from a word-for-word translation to produce a more exact and understandable equivalent meaning.

E (10) – see **Elohistic Source**.

El (2) – the name of the head creator god of the Canaanite pantheon, husband of **Asherah**.

election theology (2) – a set of beliefs surrounding God's choosing of and special protection of a people, Israel. Distinguished from **Zion theology** by its focus on God's relationship to a people rather than a place (Jerusalem).

Elephantine (11) – a Jewish colony in Egypt where ancient papyri were found that document the life and religious practices of Jews living outside the land in the **Persian period**.

Elohistic Source (10) – a *hypothesized* source of the **Pentateuch** (no separate copies have been found) that many scholars think is preserved in parts of Genesis 20–2 and other non-Priestly parts of the Pentateuch where the divine designation "Elohim" predominates (the **Priestly Source** also uses Elohim for God in Genesis, but is seen as distinct from this Elohistic Source). According to this hypothesis, this Elohistic Source was composed in the north of Israel sometime in the late ninth or eighth century, thus coming from a later time and different place from the **Yahwistic Source** (**J**). This textbook is one of a number of recent treatments that has discarded the idea that there is an identifiable E source in the Pentateuch, but there are still many references to this hypothesized source in past and some recent scholarship.

empire (2) – as analyzed in this textbook, a form of ancient social organization where a particular monarchal state dominated other states through amassed military power (often drawing on the resources of subject states), creation of interlocking economic networks, and propagandistic use of terror.

feminist criticism (1) – applied to the Bible; a range of methods aimed at analyzing biblical depictions of women (or lack of these depictions) and biblical use of feminine imagery.

form criticism (1 and 11) – the study of different types of texts, **genres**, in the Bible along with their typical social settings and purposes.

formal correspondence (Prologue) – approach that aims to produce a word-for-word translation of a (biblical) text.

former prophets (7) – see **books of the former prophets**.

gender criticism (1) – applied to the Bible, the analysis of the ways gender functions in biblical texts, both male and female, both human and non-human.

genre (11) – a type of text, such as a **lament psalm** or **prophetic call narrative**.

H (10) – a designation either for the **Holiness Code** in Leviticus 17–26 or for a broader layer of material in the **Tetrateuch** that is characterized by the central emphases of Leviticus 17–26 (e.g. the importance of Israel's holiness).

Hanukkah (13) – the Jewish holiday celebrating the rededication of the **Second Temple** by Judas Maccabee in 164 BCE after it had been temporarily transformed by Antiochus Epiphanes IV into a temple to Zeus Olympius.

Hasmonean monarchy (1) – 142–63 BCE: the period of rule of members of the Hasmonean priestly family descended from Judas Maccabeaus, who led a successful rebellion against the Hellenistic rule of Antiochus Epiphanes IV.

Hasmoneans (1 and 13) – a provincial priestly family who led a revolt against Antiochus Epiphanes IV and eventually founded the **Hasmonean monarchy**.

heavenly apocalypse (13) – a type of **apocalypse** that depicts an ancient figure receiving a tour of heavenly realms.

Hebrew Bible (Prologue) – scriptures shared by Jews and Christians.

Hellenistic period (1) – 332–167 BCE: a period when, following the conquest of the Persian empire by Alexander, Palestine was ruled by a succession of Greek kings based in Egypt (the Ptolemies), Anatolia (contemporary Turkey), or Mesopotamia (the Seleucids).

historical apocalypse (13) – a type of **apocalypse** that reviews the past eras of history, often in encoded form, leading up to the present crises and an impending divine intervention. Though written during a given crises, they often are attributed to a more ancient sage (see **pseudepigraphy**), who is depicted as receiving the revelation in the distant past as a coded prophecy of *future* eras, crisis and intervention (e.g. Daniel 10–12).

historical criticism (1) – a family of historical methods that analyzes how and where the biblical texts (and oral traditions in them) were composed.

history of interpretation (1) – study of how biblical texts have been interpreted, especially in faith communities (e.g. Judaism, Christianity, Islam). The particular emphasis on interpretation in faith communities distinguishes history of interpretation from **cultural critical** study of how such texts are reflected in popular culture.

history of religions (10) – a term used in biblical scholarship to refer to the study of ideas and themes relating to gods and ritual in ancient Near Eastern cultures outside Israel so that we might better understand biblical religious ideas and practices.

Holiness Code (10) – a collection of laws in Leviticus 17–26 *hypothesized* to have once existed separately (no separate copies have been found) and characterized by a frequent focus on the need for the people of Israel to preserve its holiness. Many recent scholars believe instead that the language and themes predominant in Leviticus 17–26 are characteristic of a broader layer of **H** material spanning the rest of material in the **Tetrateuch** assigned by others to **P**.

hybridity (7 and 13) – a concept drawn from postcolonial theory that designates the blending of self-determination with elements drawn from the culture of the past oppressor. It is not identical with mere mixing of different cultural elements in identity. Instead, it refers to the complex identity formed in the midst and wake of the experience of domination.

hymn of praise (11) – sometimes referred to just as "hymn," this is a psalm that focuses on praise of God. It often features a focus on creation and/or is characterized by refrains calling for praise of God.

hymn of trust (11) – a type of psalm that expresses trust in God's protection and provision.

ideological criticism (1) – the analysis of ways that biblical texts can be, have been, and should be read in the midst of systemic structures of power. As such it overlaps with other methods (e.g. **history of interpretation**), but with a particular accent on analysis of ideology and power.

inclusio (9) – a literary structure where a text begins and ends with similar elements that enclose a larger middle. Also known as an "envelope structure," where the shorter and similar beginning and ending provide the envelope for the middle.

intertextuality (9) – a word used to refer to the myriad ways different texts can be related to each other. It can refer to conscious or unconscious ways that texts draw on the wording of earlier texts, but also to the ways that the readings of any text can be influenced by what the reader (or reading community) knows of other texts, whether texts dated before or after the text being read.

Israel (1) – two meanings: refers more narrowly to the tribal groups settled in the northern highlands of Canaan or more broadly to Judah (in the south) along with those northern groups.

J (4 and 10) – the one-letter designation of the hypothesized **Yahwistic Source**. The prominent use of the divine "Yahweh" in the Yahwistic Source is only one indicator used to argue for the existence of the source, but it has led to the frequent designation of the source as "J" (the German letter for the "y" sound at the outset of Yahweh).

JE (10) – a hypothesized combination of the **J** and **E** hypothesized sources for the **Tetrateuch**. The texts included in what some scholars discuss as "JE" are similar to the non-**P** texts discussed in this textbook as part of **L**. The main difference is that this textbook does not see this body of texts as having been created out of a combination of J and E sources. Therefore the term JE, though found in many commentaries and introductions, is not used in this book or in a number of other recent discussions.

Josiah's reform (7) – approximately 623 BCE: a socio-religious reform that Josiah is said to have undertaken in the wake of the decline of Assyrian influence over the area (2 Kings 23; compare 2 Chronicles 34), eliminating sanctuaries outside Jerusalem and laying claim to some of the territories of the former northern kingdom.

King James Version (Prologue) – an authorized translation of the Christian Bible completed under royal sponsorship by the church of England in 1611.

Koran (Prologue) – the holiest text in Islam, seen in that faith as the collected recitations by Muhammad, the prophet, of his revelations from God. These recitations refer to biblical traditions, often as filtered through early Jewish and/or Christian interpretation of those traditions.

L (10) – see **Lay Source**.

lament (11) – though this term sometimes is used to refer to a **lament psalm**, it applies more properly to cries over irreversible bad events, such as David's mourning over the death of Saul in 2 Sam 1:18–27 or the book of Lamentations.

lament psalm (11) – a type of psalm that is a cry for God's help and typically includes most of the following elements: complaint, plea for help, vow, statement of trust in God's help, and thanksgiving for God's help. Though some refer to such lament psalms simply as "**laments**," the cry for help typical of a lament psalm is distinguished from a lament proper by the fact that it does not mourn something that is already finished (e.g. a death). Instead, it is a plea that things may get better. Because of this difference, some scholars prefer to call these lament psalms **complaints** or **supplications**.

Lay Source (10) – a term used in this textbook to designate a *hypothesized* source of the **Pentateuch** (no separate copies have been found) that included most of the material in the Pentateuch not assigned to the **Priestly Source** (**P**) in the **Tetrateuch**, along with Deuteronomy. In this book, this material is called the lay source (**L**) because it seems to have been put together and transmitted by authors outside the priesthood. Most other scholars would designate this body of texts simply as non-Priestly (or non-P) or – if they follow older models for the formation of the Pentateuch – as **JE**.

literary criticism (1) – the use of methods from modern study of literary texts (e.g. attention to plot, characterization, signification) to illuminate the poetic-narrative dynamics of biblical texts.

LXX (Prologue) – an abbreviation for **Septuagint**.

Maccabbees (1, 13) – another word for the **Hasmoneans**.

major prophets (6) – the three larger prophetic books: Isaiah, Jeremiah, and Ezekiel.

manuscript witness (Prologue) – an ancient copy of a biblical book or quotation of a biblical book (in the original language or translation).

Masoretic text (Prologue) – the authoritative version of the Hebrew text of the **Tanach** or Hebrew Bible produced by Jewish scribes in the medieval period and used as the base text in most translations.

messiah (11) – a Hebrew word meaning "anointed one," which during the **Second Temple** period came to designate a hoped-for anointed king who would deliver Jews from domination and/or a hoped-for anointed priest to replace the priests in Jerusalem, who were perceived by some to be corrupt.

minor prophets (5) – 12 smaller prophetic books (Hosea, Joel, Amos, Obadiah, Jonah, Micah, Nahum, Habakkuk, Zephaniah, Haggai, Zechariah, and Malachi) that follow the three books of the **major prophets** (Isaiah, Jeremiah, Ezekiel) in the Jewish **Tanach** and appear at the end of the Christian Bible.

monarchal city-state (2) – a state based in a walled city (and often supported by other fortified settlements) and ruled by a hereditary monarchic dynasty. This ancient form of social organization allowed an amassing of military resources and wealth not possible for more decentralized tribal groups.

monotheism (9) – a term referring to the belief that there is only one god and that all other gods are false. This is to be distinguished from the idea, attested in the late pre-exilic period, that a given people should worship only one god among the various gods that exist, an idea sometimes designated as "henotheism."

moral act-consequence (4) – the idea that the cosmos is morally coherent; that is, morally good actions eventually lead to good results for the doer(s), while morally bad actions lead to disaster.

MT (Prologue) –an abbreviation for the **Masoretic text**.

non-P and **non-Priestly** (10) – terms used to refer to texts in the **Pentateuch** (especially the **Tetrateuch**) not assigned to P. It covers many of the same texts included in the older designation JE but is used by scholars who no longer believe in the existence of the early **J** and **E** sources.

Old Testament (Prologue) – Christian term for the scriptures originating in ancient Israel, each consisting of nearly identical books (with some exceptions) in a different order that culminates in Malachi's prophecy of Elijah (leading into Matthew 3).

oral traditions (2) – traditions important at every stage in the formation of the Bible, especially if one includes the oral aspects of written traditions, since even the latter often were memorized and performed. More specifically, we see some reflections in the written traditions of the Bible of exclusively oral traditions, and these reflections are the typical focus of biblical **tradition criticism**.

P (4 and 10) – see **Priestly Source**.

Pentateuch (Prologue and 4) – the first five books of the Bible, namely Genesis, Exodus, Leviticus, Numbers, and Deuteronomy, otherwise known as the (written) **Torah**.

Persian governmental authorization (11) – a practice seen in different parts of the Persian empire whereby local leaders sought and received official recognition from the Persian authorities of their local laws as Persian law. Some scholars think that Judean **post-exilic period** lay and priestly leaders may have sought such Persian recognition for their traditions, and that this process may stand behind the present combination of **Priestly** and non-Priestly strands of the **Pentateuch**.

Persian period (1) – 538–332 BCE: a time of Persian rule of Judah, when the Persians are recorded in the Bible as helping the Judeans who returned to rebuild the temple and walls of Jerusalem and establish the **Torah** as the authoritative law of the returnee community.

postcolonial criticism (1 and 7) – study that examines ways in which texts such as the Bible were formed in imperial contexts and/or how biblical texts later functioned in colonial or imperial contexts (e.g. missionary efforts).

post-exilic period (1 and 11) – from 538 BCE: the period following the forced exile to Babylon, starting with the **Persian period**. Often the Persian period is the primary one meant when referring to the post-exilic period. Note: despite the term *post*-exilic, it is clear that many Judeans still lived outside the land after 538 BCE.

pre-state tribal period (1) – 1250–1000 BCE: a time when Israel lived in villages (joined loosely in larger tribal affiliations) in the hill country without any monarch over them.

Priestly Source (4 and 10) – a *hypothesized* source of the **Pentateuch** (no separate copies have been found) which most scholars agree contained texts such as the Genesis 1 creation story, genealogies such as Genesis 5, a strand of the flood narrative where no sacrifice happens (e.g. Gen 6:9–22 to 9:1–17), the covenant of circumcision with Abraham (Genesis 17), the second call of Moses (Exod 6:2–8), the whole section about Sinai (Exodus 19 to Num 10:10), and many other texts in the **Tetrateuch** with similar language and themes (though not all focusing on priests). Though this layer contains much earlier traditions, most scholars agree that the broader Priestly Source was not composed until the **Babylonian exile** or early **post-exilic period**.

primeval history (4) – the stories of creation, flood and other events concerning early humanity in general found in Genesis 1–11.

prophetic call narrative (6) – a story, usually told in the first person, where a prophetic figure tells of how he was authorized by God to be a prophet, usually including some or all of the following elements: an appearance of God, introductory word by God to the one to be called, call of the prophet, objection by the prophet that he is somehow unfit for the task, divine reassurance, and sign reinforcing the divine reassurance. Examples include Isaiah 6; Jer 1:4–10; and Ezekiel 1–3, though some scholars dispute whether some of these texts are proper "call narratives," and disagree about whether "call" (a term whose home is in later Christian theology) is appropriate for these ancient Hebrew narratives.

Psalter (11) – another word for the book of Psalms.

pseudepigraphy (13) – attribution of a later text to a more ancient author. This was particularly common in the Hellenistic period, when Judaism came into contact with a Greek culture that was more focused on establishing ancient authorship of authoritative texts.

rebuilding of the Jerusalem Temple (11) – 515 BCE (completion), described in the Bible as done over a period of years with Persian sponsorship: this **Second Temple** represented an important center of leadership and social organization in **post-exilic period** Judah in the years after the destruction of the monarchy.

reception history (1) – the study of the complete variety of ways that texts are used over time, in both textual and other (e.g. artistic) media and in various faith community and other contexts. It thus encompasses the range of both **history of interpretation** and **cultural criticism**.

redaction criticism (1) – the attempt to identify the ways in which the author or redactors of the present biblical books created those wholes through arrangement, transformation, and extension of earlier source materials. It is a form of **transmission history**.

royal psalms (3) – a set of psalms in the **Psalter** that focus on the king and God's special relationship to him (see **royal theology**).

royal theology (3) – a set of beliefs and images surrounding God's appointing of the king as ruler and high priest, God's equipping of the king with power, justice, and blessing, and God's granting the king anything he wishes, particularly military victory and long life.

satan (11) – a Hebrew term referring in Job to an accuser working *for* God, who roams God's realm and checks up on God's subjects. Though this term is translated in Job with a capital "S," thus leading readers to confuse the "satan" or accuser of Job with the demon Satan of later Jewish and Christian theology, the word is not a proper name in Job and does not refer to the prince of darkness.

Second Isaiah (9) – alternatively **Deutero-Isaiah**: term used to refer to chapters 40–55 of the book of Isaiah, a section that shows many signs of being composed during the time of **Babylonian exile** (with parts possibly even later). Almost no scholars today think that the author of these later chapters was named "Isaiah." The term "Second Isaiah" reflects the fact that this portion of the book of Isaiah was the first one to be distinguished from the words of the first "Isaiah," which are now to be found particularly in portions of Isaiah 1–11 and 28–32.

Second Temple (11) – the Temple rebuilt under Persian sponsorship by 515 BCE and eventually destroyed by the Romans in 70 CE, a center for Judean leadership and social organization throughout the intervening period.

seconding (3) – a term coined by James Kugel in *The Idea of Biblical Poetry* (New Haven: Yale University Press, 1981) for the multiple and complex ways that the final line of a **couplet** or **triplet** can build on the meaning of the initial lines of the given poetic unit. Many find this to be a more flexible and accurate designation for this phenomenon in Hebrew poetry than older and more commonly used terms such as "parallelism."

segmentary society (2) – a term designating the kind of decentralized, horizontal social framework that tribal Israel had prior to the onset of the monarchy.

Septuagint (Prologue) – an ancient set of translations of Old Testament books into Greek.

servant (9) – a term used in parts of **Second Isaiah** that seems to refer to a specific entity or individual, particularly in the **servant songs** of Isaiah. Scholars debate whether this "servant" is a reference to a particular individual or a metaphor in these texts for the people (or sub-group of the people).

servant songs (9) – a set of texts in Isa 42:1–8; 49:1–6; 50:4–9; and 52:13–53:12 that focus on a "**servant**" figure. Some scholars have thought these servant songs might represent a separate literary layer in **Second Isaiah**.

Sirach (13) – see **Ben Sira**.

social-scientific analysis (9) – when applied to the Bible, analysis that draws on contemporary sociological and anthropological studies to provide a more nuanced picture of ancient Israel.

source criticism (1) – the attempt to reconstruct the (now lost) written sources used by the authors of the present biblical texts. It is a type of **transmission history**.

succession narrative (7) – a *hypothesized* older narrative (no separate copies have been found) located in 2 Samuel 9–20 and 1 Kings 1–2 describing the process of succession to David. It is thought to have been written around the time of Solomon.

suffering servant (9) – the particular image of the **servant** in **Second Isaiah** found in Isa 52:13–53:12, an image that often has been interpreted by Christians to refer to the crucifixion and resurrection of Jesus Christ.

supersessionism (Prologue) – the idea that Christianity and the Christian church have superseded and thus replaced Judaism and the people of Israel.

supplication (11) – for discussion see **lament psalm**.

Syro-Ephraimite war (5) – a war occurring around 735 BCE in which Syria and the northern kingdom of Israel laid siege to Jerusalem and thus attempted to force Judah, under King Ahaz, to join a coalition of local states resisting Assyrian rule (though Judah was not yet under Assyrian rule). Ahaz appealed for and received help from Assyria in repelling the Syrian–Israelite alliance, but became subject to Assyria in return for the aid.

Tanach (Prologue) – the Jewish term for the Hebrew scriptures, referring to the three main parts of those scriptures: the **Torah**, Neviiim (Hebrew for "prophets"), and Ketuvim (Hebrew for "writings"). The arrangement of the Jewish Tanach culminates in Cyrus's promise to rebuild the Temple at the end of 2 Chronicles.

TaNaK (Prologue) – another way of writing **Tanach**.

Tetrateuch (4 and 10) – the first four books of the Bible, namely Genesis, Exodus, Leviticus, and Numbers. The portion of the **Pentateuch** that precedes Deuteronomy is formed out of combined **P** and **L** sources.

textual criticism (Prologue) – the collection and analysis of different manuscript readings, e.g. different readings in Hebrew manuscripts and early translations of Hebrew manuscripts of books in the Hebrew Bible.

thanksgiving song (11) – a type of psalm that praises God for deliverance from suffering, and calls on others to join that praise.

theophany (6) – a divine appearance. This term also often refers to a text that describes a divine appearance.

Third Isaiah (12) – a designation for chapters 56–66 of the book of Isaiah, a section distinguished from **Second Isaiah** by more explicit indicators that it addressed the situation of **post-exilic period** Judah.

Torah (Prologue) – the first five books of the Bible, namely Genesis, Exodus, Leviticus, Numbers, and Deuteronomy. Jews often distinguish between this "written Torah" and the "oral Torah" given to Moses, transmitted through the sages, and embodied in the Mishnah and other authoritative Jewish writings.

tradition criticism (1) – the attempt to recover, via the written texts of the Bible, the traditions that stand behind them, usually with a particular focus on the **oral traditions** reflected in the written texts.

tradition history (2) – a history of traditions that existed before and often alongside the written texts now in the Bible. Though such traditions can be written as well as oral, the term often refers primarily to the history of pre-biblical **oral traditions** reconstructed through **tradition criticism**.

transmission history (1) – an umbrella term for the study of the different processes leading up to the final composition of biblical books. It can include **tradition criticism**, **source criticism**, and **redaction criticism**.

trickster (2) – a character whose ability to survive through trickery and even lawbreaking is celebrated in religion, literature, or another part of culture.

triplet (3) – along with the more common **couplet**, a basic unit of Hebrew poetry. In it, the first two lines set the stage for the climactic third line. Many translations identify the second and third lines of triplets by indenting the beginning of the second line a few spaces.

tsedeqah (3) – a Hebrew word often translated as "righteousness," but perhaps better rendered as "social responsibility," fulfilling one's obligations to others in the society, particularly those most vulnerable.

united monarchy (1) – 1000–930 BCE: the time when David and Solomon ruled both north and south (and dominated some neighboring areas) from Jerusalem.

vassal treaty (5 and 7) – a type of ancient **covenant** imposed by a superpower on one or more nations that it dominated. Such a treaty typically required the subject king or nation to pay tribute to the king of the superpower, maintain constant and exclusive allegiance to him, and incur curses if the subject nation failed to be exclusively and constantly loyal to the dominating power.

village (2) – an unwalled settlement inhabited by a few clans (50–300 people total) living in pillared houses in various extended family units. Though this ancient form of social life is introduced in the discussion of pre-state Israel in Chapter 2, it was the most common way for people to live throughout the history of Israel.

wisdom psalm (11) – a psalm particularly characterized by explicit educational elements, often featuring language in common with other explicit teaching literature such as Proverbs.

Yahweh (1) – the name of the god of Israel, often translated as "LORD" in English translations. This name came to be seen as especially holy in Jewish tradition.

Yahwistic Source (4 and 10) – a *hypothesized* early source of the **Pentateuch** (no copies have been found) that some scholars think starts with the garden of Eden and materials about Abel and Cain (Gen 2:4b–4:26), continues with a version of the flood story parallel to **P** (e.g. Gen 6:1–4; 7:1–5 to 8:20–2), and continues to include the story of

Noah and his sons, large portions of the Abraham story (the bulk of Genesis 12–13, 16–19) along with various **non-Priestly** portions of the rest of the **Tetrateuch** where the divine name **Yahweh** is used (translated as "LORD" in most English translations). According to this hypothesis, this source was composed in the early monarchal south, probably sometime during the tenth century. *Within this textbook* the probability of the existence of this broader **J**/Yahwistic Source is denied, though this book does affirm the probable existence of a J/Yahwistic strand exclusively in the **primeval history**, possibly composed in the early monarchal south.

Zion (3) – the name of a holy mountain on which the fortress and temple of Jerusalem stood. It often comes to serve as a synonym for Jerusalem.

Zion psalms (3) – a set of psalms in the biblical **Psalter** that focus on Zion/Jerusalem and emphasize themes of **Zion theology**.

Zion theology (3) – a set of beliefs surrounding the idea that God lives in Jerusalem, holds Jerusalem to a high ethical standard, and will prevent Jerusalem from being destroyed by any enemy. Note: this is *not* "Zionist" theology.

INDEX

The letter b after a page reference indicates that the topic appears in a textbox. Page numbers in *italics* refer to illustrations.